Thoughts on Machiavelli

FOREVER HONORED

REMEMBER

Photo by SLIDEWAYS/R.E. Bulson.

No. 141 ($1.00/doz.; $7.00/100 + postage)
THE TRACT LEAGUE
GRAND RAPIDS MI 49534-1329
www.tractleague.com

You may know someone who has died in the service of our country. Almost every city has a monument to remind us that many of the things we enjoy were won for us by someone's painful and bloody death.

Of all the sacrifices ever given on our behalf, none has surpassed the sacrifice of Jesus Christ. The only Son of God left his heavenly home to be born as a baby. After his brief ministry, he took upon himself our punishment and willingly suffered an agonizing death and separation from his heavenly Father in order that all who believe may come into the family of God and reign with him.

With his death and resurrection, Jesus ushered in a new world order. God's reign is breaking forth into our world and nothing can stop him. Each day as we march towards the end of history God is claiming more and more lost territory.

And that is the reason I am giving this tract to you. I want to invite you join me in this awesome event. If you give your life to Jesus and his Father's work, you will never be the same. Every part of your life will change as you begin to see what Jesus is doing to prepare the world for his spectacular return. This is a far greater issue than being religious or belonging to a church or being a good person. This is an invitation to leave your old life behind and follow Jesus. It is so radical, the Bible calls it being "Born Again".

Of all the sacrifices ever given on our behalf, none has surpassed the sacrifice of Jesus Christ.

Now you have to make decision: To live out your remaining days in pursui of money and pleasure; or to open yo life to the reality of a living Jesus, to accept his sacrifice for you, and to j him in the march to a new world. D put it off--this is too good an oppor to pass by.

If you are ready, tell God him to open your eyes to what he doing. Tell him that you are read accept Jesus' sacrifice for you, Jesus to lead you into this new

Thoughts on

MACHIAVELLI

LEO STRAUSS

THE UNIVERSITY OF CHICAGO PRESS
Chicago and London

The University of Chicago Press, Chicago 60637
The University of Chicago Press, Ltd., London

Copyright © 1958 by Leo Strauss
All rights reserved. Published 1958
Paperback Edition 1978.
Printed in the United States of America
00 99 98 97 96   7 6 5 4

ISBN: 0-226-77702-2
LCN: 78-55044

Preface

THIS is an expanded version of four lectures which I delivered at the University of Chicago in the fall term 1953, under the auspices of the Charles R. Walgreen Foundation.

I am grateful to the Charles R. Walgreen Foundation and especially to its chairman, Professor Jerome G. Kerwin, for giving me the opportunity to present my observations and reflections on the problem of Machiavelli. I am also grateful to the Walgreen Foundation for generous clerical assistance.

Chapter II of this study has been published previously in the *American Political Science Review* (March, 1957).

L.S.

Chicago, Illinois, December, 1957

Contents

Preface   5

Introduction   9

I.   The Twofold Character of Machiavelli's Teaching   15

II. Machiavelli's Intention: The *Prince*   54

III. Machiavelli's Intention: The *Discourses*   85

IV. Machiavelli's Teaching   174

     Notes   301

     Index   347

Introduction

We shall not shock anyone, we shall merely expose ourselves to good-natured or at any rate harmless ridicule, if we profess ourselves inclined to the old-fashioned and simple opinion according to which Machiavelli was a teacher of evil. Indeed, what other description would fit a man who teaches lessons like these: princes ought to exterminate the families of rulers whose territory they wish to possess securely; princes ought to murder their opponents rather than to confiscate their property since those who have been robbed, but not those who are dead, can think of revenge; men forget the murder of their fathers sooner than the loss of their patrimony; true liberality consists in being stingy with one's own property and in being generous with what belongs to others; not virtue but the prudent use of virtue and vice leads to happiness; injuries ought all to be done together so that, being tasted less, they will hurt less, while benefits ought to be conferred little by little, so that they will be felt more strongly; a victorious general who fears that his prince might not reward him properly, may punish him for his anticipated ingratitude by raising the flag of rebellion; if one has to choose between inflicting severe injuries and inflicting light injuries, one ought to inflict severe injuries; one ought not to say to someone whom one wants to kill "Give me your gun, I want to kill you with it," but merely, "Give me your gun," for once you have the gun in your hand, you can satisfy your desire. If it is true that only an evil man will stoop to teach maxims of public and private gangsterism, we are forced to say that Machiavelli was an evil man.

Machiavelli was indeed not the first man to express opinions like those mentioned. Such opinions belong to a way of political thinking and political acting which is as old as political society itself. But Machiavelli is the only philosopher who has lent the weight of his name to any way of political thinking and political acting which is as old as political society itself, so much so that his name is commonly used for designating such a way. He is notorious as the classic of the evil way of political thinking and political acting. Callicles and Thrasymachus, who set forth the evil doctrine behind closed doors, are Platonic characters, and the Athenian ambassadors, who state the same doctrine on the island of Melos in the absence of the common people, are Thucydidean characters. Machiavelli proclaims openly and triumphantly a corrupting doctrine which ancient writers had taught covertly or with all signs of repugnance. He says in his own name shocking things which ancient writers had said through the mouths of their characters.[1] Machiavelli alone has dared to utter the evil doctrine in a book and in his own name.

Yet however true the old-fashioned and simple verdict may be, it is not exhaustive. Its deficiency justifies to some extent the more sophisticated views which are set forth by the learned of our age. Machiavelli, we are told, was so far from being an evil teacher of evil that he was a passionate patriot or a scientific student of society or both. But one may wonder whether the up-to-date scholars do not err much more grievously than the old-fashioned and simple, or whether what escapes the up-to-date scholars is not much more important than what escapes the simple and the old-fashioned, although it may be true that the one thing needful which is ignored by the sophisticated is inadequately articulated and therefore misinterpreted by the men of noble simplicity. It would not be the only case in which "a little philosophy"[2] generates prodigious errors to which the unphilosophic multitude is immune.

• It is misleading to describe the thinker Machiavelli as a patriot. He is a patriot of a particular kind: he is more concerned with the salvation of his fatherland than with the salvation of his soul.' His patriotism therefore presupposes a comprehensive reflection regarding the status of the fatherland on the one hand and of the soul on the other. This comprehensive reflection, and not patriotism, is the core of Machiavelli's thought. This comprehensive reflection, and not his patriotism, established his fame and made him the teacher of many men in all countries. The substance of his thought is not Florentine, or even Italian, but universal. It concerns, and it is meant to concern, all thinking men regardless of time and place. To speak of Machiavelli as a scientist is at least as misleading as to speak of him as a patriot. The scientific student of society is unwilling or unable to pass "value-judgments," but Machiavelli's works abound with "value-judgments." His study of society is normative.

But even if we were forced to grant that Machiavelli was essentially a patriot or a scientist, we would not be forced to deny that he was a teacher of evil. Patriotism as Machiavelli understood it is collective selfishness. The indifference to the distinction between right and wrong which springs from devotion to one's country is less repulsive than the indifference to that distinction which springs from exclusive preoccupation with one's own ease or glory. But precisely for this reason it is more seductive and therefore more dangerous. Patriotism is a kind of love of one's own. Love of one's own is inferior to love of what is both one's own and good. Love of one's own tends therefore to become concerned with one's own being good or complying with the demands of right. To justify Machiavelli's terrible counsels by having recourse to his patriotism, means to see the virtues of that patriotism while being blind to that which is higher than patriotism, or to that which both hallows and limits patriotism. In referring to Machiavelli's patriotism one does not dispose of a mere semblance of evil; one merely obscures something truly evil.

As regards the "scientific" approach to society which many of its adherents trace to Machiavelli, it emerges through the abstraction from the moral distinctions by which we take our bearings as citizens and as men. The indispensable condition of "scientific" analysis is then moral obtuseness. That obtuseness is not identical with depravity, but it is bound to strengthen the forces of depravity. In the case of lesser men, one can safely trace such obtuseness to the absence of certain intellectual virtues. This charitable explanation could not be tolerated in the case of Machiavelli, who was too thoughtful not to know what he was doing and too generous not to admit it to his reasonable friends.

We do not hesitate to assert, as very many have asserted before us, and we shall later on try to prove, that Machiavelli's teaching is immoral and irreligious. We are familiar with the evidence which scholars adduce in support of the contrary assertion; but we question their interpretation of the evidence. To say nothing of certain other considerations, it seems to us that the scholars in question are too easily satisfied. They are satisfied that Machiavelli was a friend of religion because he stressed the useful and the indispensable character of religion. They do not pay any attention to the fact that his praise of religion is only the reverse side of what one might provisionally call his complete indifference to the truth of religion. This is not surprising since they themselves are likely to understand by religion nothing other than a significant sector of society, if not an attractive or at any rate innocuous piece of folklore, to say nothing of those sincerely religious people who are gratified by any apparent benefit conferred upon religion. They misinterpret Machiavelli's judgment concerning religion, and likewise his judgment concerning morality, because they are pupils of Machiavelli. Their seemingly open-minded study of Machiavelli's thought is based on the dogmatic acceptance of his principles. They do not see the evil character of his thought because they are the heirs of the Machiavellian tradition; because they, or the forgotten teachers of their teachers, have been corrupted by Machiavelli.

One cannot see the true character of Machiavelli's thought unless one frees himself from Machiavelli's influence. For all practical purposes this means that one cannot see the true character of Machiavelli's thought unless one recovers for himself and in himself the pre-modern heritage of the western world, both Biblical and classical. To do justice to Machiavelli requires one to look forward from a pre-modern point of view toward an altogether unexpected and surprising Machiavelli who is new and strange, rather than to look backward from today toward a Machiavelli who has become old and our own, and therewith almost good. This procedure is required even for a purely historical understanding. Machiavelli did know pre-modern thought: it was before him. He could not have known the thought of the present time, which emerged as it were behind his back.

We thus regard the simple opinion about Machiavelli as indeed decisively superior to the prevailing sophisticated views, though still insufficient. Even if, and precisely if we are forced to grant that his teaching is diabolical and he himself a devil, we are forced to remember the profound theological truth that the devil is a fallen angel. To recognize the diabolical character of Machiavelli's thought would mean to recognize in it a perverted nobility of a very high order. That nobility was discerned by Marlowe, as he ascribed to Machiavelli the words "I hold there is no sin but ignorance." Marlowe's judgment is borne out by what Machiavelli himself, in the Epistles Dedicatory to his two great books, indicates regarding his most precious possession. We are in sympathy with the simple opinion about Machiavelli, not only because it is wholesome, but above all because a failure to take that opinion seriously prevents one from doing justice to what is truly admirable in Machiavelli: the intrepidity of his thought, the grandeur of his vision, and the graceful subtlety of his speech. Not the contempt for the simple opinion, nor the disregard of it, but the considerate ascent from it leads to the core of Machiavelli's thought. There is no surer protection against the understanding of anything than taking for granted or otherwise despising the obvious and the surface. The problem inherent in the surface of things, and only in the surface of things, is the heart of things.

There are good reasons for dealing with Machiavelli in a series of Walgreen lectures. The United States of America may be said to be the only country in the world which was founded in explicit opposition to Machiavellian principles. According to Machiavelli, the founder of the most renowned commonwealth of the world was a fratricide: the foundation of political greatness is necessarily laid in crime. If we can believe Thomas Paine, all governments of the Old World have an origin of this description; their origin was conquest and tyranny. But "the Independence of America [was] accompanied by a Revolution in the principles and practice of Governments": the foundation of the United States was laid in freedom and justice. "Government founded on a moral theory, on a system of universal peace, on the indefeasible hereditary Rights of Man, is now revolving from west to east by a stronger impulse than the Government of the sword revolved from east to west."[8] This judgment is far from being obsolete. While freedom is no longer a preserve of the United States, the United States is now the bulwark of freedom.⁕And contemporary tyranny has its roots

. in Machiavelli's thought, in the Machiavellian principle that the good end justifies every means.* At least to the extent that the American reality is inseparable from the American aspiration, one cannot understand Americanism without understanding Machiavellianism which is its opposite.

But we cannot conceal from ourselves the fact that the problem is more complex than it appears in the presentation by Paine and his followers. Machiavelli would argue that America owes her greatness not only to her habitual adherence to the principles of freedom and justice, but also to her occasional deviation from them. He would not hesitate to suggest a mischievous interpretation of the Louisiana Purchase[4] and of the fate of the Red Indians. He would conclude that facts like these are an additional proof for his contention that there cannot be a great and glorious society without the equivalent of the murder of Remus by his brother Romulus. This complication makes it all the more necessary that we should try to reach an adequate understanding of the fundamental issue raised by Machiavelli.

We may seem to have assumed that Machiavelli is the classic exponent of one of the two fundamental alternatives of political thought. We did assume that there are fundamental alternatives, alternatives which are permanent or coeval with man. This assumption is frequently denied today. Many of our contemporaries are of the opinion that there are no permanent problems and hence no permanent alternatives. They would argue that precisely Machiavelli's teaching offers ample proof for their denial of the existence of permanent problems: Machiavelli's problem is a novel problem; it is fundamentally different from the problem with which earlier political philosophy was concerned. This argument, properly elaborated, has some weight. But stated baldly, it proves merely that the permanent problems are not as easily accessible as some people believe, or that not all political philosophers face the permanent problems. Our critical study of Machiavelli's teaching can ultimately have no other purpose than to contribute towards the recovery of the permanent problems.

The Twofold Character of Machiavelli's Teaching

MACHIAVELLI presented his political teaching in two books, the *Prince* and the *Discourses on the First Ten Books of Livy*. Plato too presented his political teaching in two books, the *Republic* and the *Laws*. But Plato made it perfectly clear that the subject-matter of the *Laws* is of lower rank than that of the *Republic* or that the *Laws* is subordinate to the *Republic*. Hobbes went so far as to present his political teaching in three books. But it is easy to see that these three books are the result of three successive efforts to expound the same political teaching. The case of Machiavelli's two books is different. Their relation is obscure.

At the beginning of the *Prince*, Machiavelli divides all states into two classes, republics and principalities. It appears from the title, the Epistle Dedicatory, and the chapter headings of the *Prince* that that book is devoted to principalities. Above all, Machiavelli says explicitly that in the *Prince* he will deal solely with principalities and will not discuss republics there since he has done so elsewhere at length.[1] The reference to a work on republics fits the *Discourses*, and fits no other work by Machiavelli which is extant or known to have been extant, completed or fragmentary. It therefore seems reasonable to describe the relation of the two books as follows: the *Prince* is devoted to principalities, the *Discourses* to republics.

Yet if the case is so simple, why did Machiavelli not call his treatise on republics simply *De Republica*? It might be suggested that when Machiavelli wrote, republics were not timely in Florence, in Italy, or anywhere else on earth; principalities were in the ascendancy; republics were rather a matter of the past. Machiavelli could find such models of princely rulers in his time as Cesare Borgia or Ferdinand of Aragon, but the model of republican rule was supplied by ancient Rome.[2] In accordance with this suggestion we find what we may call a preponderance of modern examples in the *Prince* and a preponderance of ancient examples in the *Discourses*.[3] From this we might understand why the *Prince* ends with, or culminates in a passionate call to action: Machiavelli exhorts an Italian prince of his time to liberate Italy from the barbarians who have subjugated her; but the end of the *Discourses* is strangely dispassionate. In brief, it makes sense at the outset to describe the relation of the two books in terms of a difference of subject-matter.

But we are compelled almost immediately to qualify this description. It is not true that Machiavelli regarded republics as a matter of the past. He wrote the *Discourses* in order to encourage imitation of ancient republics. He hoped for the rebirth, in the near or distant future, of the spirit of ancient republicanism.[4] Hence his writing *Discourses on Livy* instead of a *De Republica*, cannot be explained by his despair of a republican future. Apart from this the *Discourses* certainly deal with both republics and principalities. The stated purpose of the book is to pave the way for the imitation not only of the ancient republics but of the ancient kingdoms as well.[5] As for the *Prince*, it abounds with references to republics. Machiavelli urges princes to take the Roman republic as their model in regard to foreign policy and military matters.[6] One obscures the difficulty by saying that the *Prince* deals chiefly with principalities and the *Discourses* deal chiefly with republics. It would be better to say that Machiavelli treats in the *Prince* all subjects from the point of view of the prince whereas in the *Discourses* he treats numerous subjects from both the princely and the republican point of view. One is therefore inclined to suggest that in the *Discourses* Machiavelli presents the whole of his political teaching whereas in the *Prince* he presents only a part of it or perhaps discusses only a special case; one is inclined to suggest that the *Prince* is subordinate to the *Discourses*. This suggestion seems to be generally favored today. While for the reason stated it is superior to the view that the relation of the two books corresponds literally to the relation of principalities and republics, it is inferior to that view because it is not based on Machiavelli's own statements. The relation of the two books is still obscure.

To gain some clarity, let us return once more to the surface, to the beginning of the beginning. Both books begin with Epistles Dedicatory. In the Epistle Dedicatory of the *Prince*, Machiavelli says that the book contains everything that he has found out for himself and learned from others, i.e., everything he knows. In the Epistle Dedicatory of the *Discourses* he says that the book contains as much as he knows and as much as he has learned of the things of the world. Hence the relation of the two books cannot possibly be understood in terms of a difference of subject-matter. The *Prince* is as comprehensive as the *Discourses*: each book contains everything that Machiavelli knows. We must add that Machiavelli raises this claim only on behalf of the *Prince* on the one hand and of the *Discourses* on the other, as can be seen from the Epistles Dedicatory of his other works.

In the ambiguous remark of the Epistle Dedicatory of the *Discourses*, Machiavelli might seem to present his knowledge as limited to "the things of the world." Knowledge of the things of the world is distinguished from book-learning on the one hand, and from knowledge of things natural and supernatural on the other. On one occasion Machiavelli seems explicitly to disclaim knowledge of things natural and supernatural. The things of the world are distinguished in particular from "chance and God" and from "Heaven." They are identical with the *res humanae*, the human things or human affairs. Instead of only "the things of the world" Machiavelli also uses the expression "the actions of the world." But the things of the world do not consist exclusively of actions; states and religions, or "mixed bodies" as distinguished from "simple bodies" (i.e., natural bodies), also are included among the things of the world. Someone said of the Florentines that they understood nothing of the things of the world. Savonarola's sermons were full of accusations and invectives against the worldly wise. Machiavelli on the other hand desires to make his readers "better knowers of the world."[7] For the things of the world are of course also distinguished from the heavenly things, or rather they are distinguished as the things of "this world" from those of "the other world."[8] In the Epistle Dedicatory of the *Prince*, Machiavelli speaks not of the things of the world, but of modern things and ancient things. The things of the world are variable; hence the modern things differ from the ancient things. But "the things of the world" is a more comprehensive expression than "things ancient and modern," for not all things of the world are affected by the difference between antiquity and modernity. As Machiavelli informs us in the Epistle Dedicatory of the *Prince*, there is a "nature of princes" and a "nature of the peoples," which natures are invariable. There is a "nature" which is the same in all men. There are natural characteristics of nations, natural inclinations, natural necessities with which the student of human affairs must be thoroughly familiar. With a view to the political significance of miracles, it is, to say the least, desirable that the statesman, and hence *a fortiori* the teacher of statesmen, should even be "a knower of the natural things," i.e., of such natural things as do not necessarily pertain to the nature of man in particular.[9] Machiavelli knows then not only the variable "things of the world" but the invariable "world" itself. He knows that heaven, the sun, the elements and man always have the same movement, order and power. He knows that the things of the world follow a course which is ordained for them by heaven so much so that all things of the world have in every age a fundamental agreement with ancient times. In a way, then, Machiavelli possesses knowledge of "all natural things." He could not know that all things of the world depend for their order on heaven unless he had some knowledge of heaven. He could not know the mixed bodies as such unless he had some knowledge of the simple bodies. It is true that what he knows of simple bodies he has learned from the physicians, among others, whereas what he knows of mixed bodies he has learned by himself. But this does not do away with the fact that he possesses knowledge both of simple bodies and of mixed bodies. The things of the world are somehow governed by chance and by God. Machiavelli is therefore compelled to give thought to the character of that government and to reach a judgment on its character, just as he is compelled to give thought to the question of whether the world, i.e., the visible universe, was created or is eternal.[10] In matters like these, his judgment does not rely on the teachings of other men, or on a science preceding his own in the order of the sciences, as it does in the case of simple bodies; in matters like these, he is compelled to judge for himself. To summarize, it is difficult to assign precise limits to Machiavelli's knowledge of "the things of the world." It is certainly imprudent to assume that his knowledge of the things of the world is limited to things political and military in the narrow sense. It is more prudent to assume that his knowledge, and hence his teaching in either the *Prince* or the *Discourses,* is all-comprehensive. In other words, it is prudent to assume that, in either book, he has excluded from consideration only such subjects that could possibly be relevant for the understanding of the nature of political things as he explicitly excludes. There is only one subject which he explicitly excludes from discussion: "How dangerous a thing it is to make oneself the head of a new thing which concerns many people, and how difficult it is to manage it and to bring it to its consummation and after it has been brought to its consummation to maintain it, would be too large and too exalted a matter to discuss; I reserve it therefore for a more convenient place."[11] All other important themes therefore are not sufficiently large and exalted to preclude their being discussed. All other important themes must be presumed to have been dealt with, if only cursorily or allusively, in each of the two books. This conclusion is perfectly compatible with the fact that the bulk of the two books is obviously devoted to political subjects in the narrow sense: we have learned from Socrates that the political things, or the human things, are the key to the understanding of all things.

In order to see how Machiavelli can treat "everything" in each of the two books, we have only to remind ourselves of their obvious subject-matter. The guiding theme of the *Prince* is the new prince. But the most important species of new princes consists of the founders of societies. In discussing the new prince, Machiavelli discusses the foundation of every society regardless of whether it is merely political or political-religious. The theme of the *Discourses* is the possibility and desirability of reviving ancient virtue. Machiavelli cannot show the possibility and the necessity of reviving ancient virtue without opening the whole question regarding the ancients and the moderns which includes the question regarding paganism and the Bible.

If the two books are not clearly distinguished from each other by subject-matter, we have to consider whether they are not clearly distinguished from each other by their points of view. The Epistles Dedicatory inform us of the addressees of the two books, of the qualities of those men "to whom above all others [the books] are addressed." Epistles Dedicatory were a matter of common practice, but if not everyone, certainly an uncommon man is free to invest a common practice with an uncommon significance. The *Prince* is addressed to a prince; the *Discourses* are addressed to two young men who were private citizens. One might think for a moment that the *Prince* deals with everything Machiavelli knows from the point of view of a prince, whereas the *Discourses* deal with everything Machiavelli knows from a republican point of view. One might think, in other words, that Machiavelli is a supreme political technician who, without any predilection, without any conviction, advises princes how to preserve and increase their princely power, and advises republicans how to establish, maintain, and promote a republican way of life. By dedicating the *Prince* to a prince and the *Discourses* to private citizens he would thus foreshadow the political scientist of the imminent future who would dedicate his treatise on liberal democracy to a successor of President Eisenhower and his treatise on communism to a successor of Premier Bulganin. But Machiavelli is not a political scientist of this sort. He did not attempt to be neutral towards subjects the understanding of which is incompatible with neutrality. As a matter of principle he preferred, in his capacity as an analyst of society, republics to monarchies. Besides, it is not true that in the *Discourses* he considers his subjects solely from a republican point of view; in numerous passages of that book he considers the same subject from both the republican and the princely point of view.[12] Above all, the private citizens to whom the *Discourses* are addressed are described in the Epistle Dedicatory as men who, while not princes, deserve to be princes, or as men who understand how to govern a kingdom. They stand in the same relation to actual princes as that in which Hiero of Syracuse, while he was still a private citizen, stood to Perseus of Macedon while the latter was a king: Hiero while a private citizen lacked nothing of being a prince or king except the power of a prince or king. The same Hiero is presented to the addressee of the *Prince* as the model of a prince comparable to Moses and to David.[13] Just as the addressee of the *Prince* is exhorted to imitate not only the ancient princes but the ancient Roman republic as well, the addressees of the *Discourses* are exhorted to imitate not only the ancient Roman republicans but the ancient kings as well. Thus, the *Prince* and the *Discourses* agree not only in regard to their subject matter but in regard to their ultimate purpose as well. We shall then try to understand the relation of the two books on the assumption that the *Prince* is that presentation of Machiavelli's teaching which is addressed to actual princes, while the *Discourses* are that presentation of the same teaching which is addressed to potential princes.

The actual prince in a given state can be only one man: the *Prince* is addressed to one man. But there may be more than one potential prince in a given state: the *Discourses* are addressed to two men.[14] An actual prince must be supposed to be very busy: the *Prince* is a short book, a manual which, while containing everything that Machiavelli knows, can be understood within a very short time. Machiavelli achieved this feat of condensation by forgoing every kind of adornment and by depriving the book of every grace except that inherent in the variety of its matter and the weight of its theme. Potential princes have leisure: the *Discourses* are more than four times as long as the *Prince*. In addition, it is not even obvious that the *Discourses* are complete: their end appears to be a cessation rather than a culmination; and, withal, there is the fact that Machiavelli almost promises a continuation. Accordingly, in the *Prince*, extensive discussion is limited to subjects which are most urgent for an actual prince, and Machiavelli promptly specifies the subject of the book in the Epistle Dedicatory. The *Discourses* on the other hand contain extensive discussions of many details, and the Epistle Dedicatory does not specify any subject, but does contain a reference to classical writers.[15] Since the *Prince* is addresssed to an actual prince, it reasonably issues in a call to action, i.e., to the most appropriate action then and there: an actual Italian prince can be imagined to be in a position to liberate Italy. But the *Discourses*, which are addressed to merely potential princes do not issue in a call to action: one cannot know whether and in what circumstances a potential prince may become an actual ruler. Hence the *Discourses* rather delineate a long range project whose realization would require leisurely preparations and a time-consuming recovery or rebirth of the spirit of antiquity. In this light we may better understand why there is a certain preponderance of modern examples in the *Prince* and a certain preponderance of ancient examples in the *Discourses*.

The actual prince to whom the *Prince* is dedicated is Machiavelli's master, Lorenzo de' Medici. Machiavelli approaches him with the signs and in the posture of a supplicant. He is a humble subject dwelling in the lowest depth, toward which the prince, who stands on the summit of life, is not likely to turn his gaze unless he is induced to do so by some audible or strange action of the supplicant. Machiavelli tries to draw his master's attention to himself by humbly submitting to him an unusual gift, his *Prince*. The gift is unsolicited: the initiative for writing the *Prince* is entirely Machiavelli's. But Machiavelli acts under the compulsion caused by that great and continual malice of chance which oppresses him. The *Discourses* are addressed to Machiavelli's friends. Those friends compelled him to write the book: Machiavelli did not write it on his initiative. Whereas through the *Prince* he solicits a favor, he expresses through the *Discourses* his gratitude for favors received. He knows that his friends have done him favors, whereas he does not know whether his master will grant him any favor. In the same way he knows in advance that the *Discourses* will interest their addressees and will be taken seriously by them, whereas he does not know whether the *Prince* will interest its addressee and will be taken seriously by him. Machiavelli leaves us uncertain, and he himself may be uncertain, as to whether the addressee of the *Prince* is likely to be interested in that book or for that matter in any serious thought, and whether he would not be more pleased by receiving a beautiful horse. After all, whereas the addressees of the *Discourses* deserve to be princes while they are not princes, it is an open question whether the actual prince to whom the *Prince* is dedicated deserves to be a prince. There is a better prospect that Machiavelli will be understood by his tested friends than by his untested master.

In order to understand the meaning of these differences, we need only attend to what Machiavelli explicitly says about speaking of actual princes. "Of peoples everyone speaks evil without fear and freely, even while they reign: of princes one always speaks with a thousand fears and a thousand respects." The few who are able to discern the harsh truth about an actual prince do not dare to oppose the opinion of the many who are unable to discern that truth; hence when referring to the outstanding faithlessness of a contemporary prince, Machiavelli refrains from mentioning his name: "it is not good to name him."[16] What is true about speaking of actual princes is still more true about speaking to actual princes, and even more true about speaking to an actual prince who is one's dreaded master. On the other hand, it goes without saying that speaking to friends means speaking frankly. Machiavelli is then likely to be reserved in the *Prince* and straightforward in the *Discourses*.[17] Reservedness goes well with brevity. In the *Prince*, Machiavelli's treatment of everything he knows is laconic. Since to be reserved means to follow convention or tradition, the *Prince* is more conventional or traditional than the *Discourses*. The *Prince* continues a conventional or traditional genre, the mirrors of princes. The book begins like an academic or scholastic treatise. As Machiavelli says in the Epistle Dedicatory, his intention is to regulate, or to give rules for, princely government, i.e., to continue the tradition of political philosophy, especially the Aristotelian tradition.[18] Perhaps the title of the *Prince*, certainly the headings of its chapters and even of the Epistle Dedicatory are written in Latin, the language of the schools and the Church. It is true that the *Prince*, unlike a scholastic treatise, ends with an Italian quotation from a patriotic poem. But Italian patriotic poetry too had a solidly traditional character: the *Prince* moves between scholastic treatises and patriotic poems, i.e., between two traditional genres. The first word of the *Prince* is *Sogliono* ("It is customary"). But the first word of the *Discourses* is *Io* ("I"): the individual Machiavelli steps forth. In the Epistle Dedicatory of the *Prince* Machiavelli indicates that he deviates from custom in two respects: he does not offer to the prince, as most supplicants would, ornaments worthy of the greatness of the prince, but he offers the *Prince;* and he does not use external ornaments within the book itself. But in the Epistle Dedicatory of the *Discourses*, he disparages the very custom of dedicating books to princes, a custom with which he had complied in the *Prince*. The body of the *Discourses* opens with a challenge to tradition, with a statement proclaiming the entire novelty of Machiavelli's enterprise. Its parallel in the *Prince* is hidden away somewhere in the center of that book. The chapter headings of the *Prince* do not express any novel or controversial thought, whereas some chapter headings of the *Discourses* do; in two chapter headings of the *Discourses* Machiavelli openly and explicitly questions received opinions.[19] In the *Discourses* we find at least nine unambiguous references to modern writings; in the *Prince* we find only one such reference.[20] In the *Prince* all quotations from ancient writers are given in Latin; in the *Discourses* there are some cases in which quotations from ancient writers are given in Italian.[21] It is almost superfluous to say that both the title and the headings of the chapters as well as of the Epistle Dedicatory of the *Discourses* are written in the vulgar tongue. The form of the *Discourses*, a mixture of a political treatise and something like sermons on Livian texts, was certainly not conventional although it gave rise to a convention.

The foregoing remarks are not to deny that the *Prince* is a "revolutionary" book, although they are to deny that the *Prince* is more "revolutionary" than the *Discourses*. For the present we merely contend that the most external or superficial character of the *Prince*, as intended by Machiavelli, is more traditional than the surface of the *Discourses*, and furthermore, that the surface of a book as intended by its author, belongs as much to the book as does its substance. As regards the substance, the *Prince* is as much animated by admiration for antiquity, and owes its existence as much to the study of antiquity, as do the *Discourses*.[22]

We have arrived at the provisional conclusion that the *Prince* is more reserved than the *Discourses*. In the *Prince*, Machiavelli frequently fails to mention important facts, facts very relevant to the subject-matter of the book, which he does mention in the *Discourses*. We find in the *Discourses* a number of statements to the effect that republics are superior to principalities; we do not find in the *Prince* a single statement to the effect that principalities are superior to republics (or vice versa), although the first sentence of the *Prince*, as distinguished from the first sentence of the *Discourses*, draws our attention to the fundamental difference between republics and principalities. Machiavelli is silent in the *Prince* as to whether and to what extent princely rule is superior to popular rule, a question which he does not hesitate to answer very explicitly and very clearly in the *Discourses*: princes are superior to peoples as regards the founding of states, peoples are superior to princes as regards the preservation of states; in the *Prince* he limits himself to answering the question of what kind of prince is necessary for the founding of states and what kind of prince is preferable for the preservation of states.[23] He does speak in the *Prince* of the advantages of hereditary principalities—to hereditary princes; but he suppresses the discussion, transmitted through the *Discourses*, of the essential defects of hereditary principalities. In the *Prince* he merely alludes to the fact that the preservation of hereditary principalities requires neither virtue nor distinction: he treats two different dukes of Ferrara as if they were even numerically identical or altogether indistinguishable.[24] He discusses the Roman emperors coherently in both books. In the *Discourses* he emphasizes the difference between the emperors who were heirs proper and those who were the adopted sons of their predecessors, in order thus to show the defects of hereditary succession; but in the *Prince* he merely alludes to this difference. In the *Discourses* he states explicitly that of the 26 emperors mentioned there, 16 were murdered and 10 died an ordinary death, whereas in the *Prince* he compels the reader to make the effort of computing by himself that of the 10 emperors mentioned there, only 2 had a good end but 8 had a bad end. In the *Discourses* he extends the list of the Roman emperors so that it includes the golden age lasting from Nerva to Marcus Aurelius, whereas in the *Prince* he makes the list begin as late as Marcus Aurelius: he shifts the emphasis silently, but only silently, to the bad emperors.[25] In the *Discourses* he insists on the fundamental difference between kings and tyrants; in the *Prince* he silently drops this distinction: individuals who are called tyrants in the *Discourses* are called princes in the *Prince;*[26] the term "tyrant" never occurs in the *Prince;* "tyrant" is too harsh a word to use within the hearing of the prince. In the *Discourses* Machiavelli sometimes acts explicitly as an adviser of tyrants;[27] in the *Prince* he acts in this capacity only silently. Just as, in the *Prince,* he never mentions the distinction between kings and tyrants, so he never mentions in that book the common good,[28] or for that matter the conscience. In discussing the various kinds of principalities, he uses the past tense in the heading of only that chapter that deals with principalities acquired by crime: no present prince's title or good repute must be questioned. The chapter explicitly devoted to the subject of flatterers is in fact chiefly devoted to the subject of advisers. In the *Prince* he speaks of the greatness and the success of Agathocles without even alluding to his pitiable end; he speaks of Nabis' extraordinary successes, which were due to his popular policy, without alluding to the fact that he perished through a conspiracy.[29] In his discussion of conspiracies in the *Prince* he emphatically limits himself to mentioning a single example which of course is not a Florentine example; the example follows the assertion that no one would dare to conspire against a popular prince; but the example silently disproves the assertion. He praises the French laws which are the cause of "the liberty and the security of the king" or of "the security of the king and of the kingdom": he is silent about the liberty of the kingdom as distinguished from the liberty of the king.[30] In the *Prince* he omits, within the limits of the possible, everything which it would not be proper to mention in the presence of a prince. He dedicated the *Prince* to a prince because he desired to find honorable employment; the book therefore exhibits and is meant to exhibit its author as a perfect courtier, a man of the most delicate sense of propriety. Features like those mentioned supply the strongest support for the view, held by men of the competence of Spinoza and Rousseau, according to which the *Prince* is a satire on princes. They also support the view, more characteristic of our age, according to which we find the full presentation of Machiavelli's teaching in the *Discourses,* so much so that we must always read the *Prince* in the light of the *Discourses* and never by itself. I do not believe that we can follow these lines of interpretation: the older view is insufficient and the later view is altogether misleading.

If it is true that of princes one always speaks with a thousand fears and a thousand respects, then the *Discourses* cannot be altogether unreserved. While we must not forget that speaking to a prince is governed by stricter rules than speaking about princes, we should remember that the *Discourses* too were written by the subject of a prince. The *Discourses* first come to view as a republican book on republics, but it soon appears that this character of the book is overlaid by other characters. The book seems to be devoted primarily to the Roman republic, to a republic which had existed in the remote past; its primary theme could seem to be of merely antiquarian or humanistic interest. But Florence herself had been a republic until a short time ago, and "in republics there is greater life, greater hatred and more desire for revenge, and the memory of ancient liberty does not let them and cannot let them remain quiet." In perfect agreement with this republican passion driven underground, Machiavelli devotes to conspiracies that chapter of the *Discourses* which is by far the most extensive, and the bulk of that chapter to conspiracies against princes. After stressing the very great dangers incurred by those who conspire against a prince, he goes on to show in what manner such attempts at regicide or tyrannicide can be brought to a happy consummation. The chapter on conspiracies may be described as a manual of tyrannicide. An outstanding example of a conspiracy that failed was the conspiracy of the Pazzi against Lorenzo and Giuliano de' Medici in 1478. It failed because the conspirators succeeded in murdering only one of the two princes. This famous Florentine conspiracy reminds Machiavelli of two similar conspiracies, one in Athens and one in Heraclea both of which failed in the same manner. In the example of Heraclea (which is the central example) the conspirators were pupils of Plato, just as in the case of the conspiracy against Galeazzo, duke of Milan, the conspirators were pupils of a humanist who taught that all famous men were bred in republics and not under princes. But Machiavelli discusses the failure of conspiracies in order to show how they might have succeeded. Accordingly he shows that conspiracies against two or even more tyrants are by no means doomed to failure: a conspiracy in Thebes against ten tyrants had a most happy issue because the adviser of the tyrants was in his heart their enemy.[31]

But let us return once more to the surface. The *Prince* is written

for princes or for a prince. According to the *Prince*, a prince must
be able to act like a beast; he must not be altogether human or
humane; he cannot afford to be a perfect gentleman. Machiavelli
wants to be taken seriously and to be listened to by a man of this
kind. He must therefore speak the language of princes as distinguished from subjects: "great men call it disgrace to lose;
they do not call it disgrace to gain by deceit." He would ruin
every prospect of establishing his character as a competent adviser of princes if he were to speak the language of a saint, a
gentleman, or a professor of moral philosophy. For a prince who
could in any way be benefited by Machiavelli's advice must have
some awareness of what it means to be a prince in Machiavelli's
sense of the term. He must have been corrupted to some extent
by the exercise of princely power before he could bear to listen
to Machiavelli. But let us assume that there is some truth in the
princely understanding of things, or that princes can be presumed
to know certain harsh truths which gentlemen must not be presumed to know. In that case Machiavelli could be more frank
when addressing a prince, an actual prince, than when addressing
men who lack the experience of princely life. Whereas gentlemen
would first have to be broken in to the *arcana imperii*, or to be
led gradually toward realizing the problematic character of the
common good or of the conscience or of the distinction between
king and tyrant, princes might take it for granted that those generally received notions are merely popular or provisional. It is
then barely possible that the *Prince* is in some respects more outspoken than the *Discourses*. One may find a sign of this in the
facts that the title of the *Prince* reveals the subject-matter of the
book to a higher degree than does the title of the *Discourses*, and
that the plan of the *Prince* is less obscure than the plan of the
Discourses. It suffices here to mention a single obvious example.
Machiavelli explicitly excludes only one subject from discussion:
"How dangerous a thing it is to make oneself the head of a new
thing which concerns many people, and how difficult it is to
manage it and to bring it to its consummation, and after it has
been brought to its consummation, to maintain it, would be too
large and too exalted a matter to discuss; I reserve it therefore for
a more convenient place." This is said in the *Discourses*. But in
the *Prince*, where he discusses the most "exalted examples," he

does not hesitate to discuss what he calls in the *Discourses* a matter too large and too exalted to discuss. He opens the discussion as follows: "One must consider how nothing is more difficult to treat, more doubtful of success and more dangerous to handle than to make oneself the head of new orders. . . ." Machiavelli then discusses in the *Prince* and not in the *Discourses,* the only subject of which he ever says that it is too exalted for discussion. But even in the *Prince* he does not discuss it completely: he fails to discuss there how new orders can be maintained beyond the death of the founder.[32]

To summarize, Machiavelli presents in each of his two books substantially the same teaching from two different points of view, which may be described provisionally as the points of view of the actual prince and of potential princes. The difference of points of view shows itself most clearly in the fact that in the *Prince* he fails to distinguish between princes and tyrants and he never speaks of the common good nor of the conscience, whereas in the *Discourses* he does distinguish between princes and tyrants and does speak of the common good and of the conscience. We are therefore compelled to raise this question: does he regard the distinction between princes and tyrants as ultimately valid or not? does he regard the common good as the ultimate criterion or not? or does he think that these questions do not permit of a simple answer but require for their answer a distinction? We are compelled to raise the question as to whether Machiavelli's perspective is identical with that of the *Prince* or with that of the *Discourses* or whether it is different from both perspectives. Under no circumstances are we permitted dogmatically to assume, as most contemporary students do, that Machiavelli's point of view is identical with that of the *Discourses* as distinguished from that of the *Prince.*

The question which we raised can be answered only by reading Machiavelli's books. But how must we read them? We must read them according to those rules of reading which he regarded as authoritative. Since he never stated those rules by themselves, we must observe how he applied them in reading such authors as he regarded as models. His principal author being Livy, we must pay special attention to the way in which he read Livy. His manner of reading Livy may teach us something about his manner of writing. He did not read Livy as we are wont to read Livy. For Machiavelli,

Livy's work was authoritative, as it were, his Bible. His way of reading Livy was nearer to the way in which all theologians of the past read the Bible than to our way of reading either Livy or the Bible. Someone may object that precisely if Livy was an authority for Machiavelli, he, being something like a commentator on an authoritative text, would write differently than did his authority. This objection overlooks the possibility that Machiavelli may have intended his *Prince* and his *Discourses* to become authoritative texts of a kind.

Almost exactly in the center of the *Discourses*, Machiavelli tries to prove, as he indicates at the outset in the heading of the chapter in question, that money is not the sinews of war, as it is thought to be by common opinion. After thus openly challenging common opinion in the very heading of the chapter, and refuting that opinion within the chapter, he turns, near the end of the chapter, to the authority of Livy: "But Titus Livius is a truer witness to this opinion than anyone else. In the place where he discusses whether Alexander the Great, if he had come to Italy, would have vanquished the Romans, he shows that three things are necessary in war: many good soldiers, prudent captains and good luck. Examining there whether the Romans or Alexander were superior in these things, he then draws his conclusion without ever mentioning money." Livy does not mention money in a context in which he would have mentioned it if he had regarded it as important. This fact by itself establishes not only a vague presumption in favor of Livy's having held the sound opinion on the subject of money; it makes him the truest witness, the most important authority for that opinion. Livy's silence is more impressive than his explicit statement would have been.[33] Livy reveals an important truth most effectively by silence. The rule which Machiavelli tacitly applies can be stated as follows: if a wise man is silent about a fact that is commonly held to be important for the subject he discusses, he gives us to understand that that fact is unimportant. The silence of a wise man is always meaningful. It cannot be explained by forgetfulness. The view from which Livy deviates is the common view. One can express one's disagreement with the common view by simply failing to take notice of it; this is, in fact, the most effective way of showing one's disapproval.

Let us apply this lesson to Machiavelli's practice. In the *Prince* he fails to mention the conscience, the common good, the distinction between kings and tyrants, and heaven. We are reluctant to say that he forgot to mention these things, or that he did not mention them because there was no need to mention them since their importance is a matter of course or known to the meanest capacities. For if this reasoning were sound, why did he mention them in the *Discourses?* We suggest that he failed to mention them in the *Prince* because he regarded them as unimportant within the context of the *Prince.* There are, however, certain subjects which he fails to mention, not only in the *Prince* but in the *Discourses* as well, whereas he does mention them in his other works. He does not in either book mention the distinction between this world and the next, or between this life and the next; while he frequently mentions God or gods, he never mentions the devil; while he frequently mentions heaven and once paradise, he never mentions hell; above all, he never mentions the soul. He suggests by this silence that these subjects are unimportant for politics. But since each of the two books contains everything he knows, he suggests by this silence that these subjects are unimportant simply, or that the common opinion according to which these subjects are most important, is wrong. Yet this very contention is obviously of the greatest importance. That is to say, his silence concerning subjects which, according to common opinion, are very important, shows that he regards the question concerning the status of these subjects or concerning their truth or their reality, as very important. He expresses his disapproval of common opinion most effectively by silence.

The 65th chapter of the *Discourses* (II 5) opens with a reference to the grave issue of the eternity of the world, to the issue of whether the visible universe exists from eternity to eternity or whether it had a beginning. Machiavelli refers to one argument in favor of the view that the visible universe had a beginning, i.e., of the commonly held view, and then indicates that this argument has no force. He leaves it at this—at four or five lines. One cannot help wondering what Machiavelli might have thought of the other arguments in favor of the orthodox belief in creation, and what he thought of that orthodox belief itself: did he regard that belief as sound or as unsound? He does not answer these questions. He does not even raise them in so many words. But he raises them by his silence. He draws our attention to them by his silence, his half silence. The reader must keep them in mind, i.e., he must keep in mind the possibility that Machiavelli believed in the eternity of the visible universe or that he took the side of Aristotle as over against the Bible. By opening his mind to this possibility and facing it boldly, the reader may be able to understand passages which otherwise he would not appreciate. He will not be so reckless as to overlook Machiavelli's declaring, in the remaining part of the chapter, that all religions, Christianity included, are of human, not of heavenly origin and have a life span of between 1666 and 3000 years. There is an obvious connection between the question concerning the duration of the world *a parte ante* and the question concerning the source of revealed religion: the orthodox answer rests upon the belief in the superhuman origin of the Bible.

In the first chapter of the *Prince*, Machiavelli says that principalities are either hereditary or new. The distinction is obviously incomplete: it is silent regarding elective principalities. What this silence means appears from a remark that Machiavelli makes in the nineteenth chapter. When mentioning there the kingdom of the Sultan he says that it is neither hereditary nor new but elective, and therefore resembles no other principality except the Christian Pontificate. The Christian Pontificate may be said to be the theme of a special chapter of the *Prince* (chapter 11). Machiavelli's silence in the first chapter regarding the genus to which the Christian Pontificate belongs draws our attention to the chapter dealing with the Christian Pontificate—to a chapter which to the superficial reader could appear to be the product of an afterthought. By silently pointing to the theme of that chapter at the very beginning of the book, he causes us to appreciate the significance which that theme has for the whole argument of the *Prince*.[34] It almost goes without saying that Machiavelli does not speak in chapter 11 of the fact that the kingdom of the Sultan and the Christian Pontificate belong to the same genus of principalities.

Machiavelli is justly notorious or famous for the extraordinary boldness with which he attacked generally accepted opinions. He has received less than justice for the remarkable restraint which he exercised at the same time. This is not to deny that that restraint was, in a way, imposed upon him. In the tenth chapter of the

Discourses, which immediately precedes his explicit discussion of religion, he calls the age of the good Roman emperors, the period from Nerva to Marcus Aurelius, the golden times when everyone could hold and defend whatever opinion he wished. He thus indicates not only how great a value he assigned to freedom of thought or of discussion, but likewise how rarely that freedom is to be found. It certainly was not found in his time, as is shown sufficiently by the difficulties which Pietro Pomponazzo encountered because of his book on the immortality of the soul. That freedom would not be found, according to Machiavelli, in a well-ordered republic; in the very center of his *Florentine Histories* he praises Cato for having provided that no philosopher should be received in Rome.[35] One may wonder whether according to him freedom of discussion could be found in any society: in the same chapter in which he praises the age of the good Roman emperors as the epoch of perfect freedom of discussion, he as it were retracts this praise by saying that as long as the Roman emperors ruled, writers were not permitted to speak freely about Caesar, since Caesar was the source of the emperors' authority. In the same chapter he illustrates how restrictions on freedom of speech affect writers whose minds are free. Since under the Roman emperors free writers could not blame Caesar, they blamed Catiline, Caesar's luckless prefiguration, and they celebrated Brutus, Caesar's enemy. After having indicated the principle, Machiavelli immediately turns to applying it by praising the pagan Roman religion, the enemy of the Biblical religion: his praising the religion of the pagans while he was subject to the Christian Church is almost the exact counterpart of a Roman republican's praising the murderer of Caesar while being subject to the Roman emperors.[36] For what is true of the situation under the Roman emperors is equally true of all other situations: at all times there exists a ruling power, a victorious power which dazzles the eyes of most writers and which restrains the freedom of those few writers who do not desire to become martyrs. Restriction on freedom of discussion compels writers whose minds do not succumb to the glamor or the frowning of authority to present their thoughts in an oblique way. It is too dangerous for them to attack the protected opinions openly or frontally. To a certain extent they are even compelled to express the protected opinions as their own opinions. But to adopt opinions of

which one is certain that they are false, means to make oneself
more stupid than one is, or to play the fool: "one plays the fool
sufficiently if you praise, speak, see, and do things against your
opinion in order to please the prince." For to speak the truth is
sensible only when one speaks to wise men.[37]

Machiavelli was compelled to be restrained because he was bold.
His boldness consisted in questioning the established modes and
orders and in seeking new modes and orders. He compares the
search for new modes and orders to the search for unknown seas
and lands, but he indicates this difference between the two kinds
of quest: in the case of new modes and orders, it is not so much the
seeking as the finding that is dangerous. The danger is caused by
the envy of men who begrudge the glory of him who discovered
the new modes and orders. It is then not so much the discovery
as the communication of the discovery which is dangerous. These
indications with which Machiavelli opens the *Discourses* give an
insufficient notion of the risks run by the proposer of new modes
and orders. Toward the end of the *Discourses*, Machiavelli declares
that he will not discuss how dangerous it is to make oneself the
head of novelties which are of public concern: to discuss those
dangers would increase them. He is more informative in the *Prince*,
in which he does not say that he has discovered new modes and
orders and in which therefore the question of the dangerous character of such discovery is not explicitly linked to his own case. In
the *Prince* he says that the opponents of the new modes and orders
have on their side the laws, the majesty of the laws, and of what
gives majesty to the laws. The innovator arouses the indignation of
the overpowering multitude, which clings to the established order.
His situation would be hopeless if there were no disagreement as
to how the obtaining law is to be interpreted, or if the defenders of
the ancient were not split into opposing parties. This being the
case, Machiavelli expresses with the greatest boldness such views
as are tolerable to one party but he is very cautious in regard to
views which have no respectable support whatever. More precisely,
he conceals the ground on which he partly agrees with one party.
His enterprise being difficult, he says, he will nevertheless carry
it out in such a manner that there shall remain to another man a
short road to go towards the destination: Machiavelli does not go
to the end of the road; the last part of the road must be travelled

by the reader who understands what is omitted by the writer. Machiavelli does not go to the end; he does not reveal the end; he does not fully reveal his intention.[38]

But he intimates it. It is indispensable that we should discuss some examples of Machiavelli's modes of intimating what he is unable to state. Almost at the end of the *Discourses* (III 48) he notes, after having cited a single example, that "the leader of an army must not believe in an error which an enemy evidently commits, for there will always be fraud beneath it, it not being reasonable that men should be so uncautious." Immediately after having stated this allegedly universal rule, he cites an example—the central example of the chapter—in which an enemy committed a manifest blunder without a tincture of fraud; the example shows in effect that enemies sometimes commit grave blunders out of panic or cowardice. The absurdity of Machiavelli's universal rule is underlined by the contrast between the rule as stated within the chapter and the rule as stated in the heading of the chapter. The heading soberly says that "when one sees an enemy commit a grave blunder, one ought to believe that there is deception beneath it"; for "to believe" means merely "provisionally to assume." Besides, Machiavelli had earlier used the crucial example in order to show that "fortune sometimes blinds the minds of men": the manifest blunder in question was caused not by human calculation, but by human blindness.[39] It is of no importance to us that Machiavelli restates the rule elsewhere so that it becomes reasonable: if a prudent and strong enemy commits a manifest blunder, there will always be fraud beneath it.[40] What is important is the fact that Machiavelli, in the act of speaking of manifest blunders, himself commits a manifest blunder. He does what, as he says, enemies sometimes do. His action ceases to be absurd if he himself is an enemy, a clever enemy. And can we doubt that he is an enemy? As the friend or father of new modes and orders, he is of necessity the enemy of the old modes and orders, and therewith also the enemy of his readers who would not have to learn from him if they were not adherents of the old modes and orders. Machiavelli's action is a kind of warfare. Some things which he says about strategy and tactics in ordinary warfare apply to his own strategy and tactics in what we may call his spiritual warfare. By committing a manifest blunder when speaking of such manifest blunders as conceal fraud, he gives us to understand that there is deception beneath his own manifest blunders, or that his manifest blunders are intentional: they indicate his intention.

We arrive at this solution by taking most seriously what Machiavelli says at the very beginning of the *Discourses:* that he has discovered new modes and orders, that such discovery is dangerous if it is communicated, and that he will nevertheless communicate his discovery. This most obvious and explicit, if initial and provisional statement concerning his intention guides us towards the adequate understanding of his intention, provided "we put 2 and 2 together" or do some thinking on our own. Regarding the example discussed above, we thus arrive at a solution which acquits Machiavelli of the disgrace of committing blunders of which an intelligent high school boy would be ashamed. Some readers will feel that this solution is to be rejected because it does not do credit to Machiavelli's morality. As we have indicated from the outset, we are doubtful of his morality. To the readers who would raise the difficulty mentioned we may reply using Machiavelli's own words: "For some time I never say what I believe and I never believe what I say; and if it sometimes occurs to me that I say the truth, I conceal it among so many lies that it is hard to find it out."[41] To discover from his writings what he regarded as the truth is hard: it is not impossible.

Machiavelli's work is rich in manifest blunders of various kinds: misquotations, misstatements regarding names or events, hasty generalizations, indefensible omissions and so on. It is a rule of common prudence to "believe" that all these blunders are intentional and in each case to raise the question as to what the blunder might be meant to signify. The simplest case of manifest blunder is the author's self-contradiction and especially self-contradiction on one and the same page. In *Discourses* I 28, Machiavelli raises the question as to why the Romans were less ungrateful to their fellow citizens than were the Athenians. His answer is based on a number of premises, among which the following is particularly important in the present context: Athens was deprived of her liberty by Pisistratus during her most flourishing period, whereas Rome was never deprived of her liberty by any of her citizens between the expulsion of the kings and the time of Marius and Sylla. Seven chapters later he says that the ten citizens elected for making laws by the free votes of the Roman people became tyrants of Rome. We are not at present concerned with the fact that this self-contradiction makes doubtful Machiavelli's explanation of Roman gratitude and Athenian ingratitude.[42] We merely raise the preliminary question concerning the most obvious implication of Machiavelli's obvious blunder. The temporary disregard of the Decemvirate amounts to a temporary overstatement concerning the goodness of the Roman republic; for long and continuous duration of freedom is, according to Machiavelli, a great good.[43] We are then compelled to wonder why Machiavelli temporarily overstates the case in favor of the Roman republic. We observe that in the same short chapter (I 28) he calls the period of Pisistratus first "the most flourishing time" of Athens, and, about a page later, Athens' "first times and prior to Athens' growth." He thus suggests that the most flourishing period of a city is the period preceding its growth, i.e., the first time or its beginning. This agrees with his earlier remark that at the birth of a republic, as distinguished from later periods, "men are good," and with his emphatic praise, in the first chapter, of the kings of Egypt who ruled that country "in the most ancient antiquity." The praise of the beginnings or origins, which, as we shall see later, is contradicted elsewhere in the Discourses, is the context within which Machiavelli's deliberately exaggerated praise of the Roman republic must be understood. He challenges the established modes and orders, whose primary claim to reverence rests on their antiquity, primarily by appealing not to the good as such but to a more ancient antiquity, if not to "the most ancient antiquity." For he who desires to introduce new modes and orders, is compelled to retain at least a shadow of ancient modes and orders, if he is unable or unwilling to use force and nothing but force.[44]

An author may reveal his intention by the titles of his books. The titles of Machiavelli's two books are most unrevealing in this respect. The same is almost equally true of the chapter headings, which occupy an intermediate position between the titles of the books and their substance. We have noted that the chapter headings of the Discourses, to say nothing of those of the Prince, reveal hardly anything of the daring quality of his thought.[45] In discussing a passage from the Discourses (III 48), we observed a striking difference between the rule of conduct stated in the heading and the rule as restated within the chapter: the rule as stated in the heading does not stimulate thought, whereas the restatement arouses thought not to say indignation. The heading of I 48 reads, "He who wishes that a magistracy be not given to someone base or bad, induces either someone exceedingly base and exceedingly bad or someone exceedingly noble and exceedingly good to apply for it." The argument of the chapter leads to the conclusion that while the people deceive themselves as to generalities, they do not deceive themselves as to particulars. But at the end of the preceding chapter, Machiavelli says that I 48 is meant to show how the Roman senate went about to deceive the people in regard to the distribution of ranks and dignities among candidates, i.e., in regard to particulars. The heading of I 13 reads, "How the Romans used religion for reordering the city and pursuing their enterprises and stopping tumults"; the heading does not give the slightest indication of the fact that the body of the chapter deals chiefly with the question of how the Roman nobility used religion for controlling the plebs. In the heading of I 26 Machiavelli speaks of "a new prince"; neither in the heading nor in the body of the chapter does he say what he says at the end of the preceding chapter, namely, that I 26 is devoted to the phenomenon generally known by the name of tyranny. In the heading of I 30, he uses the expression "the vice of ingratitude"; at the beginning of the chapter itself he replaces this expression by "the necessity . . . to be ungrateful": the thought that men's vices (and virtues) are due to necessity rather than to election is in no way suggested by the heading. In the heading of I 9, he says that "It is necessary to be alone if one wishes to order a republic afresh"; there is not the slightest indication here that being alone can be achieved by murdering one's only brother, as is developed at great length within the chapter; in fact, the lesson to be learned from Romulus's slaying of his brother may be said to be the chief theme of the chapter.

The heading of *Discourses* III 18 makes one expect that Machiavelli will discuss in that chapter the importance as well as the difficulty of understanding the enemy's intentions. On the basis of our previous observations we are not surprised to see that he drops this subject immediately after having referred to it, and replaces it by the difficulty of knowing the enemy's actions, and not merely his actions in the past and in remote places but his "present and near" actions. He cites four examples to prove his point. There is a strict parallelism among the examples: twice an ancient example is followed by a modern example. The first two examples deal with defeats caused by errors as to the enemy's present and near actions; the last two examples deal with victories due to correct information as to the enemy's present and near actions: in both the latter examples, possession of true knowledge alone was decisive for victory. In both the latter examples, the victory lacked splendor and the acquisition of knowledge lacked merit. The ancient victory had this character: there had been a drawn battle between the Romans and the Aequi; each army believed that the enemy had won and each therefore marched home; by accident a Roman centurion learned from some wounded Aequi that the Aequi had abandoned their camp; he therefore sacked the deserted camp of the enemy and returned home a victor. The modern victory had this character: a Florentine and a Venetian army had been facing each other for several days, neither daring to attack the other; since both armies began to suffer from lack of victuals, each decided to retire; by accident the Florentine captains learned from a woman who, being "secure because of her age and her poverty," had gone to see some of her people in the Florentine camp, that the Venetians were retiring; the Florentines therefore became courageous, went after their enemies, and wrote to Florence that they had repulsed the enemy and won the war. In the ancient example we find then a bloody battle, wounded enemy soldiers, and the plundering of the enemy camp. In the modern example we find a phony battle, an old and poor woman, and a boastful letter. The contrast which is not made explicit, between the ancient and the modern example teaches us nothing about the superiority of the virile ancients to the effeminate moderns that Machiavelli does not tell us with the utmost explicitness in many other passages of the *Discourses*. That silent contrast, therefore, does not teach us anything new as to his primary intention, which is to contribute toward the rebirth of the spirit of antiquity. Yet that silent contrast performs a function, or rather it performs two different, if related functions. In the first place, it draws our attention to the fact that the chapter under consideration is secretly devoted to some aspect of the central problem regarding the difference between the ancients and the moderns. Secondly, it presents the general lesson in a mode which is less obvious throughout the *Discourses* and the *Prince*, than the opposite mode. Every reader, however superficial, of either of the two books cannot but become aware of the gravity of Machiavelli as a teacher of princes and statesmen. It is then of some importance to realize that the spirit of comedy, not to say levity, is not absent from his two most serious books. In fact, gravity and levity are combined in these two books "in a quasi-impossible combination," just as they were in the man Machiavelli.[46] If it is true that every complete society necessarily recognizes something about which it is absolutely forbidden to laugh,[47] we may say that the determination to transgress that prohibition *sanza alcuno rispetto*, is of the essence of Machiavelli's intention.

He does not reveal this intention. He even refuses to reveal the difficulties that bar the understanding of the enemy's intention. But he adumbrates those difficulties by suggesting a hierarchy of the difficulties that prevent one from knowing the enemy's present and near actions. In the last of the four examples, no error was committed by anyone because no action was taken during the night. In the first three examples errors, and in the first two examples even disastrous errors, were committed because darkness had supervened. In the last two examples, present and near daytime actions of the enemy were discovered by sheer accident. All four examples deal with present and near actions. The difficulties increase infinitely when one is concerned with discovering the truth about nocturnal enemy actions done in remote countries and in the remote past. But even these difficulties are surpassed by those obstructing the discovery of the intentions of clever enemies: they can never be discovered by accident.[48] This is not to deny that accessible writings of clever enemies partly partake of the character of present and near daytime actions of the enemy.

In a deliberate self-contradiction an author says incompatible things or, more generally stated, different things about the same subject to different people, and in some cases to the same people in different stages of their understanding. But to speak differently to different people may be said to be irony in the primary sense of the word.[49] Whatever may be the relation between irony and parody in general, certainly subtle parodies may fulfill the demands of irony proper. *Discourses* II 12 is a parody of this kind, a subdued parody of scholastic disputations. Machiavelli discusses there the question of whether it is better, if one apprehends an attack, to assail the enemy in his country, or to await him in one's own country. The discussion consists of four parts: arguments from authority for either side, arguments from reason for either side, a solution based on a distinction, and a defense of the solution against an adverse argument. It is a parody of a scholastic disputation both because it applies scholastic procedure to a non-scholastic subject and because the central authority in favor of the superior alternative is a "poetic fable": the place of the Bible is taken by poetic fables. Machiavelli would seem to have inferred from the human, not heavenly, origin of Biblical religion to which he had alluded seven chapters earlier, that the dogmatic teaching of the Bible has the cognitive status of poetic fables.[50] We are at present much more concerned, however, with the seemingly trivial circumstance that he hesitates in *Discourses* II 12 to call the arguments from authority by that name: in that place he somewhat blurs the difference between authority and reason.[51] He stresses that difference six chapters afterward in a rather striking manner. In the heading of II 18, he refers to "the authority of the Romans and the example of the ancient militia," but he replaces this expression in the first line of the chapter by "many reasons and many examples." Shortly afterward, he quotes a Latin sentence, an extremely simple Latin sentence, and then adds to the quotation its Italian translation, something he does nowhere else in either book: after having replaced "authority" by "reasons," he goes on to replace the language of authority by his own native tongue.[52] In the immediate sequel he says, "*if* one must follow authority . . . Apart from authority, there are manifest reasons." After having established his opinion by reason alone, he refers—and this is another unique occurrence —to "the authority of those who regulate political things," i.e., to "the authority" of the traditional political theorists. One must bear in mind the presence of the problem of authority in this section of the *Discourses*, a section which may be said to be opened by the remark, discussed above, as to the meaning of Livy's silence. Otherwise, one may fail to understand, among other things, the following irregularities occurring in an intervening chapter. *Discourses* II 13 is meant to prove that one ascends from a low to a high position through fraud rather than through force. Machiavelli gives some details concerning only two individuals who rose from an abject or low condition to great political power. Both individuals were nephews (*nepoti*) of the absolute rulers who preceded them; they cannot be said to have risen to their commanding height from an abject or low place. That is to say, the examples are not apt: we are compelled to wonder which were the apt examples that Machiavelli had in mind. In the same chapter he asserts that not only princes but the Roman republic as well rose to pre-eminence initially by fraud, and he proves this by quoting from Livy a speech by an enemy of the Romans; Livy is presented as revealing the truth about Roman fraud by putting certain words into the mouth of an enemy of Rome. Could a respectable Roman have been unable to say the truth about Rome except by making an enemy of Rome his mouthpiece, just as a subject of the Roman emperors was unable to say the truth about Caesar except by praising Caesar's enemy? Could a citizen of the *respublica Christiana* have been unable to say what he regarded as the truth about Christianity except by employing an enemy of Christianity or a pagan, such as Livy, as his mouthpiece? Machiavelli certainly tries to establish the truth about the Hebrew conquest of Canaan by referring to an account about Joshua which goes back to enemies of the Hebrews and which flagrantly contradicts the Hebrew account.[53]

When an author deliberately contradicts himself in a subtle manner, he may be said to repeat an earlier statement of his while varying it in a way which for some reason is not easily noticed. Machiavelli discusses in the *Discourses* the policy of Florence toward Pistoia more than once. In the first statement (II 21) he says that the city of Pistoia came voluntarily under the sway of Florence because the Florentines had always treated the Pistoians as brothers. In the second statement (II 25) he says that the city of Pistoia came under the sway of Florence by means of the following "peaceful artifice." Pistoia being divided into parties, the Florentines favored now one, now the other party and thus led the Pistoians to become so tired of party strife that they threw themselves voluntarily into the arms of Florence. The peaceful art used by the Florentines is described in the context as that of dividing and conquering. In the second statement Machiavelli draws our attention to the difference between the two accounts of the Florentine policy toward Pistoia by referring to what he had said on this subject in another chapter and "for another purpose." The cross reference is striking since it is the only one of this character that occurs in the *Discourses*. Machiavelli must indeed have had more than one purpose if he could describe the same policy first as an expression of fraternity and liberality, and then as an application of the rule "divide and conquer." What first comes to sight as fraternity and liberality, reveals itself on reflection as shrewd "power politics." The first statement agrees with the common view according to which morality can control and ought to control political life; the second statement read in conjunction with the first suggests doubt of the common view. No one, I believe, questions the opinion that Machiavelli did doubt the common view regarding the relation between morality and politics, for every one has read chapters 15 ff. of the *Prince*. The cross-reference under discussion is important to us at present not because it throws light on the substance of his teaching but because it reveals to some extent his way of presenting it. The substance of his teaching is bound to be misunderstood if one does not realize that he reveals his teaching, to the extent to which he does reveal it, only in stages: he ascends from "first statements," which are, to exaggerate for the purpose of clarification, in all cases respectable or publicly defensible, to "second statements" of a different character. If one does not realize the difference of "purpose" between "first statements" and "second statements," one may read the "second statements" in the light of the "first statements" and thus blunt the edges of his teaching; one will at any rate ascribe the same weight to both kinds of statements; and since the "first statements" are more or less traditional or conventional, one will not grasp the magnitude or enormity of Machiavelli's enterprise. It is necessary, at least wherever Machiavelli refers to earlier statements on a given subject by using expressions like "as has been said," carefully to compare the restatement with the original statement and to see whether the restatement does not imply a considerable modification of the first statement. To give an example the complexity of which is proportionate to its importance, Machiavelli repeatedly discusses in the first book of the *Discourses* the subject of "founders" or of men who established "new orders." In the first statement (I 9-10), he contends that a founder who is concerned with the common good, as distinguished from a tyrant, cannot be blamed if he commits murder in order to achieve his good end; the discussion is based on the fundamental and traditional distinction between the prince and the tyrant, between the common good and the private good, between virtue and ambition; Caesar, in contrast to Romulus, appears as the outstanding example of a most blameworthy tyrant. In the second statement (I 16-18), Machiavelli makes use of the distinction between corrupt and uncorrupt peoples, and in connection with this blurs the distinction between princes and tyrants: was Caesar's tyranny not inevitable, and therefore perfectly excusable, given the corruption of Rome in his time?[54] And what do corruption and its opposite mean if, to say nothing of other things, the uncorrupt character of the earliest Rome permitted Romulus "to color his design" whereas Caesar presumably was under no compulsion to do this? Was then Romulus's design not to promote the common good? In the third statement (I 25-27), Machiavelli indicates that "tyranny" is a traditional term, i.e., a term not necessarily required by, or compatible with, his intention. In a chapter which is explicitly devoted to what "the writers call tyranny," he treats the godly King David as an example of a tyrant; and in the chapter following he makes it clear that a very wicked ruler who cannot be presumed to be guided by any concern with the common good, may nevertheless earn eternal glory by doing deeds which are conducive to the common good. We are led to conclude that the primary distinction between public-spirited virtue and selfish ambition is irrelevant since selfish ambition on the broadest scale can be satisfied only by actions from which very many people profit. In all these statements it is assumed that foundation is a unique act at the inception of a commonwealth or a regime. But Machiavelli eventually questions this assumption: foundation is, as it were, continuous foundation; not only at the beginning, but "every day," a commonwealth needs "new orders."[55] Once one realizes this, one sees that the founders of a republic are its leading men throughout the ages, or its ruling class. One sees therefore, that the section devoted to the ruling class (I 33-45) is as it were the true and final statement concerning founders.[56] We may draw a further lesson from Machiavelli's twofold discussion of the policy of Florence toward Pistoia. He suggests mutually exclusive interpretations of the same fact: what is important is not the fact itself but the opportunity which it provides for making a point. Thus we understand that Machiavelli is not always concerned with historical truth, and frequently changes at will the data supplied by the histories: if there are examples which are both beautiful and true,[57] there may be examples which are beautiful without being true. In the language of our time, Machiavelli is an artist as much as he is an historian. He is certainly very artful.[58]

Machiavelli's examples are not always apt nor always true. I do not believe that we can infer from this that they are not always well chosen. He frequently uses expressions like "I wish to leave it at this example." It is always necessary to wonder why he preferred the example or the examples which he adduces: were they the most apt or the most suggestive examples?[59] For what we know in such cases is merely the fact that Machiavelli did not wish to mention other examples; we do not know the reason why he did not wish to mention them. As regards the *Discourses* in particular, the primary intention of which would suggest an even distribution of Roman and modern examples, one must pay attention to the actual distribution which is highly irregular. We must do this even independently of whether Machiavelli explicitly refers to his wishing to leave it at the examples adduced. Expressions of the type "I wish to leave it at . . ." may be said to indicate "exclusions," since they exclude from mention, or from further discussion, what might well deserve to be, but what could not conveniently or with propriety be, mentioned or discussed at greater length. The opposite of exclusions are digressions. A typical expression indicating a digression is the remark "But let us return to our subject-matter." In a digression an author discusses something which he characterizes as not belonging to the subject-matter strictly understood. In books like the *Prince* and the *Discourses*, the digressions contain discussions which would not be required to further the primary, explicit, ostensible or partial intention but are required to further the full or true intention. The primary or partial intention of the *Prince* would require the treatment of only those kinds of principality or of the acquisition of princely power which are mentioned in the first chapter; that is to say, the first chapter leads us to expect the subject-matters of chapters 2-7; chapters 8-11, containing, among other things, the discussion of the acquisition of princely power by crime and the discussion of ecclesiastical principalities, come as a surprise; it is not misleading, although it is not strict, to call chapters 8-11 a digression. The statement as to the similarity between the state of the Sultan and the Christian Pontificate, in the nineteenth chapter of the *Prince*,[60] is a typical digression in the strict sense. We would not consider as a digression in the strict sense a passage which Machiavelli does not indicate to be one. We do regard as a digression however a passage which is presented as an answer to a possible question or objection of the reader.[61] A passage of this kind is Machiavelli's discussion, in the eleventh chapter of the *Prince*, of how the temporal power of the church rose to its present height. Another passage of this kind is the discussion of the Roman emperors in the nineteenth chapter of the *Prince*. A brief analysis of the latter passage may be helpful for understanding the meaning of digressions in general. In the ninth chapter Machiavelli had made it clear that there is one absolute limit to the astute use of princely power: while a prince may, under certain circumstances, safely disregard the interests of the great and even destroy the great, it is absolutely necessary for him to respect the extremely moderate demands of the common people. After having restated this rule in a mitigated form in the first part of chapter 19, Machiavelli explains in the section on the Roman emperors that that rule, even in its original form, is by no means universally valid: under the Roman empire there was a conflict of interests between the people and the soldiers; the power of the soldiers was greater than that of the people; therefore the emperors had to satisfy the demands of the soldiers rather than those of the people; hence an able Roman emperor who had the support of the soldiers was under no compulsion to consider the people at all. The last brake on wicked rulers can be rendered ineffective. The outstanding example of such a Roman emperor was Septimius Severus. If Machiavelli had at this point been able to use traditional language, he would have said that Severus was a typical tyrant who had the support of his bodyguard. Now, it is precisely Severus, this "most ferocious lion and most astute fox"—the same Severus whom he calls elsewhere a criminal—whom he holds up at the end of the chapter as a model for founders of states as distinguished from princes whose task is merely to preserve a state already founded:[62] as far as founders are concerned, the distinction between virtuous heroes and extremely able criminals has ceased to exist.

In reading Machiavelli's books one is constantly kept wondering whether he is careful or careless in the use of terms both technical and other. We have observed so many examples of his exceeding care that we venture to make this suggestion: it is safer to believe that he has given careful thought to every word he uses than to make allowances for human weakness. Considering the difference of rank between Machiavelli and people like ourselves, the rule of reading which derives from that belief may be impracticable, since we cannot possibly comply with it in all cases. It is nevertheless a good rule, for remembering it keeps us awake and modest or helps us to develop the habit of being in the proper mixture both bold and cautious. There are certain terms which require particular attention, namely, ambiguous terms. The ambiguity of "virtue" is best known. Machiavelli says of the criminal Agathocles, in two consecutive sentences, first that he lacked virtue and then that he possessed virtue; in the first case "virtue" means moral virtue in the widest sense which includes religion, and in the second case it means cleverness and courage combined. Pope Leo X is said to possess "goodness and infinite other virtues" and Hannibal is said to have possessed "inhuman cruelty together with (infinite) other virtues." To use liberality "virtuously and as one ought to use it" is distinguished from using it prudently, i.e., virtuously in a different sense of the term.[63] There is an intermediate meaning according to which "virtue" designates political virtue or the sum of qualities required for rendering service to political society or for effective patriotism. Even in accordance with this intermediate meaning, inhuman cruelty could be a virtue and ambition a vice. In many cases it is impossible to say which kind of virtue is meant. This obscurity is essential to Machiavelli's presentation of his teaching. It is required by the fact that the reader is meant to ascend from the common understanding of virtue to the diametrically opposite understanding. Equally ambiguous is "prince." "Prince" may mean a non-tyrannical monarch, or any monarch, or any man or body of men in a ruling position including the leading men in a republic, to say nothing of another meaning. "People" may mean a republican society as well as the common people. "Human beings" may mean human beings as such or male human beings, or the general run of men, or the subjects of princes.[64] "Heaven" may mean the visible heaven, the ground of all regularity or order in the sub-celestial world, a thinking and willing being that may be kind to human beings or love certain human individuals, chance, a goal of human aspiration, and the cause of catastrophes like plagues, famines or floods. "We" may mean Machiavelli, Machiavelli and his reader or readers, Machiavelli's contemporaries, the Florentines, the Christians, the contemporary Christians, the Italians, the contemporary Italians, all human beings, a society to which the speaker belongs in contradistinction to an enemy society, both a society and its enemy taken together. In some cases it is hard to decide what the first person plural pronoun precisely means, as for instance when Machiavelli calls Livy "our historian," or when he says "we, at any rate, do not have knowledge of things natural and supernatural."[65] In the last case it is not impossible that "we" means "we who are not philosophers."

The *Discourses* are devoted to the first ten books of Livy's *History*, or to the history of Rome up to about 292 B.C. Livy's *History* consisted of 142 books. Strangely, the *Discourses* consist of 142 chapters, for the prefaces to Book I and Book II are, of course, not chapters. Machiavelli would seem thus to convey his intention of elucidating the history, not only of early Rome, but of Rome from its beginning until the time of the emperor Augustus. A glance at the list of the events discussed in the *Discourses* bears out this contention.[66] The strange fact that the number of chapters of the *Discourses* is the same as the number of the books of Livy makes one wonder whether the number of chapters of the *Prince* is not also significant. Since the *Prince* consists of twenty-six chapters and the *Prince* does not give us any information as to the possible meaning of this number, we turn to the twenty-sixth chapter of the *Discourses*. That chapter is the only chapter of the *Discourses* which is devoted, according to its heading, to the "new prince," i.e., the chief theme of the *Prince*. Moreover, the chapter deals with what the authors call tyranny, as Machiavelli says at the end of the preceding chapter; but the term "tyranny" (or "tyrant") is avoided in the twenty-sixth chapter. If we turn from the twenty-sixth chapter of the *Discourses* to the *Prince*, which consists of twenty-six chapters, we observe that the terms "tyrant" or "tyranny" are avoided in the *Prince* too: the twenty-sixth chapter of the *Discourses* imitates the *Prince* in such a way as to give us a clue to the *Prince*. Since this observation leads to further relevant observations concerning the *Prince*, some of which have been noted before, we gain some confidence that in taking seriously the number 26, we are on the right path. But before pursuing this line of thought, it may be wise to dwell for a while on the twenty-sixth chapter of the *Discourses*. The first of the two examples which Machiavelli uses in that chapter is King David, according to the Gospels, the ancestor of Jesus. The measures that men like King David must employ at the beginning of their reign, i.e., in order to found or establish their states, are described by Machiavelli as "most cruel and inimical, not only to every Christian manner of living but to every humane manner of living as well." One measure of King David was to make the rich poor and the poor rich. In speaking of this measure Machiavelli quotes the following verse from the Magnificat: "He filled the hungry with good things, and sent the rich away empty." That is to say, he applies to the tyrant David an expression which the New Testament, or Mary, applies to God. Since he characterizes as tyrannical, a way of acting that the New Testament ascribes to God he leads us to the conclusion, nay, says in effect, that God is a tyrant. In his own strange way he accepts the traditional view according to which David was a godly king or walked in the ways of God. It is for the sake of making this extraordinary and shocking suggestion that he uses the only quotation from the New Testament which he ever uses in either the *Prince* or the *Discourses*.[67]

The most superficial fact regarding the *Discourses*, the fact that the number of its chapters equals the number of books of Livy's *History*, compelled us to start a chain of tentative reasoning which brought us suddenly face to face with the only New Testament quotation that ever occurs in Machiavelli's two books and with an enormous blasphemy. It would be a great disservice to truth if we were to use any other words, any weaker words for characterizing what he is doing. For it would be a mistake to believe that the blasphemy which we encountered is the only one or even the worst one which he committed. That blasphemy is, so to speak, only the spearhead of a large column. We have no compunction whatever about using a term which expresses very strong

disapproval, although its use is likely to be regarded by our fellow
social scientists as a "culture conditioned" reflex and therefore as
an aberration from the straight and narrow path of scientific cor-
rectitude; for we believe that failing to call a spade a spade is not
scientific. Someone might say in defense of Machiavelli that he
does not speak of God in the incriminated passage or that the blasphemy is so well concealed as to be non-existent for the majority
of readers. Over against this one might well urge that a concealed
blasphemy is worse than an open blasphemy, for the following
reason. In the case of an ordinary blasphemy, the hearer or reader
becomes aware of it without making any contribution of his own.
By concealing his blasphemy, Machiavelli compels the reader to
think the blasphemy by himself and thus to become Machiavelli's
accomplice. One cannot compare the situation of the reader of
Machiavelli with that of a judge or a prosecutor who likewise re-
thinks criminal or forbidden thoughts in order to bring the accused to justice and thus establishes a kind of intimacy with the
criminal without however incurring the slightest suspicion of
thus becoming an accomplice and without for a moment having a
sense of guilt. For the criminal does not desire and invite this kind
of intimacy but rather dislikes it. Machiavelli on the other hand
is anxious to establish this kind of intimacy if only with a certain
kind of reader whom he calls "the young." Concealment as practiced by Machiavelli is an instrument of subtle corruption or se-
duction. He fascinates his reader by confronting him with riddles.
Thereafter the fascination with problem-solving makes the reader
oblivious to all higher duties if not all duties. By concealing his
blasphemies, Machiavelli merely avoids punishment or revenge,
but not guilt. When we turn from the twenty-sixth chapter of
the First Book of the *Discourses* to the twenty-sixth chapter of the
Second Book, we find Machiavelli uttering strong warnings of
a calculating character against hurting men's feelings with words
of scorn; he concludes the chapter with quoting a sentence which
Tacitus pronounces when speaking of an enemy of the tyrant
Nero: "Smarting jokes, if they draw too much on truth, leave
stinging memories behind them." A liberal theologian once said
within my hearing that the traditional judgment on blasphemy is
based on too narrow a conception of God's honor. He used the
analogy of a very wise and very powerful king who would tolerate

and even enjoy jokes about himself however smarting, provided
they are graceful and do not create a public scandal. This argument
seems to us so patently inappropriate that we may dismiss it without any discussion. We prefer to submit the following consideration.
The kinds of unbelief with which we are most familiar today are
respectful indifference and such a nostalgia for lost faith as goes
with an inability to distinguish between theological truth and myth.
Are not these kinds of unbelief much more insulting to belief than
is an unbelief like Machiavelli's which takes seriously the claim
to truth of revealed religion by regarding the question of its
truth as all-important and which therefore is not, at any rate,
a lukewarm unbelief? Furthermore, if, as Machiavelli assumes,
Biblical religion is not true, if it is of human and not of heavenly
origin, if it consists of poetic fables, it becomes inevitable that one
should attempt to understand it in merely human terms. At first
glance, this attempt can be made in two different ways: one may
try to understand Biblical religion by starting from the phenomena
of human love or by starting from political phenomena. The first
approach was taken by Boccaccio in his *Decameròn*, the second
approach was taken by Machiavelli. In *Discourses* II 12, which
is a parody of scholastic disputations, he indicates how political
or military truths can be transformed into poetic fables, or how
the political or military truths underlying such fables can be
elicited: Antaeus was not the son of Earth nor therefore invincible
as long as he stood on the earth and was not lifted from the
earth; but being a son of a human mother, he was invincible as
long as he waited within the confines of his realm for the attack
of his enemy. Similarly the fable according to which the ancient
princes were taught their art by a centaur means nothing other
than that princes must be half inhuman. In the same way, "reading the Bible judiciously," Machiavelli discerns that the actions of
Moses were not fundamentally different from those of Cyrus,
Romulus, Theseus or Hiero of Syracuse: to "read the Bible judiciously" means to read it not in its own light but in the light of the
fundamental political verities.[68] But even if we grant that he was
compelled to raise the question regarding the political phenomena
or the political hopes which in principle perfectly explain the
Bible and the Biblical conception of God, we do not yet understand why he had recourse to blasphemies. After all, that ques-

tion is being discussed today and has been discussed for some generations by many scholars who are and were perfectly innocent of blasphemy. The answer is simple: for some generations, the authority of the Bible has not been generally recognized and supported by law; Machiavelli on the other hand was compelled to use subterfuges. Many features of his writings, which to us may appear to be caused by mere levity, are also caused by the necessity in which he found himself of combining simply political or military lessons with indications of what he thought to be the human or natural phenomena that make intelligible the belief in the supernatural or the desire for it. This necessity must not be disregarded when one reads his praise of necessity in general: men's hands and tongues would not have carried the works of men to the height to which they are seen to have been carried, if men had not been driven on by necessity.[69]

To repeat, we do not believe it to be accidental that the number of chapters of the *Discourses* is the same as the number of books of Livy, and hence we believe that one should wonder whether the number of chapters of the *Prince*, which is twenty-six, is not of some significance. We have seen that the twenty-sixth chapter of the *Discourses* is of eminent importance for the understanding of the *Prince*. We note that when discussing the Roman emperors in the *Discourses*, Machiavelli speaks explicitly of the twenty-six emperors from Caesar to Maximinus.[70] To say nothing of the fact that Caesar was not an emperor, Machiavelli does not give any reason for making this particular selection from among the emperors; the only evident fact is the number of the emperors selected. It might appear that there is some connection between the number 26 and "prince," i.e., monarch. This is not the place to give further examples of Machiavelli's use of the number 26 or, more precisely, of 13 and multiples of 13. It is sufficient here to mention some further features of his work which would seem to indicate that numbers are an important device used by him. There are three chapters of the *Discourses* which open with a quotation from Livy; they follow each other at an interval of 20 chapters.[71] The only two chapters of the *Discourses* which contain exclusively modern examples are the twenty-seventh and the fifty-fourth chapters. If a given chapter presents difficulties which one cannot resolve by studying its context, one will sometimes derive help by simply turning to a chapter which carries the same number either in another Book of the *Discourses* or in the *Prince*. For instance, the key passages regarding silence are chapters 10 of Book I and Book II of the *Discourses*. The key passages regarding "continuous foundation" are chapters 49 of Book I and Book III of the *Discourses*. *Discourses* III 48 deals with deceit practiced by a foreign enemy while I 48 deals with deceit practiced by domestic opponents. The parody of scholastic disputations occurs in *Discourses* II 12; *Discourses* I 12 is explicitly devoted to the harm done by the Church. The eleventh chapter of the *Prince* is devoted to ecclesiastical principalities; the eleventh chapter of the *Discourses* is devoted to the religion of the Romans. The most important discussions of M. Manlius Capitolinus occur in *Discourses* I 8 and III 8, and so on.[72] It would be foolish to apply this suggestion mechanically, for Machiavelli's devices would defeat his purpose if he had applied them mechanically. It would be almost equally foolish to try to establish the meaning of his teaching by relying exclusively or even chiefly on his devices. But it would also be imprudent to read his writings in the way in which they are usually read. Machiavelli's devices, judiciously used, lead the reader to the nerve of his argument. The order of finding is, however, not necessarily the order of proving.

To summarize: Machiavelli has presented his teaching in two books whose relation to each other is enigmatic. Each book presents "everything" he knows with a view to a specific audience or in a specific perspective. The question regarding the relation of the two perspectives cannot be answered before one has fully understood the perspective of each book and therefore before one has understood adequately each book by itself. By reading either book from the beginning in the light of the other, one arrives at some average meaning that is more superficial than even the surface meaning of either book and that can in no way claim to be authentic. Ultimately, the twofoldness of perspective reflects a twofoldness of "purpose" which is effective in each book and which corresponds to the difference between the "young" readers and the "old."

CHAPTER

I I

Machiavelli's Intention: The *Prince*

MANY WRITERS have attempted to describe the intention of the *Prince* by using the term "scientific." This description is defensible and even helpful provided it is properly meant. Let us return once more to the beginning. In the Epistle Dedicatory Machiavelli gives three indications of the subject-matter of the book: he has incorporated in it his knowledge of the actions of great men both modern and ancient; he dares to discuss princely government and to give rules for it; he possesses knowledge of the nature of princes. As appears from the Epistle Dedicatory, from the book itself, and from what the author says elsewhere,[1] knowledge of the actions of great men, i.e., historical knowledge, supplies only materials for knowledge of what princely government is, of the characteristics of the various kinds of principalities, of the rules with which one must comply in order to acquire and preserve princely power, and of the nature of princes. It is only knowledge of the latter kind that the *Prince* is meant to convey. That kind of knowledge, knowledge of the universal or general as distinguished from the individual, is called philosophic or scientific. The *Prince* is a scientific book because it conveys a general teaching that is based on reasoning from experience and that sets forth that reasoning. That teaching is partly theoretical (knowledge of the nature of princes) and partly practical (knowledge of the rules with which the prince must comply). In accordance with the fact that the *Prince* is a scientific, and not an historical book, only three of twenty-six chapter headings contain proper names.[2] When referring to the *Prince* in the *Discourses*, Machiavelli calls it a "treatise."[3] For the time being we shall describe the *Prince* as a treatise, meaning by "treatise" a book that sets forth a general teaching of the character indicated. To the extent that the *Prince* is a treatise, it has a lucid plan and its argument proceeds in a straight line without either ascending or descending. It consists at first sight of two parts. The first part sets forth the science or the art of princely government while the second takes up the time honored question of the limits of art or prudence, or the question of the relation of art or prudence and chance. More particularly, the *Prince* consists of four parts: 1) the various kinds of principalities (chs. 1-11), 2) the prince and his enemies (chs. 12-14), 3) the prince and his subjects or friends (chs. 15-23),[4] 4) prudence and chance (chs. 24-26). We may go a step further and say that the *Prince* appears, at the outset, not only as a treatise but even as a scholastic treatise.[5]

At the same time, however, the book is the opposite of a scientific or detached work. While beginning with the words "All states, all dominions which have had and have sway over men," it ends with the words "the ancient valor in Italian hearts is not yet dead." It culminates in a passionate call to action—in a call, addressed to a contemporary Italian prince, to perform the most glorious deed possible and necessary then and there. It ends like a tract for the times. For the last part deals not merely with the general question concerning the relation of prudence and chance, but it is concerned with the accidental also in another sense of the term. The chapters surrounding the explicit discussion of the relation between prudence and chance (ch. 25) are the only ones whose headings indicate that they deal with the contemporary Italian situation. The *Prince* is not the only classic of political philosophy which is both a treatise and a tract for the times. It suffices to refer to Hobbes' *Leviathan* and Locke's *Civil Government*. But the case of the *Prince* is not typical: there is a striking

contrast between the dry, not to say scholastic, beginning and
the highly rhetorical last chapter which ends in a quotation from
a patriotic poem in Italian. Could Machiavelli have had the ambition of combining the virtues of scholasticism with those of
patriotic poetry? Is such a combination required for the understanding of political things? However this may be, the contrast
between the beginning of the *Prince*, or even its first twenty-five
chapters, and its end forces us to modify our remark that the
argument of the book proceeds in a straight line without ascending
or descending. By directly contrasting the beginning and the end,
we become aware of an ascent. To the extent to which the *Prince*
is a treatise, Machiavelli is an investigator or a teacher; to the
extent to which it is a tract for the times, he assumes the role
of an adviser, if not of a preacher. He was anxious to become the
adviser of the addressee of the *Prince* and thus to rise from his
low, and even abject condition.[6] The movement of the *Prince* is
an ascent in more than one sense. And besides, it is not simply
an ascent.

In contradistinction to the *Discourses*, the *Prince* comes first
to sight as a traditional or conventional treatise. But this first appearance is deliberately deceptive. The antitraditional character
of the *Prince* becomes explicit shortly beyond the middle of the
book, and after remaining explicit for some time, it recedes again.
Hence the movement of the *Prince* may be described as an ascent
followed by a descent. Roughly speaking, the peak is in the
center. This course is prefigured in the first part of the book
(chs. 1-11): the highest theme of this part (new principalities acquired by one's own arms and virtue) and the grandest examples
(Moses, Theseus, Romulus, Cyrus) are discussed in chapter 6,
which is literally the central chapter of the first part.

But let us follow this movement somewhat more closely. At
first sight, the *Prince* belongs to the traditional genre of mirrors
of princes which are primarily addressed to legitimate princes,
and the most familiar case of the legitimate prince is the un-
disputed heir. Machiavelli almost opens the *Prince* by following
custom in calling the hereditary prince the "natural prince." He
suggests that the natural is identical with the established or customary, the ordinary and the reasonable; or that it is the opposite
of the violent. In the first two chapters he uses only contempo-

rary or almost contemporary Italian examples: we do not leave
the dimension of the familiar. We cannot help noting that in the
Discourses, which open with his declaration that he will communicate therein new modes and orders, the first two chapters are
devoted to the remote beginnings of cities and states: we immediately transcend the dimension of the familiar. In the third chapter
of the *Prince,* he continues to speak of "the natural and ordinary"
and "the ordinary and reasonable" but he now makes it clear that
nature favors the established no more than the disestablishment of
the established or, more generally stated, that the natural and
ordinary stands in a certain tension to the customary: since the
desire for acquisition is "natural and ordinary," the destruction
of "natural" princes, "the extinction of ancient blood," by an
extraordinary conqueror is perhaps more natural than the peaceful
and smooth transition from one ordinary heir to another.[7] In accordance with this step forward, foreign and ancient examples
come to the fore: the Turks and above all the Romans appear
to be superior to the Italians and even to the French. Provoked
by the remark of a French Cardinal that the Italians know
nothing of war, and thus justified, Machiavelli replied, as he reports here, that the French know nothing of politics: the Romans,
whose modes of action are discussed in the center of the chapter,
understood both war and politics. Furthermore, he transcends the
Here and Now also by referring to a doctrine of the physicians,
for medicine is an achievement of the ancients,[8] and by opposing
the wise practice of the Romans to "what is everyday in the
mouth of the sages of our times." But he is not yet prepared to
take issue with the opinion held by more than one contemporary
according to which faith must be kept. In chapters 4-6, ancient
examples preponderate for the first time. Chapter 6 is devoted
to the most glorious type of wholly new princes in wholly new
states, i.e., to what is least ordinary and most ancient. The heroic
founders discussed therein acquired their positions by virtue, and
not by chance, and their greatness revealed itself by their success
in introducing wholly new modes and orders which differed pro-
foundly from the established, familiar, and ancient. They stand at
the opposite pole from the customary and old established, for two
opposite reasons: they were ancient innovators, ancient enemies of
the ancient. Chapter 6 is the only chapter of the *Prince* in which

Machiavelli speaks of prophets, i.e., of men to whom God speaks. In the same chapter there occurs the first Latin quotation. Compared with that chapter, the rest of the first part marks a descent. The hero of chapter 7 is Cesare Borgia, who acquired his principality by means of chance. He is presented at the outset as simply a model for new princes. But, to say nothing of the fact that he failed because of a grave mistake of his, he was not a wholly new prince in a wholly new state: he is a model for such new princes as try to make changes in ancient orders by means of new modes rather than for such new princes, like the heroes of chapter 6, as try to introduce wholly new modes and orders. Accordingly, the emphasis shifts to modern examples from this point on.[9] As for chapters 8-11, it suffices to note that even their chapter headings no longer contain references to new princes; the princes discussed therein were at most new princes in old states. The last two chapters of the first part contain, as did the first two chapters, only modern examples, although the last two chapters contain also examples other than Italian.

The second part (chs. 12-14) marks an ascent from the end of the first part. The first part had ended with a discussion of ecclesiastical principalities, which as such are unarmed. We learn now that good arms are the necessary and sufficient condition for good laws.[10] As Machiavelli indicates through the headings of chapters 12-13, he ascends in these chapters from the worst kind of arms to the best. We note in this part an almost continuous ascent from modern examples to ancient ones. This ascent is accompanied by three references to the question as to whether modern or ancient examples should be chosen; in the central reference it is suggested that it would be more natural to prefer ancient examples.[11] Machiavelli now takes issue not only with specific political or military errors committed by "the sages of our times" but (although without mentioning his name) with his contemporary Savonarola's fundamental error: Savonarola erroneously believed that the ruin of Italy was caused by religious sins, and not by military sins. In this fairly short part (about 10 pages) Machiavelli refers six times to ancient literature while he had referred to it in the considerably more extensive first part (about 37 pages) only twice. Only in the second part does he come close to referring deferentially to the highest authorities of political or moral thought. He refers, not indeed to the New Testament, but to the Old, and not indeed to what the Old Testament says about Moses but to what it says about David, and not to what it says about David literally but to what it says about David, or in connection with David, figuratively. And he refers, not indeed to Aristotle, or to Plato, but to Xenophon whom he regarded however as the author of the classic mirror of princes. Besides, the Old Testament citation in chapter 13 merely supplies at most an additional example of the correct choice of arms; Xenophon's *Education of Cyrus*, mentioned at the end of chapter 14, however, is the only authority he refers to as setting forth a complete moral code for a prince. To say the least, the height reached at the end of the second part recalls the height reached in the center of the first part: the second part ends and culminates in a praise of Cyrus —one of the four "grandest examples" spoken of in chapter 6. In the first part, Machiavelli leisurely ascends to the greatest doers and then leisurely descends again; in the second part he ascends quickly to the origins of the traditional understanding of the greatest doers.

Right at the beginning of the third part (chs. 15-23) Machiavelli begins to uproot the Great Tradition. The emphasis is on a change in the general teaching: the first chapter of the third part is the only chapter of the *Prince* which does not contain any historical examples. Machiavelli now takes issue explicitly and coherently with the traditional and customary view according to which the prince ought to live virtuously and ought to rule virtuously. From this we begin to understand why he refrained in the second part from referring to the highest authorities: the missing peak above the Old Testament and Xenophon is not the New Testament and Plato or Aristotle but Machiavelli's own thought: all ancient or traditional teachings are to be superseded by a shockingly new teaching. But he is careful not to shock anyone unduly. While the claim to radical innovation is suggested, it is made in a subdued manner: he suggests that he is merely stating in his own name and openly a teaching which some ancient writers had set forth covertly or by using their characters as their mouthpieces.[12] Yet this strengthens Machiavelli's claim in truth as much as it weakens it in appearance: one cannot radically change the mode of a teaching without radically changing its substance. The argument ascends from chapter 15 up to chapters 19 or 20 and then descends again. In chapter 17 Machiavelli begins to speak again of "new princes," after a pause of 10 chapters, and he continues to do so in the three subsequent chapters; at the beginning of chapter 21 he still refers to "a quasi-new prince," but in the rest of the third part this high theme disappears completely: Machiavelli descends again to ordinary or second rate princes.[13] This movement is paralleled by a change regarding modern or ancient examples. Up through chapter 19, there is, generally speaking, an increase in emphasis on the ancient; thereafter modern examples preponderate obviously.[14] The last two-thirds of chapter 19, which deal with the Roman emperors, may be said to mark the peak of the third part. The passage is introduced as a rejoinder to what "many" might object against Machiavelli's own opinion. Chapter 19 is literally the center of the third part, just as the peak of the first part was literally its center (ch. 6). This is no accident. Chapter 19 completes the explicit discussion of the founder while chapter 6 had begun it. Hence we may justly describe chapter 19 as the peak of the *Prince* as a whole, and the third part as its most important part.[15] Chapter 19 reveals the truth about the founders, or the greatest doers almost fully.[16] The full revelation requires the universalization of the lesson derived from the study of the Roman emperors, and this universalization is presented in the first section of chapter 20. Immediately thereafter the descent begins. Machiavelli refers there to a saying of "our ancients," i.e., of the reputedly wise men of old Florence, and rejects it in an unusually cautious manner:[17] after having broken with the most exalted teaching of the venerable Great Tradition, he humbly returns to a show of reverence for a fairly recent and purely local tradition. Shortly afterwards he expresses his agreement with "the judgment of many," and immediately before questioning the wisdom of building fortresses and before showing that the practice of building fortresses had wisely been abandoned by a considerable number of Italian contemporaries, he says that he praises the building of fortresses "because it has been used from ancient times."[18] He shows every sign of wishing to pretend that he believes in the truth of the equation of the good with the ancient and the customary. Acting in the same spirit he expresses there a belief in human gratitude, respect for justice, and honesty[19] which is quite at variance with everything that went before, and especially with what he said in the third part.

Just as the movement of the argument in the third part resembles that in the first part, the movement of the argument in the fourth part (chs. 24-26) resembles that in the second part. In contrast to the last chapters of the third part, the fourth part is marked by the following characteristics: Machiavelli speaks again of the "new prince," and even "the new prince in a new principality" and he again emphasizes ancient models. Philip of Macedon, "not the father of Alexander, but the one who was defeated by Titus Quintus," i.e., an ancient prince who did not belong to the highest class of princes, is presented as vastly superior to the contemporary Italian princes who also were defeated. While the central chapter of the fourth part contains only modern examples, it compensates for this, as it were, by being devoted to an attack on a contemporary Italian belief, or rather on a belief which is more commonly held in contemporary Italy than it was in the past. In the last chapter, Moses, Cyrus, and Theseus, three of the four heroic founders praised in chapter 6, are mentioned again; Moses and Theseus had not been mentioned since. In that chapter Machiavelli speaks in the most unrestrained terms of what he hopes for from a contemporary Italian prince or from the latter's family. But he does not leave the slightest doubt that what he hopes for from a contemporary new prince in a new state is not more than at best a perfect imitation of the ancient founders, an imitation made possible by the survival of the Italians' ancient valor: he does not expect a glorious deed of an entirely new kind, or a new creation. While the last chapter of the *Prince* is thus a call to a most glorious imitation of the peaks of antiquity within contemporary Italy, the general teaching of the *Prince*, and especially of its third part, i.e., Machiavelli's understanding of the ancient founders and of the foundation of society in general, is the opposite of an imitation, however perfect: while the greatest deed possible in contemporary Italy is an imitation of the greatest deeds of antiquity, the greatest theoretical achievement possible in contemporary Italy is "wholly new."[20] We conclude, therefore, that the movement of the *Prince* as a whole is an ascent followed by a descent.

It is characteristic of the *Prince* to partake of two pairs of opposites: it is both a treatise and a tract for the times, and it has both a traditional exterior and a revolutionary interior. There is a connection between these two pairs of opposites. As a treatise, the book sets forth a timeless teaching, i.e., a teaching which is meant to be true for all times; as a tract for the times, it sets forth what ought to be done at a particular time. But the timelessly true teaching is related to time because it is new at the particular time at which it is set forth, and its being new, or not coeval with man, is not accidental. A new teaching concerning the foundations of society being, as such, unacceptable or exposed to enmity, the movement from the accepted or old teaching to the new must be made carefully, or the revolutionary interior must be carefully protected by a traditional exterior. The twofold relation of the book to the particular time at which it was composed or for which it was composed explains why the preponderance of modern examples has a twofold meaning: modern examples are more immediately relevant for action in contemporary Italy than ancient examples, and a discussion of modern examples is less "presumptuous"[21] or offensive than is a discussion of the most exalted ancient examples or of the origins of the established order which are neither present nor near. This must be borne in mind if one wants to understand what Machiavelli means by calling the *Prince* a "treatise."[22] As matters stand, it is necessary to add the remark that, in describing the *Prince* as the work of a revolutionary, we have used that term in the precise sense: a revolutionary is a man who breaks the law, the law as a whole, in order to replace it by a new law which he believes to be better than the old law.

The *Prince* is obviously a combination of a treatise and a tract for the times. But the manner in which that combination is achieved is not obvious: the last chapter does come as a surprise. We believe that this difficulty can be resolved if one does not forget that the *Prince* also combines a traditional surface with a revolutionary center. As a treatise, the *Prince* conveys a general teaching; as a tract for the times, it conveys a particular counsel. The general teaching cannot be identical, but it must at least be compatible, with the particular counsel. There may even be a connection between the general and the particular which is closer than mere compatibility: the general teaching may necessitate the particular counsel, given the particular circumstances in which the immediate addressee of the *Prince* finds himself, and the particular counsel may require the general teaching of the *Prince* and be incompatible with any other general teaching. At any rate, in studying the general teaching of the *Prince* we must never lose sight of the particular situation in which Lorenzo finds himself. We must understand the general in the light of the particular. We must translate every general rule which is addressed generally to princes, or a kind of prince, into a particular counsel addressed to Lorenzo. And conversely, we must work our way upward from the particular counsel which is given in the last chapter to its general premises. Perhaps the complete general premises differ from the general premises as explicitly stated, and the complete particular counsel differs from the particular counsel as explicitly stated. Perhaps the unstated implications, general or particular, provide the link between the general teaching as explicitly stated and the particular counsel as explicitly stated.

What precisely is the difficulty created by the counsel given in the last chapter of the *Prince*? As for the mere fact that that chapter comes as a surprise of some kind, one might rightly say that in the *Prince* no surprise ought to be surprising. In the light of the indications given in the first chapter, chapters 8-11 come as a surprise, to say nothing of other surprises. Besides, one merely has to read the *Prince* with ordinary care, in order to see that the call to liberate Italy with which the book ends is the natural conclusion of the book. For instance, in chapter 12 Machiavelli says that the outcome of the Italian military system has been that "Italy has been overrun by Charles, plundered by Louis, violated by Ferdinand, and insulted by the Swiss," or that Italy has become "enslaved and insulted."[23] What other conclusion can be drawn from this state of things than that one must bend every effort to liberate Italy after having effected a complete reform of her military system, i.e., that one ought to do what the last chapter says Lorenzo ought to do? The last chapter presents a problem not because it is a call to liberate Italy but because it is silent as to the difficulties obstructing the liberation of Italy. In that chapter it is said more than once that the action recommended to Lorenzo, or urged upon him, will not be "very difficult": almost everything has been done by God; only the rest remains to be done by the human liberator. The chapter creates the impression that the only things required for the liberation of Italy are the

Italians' strong loathing of foreign domination, and their ancient valor; the liberator of Italy can expect spontaneous cooperation from all his compatriots and he can expect that they will all fly to arms against the foreigners once he "takes the banner." It is true that Machiavelli stresses even here the need for a radical reform of the Italian military system. In fact, he devotes the whole center of the chapter, i.e., almost half of the chapter, to the military conditions for the liberation of Italy. But all the more striking is his complete silence as to its political conditions. What would be gained by all Italians becoming the best soldiers in the world if they were to turn their skill and prowess against one another or, in other words, if there were not first established a strict unity of command, to say nothing of unity of training? It is absurd to say that Machiavelli's patriotic fervor temporarily blinds him to the hard practical problems: his patriotic fervor does not prevent him from speaking in the last chapter very prosaically and even technically about the military preparation. The liberator of Italy is described as a new prince, for the liberation of Italy presupposes the introduction of new laws and new orders: he must do for Italy what Moses did for the people of Israel. But, as Machiavelli had been at pains to point out in the earlier chapters of the book, the new prince necessarily offends many of his fellow countrymen, especially those who benefit from the customary order of things, and his adherents are necessarily unreliable. In the last chapter he is silent on the subject of the inevitable offensiveness of the liberator's actions, as well as concerning the powerful resistances which he must expect. The liberator of Italy is urged there to furnish himself with his own troops who will be all the better if they see themselves commanded by their own prince: will the Venetian or the Milanese troops regard the Florentine Lorenzo as their own prince? Machiavelli does not say a word about the difficulties which might be created for the liberator by the various Italian republics and princes. He merely alludes to those difficulties by raising the rhetorical question, "what envy will oppose itself to him?" and by speaking once of "the weakness of the chiefs" in Italy. Does he mean to say that the patriotic fervor of the Italian people will suffice for sweeping aside those weak chiefs, however envious they might be? He certainly implies that before the liberator can liberate Italy, he would have to take not merely a banner, as is said in the text of the chapter, but Italy herself, as is said in the heading. It is a rare if not unique case in Machiavelli's books that the heading of a chapter should be more informative than its body.

Apart from chapters 26 and 24, the headings of which refer us to contemporary Italy, only one chapter heading in the *Prince* contains proper names and thus draws our attention to the particular. Chapter 4 is entitled: "Why the Kingdom of Darius which Alexander had seized did not rebel against Alexander's successors after his death."[24] As a consequence, the place of the chapter within the plan of the general teaching as indicated in chapter 1, is not immediately clear. Chapter 4 is the central one of three chapters which deal with "mixed principalities," i.e., with the acquisition of new territory by princes or republics, or, in other words, with conquest. The primary example in chapter 3 is the policy of conquest practiced by King Louis XII of France; but the country in which he tried to acquire new territory was Italy. In chapter 3, Machiavelli discusses the difficulties obstructing foreign conquests in Italy, a subject most important to the liberator of Italy. By discussing the mistakes which the French king committed in attempting to make lasting conquests in Italy, Machiavelli undoubtedly gives advice to foreigners contemplating conquest in his own fatherland.[25] This might seem to cast a reflection on his patriotism. But one might justly say that such advice is only the reverse side, if the odious side, of advice as to how to defend Italy against foreign domination, or how to liberate Italy. It appears from Machiavelli's discussion that but for certain grave mistakes committed by the French king, he could easily have kept his Italian conquests. The French king committed the grave mistakes of permitting the minor Italian powers to be destroyed and of strengthening a major Italian power, instead of protecting the minor Italian powers and humiliating that major power. We are forced to wonder what conclusion the liberator of Italy would have to draw from these observations. Should he destroy the minor Italian powers and strengthen the major Italian powers? The destruction of the minor powers which Machiavelli has in mind was effected by Cesare Borgia whose actions he holds up as models for Lorenzo. But would not the strengthening of the other major Italian powers perpetuate, and even increase, the difficulties of keeping the foreigner out of Italy? It is this question which is taken up in an oblique way in chapter 4. Machiavelli there distinguishes two kinds of principality: one like the Persia conquered by Alexander the Great, in which one man is prince and all others are slaves, and another kind, like France, which is ruled by a king and barons, i.e., in which powers exist that are not simply dependent on the prince but rule in their own right. He makes this distinction more general by comparing the French monarchy to Greece prior to the Roman conquest. What he is concerned with is then the difference between countries ruled by a single government from which all political authority within the country is simply derived, and countries in which there exists a number of regional or local powers, each ruling in its own right. Seen in the light of this distinction, Italy belongs to the same kind of country as France. In discussing Alexander's conquest of Persia, Machiavelli is compelled to discuss the conquest of a country of the opposite kind, i.e., the conquest of France. This, however, means that he is enabled to continue surreptitiously the discussion, begun in the preceding chapter, of the conquest of Italy.[26] Chapter 4 supplies this lesson: while it is difficult to conquer Persia, it is easy to keep her; conversely, while it is easy to conquer France, it is difficult to keep her. France (for which we may substitute in this context Italy) is easy to conquer because there will always be a discontented baron (state) that will be anxious to receive foreign help against the king (against other states within the country). She is difficult to keep because the old local or regional loyalties will always reassert themselves against the new prince. Secure possession of the country is impossible as long as the ancient blood of the local or regional lords or dukes or princes has not been extinguished. One might think for a moment that what is good for the foreign conqueror of a country of the kind under discussion is not necessarily good for the native liberator of such a country. But, as Machiavelli indicates in chapter 3, the superiority of France to Italy in strength and unity is due to the extirpation of the princely lines of Burgundy, Brittany, Gascony and Normandy. Given the urgency arising from foreign domination of Italy, the liberator cannot afford to wait until the other princely families have become extinct in the course of centuries. He will have to do on the largest scale what Cesare Borgia had done on a small scale:[27] in order to uproot the power of the old local and regional loyalties which are a major source of Italian weakness, one must extinguish the families of the obnoxious Italian princes. Cesare Borgia performs a crucial function in the *Prince* for the additional reason that he is the link between the foreign conqueror of Italy and her native, patriotic liberator: since he was not simply an Italian, he could not well be regarded as a potential liberator of his fatherland.[28] As for the Italian republics, we learn from chapter 5, the last chapter devoted to the subject of conquest, that the only way in which a prince, or a republic, can be sure of the loyalty of a conquered republican city with an old tradition of autonomy is to ruin it, and to disperse its inhabitants, and that this holds true regardless of whether the conqueror and the conquered are sons of the same country or not.[29]

The information regarding the political prerequisites of the liberation of Italy is withheld in the chapter which is explicitly devoted to the liberation of Italy because Machiavelli desired to keep the noble and shining end untarnished by the base and dark means that are indispensable for its achievement. He desired this because the teaching that "the end justifies the means" is repulsive, and he wanted the *Prince* to end even more attractively than it began. The information withheld in the last chapter is supplied in the section on conquest. To that section above all others we must turn if we desire to know what kinds of resistance on the part of his countrymen the liberator of Italy will have to overcome, and what kinds of offense against his fellow countrymen he will have to commit. To liberate Italy from the barbarians means to unify Italy, and to unify Italy means to conquer Italy. It means to do in Italy something much more difficult than what Ferdinand of Aragon had done in Spain, but in certain respects comparable to it.[30] The liberator of Italy cannot depend on the spontaneous following of all inhabitants of Italy. He must pursue a policy of iron and poison, of murder and treachery. He must not shrink from the extermination of Italian princely families and the destruction of Italian republican cities whenever actions of this kind are conducive to his end. The liberation of Italy means a complete revolution. It requires first and above everything else a revolution in thinking about right and wrong. Italians have to learn that the patriotic end hallows every means however much condemned by the most exalted traditions both philosophic and religious. The twenty-sixth chapter of the *Discourses*, which has already supplied us with more than one key to the *Prince*, confirms our present conclusion. Its heading says: "A new prince, in a city or country taken by him must make everything new." From its text we learn that just as Cesare Borgia did not become master of the Romagna except by "cruelty well used," Philip of Macedon did not become within a short time "prince of Greece" except by the use of means which were inimical not only to every humane manner of life but to every Christian manner of life as well.[31]

The major Italian power which the would-be foreign conqueror, Louis XII, mistakenly strengthened instead of humiliating, was the Church. The native liberator of Italy on the other hand, is advised to use his family connection with the then Pope Leo X in order to receive support for his patriotic enterprise from the already greatly strengthened Church. He is advised, in other words, to use the Church ruled by Leo X as Cesare Borgia, the model, had used the Church ruled by Alexander VI. But this counsel can be of only a provisional character. To see this, one has to consider Machiavelli's reflections on Cesare's successes and failures. Cesare's successes ultimately benefited only the Church, and thus increased the obstacles to the conquest or liberation of Italy. Cesare was a mere tool of Alexander VI and hence, whatever Alexander's wishes may have been, a mere tool of the papacy. Ultimately, Alexander rather than Cesare represents the contemporary Italian model of a new prince. For Cesare's power was based on the power of the papacy. That power failed him when Alexander died. Cesare's failure was not accidental, considering that the average length of a Pope's reign is ten years, that the influence of any Italian prince on the election of a new Pope is not likely to be greater than that of the great foreign powers and, above all, considering that the Church has a purpose or interest of its own which casts discredit on and thus endangers the use of the power of the Church for purposes other than strengthening the Church.[32] The liberation of Italy which requires the unification of Italy eventually requires therefore the secularization of the Papal states. It requires even more. According to Machiavelli, the Church is not only through its temporal power the chief obstacle to the unity of Italy; the Church is also responsible for the religious and moral corruption of Italy and for the ensuing loss of political virtue. In addition, Machiavelli was very much in fear of the Swiss, whose military excellence he traced partly to their sturdy piety. He draws the conclusion that if the Papal Court were removed to Switzerland, one would soon observe the deterioration of Swiss piety and morals and hence of Swiss power.[33] He seemed to have played with the thought that the liberator of Italy would have to go beyond secularizing the Papal states; he might have to remove the Papal Court to Switzerland and thus kill two birds with one stone. The liberator of Italy must certainly have the courage to do what Giovampagolo Baglioni was too vile to do, namely, "to show the prelates how little one ought to respect people who live and rule as they do and thus to perform an action whose greatness obliterates every infamy and every danger that might arise from it." He must make Italy as united as she was "in the time of the Romans."[34] The addressee of the *Prince* is advised to imitate Romulus among others. To imitate Romulus means to found Rome again. But Rome exists. Or could the imitation of Romulus mean to found again a pagan Rome, a Rome destined to become again the most glorious republic and the seminary and the heart of the most glorious empire? Machiavelli does not answer this question in so many words. When he mentions for the second time, in the last chapter of the *Prince*, the venerable models whom the addressee of the *Prince* should imitate, he is silent about Romulus.[35] The question which he forces us to raise, he answers by silence. In this connection we may note that, whereas in the *Discourses* "We" sometimes means "We Christians," "We" never has this meaning in the *Prince*. At any rate, both the explicit general teaching and the explicit particular counsel conveyed by the *Prince* are more traditional or less revolutionary than both the complete general teaching and the complete particular counsel. The two pairs of opposites which are characteristic of the *Prince*, namely, its being both a treatise and a tract for the times and its having both a traditional exterior and a revolutionary center, are nicely interwoven. The *Prince* is altogether, as Machiavelli indicates at the beginning of the second chapter, a fine web. The subtlety of the web contrasts with the shocking frankness of speech which he sometimes employs or affects. It would be better to say that the subtle web is subtly interwoven with the shocking frankness of speech which he chooses to employ at the proper time and in the proper place.

So much for the present regarding the character of the *Prince*. The subject of the book is the prince but especially the new prince. In the Epistle Dedicatory, Machiavelli indicates that his teaching is based upon his knowledge of the actions of great men; but the greatest examples of great men are new princes like Moses, Cyrus, Romulus and Theseus, men "who have acquired or founded kingdoms." In the first chapter, he divides principalities into classes with a view to the differences of materials and modes of acquisition rather than to differences of structure and purpose. He thus indicates from the outset that he is chiefly concerned with men who desire to acquire principalities (either mixed or wholly new), i.e., with new princes. There is a twofold reason for this emphasis. The obvious reason is the fact that the immediate addressee of the book is a new prince, and one who is, moreover, advised to become prince of Italy and thus to become a new prince in a more exalted sense. But what at first glance seems to be dictated merely by Machiavelli's consideration for the needs and prospects of his immediate addressee proves, on reflection, to be necessary for purely theoretical reasons as well. All principalities, even if they are now elective or hereditary, were originally new principalities. Even all republics, at least the greatest republics, were founded by outstanding men wielding extraordinary power, i.e., by new princes. To discuss new princes means then to discuss the origins or foundations of all states or of all social orders, and therewith the nature of society. The fact that the addressee of the *Prince* is an actual or potential new prince somewhat conceals the eminent theoretical significance of the theme "the new prince."

The ambiguity due to the fact that the *Prince* sometimes deals with princes in general and sometimes with new princes in particular is increased by the ambiguity of the term "new prince." The term may designate the founder of a dynasty in a state already established, i.e., a new prince in an old state, or a man who "seizes" a state, like Sforza in Milan or Agathocles in Syracuse or Liverotto in Fermo. But it may also designate a new prince in a new state or "a wholly new prince in a wholly new state," i.e., a man who has not merely acquired a state already in existence but has founded a state. The new prince in a new state in his turn may be an imitator, i.e., adopt modes and orders invented by another new prince, or in other ways follow the beaten track. But he may also be the originator of new modes and orders, or a radical innovator, the founder of a new type of society, possibly the founder of a new religion—in brief, a man like Moses, Cyrus, Theseus, or Romulus. Machiavelli applies to men of the highest order the term "prophets."[36] That term would seem to fit Moses rather than the three others. Moses is indeed the most important founder: Christianity rests on a foundation laid by Moses.

At the beginning of the chapter which is devoted to the grandest examples, Machiavelli makes unambiguously clear the fact that he does not expect the addressee of the *Prince* to be or to become an originator: he advises his reader to become an imitator or to follow the beaten track or to be a man of second rate virtue. This is not surprising: an originator would not need Machiavelli's instruction. As he states in the Epistle Dedicatory, he wishes that Lorenzo would "understand" what he himself "had come to know and had come to understand": he does not expect him to have come to know the most important things by himself. Lorenzo may have an "excellent" brain; he is not expected to have a "most excellent" brain.[37] However this may be, being "a prudent man," he is exhorted to "follow the track beaten by great men and to imitate those who have been most excellent," i.e., men like Romulus and Moses. On the other hand, the precepts which Machiavelli gives to Lorenzo are abstracted from the actions, not of Romulus or Moses, but of Cesare Borgia.[38] For, to say nothing of other considerations, Lorenzo's hoped-for rise depends upon his family connection with the present head of the Church and therewith on chance, just as Cesare's actual rise depended on his family connection with a former head of the Church, whereas Romulus and Moses rose to power through virtue as distinguished from chance. In imitating Cesare Borgia, Lorenzo would admit his inferiority to Cesare: Machiavelli's book would be somewhat out of place if meant for a man of Cesare's stature and lack of scruples. Still, Lorenzo is advised to imitate men of the stature of Romulus and of Moses. As appears from the last chapter, however, that imitation is expected less of Lorenzo by himself than of the illustrious house to which he belongs.

In the last chapter the emphasis is altogether on Moses. Machiavelli says there that God was a friend of Moses, Cyrus and Theseus. The description is applied to Moses with greater propriety than to Cyrus and to Theseus. Lorenzo is then exhorted to imitate Moses. The notion of imitating the prophets of old was familiar to Machiavelli's contemporaries: Savonarola appeared as a new Amos or as a new Moses, i.e., as a man who did the same things which the Biblical prophets had done, in new circumstances. This is not to say that there is no difference between the imitation of Moses as Savonarola meant it and the imitation of Moses as Machiavelli understood it. In order to encourage Lorenzo to liberate Italy, Machiavelli reminds him of the miracles which God had performed before their eyes: "The sea has been divided. A cloud has guided you on your way. The rock has given forth water. Manna has rained." The miracles of Lorenzo's time which indeed are attested to by Machiavelli alone, imitate the miracles of Moses' time. More precisely, they imitate the miracles which were performed, not in Egypt, the house of bondage, but on the way from Egypt to the promised land—to a land to be conquered. Differing from Savonarola, Machiavelli does not predict that Florence, or her ruler, will become the ruler of Italy,[39] for the success of the venture now depends alone on the exercise of human virtue which, because of man's free-will, cannot be foreseen. What may be imminent, Machiavelli suggests, is the conquest of another promised land, the land which Machiavelli has half-promised to Lorenzo. But alas, the imitation of Moses is bad for Lorenzo; for Moses did not conquer the promised land: he died at its borders. In this dark way, Machiavelli, the new sibyl, prophesies that Lorenzo will not conquer and liberate Italy.[40] He did not regard the practical proposal with which he concluded the *Prince* as practicable. He had measured the forces of contemporary Italy too well to have any delusions. As he states in the two Prefaces of the companion book, which in this respect takes up the thread where the *Prince* drops it, "of that ancient virtue [which is political] no trace has been left" in Italy. Not the short range project suggested at the end of the *Prince*, but rather the long range project indicated throughout the *Discourses* offers hope for success. Many writers have dismissed the last chapter of the *Prince* as a piece of mere rhetoric. This assertion—if it were followed up by an intelligent account of the enigmatic conclusion of the *Prince*—could be accepted as a crude expression of the fact that that chapter must not be taken literally or too seriously.

Machiavelli is not content with indicating his opinion by leading us to think of the inauspicious character of the imitation of Moses in respect of the conquest of a promised land. While stressing the imitative character of the work to which he exhorts Lorenzo, he stresses the fact that the liberator of Italy must be an originator, an inventor of new modes and orders, hence not an imitator. He himself hints at some far-reaching tactical innovations. But it is clear that the innovator or the inventor in these matters would be Machiavelli, not Lorenzo. The cryptic prediction of Lorenzo's failure, if he were to attempt to liberate Italy, can therefore be restated as follows: only a man of genius, of supreme virtue, could possibly succeed in liberating Italy; but Lorenzo lacks the highest form of virtue. This being the case, he is compelled to rely too much on chance. Machiavelli indicates and conceals how much Lorenzo would have to rely on chance by the religious language which he employs in the last chapter. He mentions God as often there as in all other chapters of the *Prince* taken together. He refers to the liberator of Italy as an Italian "spirit"; he describes the liberation of Italy as a divine redemption and he suggests its resemblance to the resurrection of the dead as depicted by Ezekiel; he alludes to the miracles wrought by God in Italy. However much we might wish to be moved by these expressions of religious sentiment, we fail in our effort. Machiavelli's certainty of divine intervention reminds us of his expectation of a spontaneous all-Italian rising against the hated foreigners. Just as that expectation is at variance with what earlier chapters had indicated as to the certainty of powerful Italian resistance to the liberator and unifier of Italy, so the expression of religious sentiment is at variance with earlier explicit remarks. According to those remarks, fear of God is desirable or indispensable in soldiers and perhaps in subjects in general, while the prince need merely appear religious, and he can easily create that appearance considering the crudity of the large majority of men. In the last chapter itself, Machiavelli calls the God-wrought contemporary events which resemble certain Biblical miracles not "miracles" but "extraordinary" events "without example"[41]: he thus denies the reality of those Biblical miracles and therewith, for an obvious reason, the reality of all Biblical miracles. Without such a denial, his own free invention of the contemporary "extraordinary" events would not have been possible: those invented miracles have the same status as the Biblical miracles. According to the *Prince*, miracles are happenings which are neither common nor reasonable. They are happenings that cannot be traced to secondary causes but only to God directly. Near the beginning of chapter 25 Machiavelli suggests that what is generally meant by God is in truth nothing but chance. Hence the suggestion made in chapter 26, that a number of miracles had happened in contemporary Italy is the figurative equivalent of the assertion, made explicitly in chapter 25, that chance is particularly powerful in contemporary Italy. More specifically, many "miraculous losses" have been sustained in contemporary Italy.[42] In the last chapter Machiavelli enumerates seven astonishing defeats suffered in the immediate past by Italian troops.[43] Since there is no defeat without a victor, one may speak with equal right of "miraculous losses and miraculous acquisitions" being the necessary consequence of the preponderance of Fortuna's power in contemporary Italy.[44] This means that, given the poverty of the Italian military system and the ensuing preponderance of chance, a well advised and industrious prince might have astounding temporary successes against other Italian princes, just as Pope Julius II had such successes against his cowardly enemies. In particular, Lorenzo might succeed in building up a strong power in Tuscany. But the thought of defeating the powerful military monarchies which dominate parts of Italy remains for the time being a dream.[45]

One cannot understand the meaning of the last chapter, and therewith of the *Prince* as a whole, without taking into consideration the position, the character and the aspirations of the other partner in the relationship, not to say in the dialogue, which is constitutive of the book. In proportion as the status of Lorenzo is lessened, the stature of Machiavelli grows. At the beginning, in the Epistle Dedicatory, Lorenzo appears as dwelling on the wholesome heights of majesty whereas Machiavelli must inhale the dust at his feet: the favorite of Fortuna is contrasted with her enemy. Machiavelli presents himself as a man who possesses information which princes necessarily lack and yet need. He describes that information in a way which is surprising not only to those who are forced by disposition or training to think of statistical data. He claims to possess knowledge of the nature of princes:

just as one sees mountains best from a valley and valleys best from a mountain, so one must be a prince in order to know well the nature of peoples, and one must be a man of the people in order to know well the nature of princes. In other words, while Lorenzo and Machiavelli are at opposite ends of the scale of Fortuna, they are equal in wisdom: each possesses one half of the whole of political wisdom; they are born to supplement each other. Machiavelli does not say that they should pool their resources in order to liberate Italy. Nor does he wish to hand over his share of political wisdom to Lorenzo as a pure gift. He desires to receive something in return. He desires to better his fortune. Looking forward to the end of the book, we may say that he desires to better his fortune by showing Lorenzo how to better his fortune through becoming prince of Italy. For, as he says already in the Epistle Dedicatory, chance and Lorenzo's other qualities promise him a greatness which even surpasses his present greatness. He dedicates the *Prince* to Lorenzo because he seeks honorable employment. He desires to become the servant of Lorenzo. Perhaps he desires to become an occasional or temporary adviser to Lorenzo. Perhaps he is even thinking of the position of a permanent adviser. But the absolute limit of his ambition would be to become the minister of Lorenzo, to be to Lorenzo what Antonio da Venafro had been to Pandolfo Petrucci, prince of Siena. His desire would be wholly unreasonable if he did not see his way toward convincing his master of his competence. The proof of his competence is the *Prince*. But competence is not enough. Lorenzo must also be assured of Machiavelli's loyalty or at least reliability. Machiavelli cannot refer, not even in the Epistle Dedicatory, to the fact that he had once had honorable employment in which he served loyally. For he was a loyal servant of the republican regime in Florence, and this by itself might compromise him in the eyes of his prince. He faces this difficulty for the first time in the chapter on civil principalities, i.e., on the kind of principality of which Lorenzo's rule is an example. He discusses there the question of how the prince ought to treat the notables among his subjects. He distinguishes three kinds of notables, the central one consisting of men who do not commit themselves entirely to the cause of the prince because they are pusillanimous and have a natural defect of courage. Machiavelli advises the prince to employ men of this kind provided they are men of good counsel, "for in prosperity you are honored on account of this and in adversity you have nothing to fear from them." Men of good counsel will have the required pusillanimity if the power of the prince has strong popular support: the few who can see with their own eyes "do not dare to oppose themselves to the opinion of the many who have the majesty of the state on their side." Since Machiavelli was suspected of having participated in a conspiracy against the Medici, it was particularly necessary for him to show through the *Prince* that men of his kind would never have the temerity to engage in such dangerous undertakings for they would think only of the probable outcome of the deed and not of its possible intrinsic nobility. He almost presents the spectacle of a conversation between himself and a potential conspirator against the prince in which he tries to convince the conspirator of the folly of his imaginings—a spectacle the very suggestion of which must have edified and reassured Lorenzo should he have read the *Prince*. Eventually, Machiavelli does not refrain from speaking explicitly about how a new prince should treat men who in the beginning of his reign had been suspect because of their loyalty to the preceding regime. He urges the prince to employ men of this kind. "Pandolfo Petrucci, prince of Siena, ruled his state more with those who were suspected by him than with others." The mere fact that such men are compelled to live down a past makes them willing to be reliable servants of the prince. But by proving so completely his reliability in addition to his competence, Machiavelli might seem to have overshot the mark. His potential employer might well wonder whether a man of Machiavelli's cleverness, if employed as an adviser or minister, would not receive all credit for wise actions of the government and thus by contrast render the less wise prince rather contemptible. Machiavelli reassures him, as well as he can, by setting up the infallible general rule that a prince who is not himself wise cannot be well advised.[46] Considering the great hazards to which Machiavelli exposes himself by trying to enter the service of a new prince, one may wonder whether according to his principles he ought not to have preferred poverty and obscurity. He answers this question in the *Discourses* since it cannot be answered with propriety in the *Prince*. Men in his position, he indicates, live in continuous danger if they do not seek employment with the prince; in trying to give advice to the prince, they must indeed "take things moderately," i.e., they must avoid standing forth as the chief or sole promoters of a bold scheme. Only if the bold scheme is backed by a strong party can some risks be safely taken.[47] The particular counsel which Machiavelli gives to Lorenzo explicitly, i.e., the counsel which he gives in the last chapter of the *Prince,* is moderate both because it is silent concerning the extreme measures required for the liberation of Italy and because it cannot but be very popular with very many Italians.

We have not yet considered Machiavelli's strange suggestion that he possesses one half of political wisdom, namely, knowledge of the nature of princes, whereas Lorenzo may possess the other half, namely, knowledge of the nature of peoples. He makes this suggestion in the same context in which he declares his intention of giving rules for princely government. But to give rules to princes as to how they ought to rule, means to teach them how they ought to rule their peoples. Machiavelli cannot then teach princes without possessing good knowledge of the nature of peoples as well. In fact, he gives much evidence of his possessing such knowledge inasmuch as he transmits it in the *Prince* to his princely pupil. He knows then everything of relevance that the prince knows, and in addition he knows much that is relevant of which the prince is ignorant. He is not merely a potential adviser of a prince but a teacher of princes as such. In fact, since more than one of his precepts is not required for princes at all, because princes would know such things without his instruction, he also, through the *Prince,* teaches subjects what they should expect from their prince, or the truth about the nature of princes.[48] As an adviser of a prince, he addresses an individual; as a teacher of political wisdom, he addresses an indefinite multitude. He indicates his dual capacity and the corresponding duality of his addressees by his use of the second person of the personal pronoun: he uses "Thou" when addressing the prince, and even the man who conspires against the prince, i.e., when addressing men of action, while he uses "You" when addressing those whose interest is primarily theoretical, either simply or for the time being. The latter kind of addressees of the *Prince* are identical with the addressees of the *Discourses,* "the young."[49]

Machiavelli mentions only one teacher of princes, namely, Chiron the centaur who brought up Achilles and many other ancient princes. Machiavelli's own model is a mythical figure: he returns to the beginnings not only by making the heroic founders his most exalted theme and the foundation of society his most fundamental theme, but likewise in understanding his own doing. His model is half beast, half man. He urges princes, and especially new princes, first to make use of both natures, the nature of the beast and the nature of man; and in the repetition, simply to imitate the beast, i.e., to use the person of the fox and the lion, or to imitate those two natures.[50] The imitation of the beast takes the place of the imitation of God. We may note here that Machiavelli is our most important witness to the truth that humanism is not enough. Since man must understand himself in the light of the whole or of the origin of the whole which is not human, or since man is the being that must try to transcend humanity, he must transcend humanity in the direction of the subhuman if he does not transcend it in the direction of the superhuman. *Tertium*, i.e., humanism, *non datur*. We may look forward from Machiavelli to Swift whose greatest work culminates in the recommendation that men should imitate the horses,[51] to Rousseau who demanded the return to the state of nature, a sub-human state, and to Nietzsche who suggested that Truth is not God but a Woman. As for Machiavelli, one may say with at least equal right that he replaces the imitation of the God-Man Christ by the imitation of the Beast-Man Chiron. That Beast-Man is, as Machiavelli indicates, a creation of the writers of antiquity, a creature of the imagination. Just as Scipio, in imitating Cyrus, in fact imitated a creation of Xenophon,[52] so the princes in imitating Chiron, will in fact imitate, not Chiron, but the ancient writers, if the carrying out of a teaching can justly be called an imitation of that teaching. But whatever may be true of princes or other actors, certainly Machiavelli, by teaching princes what Chiron was said to have taught, imitates Chiron or follows the creators of Chiron. Yet, as we have noted before, merely by teaching openly and in his own name what certain ancient writers had taught covertly and by using their characters as their mouth-pieces, Machiavelli sets forth an entirely new teaching. He is a Chiron of an entirely new kind.

As a teacher of princes or of new princes in general, Machiavelli is not especially concerned with the particular problems facing contemporary Italian princes. Those particular problems would be of interest to him only as illustrations of typical problems. The primary purpose of the *Prince* then is not to give particular counsel to a contemporary Italian prince, but to set forth a wholly new teaching regarding wholly new princes in wholly new states, or a shocking teaching about the most shocking phenomena. From that fact we understand the meaning of the last chapter. The particular counsel there given serves the purpose of justifying the novel general teaching before the tribunal of accepted opinion: a general teaching, however novel and repulsive, might seem to be redeemed if it leads up to a particular counsel as respectable, honorable and praiseworthy as that of liberating Italy. But how is this transformation achieved? Machiavelli does not merely suppress mention of the unholy means which are required for the achievement of the sacred end. He surreptitiously introduces a new end, an end not warranted by the argument of the first twenty-five chapters. He urges Lorenzo to liberate Italy on patriotic grounds or, to use a term to which he alludes near the beginning of chapter 26, on grounds of the common good. He thus creates the impression that all the terrible rules and counsels given throughout the work were given exclusively for the sake of the common good. The last chapter suggests then a tolerable interpretation of the shocking teaching of the bulk of the work. But the first twenty-five chapters had observed complete silence regarding the common good. The allusion to the common good near the beginning of chapter 26 has the same status as the other surprising features of that chapter: the expectation of a spontaneous all-Italian rising against the foreigners and the expression of religious sentiment. It is only when one subjects the particular counsel given in the last chapter to political analysis along the lines demanded by the earlier chapters that one realizes that one must have broken completely with traditional morality and traditional beliefs in order even to consider that counsel. But the judicious reader cannot be satisfied with raising the question of how that particular counsel could be put into practice and thereafter whether it can be put into practice under the given circumstances. He must raise this further and more incisive question: would Machiavelli condemn the im-

moral policies recommended in the bulk of the book if they did
not serve a patriotic purpose? Or are those immoral policies barely
compatible with a patriotic use? Is it not possible to understand
the patriotic conclusion of the *Prince* as a respectable coloring of
the designs of a self-seeking Italian prince? There can be no doubt
regarding the answer; the immoral policies recommended throughout the *Prince* are not justified on grounds of the common good,
but exclusively on grounds of the self-interest of the prince, of
his selfish concern with his own well-being, security and glory.[53]
The final appeal to patriotism supplies Machiavelli with an excuse
for having recommended immoral courses of action. In the light
of this fact, his character may very well appear to be even blacker
than even his worst enemies have thought. At the same time however, we are not forced to leave the matter with the remark that
the last chapter of the *Prince* is a piece of mere rhetoric, i.e., that
he was not capable of thinking clearly and writing with con-
summate skill.

These observations are not to deny that Machiavelli was an
Italian patriot. He would not have been human if he had not loathed
the barbarians who were devastating and degrading his fair country. We merely deny that his love for his fatherland, or his fatherland itself, was his most precious possession. The core of his
being was his thought about man, about the condition of man
and about human affairs. By raising the fundamental questions he
of necessity transcended the limitations and the limits of Italy,
and he thus was enabled to use the patriotic sentiments of his
readers, as well as his own, for a higher purpose, for an ulterior
purpose. One must also consider an ambiguity characteristic of
Machiavelli's patriotism. In the *Prince* there are eight references
to "the fatherland." In one case Italy is described as a fatherland.
In six cases the fatherlands mentioned are, not countries, but cities.
In one case, four fatherlands are mentioned; two are cities (Rome
and Athens) and two are countries; one of the countries is Persia;
as regards the other country, the fatherland nobilitated by Moses,
it is unclear whether it is Egypt or Canaan, the land of his birth
or the land of his aspiration.[54] When we apply this observation
to Machiavelli, we become aware of a tension between his Italian
patriotism and his Florentine patriotism. Or should one not rather
speak of a tension between his Roman patriotism and his Tuscan

patriotism? There exists a close connection between the transpatriotic core of his thought and his love for Italy. Italy is the soil out of which sprang the glory that was ancient Rome. Machiavelli believed that the men who are born in a country preserve through all ages more or less the same nature. If the greatest political achievement which the world has ever known was a fruit of the Italian soil there is ground for hope that the political rejuvenation of the world will make its first appearance in Italy: the sons of Italy are the most gifted individuals; all modern writers referred to in either the *Prince* or the *Discourses* are Italians. Since that political rejuvenation is bound up with a radical change in thought, the hope from Italy and for Italy is not primarily political in the narrow sense. The liberation of Italy which Machiavelli has primarily in mind is not the political liberation of Italy from the barbarians but the intellectual liberation of an Italian elite from a bad tradition. But precisely because he believed that the men who are born in a country preserve through all ages more or less the same nature, and as the nature of the Romans was different from that of the Tuscans, his hope was also grounded on his recollection of Tuscan glory:[55] the old Etrurians had made a decisive contribution to the religion of the Romans. He seems to have regarded himself as a restorer of Tuscan glory because he too contributed toward supplying Rome with a new religion or with a new outlook on religion. Or perhaps he thought of Tarquinius Priscus who, coming from Etruria, strengthened the democratic element of the Roman polity.

Furthermore, once one grasps the intransigent character of Machiavelli's theoretical concern, one is no longer compelled to burden him with the full responsibility for that practical recklessness which he frequently recommends. The ruthless counsels given throughout the *Prince* are addressed less to princes, who would hardly need them, than to "the young" who are concerned with understanding the nature of society. Those true addressees of the *Prince* have been brought up in teachings which, in the light of Machiavelli's wholly new teaching, reveal themselves to be much too confident of human goodness, if not of the goodness of creation, and hence too gentle or effeminate. Just as a man who is timorous by training or nature cannot acquire courage, which is the mean between cowardice and foolhardiness, unless he drags himself in the direction of foolhardiness, so Machiavelli's pupils must go through a process of brutalization in order to be freed from effeminacy. Or just as one learns bayoneting by using weapons which are much heavier than those used in actual combat,[56] one learns statecraft by seriously playing with extreme courses of action which are rarely, if ever, appropriate in actual politics. Not only some of the most comforting, but precisely some of the most outrageous statements of the *Prince* are not meant seriously but serve a merely pedagogic function: as soon as one understands them, one sees that they are amusing and meant to amuse. Machiavelli tries to divert the adherence of the young from the old to the new teaching by appealing to the taste of the young which is not the best taste or, for that matter, to the taste of the common people:[57] he displays a bias in favor of the impetuous, the quick, the partisan, the spectacular, and the bloody over and against the deliberate, the slow, the neutral, the silent, and the gentle. In the *Prince* he says that a prince who has conquered a city which was wont to live free must destroy that city if he cannot make it his residence. In the *Discourses* he says that precisely a prince (if he is not a barbarian) as distinguished from a republic would spare and protect conquered cities and would leave their autonomy intact, as much as possible.[58] Another resolute course of action recommended in the *Prince* is to avoid neutrality when two powerful neighbors come to blows: to take sides is always better than to remain neutral. Machiavelli gradually discloses the limitations of this advice. He admits first that neutrality is not always fatal. He then states that because of the power of justice, to take sides is safer than to remain neutral. Thereafter he makes clear that under certain conditions it is most unwise to abandon neutrality in case of conflict between two powerful neighbors. Finally he admits that no course of action is perfectly safe or, in other words, that the power of justice is not as great as he previously indicated.[59] He suggests very strongly in the *Prince* that the one thing needful is good arms; he speaks less loudly of the need for prudence.[60]

We must return once more to Machiavelli's suggestion that he possesses adequate knowledge of the nature of princes, whereas Lorenzo may possess adequate knowledge of the nature of peoples. As we have said, this suggestion is absurd: since to be a prince means to rule the people, it is impossible to know princes well without knowing peoples well; to say nothing of the facts that

Machiavelli displays knowledge of the nature of peoples throughout the *Prince* and, as he says explicitly in the *Discourses*, there is no difference of nature between princes and peoples.[61] Since he knows well the nature of peoples, he intimates by his strange suggestion that he is a prince. This intimation will appear strange only to those who lack familiarity with Xenophon or Plato: he who knows the art of ruling is more truly a ruler than men who rule merely by virtue of inheritance or force or fraud or election by people who know nothing of the art of ruling.[62] But if Machiavelli is a prince, he is a new prince and not one who imitates the modes and orders found by others, but rather an originator, a true founder, a discoverer of new modes and orders, a man of supreme virtue. In fact, if it is proper to call prophet the founder of a new social order which is all-comprehensive and not merely political or military, then Machiavelli is a prophet. Not Lorenzo, but Machiavelli is the new Romulus-Numa or the new Moses, i.e., a man who does not merely repeat in new circumstances what Romulus-Numa or Moses had done in the olden times, but who is as original as they were. In the last chapter of the *Prince*, he attests to certain miracles which had happened somewhere in contemporary Italy—miracles which resemble those of the time of Moses. The ancient miracles happened on the way from the house of bondage to the promised land: they happened immediately before the revelation on Mount Sinai. What is imminent, Machiavelli suggests then, is not the conquest of a new promised land, but a new revelation, the revelation of a new code, of a new decalogue. The man who will bring the new code, cannot be Lorenzo or any other prince in the vulgar sense. The bringer of the new code is none other than Machiavelli himself: he brings the true code, the code which is in accordance with the truth, with the nature of things. Compared with this achievement, the conquest of the promised land, the liberation of Italy, is a *cura posterior*: it can wait, it must wait until the new code has regenerated the Italians. The new Moses will not be sad if he dies at the borders of the land which he had promised, and if he will see it only from afar. For while it is fatal for a would-be conqueror not to conquer while he is alive, the discoverer of the all-important truth can conquer posthumously.[63]

Concerning prophets in general, Machiavelli remarks that all armed prophets have conquered and the unarmed prophets have failed. The greatest armed prophet is Moses. The only unarmed prophet mentioned is Savonarola. But as is shown by the expression "all armed prophets . . . and the unarmed ones," he thinks not only of Savonarola. Just as he, who admired so greatly the contemporary Muslim conquerors, could not help thinking of Muhammad when speaking of armed prophets, so he must have thought of Jesus when speaking of unarmed prophets. This is perhaps the greatest difficulty which we encounter when we try to enter into the thought of the *Prince*: how can Machiavelli, on the basis of his principles, account for the victory of Christianity? Certain of his successors attempted explicitly to explain the victory of Christianity in purely political terms. To quote from a present-day historian: "In the most starkly Erastian utterance of the [seventeenth] century, [Henry] Parker all but maintained that it was Constantine, and not the preaching or the miracles of the early Church, that won Europe to the Christian fold."[64] But we cannot bring ourselves to believe that a man of Machiavelli's intelligence would have been satisfied with an answer of this kind, which merely leads to this further question: what motivated Constantine's action? must Christianity not already have been a power in order to become an attraction or a tool for a politician? To see how Machiavelli could have accounted for the victory of Christianity, we have to consider a further difficulty which is no less obvious. All unarmed prophets, he says, have failed. But what is he himself if not an unarmed prophet? How can he reasonably hope for the success of his enormous venture—enormous in itself and productive of infinite enormities—if unarmed prophets necessarily fail? This is the only fundamental question which the *Prince* raises in the reader's mind without giving him even a suspicion of Machiavelli's answer. It reminds one of the question, likewise left unanswered in the *Prince*, as to how new modes and orders can be maintained throughout the ages.[65] For the answer to it, we must turn to the *Discourses*.

Machiavelli's Intention:
The *Discourses*

SUPERFICIAL readers of the *Prince* who are not altogether careless will approach the *Discourses* with the expectation that that book is devoted to republics or to peoples as distinguished from princes. This expectation will not be altogether disappointed. Since to speak about peoples is less dangerous than to speak about princes, the *Discourses* can be expected to be more outspoken than the *Prince*. We have seen that it is so in an important respect: our information concerning Machiavelli's manner of writing is derived primarily and chiefly from the *Discourses*.

The *Discourses* cannot be described simply as a book on republics. At the beginning, Machiavelli indicates the intention of the book by presenting himself as another Columbus, as the discoverer of a hitherto unexpected moral continent, as a man who has found new modes and orders. But just as men generally were good at the beginning of the world or of societies, Machiavelli, who imitates in his books "the things of the world," is good at the beginnings of his books. Accordingly, at the beginning of the *Discourses* he appears to proclaim the daring character of his enterprise without any reserve: he does not seem to conceal anything.

He seems to explain his daring action by his concern with the common good: he did not write the *Discourses* in order to better his fortune. Above all, the new modes and orders prove to be the modes and orders of antiquity and hence very old modes and orders.

The ancient modes and orders are new because they have been forgotten, or buried like ancient statues. Machiavelli must then disinter them: no trace of ancient virtue, the origin and progeny of the ancient modes and orders, remains. But he does not claim that he is the first or the only modern man to become aware of the ancient modes and orders. Everyone knows of them and many admire them. But everyone thinks that they cannot be imitated by modern man. The purpose of the *Discourses* is not simply to bring to light the ancient modes and orders but above all to prove that they can be imitated by modern man. Machiavelli's enterprise therefore requires knowledge of things modern as well as of things ancient; it cannot be the work of a mere antiquarian. The prevailing unbelief concerning the possibility of imitating ancient virtue is partly due to the influence of Christianity. Modern men do not believe that ancient virtue can be imitated because they believe that man now belongs to a different order of things than formerly or that his status has changed or that he has been miraculously transformed. Machiavelli does not deny that modern men differ from ancient men. But this difference, he holds, is due entirely to a difference in education and in knowledge of "the world." If modern men were properly educated and properly taught, they could imitate the ancients. Modern men regard the imitation of antiquity as not so much physically as morally impossible. They believe that the ancient modes and orders ought not to be imitated: they have been taught to regard the virtues of the ancients as resplendent vices or to reject the concern of the ancients with worldly glory in the name of the Biblical demands for humility and charity.[1] It is therefore not sufficient for Machiavelli to exhibit specimens of ancient virtue; it is incumbent upon him to prove that the virtue of the ancients is genuine virtue. To prove that ancient virtue can be imitated and ought to be imitated is tantamount to refuting the claims of Biblical religion.

According to an opinion which is venerable because of its age, Machiavelli's intention in the *Discourses* is to reduce the lessons implicitly or even unconsciously conveyed through the narrative of an ancient historian to general rules which even very mediocre minds can easily understand. This opinion is misleading for a number of reasons. In the first place, it arises from disregarding the major obstacle which has to be overcome before the general rules derived from ancient practice can be accepted as good rules. Secondly, it arises from disregarding what Machiavelli explicitly says concerning the intention of his book. In the Preface to the First Book where he indicates his intention, he speaks of the examples of the ancients but not of rules derived from those examples. On a later occasion he says: "And truly, not without cause do the good historians . . . put down certain cases with particulars and distinctly so that posterity can learn how to defend itself in similar situations." This would indicate that the reduction to rules of what the good historians teach is a trivial or pedantic business altogether unbecoming a new Columbus. Machiavelli does say in the Preface to the First Book that "the civil laws are nothing but decisions given by the ancient jurists which, reduced to order, teach our present jurists to judge." But he does not make this remark on the jurists in order to say that he will do in regard to ancient political practice what the present-day jurists do (or perhaps what their ancient and medieval teachers did) in regard to ancient judicial practice. He makes that remark in order to show that in limited or subordinate matters modern men do imitate the ancients and thus to lead up to the demand that modern man should imitate the ancients in the greatest matters. He goes on to say that "Medicine is nothing but the experiences made by the ancient physicians on which the present physicians found their judgments." The modern physicians, who are more interesting to Machiavelli than the modern lawyers, differ from the ancient physicians not because they reduce to rules what the ancient physicians did but because they do not have access to certain experiences or observations except through the reports of the ancient physicians, probably because dissection is no longer practiced but rather frowned upon. The ancient physicians then are not truly imitated by the modern physicians. The true imitator of the ancient physicians is Machiavelli: the ancient physicians' anatomy of simple bodies is the model for his anatomy of mixed bodies. The anatomy of mixed bodies itself is wholly new. The anatomy of the mixed bodies is the indispensable

condition for elaborating any reliable rules regarding the treatment of mixed bodies, whereas no equivalent of anatomy is needed
in order to reduce to rules the decisions of the ancient lawyers:
the lawyers can and must take for granted the law, the positive
law which is not a mixed body but a product of a mixed body, and
they cannot go back behind that product. In the context, the
reference to something like rules in the case of the lawyers and
the complete silence about rules in the case of the physicians is a
sign of the fact that law occupies a lower rank than medicine.
While differing from the modern physicians by the fact that he
is an anatomist, Machiavelli is in the same position as they are insofar as he too is compelled to rely on reports by the ancients:
to anatomize an excellent republic is not possible for him on the
basis of immediately available phenomena since no excellent republic is at present near at hand. It goes without saying that in
speaking about modern pursuits which in one way or another imitate ancient pursuits, Machiavelli does not speak of theology: "the
Christian sect . . . has destroyed every memory of ancient theology." But it is noteworthy that he does not mention in this context
the fourth of the four faculties: he does not suggest that the present
philosophers imitate the ancient philosophers.[2]

The ancient modes and orders which Machiavelli desires to
show can be imitated and ought to be imitated by modern men are
those of ancient Rome. The Roman historian of Rome's glory is
Livy. For the experience, the first-hand knowledge, of the mixed
body to be dissected, Machiavelli will rely on Livy. The *Discourses*
are explicitly devoted to the first ten Books of Livy. Machiavelli
seems to promise a continuation to be devoted to the other Books
of Livy which have been preserved.[3] But as he indicates by making
the number of the chapters of the *Discourses* equal to the number
of Books of Livy's *History*, the *Discourses on the First Ten Books
of Livy* are meant to cover the whole ground covered by Livy's
whole work. Machiavelli's analysis of the Roman republic would
be incomplete if it did not include an analysis of the destruction
of the Roman republic and therewith, as matters stand, of the
destruction of vigorous republican life in the world for at least a
millennium and a half, but the *Discourses* include such an analysis.[4] In other words the *Discourses*, imitating Livy's *History*, follow
Rome from her beginning until the beginning of Christianity. Yet

Machiavelli may have had an additional reason for creating the impression that he was dealing merely with the events recorded in Livy's first ten books. It is not sufficient to say that he was particularly concerned with the Roman republic in its state of incorruption, for according to him Rome was still incorrupt at the time of the Second Punic War and even by the middle of the second century B.C.[5] He indicates his true reason by saying that Rome reached her ultimate greatness in about 266 B.C.,[6] i.e., immediately before the outbreak of the First Punic War. The period immediately preceding the First Punic War was treated by Livy in his second decade, which is lost. Machiavelli then was particularly concerned with Livy's first ten books because they are the only remains of the only Livian books which deal with the rise of Rome from her humble origins up to her ultimate greatness: the growth of Rome up to its completion naturally takes precedence over her decay. Rome reached her ultimate greatness when she ruled (most of) Italy and had not yet embarked on foreign conquests. Hence the full title of the *Discourses* draws our attention to a united and free Italy, freed and united by a hegemonial republic, be it Rome or Florence, and not by a prince. In a becomingly subdued manner, Machiavelli suggests a practical alternative to the practical proposal proclaimed in the last chapter of the *Prince*.

In order to show that the Roman modes and orders can be imitated and ought to be imitated by modern men, Machiavelli would have to show in each case that the Roman practice was sound and the corresponding modern practice is unsound. He also would have to show that one or another modern state successfully followed the Roman practice, unless he could presuppose or establish that what men did once they can do always. At any rate, through understanding the intention of the *Discourses* one is led to a definite expectation regarding the general character of each of its 142 discourses or chapters. This expectation must be modified immediately with a view to the very great dissimilarities among those chapters. There are chapters which contain only ancient examples; there are chapters which contain only modern examples; there are chapters which contain only ancient examples none of which is Roman; there are chapters which contain only ancient and Turkish examples.[7] The longest chapter (III 6) is about 72

times as long as the shortest chapter (I 48). It is curious that the
longest chapter is the one which has the shortest chapter heading
(two words) ever to occur in the book;[8] at the opposite pole we
find two chapters (I 55, III 30) whose headings consist of thirty-
five words. Thirty-nine chapter headings contain proper names;
in thirty-seven cases the men or societies mentioned are ancient,
in one case (I 12) they are modern, and in one case (III 36) they
are both ancient and modern. Connected with this is the fact that
only thirty-three chapter headings refer to the past by the tense in
which they are framed.

In spite or rather because of these and other irregularities, one
is entitled to speak of the typical chapter of the *Discourses* and to
seek for it. That chapter which at first glance is the most atypical
is the chapter on conspiracies (III 6). It is followed by a chapter,
the 100th chapter of the book, which, I am inclined to think, is
meant to be the typical chapter. That chapter stands out from the
group of chapters to which it belongs (III 1-10) because it is
the only one in that group that is not explicitly connected with the
following or the preceding chapter by a reference at its end or
at the end of the preceding chapter. The typical chapter of the
Discourses is "unconnected" in this sense. The heading of the
typical chapter does not contain any proper names and it is framed
in the present tense: it expresses a permanent fact regarding man
as man. The heading is less shocking than the body of the chapter:
while in the heading of *Discourses* III 7 Machiavelli uses the expression "without blood," he speaks in the body of the chapter of
"the blood and the death" of "innumerable men"; of one kind of
change of regime he says that those changes were always such as
to make him shudder who reads of them, to say nothing of someone else. Machiavelli desires to remain silent about those changes,
not however because they are so appalling but because the histories
are full of them: the *Discourses* do speak of things which make
shudder him who reads of them, to say nothing of him who is
faced by them, provided those horrible things are not well known;
the *Discourses* deal with the hidden causes of those horrors or
with the terrors inherent in the ultimate causes or with the initial
terror. In the chapter under consideration, one Roman and one
modern (Florentine) example are mentioned. The Roman example
occurs in Livy. But no reference is made to Livy (or to any other

writer) in any manner or form nor is any passage from Livy (or any other writer) quoted in the original or in the Italian. In the chapter the two references to "the histories" underline the fact that no reference is made to Livy in particular: every reference to Livy (or to any other writer) and every quotation from Livy (or from any other writer) requires an explanation. The examples used are parallels, not specimens of opposites; the same kind of event happened in ancient Rome and in modern Florence. While knowledge of the events is supplied by "the histories" or by the author's experience, Machiavelli selects the parallel events, lets us see that the ancient and the modern examples are identical in the decisive respect, and indicates the identical cause. These mental operations culminate in the formulation of a rule which reveals the connection between one typical phenomenon as the cause and another typical phenomenon as its effect. The rule in question could not have been discovered through the study of ancient political practice because it is derived from a comparison of an ancient and a modern event. We are thus induced to wonder whether it is the ultimate intention of the *Discourses* to prove the superiority of the ancients to the moderns.

But let us return to the beginning. The initial impression according to which the author of the *Discourses* is a bold innovator is immediately afterward overlaid by the impression that he is merely the restorer of something old. Certainly the primary purpose of the book is to prove that the ancient modes and orders can and ought to be imitated or that those modes and orders are the best. The book as a whole constitutes this proof. But one cannot begin to prove anything if one cannot start from principles which are universally or generally granted. The readers of Machiavelli, being adherents of the established modes and orders, are opposed to the modes and orders which he recommends. He must appeal to principles which those readers will grant him. We learn from the Preface to the First Book that those readers, besides being adherents of the established modes and orders, are also admirers of classical antiquity. There exists a prejudice in favor of classical antiquity to which Machiavelli can appeal. He fully enters into the spirit of this prejudice as a prejudice. It is significant that whereas the *Epistle Dedicatory* of the *Prince* refers to the difference between the ancients and the moderns, the *Epistle Dedicatory*

of the *Discourses* is silent about that difference. We are expected
to lose sight of modernity, to lose ourselves in antiquity, in the
admiration for antiquity and in the imitation of antiquity. Machiavelli demands that the admirers of antiquity be consistent and imitate antiquity not only in subordinate matters but in the most important matters as well. He desires to make admiration for antiquity
complete: the last and most important part of the return to antiquity,
or of the ascent to antiquity, will take place under the guidance
of the most competent ancient, of Livy. Machiavelli argues dia-
lectically or ironically.

The appeal to the half-hearted admirers of antiquity, to the
followers of the *via del mezzo*, is insufficient. Not all readers can
be presumed to be "humanists." Let us not forget the many who
could read and who had followed Savonarola. Savonarola had
praised Pope Gregory the Great for having burned the works of
Livy.[9] From this we understand why in the early part of the
Discourses, in the first 36 chapters of the 142 devoted to Livy,
Machiavelli is very hesitant to refer to Livy, to say nothing of
quoting from Livy. His first task is to establish the authority of
Livy and, prior to this, the authority of classical Rome. He does
this by appealing to what is common to both opposite parties.
Both appeal to antiquity, be it classical or Biblical antiquity. In
some way they seem to assume that the good is the old, be it the
old established or something disestablished. Machiavelli begins his
argument by appealing to the equation, so natural to man, of the
good and the old. If the good is the old, the best must be the
oldest. From this we understand why Machiavelli in the first chapter praises the kingdom of Egypt so highly. The kings of Egypt
or their subjects deserve higher praise than even Alexander the
Great, for the kingdom of Egypt existed "in the most ancient
antiquity." It goes without saying that this praise is entirely provisional. When, in the beginning of the Second Book, he surveys
the temporal sequence in which virtue resided in different ancient
kingdoms, he assigns the first place to Assyria and is silent about
Egypt. Even if Egypt as the oldest kingdom had been the best
kingdom, we could not know this in any precise and useful way;
the ancient Egyptians would deserve higher praise than Alexander the Great if we knew more about them.[10] Granting that
the best is the oldest, one is compelled to be satisfied with that

oldest which is sufficiently known. Since one must then compromise, one might as well prefer to the oldest simply that oldest
which is one's own. For the Tuscan Machiavelli this would seem
to mean that he should choose old Etruria. In fact he recommends
to the present Tuscans that they imitate the ancient Tuscans. The
ancient Tuscans resembled the present Swiss since they too were
sturdy republicans and formed a league of independent and equal
republics. Besides, being most powerful on sea and on land, the
Tuscans controlled a large part of Italy and were prevented by
their political organization from acquiring territory outside of
Italy. Ancient Etruria endured for a long time, famous for empire,
arms, religion and virtue while having her own customs and her
own ancestral language. But what is true of the exceedingly pious
ancient Egyptians, is almost equally true of the almost equally
pious ancient Tuscans: hardly any reliable reports about them
remain.[11] No choice then is left to Machiavelli except to return
to ancient Rome: ancient Rome satisfies the conditions both of
being the heritage of the Italian Machiavelli and of being sufficiently
known. It is sufficiently known through Livy. We shall then follow
Livy. In meditating upon things Roman we shall cling as much
as possible to the sequence of events as recorded by Livy. We
shall defer to the text of Livy. We shall cherish it. We shall
harken to it in filial affection, in patient docility, in pious reverence
until it has revealed to us its full message. In pious reverence we
shall avert our eyes from Livy's own references to the derivative
or untrustworthy character of many of the tales which he retells:
we shall not even allude to those jarring references. We shall use
Livy in the way in which the theologians use the Bible. Just as
Livy is Machiavelli's Bible, the Romans are his chosen people: a
man who dares to promise a land will not hesitate to choose a
people. Just as the Bible does not teach that the best modes and
orders were the oldest, neither does Livy teach it; nothing prevents
us from believing that the Roman republic marks a great advance
beyond the Roman kingship.

The Bible, reputedly the oldest record of the most ancient antiquity and the authentic record of the Mosaic laws and orders,
is bypassed by Machiavelli as he moves from ancient Egypt to
ancient Rome. He mentions Moses in the first chapter of the *Discourses* when speaking of peoples which are compelled to leave

their native land and to seek a new homeland for themselves. In the same chapter he draws our attention to the question of the goodness of the Mosaic laws but he does not answer it there or elsewhere in the *Discourses*. He says later on that Moses framed laws with a view to the common good, but he says the same thing of Solon whose laws he criticizes severely: the goodness of laws requires more than that the end of the laws be good. On the other hand he bestows the highest praise on Moses' native land and its ancient kings. Those ancient kings would deserve more praise than "others whose memory is still fresh." This praise of the ancient Egyptians is immediately followed by praise of the kingdom of the Sultan and the order of the Mamelukes, i.e., by praise of infidels.[12] It is clear that Machiavelli fails to imitate Biblical antiquity or at any rate to recommend its imitation. But the indications mentioned do not show the reasons for this refusal. The problem posed by Biblical antiquity remains behind him like an unconquered fortress.

The deeds and institutions which Livy celebrates are not always of such a nature as to command instant approval and admiration. At first glance the Roman modes and orders appear to be inferior to those of Sparta. The Spartan polity was established by a single wise man at one stroke in the beginning; hence Sparta was never in need of improvement and therefore of dangerous change; she was always perfectly stable; she preserved her polity and her freedom without any corruption for more than eight hundred years. But the Roman polity was established in a fortuitous manner and in answer to accidents as they arose; therefore Rome was unstable and constantly imperiled; her liberty lasted for less than four hundred years. In Sparta there was harmony between the nobility and the commons because she kept all her citizens poor and hence virtuous; Rome was constantly shaken by the conflict between her insolent nobles and her ambitious plebs. Sparta was organized for just defense whereas Rome was organized for unjust expansion. Machiavelli must therefore defend the Roman polity against its critics. He is strangely reticent as to the identity of those critics; in the crucial context he does not mention a single proper name. Before discussing the quality of the Roman republic he refers to "those who have written of republics," i.e., to the traditional political philosophers.[13] It is on the basis of what is taught by the most famous traditional political philosophers that Rome necessarily appears inferior to Sparta or that "many condemn" the Romans. Machiavelli is then compelled to defend the Roman polity against the ancient philosophers just as the theologians are compelled to defend the Bible and its teachings against the ancient philosophers. He is compelled to attack the philosophers in the name of his authority. His argument in *Discourses* I 2-6 is reminiscent of theological apologetics. However, since he defers to the prejudice in favor of antiquity, he must proceed cautiously in taking issue with ancient philosophy. His refusal to identify "those who have written of republics" is a consequence of this caution. But how cautious a man can be often depends more on the conduct of others than on himself. As Machiavelli informs us, there is disagreement among the traditional political philosophers: it is not his fault that he must take sides. But he is not so presumptuous as to settle the controversy by himself. Taking the safest course, he adopts the opinion of those political philosophers who "according to the opinion of many" are wiser than their opponents. Those wiser thinkers had preferred mixed polities to simple polities. Machiavelli reproduces their doctrine and adopts it. He merely alludes to his disagreement with them by indicating a difference between his own reason and that given by the classical writers for the inadequacy of simple aristocracy. Immediately after making this barely noticeable allusion, he explicitly and emphatically accepts a premise which has been demonstrated by all political philosophers. Arguing from this premise, he then explicitly takes issue with the anti-Roman "opinion of many" and even dares to say that "many inconsiderately condemn" the violent strife between the Roman nobility and the Roman plebs; that violent strife, he contends, was the cause of Roman freedom and Roman greatness. Yet at the end of this wholly new praise of discord, he turns for support and comfort to Cicero's *On Friendship*.[14] Only after so much preparation does he meet the issue posed by the seeming superiority of Sparta to Rome: is not the less democratic and more stable Spartan polity preferable to the more democratic and less stable Roman polity? Here he is confronted with the difficulty that democracy was controversial within Rome herself, between the people and the senate. He is compelled to choose not between two sects of ancient philosophers but between

two parties into which his own authority is divided; this division
seems to render nugatory that authority. He is compelled to fall
back on his own reason. He reaches a decision in favor of Rome
and against Sparta. The decision seems to depend on demonstration, but in setting forth the decision Machiavelli says four times
"I believe."[15] Has he then demonstrated the superiority of Rome
to Sparta, or has he merely shown that, before the tribunal of
unassisted reason, the case for Rome is as strong as the case for
Sparta, so that one is free to believe in the superiority of Rome?
Does he imitate an apparent ambiguity of theological apologetics?
However this may be, the first step of Machiavelli's argument consists in establishing through demonstration, or faith, or both, the
authority of ancient Rome and therewith the authority of Livy
who celebrated ancient Rome. Only after he has taken this step
can he as it were identify himself with Livy and enter on those
discourses which are properly and even explicitly discourses on
Livy.

Machiavelli cannot identify himself with Livy completely. The
intention of the *Discourses* cannot be identical with that of Livy's
History. This is true on at least two levels. The intention of an
apologist is not identical with that of his authoritative text; the
apologist is confronted with such arguments against his authoritative
text as are not met by that text. Besides, Livy's purpose is to set
forth the greatness of ancient Rome but not to prove the superiority
of ancient Rome to modernity. Machiavelli cannot then be a commentator on Livy; he has to perform an important task which
Livy did not perform. Machiavelli does not emphasize this point;
not before the 91st chapter of the *Discourses* does he explicitly
indicate the difference between Livy's theme and his own purpose.
He there mentions an event which Livy had mentioned with an
apology for mentioning it. The event was a war waged on Italian
soil, but not a war in which Romans were engaged: Livy's theme
is strictly Roman. Machiavelli's purpose, on the other hand, does
not limit him to things Roman. In the chapter in question, he discusses "How vain both the faith and the promises of those are who
find themselves outside of their fatherland." He explicitly limits
himself to two examples while indicating that there are other examples. Neither example is Roman or modern. Both examples contain references to Asia. Not only is Machiavelli's subject not

limited to Rome; it includes things which happened in Asia; ultimately his subject is not Roman at all. In the present case we may wonder whether the fatherland which he has in mind is any fatherland on earth. At any rate, Machiavelli reasons about matters of state, while Livy is an historian. Machiavelli knows important historical facts which Livy could not have known. He must then make important additions to Livy. On the other hand, it goes without saying that he will not repeat what Livy has made sufficiently clear.[16]

Since Machiavelli's intention is not identical with Livy's, it cannot be expected that the plan of the *Discourses* should be identical with the order of Livy's *History*. Machiavelli divides the *Discourses* into three Books, each of which is devoted to a subject of its own: the internal affairs of Rome that were transacted on the basis of public counsel (I), the foreign affairs of Rome that were transacted on the basis of public counsel (II), both private and public affairs of Romans that were transacted on the basis of private counsel (III).[17] At the beginning of the 9th chapter he indicates the following division of subject matter: founders, religion, militia. At the beginning of the 66th chapter he indicates that the preceding chapters of the Second Book had dealt with the Roman policy of aggrandizement but in the sequel he will go on to discuss the Roman procedure in the waging of war. These remarks show that he desires to order the happenings which Livy narrates in their temporal sequence and therefore somewhat chaotically; he desires to follow not the Livian sequence but the essential order of subject matter. He follows a plan of his own. He therefore selects Livian stories with a view not only to their throwing light on the nature of political things but likewise to their fitting into his plan. Hence there occur a considerable number of cases in which the examples taken from Livy follow one another in the *Discourses* in a way altogether different from the way in which they follow one another in Livy; and likewise there occur a considerable number of cases in which a series of chapters of the *Discourses* is manifestly held together by no other bond than that supplied by the identity of trans-historical subject matter (gratitude, character of the multitude, etc.). When Machiavelli says that something will be discussed "in its place," he means that it will be discussed in its place within his plan and not in its temporal place.[18]

At the same time he betrays an unmistakeable tendency to follow the order of Livy's *History*. At the beginning of the 8th chapter he retells a Livian story without making any reference to his source; yet he introduces his discourse on that story as a remark on "this text"; he thus leads us to expect that every discourse is related to some Livian text regardless of whether this is explicitly said or not. The 113th chapter deals with a subject that Machiavelli had sufficiently treated in another work; he discusses that subject in the *Discourses* only because a certain Livian passage invites such a discussion; in Livy's *History* that Livian passage immediately follows the Livian passage discussed in the preceding chapter of the *Discourses*. The 130th chapter begins with a reflection which is said to have been occasioned by a remark of Livy. The subject of the 60th chapter is introduced with a view to "the order of the history"; "the order of the history" is not the same as "our order," the order established by Machiavelli of which he speaks elsewhere.[19] What then, in general, is the relation between the Livian order and the Machiavellian order? Let us begin at the beginning. The first 15 chapters are manifestly ordered according to Machiavelli's own plan; that plan is to some extent made explicit; Machiavelli draws our attention to it by noting that he has deviated from the Livian order and that he may have deviated from his own plan.[20] In the rest of the First Book there no longer appears a manifest plan. Yet one cannot say that Machiavelli therein simply follows the Livian order: discourses related to the expulsion of the Roman kings (I 16-18) precede discourses related to the first three Roman kings (I 19-24). However if we consider the references to Livy in I 16-60, we see that they strictly follow the Livian order; they lead us in a straight way from the beginning of Livy II towards the end of Livy VII.[21] On the other hand, Machiavelli does not follow the Livian order in I 1-15, i.e., in a group of chapters which is manifestly governed by a clear and even partially explicit plan. The authority of the Livian order asserts itself in proportion as the light coming from Machiavelli's own plan is dimmed. Yet we must not overlook the fact that only 13 of the 45 chapters in I 16-60 and more specifically only 3 of the 24 chapters in I 16-39 contain references to Livy: the Livian order ruling these sections resembles a thin cover which is torn in many places rather than a strong bond; Machiavelli merely pretends to follow the Livian order. Hence Machiavelli's manner of following the Livian order constitutes a problem: when the Livian order is followed, there must be a Machiavellian reason for it. When a number of chapters are linked exclusively by the Livian order, i.e., when the study of their subject matter, conducted with ordinary care, reveals no other link between the chapters than the Livian order, one ought not to assume that these chapters are not governed by Machiavelli's own plan; one should rather assume that Machiavelli's own plan has gone completely underground. Or, to state without reservation what we believe, the Livian order conceals Machiavelli's plan. There are three ways in which Machiavelli indicates his plan. In the first place, he sometimes connects a number of chapters by explicitly referring in one chapter to the next until the true or apparent end of a section has been reached. In this way he suggests that I 2-8, I 25-27, III 1-6, III 8-10, and III 19-23 each form a section.[22] The second and most important way in which one can discover Machiavelli's plan is the study, conducted with the proper care, of the subject matter discussed. It is not sufficient to understand the purport of a given chapter taken by itself. *Par operi sedes*:[23] it is also necessary to raise the question of why the teaching concerned is transmitted in the context in which it is transmitted, and not to let this question drop if the event commented upon follows temporally or in the Livian order an event commented upon in the preceding chapter: the second event seldom immediately follows the first event in Livy's narrative; hence one must raise the question regarding the principle which guides Machiavelli's selection of events. In *Discourses* I 39 Machiavelli shows that the same accidents can frequently be observed among different peoples. The accidents which he uses as examples illustrate the foolish humors of the people, i.e., of the common people; the same kind of accident due to the foolish humors of the common people happened both in modern Florence and in ancient Rome. The preceding chapter had dealt with the difference between Florence as a weak republic and Rome as a strong republic. Remembering the preceding chapter, one realizes in reading I 39 that the difference between strong Rome and weak Florence cannot be due to the difference of the popular humors in the two cities but must be traced to the dissimilarity of their ruling classes. Accordingly, the function of I 39 is to contribute toward the exposition of the essential character of a virtuous ruling class: that chapter proves to be the central chapter of the section devoted to the essential character of a virtuous ruling class as exemplified by the Roman ruling class or the continuous founders of Rome. This conclusion is not contradicted by the fact that I 39 is connected by an emphatic reference with I 13, the central chapter of the section manifestly devoted to religion; the Florentine ruling class differs from the Roman ruling class precisely in regard to religion: the Roman ruling class made "a good use" of religion. The third way in which Machiavelli indicates his plan is by the use of hints. But this subject is better relegated to a note.[24]

The Second Book confronts us with a somewhat different situation: by the time we have reached the Second Book, we are supposed to have learned something about the substance as well as the mode of Machiavelli's teaching; therefore the devices used by the author can and must be varied to some extent. In the beginning of the Second Book we are not welcomed, as we were in the beginning of the First Book (I 2-8), by a series of explicitly connected chapters. On the other hand, the beginning of the Second Book does present the same disregard of the Livian order and the same degree of explicitness regarding Machiavelli's own plan as does the beginning of the First Book.[25] The number of chapters which contain references to Livy is proportionately much greater in the Second Book than it was in the First: while of the 60 chapters in the First Book only 18 contain such references, of the 33 chapters of the Second Book 22 chapters do.[26] If we take into account the fact, which we explained above, that Machiavelli could not well refer to Livy in the opening chapters of the *Discourses*, and if we therefore compare the 33 chapters of the Second Book with the last 33 chapters of the First Book, we notice more clearly the amazing progress in the emphatic use of Livy: of the last 33 chapters of the First Book only 11 contain references to Livy. All the more noticeable is the fact that the references to Livy in the Second Book do not strictly follow the Livian order through a long series of chapters as they did in the bulk of the First Book; the equivalent of the order of Livy references in I 16-60 which leads us in a straight way from the beginning of Livy II toward the end of Livy VII, is the order of Livy references in II 28-32, which leads us in a straight way from about the last third of Livy V toward the end of Livy X. In spite of, or because of this, Machiavelli adapts his own plan to the Livian order in the Second Book more closely than he had done in the First Book; in the Second Book he sometimes uses the Livian order as a means for indicating his own plan, which is not guided by chronology; he indicates beginnings of new sections by deviating from the Livian order, or, more precisely, by returning in the order of his Livy references from a later Livian passage (say, Livy IX 20) to an earlier Livian passage (say, Livy VIII 13).[27] At the same time, he continues to use such devices for indicating his plan as he had already used in the First Book, namely, the expressions "in the following chapter" occurring at the end of chapters,[28] "not foreign to (my) purpose" occurring at the beginning or end of chapters,[29] and "everyone knows."[30] A particular difficulty is created by Machiavelli's remark in II 4 that a certain point will be made "at the end of this matter," for the remark cannot refer to the end of the section to which II 4 belongs, namely the end of II 5. He thus indicates that the division of the Second Book into sections interferes somehow with the unity of a certain "matter" or that in the Second Book he discusses a broad subject whose treatment requires, to say the least, more than one section. At the beginning of II 15 he connects that chapter with the preceding one by speaking of "this same matter and . . . these same beginnings of the war between the Latins and the Romans"; he thus may indicate that the "matter" in question is not identical with a historical subject like a given war or the beginnings of a given war.[31] For in itself "a matter" may of course mean both a historical subject like the Roman Decemvirate and a trans-historical subject like ingratitude.[32] In other words, "a matter" may mean a Livian story or a Machiavellian topic. When Machiavelli says toward the end of I 34, "to turn to our matter, I conclude," and thus distinguishes between "our" matter and "my" conclusion, he means "to turn from my discourse to the matter reported by Livy"; he thus supplies us incidentally with the simple formula for his use of Livy and the Livian order: Machiavelli impresses his form on the matter supplied by Livy. But to return to the cryptic expression "at the end of this matter" which occurs in II 4, the context makes it clear that the "matter" in question is the contrast between the unarmed modern states and the armed ancient states and the demand following from the understanding of that contrast, that the modern states ought to imitate the ancient modes and orders. If one assumes that "the end of this matter" will coincide with the end of some chapter, one notices that it is impossible to decide without guessing what Machiavelli means by "the end of this matter"; and if one does not make that assumption, one will be confronted by an even greater difficulty. The ends of the following chapters meet the requirement stated in II 4: II 18, 20, 24, 30, 33, III 15, 27, 31, 36. We believe that "the end of this matter" is the end of the Second Book (II 33), and that the cryptic statement in II 4 therefore gives us more precise information concerning the subject matter of the whole Second Book than do the thematic statements. That subject matter is not merely Roman foreign policy insofar as it was directed by public counsel or, as Machiavelli suggests elsewhere, the militia;[33] the Second Book is devoted in a much higher degree than the two other Books to the contrast between the armed ancient states and the unarmed modern states, between "the weak world" of modernity and the strong world of antiquity, between "the unarmed heaven"[34] and the armed heaven, i.e., to the causes, the origin, and the essential character of the contrast between the moderns and the ancients. In spite of a certain preponderance of ancient "matter" in the Second Book, we are entitled to say that the theme of that Book is the critical analysis of modernity or, as Machiavelli intimates by occasionally using "modern" and "Christian" synonymously, of Christianity; for the ancient examples are necessary to provide a provisional standard for the judgment on modernity.[35] The Second Book would then have a twofold function: it is devoted to the foreign policy and the wars of the Romans or to the militia, and it is devoted to the critical analysis of modernity. To see the connection between the two themes one has merely to remember these three points. There is a certain similarity between warfare proper and spiritual warfare, or between a militia proper and a spiritual militia. The problem concerning the militia proper can be reduced to the alternatives of a citizen army and an auxiliary army; these alternatives have a certain similarity with the alternatives of a citizen priesthood and a priesthood subject to a foreign head. According to Machiavelli, there is a certain similarity between the rule exercised by ancient Rome over other cities and countries and that exercised by papal Rome: the rule of both is to some extent indirect.[36]

The Third Book combines external features of the first two

Books.[37] It also combines their subject matter; in the Third Book, chapters devoted to domestic affairs alternate in an irregular way with chapters devoted to foreign affairs or war. This is not altogether surprising, for the domestic affairs of the Romans are characterized by the enmity or the conflict between the nobility and the plebs.[38] At any rate, the Third Book "repeats" the two preceding Books from a new point of view. In his first statement relating to the organization of the *Discourses* as a whole, Machiavelli had made use of two divisions: the division into domestic and foreign affairs and the division into public and private counsel; and he had assigned to the First Book the combination of "domestic affairs" and "public counsel"; in the second statement he had in fact assigned to the Second Book the combination "foreign affairs" and "public counsel"; one could therefore expect that a Third and a Fourth Book would each be devoted to one of the two remaining combinations; in his last statement which occurs near the beginning of the Third Book he makes it clear by speaking of "this third book and last part" that the Third Book will deal with both the domestic and foreign affairs of the Romans as far as they were based on private counsel.[39] While this description is provisional, it is not therefore unimportant: proper names of individual human beings occur in chapter headings only in the Third Book.[40] Yet Machiavelli does not speak in the last statement of "private counsel"; he mentions in it however "private benefits." Could the Third Book deal primarily with private deliberations of Romans which were directed toward the private benefit of the individuals concerned? In his second statement he distinguishes between the deliberations, discussed in the First Book, of "the Romans" concerning domestic affairs and the deliberations of "the Roman people" concerning foreign affairs. Could he have already dealt in the First Book with private deliberations of the Romans? A central chapter of the First Book is explicitly devoted to the violent struggle in Rome over the agrarian law; Machiavelli there praises the patience and industry with which the Roman senate or nobility prevented the enactment of the agrarian law; the Roman nobles opposed the agrarian law because they loved property, i.e., because each Roman noble loved his property. One of the means which they employed was to oppose a tribune of the plebs to that tribune who had proposed the agrarian law. In a passage to which Machiavelli does not refer, Livy says

that certain senators who had some private claims on certain tribunes used this influence in order to gain the support of those tribunes; this would seem to constitute a kind of private deliberation
not wholly divorced from thought about the private benefit of the
individuals concerned. As we learn from the sequel in Livy, there
soon came a moment when the ordinary means employed by the
senate appeared to be inadequate; the senators therefore abandoned
"public counsels" and resorted to "private counsels" which were
guided by the consideration that the nobles must reach their immediate objective "by fair means or foul"; the result was the murder
of an obnoxious tribune of the plebs.[41] Machiavelli does not say a
word about this "Machiavellian" deed, about this classic example
of private counsel. Instead he devotes the next chapter to the praise
of "the generosity and prudence of the senate." This obtrusive silence teaches us more than one lesson. In the first place, we see
that if the First Book deals with such private deliberations as were
directed toward private benefits, it deals with them only in a very
subdued manner, and hence that private deliberations of this kind
may very well be the peculiar theme of the Third Book. Above all,
we see that the common way of studying the relation of the *Discourses* to Livy is defective because it disregards that Machiavellian
use of Livy which reveals itself only through the suppression of
Livian stories. This was the reason why, in considering the relation
between Machiavelli's plan and the Livian order, we limited ourselves so strictly to the references to Livy as distinguished from
the mere use of Livian passages: whether Machiavelli refers or does
not refer to Livy in a given place can easily be seen, and the collection of his references to Livy is a finite piece of work; but to
achieve clarity about his use of Livy is an infinite task: its completion would require complete understanding of every sentence of
the *Discourses* and of Livy; for Machiavelli can be presumed to
have read Livy with infinitely greater penetration than people like
ourselves are capable of.

The first eight chapters of the Third Book deal with the question of how to maintain a regime and a religion and how to establish
a regime; they take up the theme of the founder.[42] The 9th chapter "depends"[43] on the 8th, and the 10th chapter "depends" on the
9th; the 9th and 10th chapters prepare and even constitute the almost insensible transition from the theme "founder" to the theme

"captain" which is manifestly discussed in chapters 12-15. We suggest that III 1-15 constitute the first section of the Third Book, and that this section is devoted to the theme "the founder-captain."[44] The next section begins with emphatic references to the themes "true virtue" and "republic." Instead of "republic" we may also say "the people" or "the multitude."[45] Since according to Machiavelli, the multitude is the locus of morality and of piety the argument shifts insensibly to a discussion of the moral qualities. Or, perhaps more precisely, since the founder-captain is a prince, and prince and people are correlative, certain characteristics of the founder-captain can only be brought out in the context of a discussion of the moral qualities which are required for ruling the multitude. This context gives occasion for throwing light on the two types of founder-captains which are figuratively represented by Hannibal and Manlius Torquatus on the one hand, and by Scipio and Valerius Corvinus on the other.[46] The section beginning with the 16th chapter ends with the 34th chapter, i.e., with a chapter which repeats the theme of I 58, the most important chapter of the section on the multitude in the First Book. The last section of the Third Book begins with a remark which must be quoted again: "How dangerous a thing it is to make oneself the head of a new thing which concerns many people, and how difficult it is to manage it and to bring it to its consummation and, after it has been brought to its consummation, to maintain it, would be too long and too exalted a matter to discuss; I reserve it therefore for a more convenient place." Who will be so inhuman as to believe that Machiavelli was so inhuman as to whet the appetite of the earnest reader and leave it completely unsatisfied? We believe him on his word that he will not "discuss that long and exalted matter." But is there no mean between discussion and complete silence? Is there no "place" other than the lines of a book? Is a series of intimations not "a convenient place" for transmitting "a matter too long and too exalted to discuss"? Seeing that Machiavelli is a discoverer of new modes and orders, of something new which concerns many people, who desires that these new modes and orders be adopted and maintained and who therefore must give thought to the question by what procedures they may be adopted and maintained, the matter too long and too exalted to discuss is his own enterprise insofar as it depends upon the cooperation of "the young." In a word, we believe that the last section of the *Discourses* deals obliquely with Machiavelli's enterprise: he selects from Livy VII-X such stories as properly understood throw light on his strategy and tactics. He conceals the most exalted theme by scattering its parts, i.e., by presenting its parts not according to their intrinsic order but according to the purely accidental order of their Livian equivalents.[47] We have discussed an example of his intimations—his discussion of manifest blunders committed by an enemy (III 48)—on an earlier occasion. At present, it is necessary to note that the last sections of the First and Second Books have the same theme as the last section of the Third Book.[48] The last section of the First Book will be discussed in the proper place. Here we shall discuss briefly the last section of the Second Book.

Machiavelli begins the last section of the Second Book, i.e., the 33rd chapter, with a remark as to what one ought to do in order to profit from reading "this Livian history," i.e., Livy's work in general; this is the only reference to Livy which occurs in the chapter. While leading us to expect that he will in that chapter discuss more than one procedure of the Roman people and senate, he in fact discusses only one such, namely, their giving very great discretionary power to the captains of their armies. He then speaks of what the Romans did when they had decided upon a war, "for instance, against the Latins," but in the chapter he discusses only an incident in a war against the Tuscans. That incident was the conduct of the consul Fabius who had crossed the Ciminian Forest with his army without having had permission from the senate. On his return from the expedition he found two legates who ordered him in the name of the senate not to cross the Ciminian Forest. This order of the senate does not exactly support the thesis, stated in the heading and restated more forcefully within the chapter, that the Romans gave the captains of their armies great discretionary powers. When we turn to the Livian text, we see that Machiavelli has made a minor change: Livy speaks not of two legates but of "five legates with two tribunes of the plebs." But this minor change indicates a major change or a major silence. Machiavelli does not tell us how the difficulty obstructing the passage through the Ciminian Forest was overcome. The Ciminian Forest was thought to be impassable and no Roman had ever entered it. The consul's brother, M. Fabius, offered to explore it. M. Fabius had been educated in Tuscany, was learned in Tuscan letters, and knew the Tuscan language well. So he ventured among the Tuscans "in a bold disguise." What secured him against detection was however less Tuscan learning, or even his disguise, than the fact that "it was repugnant to belief that an outsider would enter the Ciminian Forest."[49] Machiavelli is another Fabius: it is the incredibility of his enterprise which secures him against detection, i.e., against the detection of the intransigence and awakeness with which he conducts his exploration of hitherto unknown territory and thus prepares the conquest of that territory by his brothers.

We agree with the commonly held opinion according to which Machiavelli, having decided to write *Discourses on Livy*, must at some point or other begin to refer to Livy or even to quote Livy. But it cannot be indifferent to us at what precise point he for the first time introduces Livy. The first reference to Livy or the first Latin quotation from Livy will be no longer for us a trivial fact but an amazing occurrence; it will elicit neither empty curiosity nor yawning but disturbing wonder. Since, other things being equal, a Latin quotation from Livy which occurs in an Italian book reveals a more powerful presence of Livy than does an Italian summary of a Livian passage, we turn our attention first to the first Latin quotations from Livy. These quotations occur in the section which is explicitly devoted to the Roman religion (I 11-15). Their introduction was properly prepared. Machiavelli had established the authority of the Roman republic by taking issue with classical political philosophy and with the aristocratic Roman tradition. In that context he had criticized certain critics of ancient Rome but had not openly criticized any ancient writers in his own name. In the section which immediately precedes the section on religion, i.e., in the section explicitly devoted to the founders (I 9-10), he takes issue with the opinion "perhaps" held by "many" according to which Romulus is to be blamed for having murdered his brother; he refutes that opinion by having recourse, not to any authority, but to "a general rule" without however saying a word as to whether that general rule is generally accepted. When, in chapter 4, he had attacked the opinion of "many" which condemned Rome for the discord between the plebs and the senate, he had eventually referred to the authority of Cicero. But now, when the deed to be excused is no longer shouting in the streets or the closing of shops, as it was in the fourth chapter, but murder, the murder of one's only brother, he does not betray any need for support by authority. Or, if one wishes, one might say that the authority of the divine founder of Rome enables Machiavelli to oppose to the false general rule which unconditionally forbids murder the true general rule which allows murder under certain conditions. Thereafter, he openly blames in his own name those ancient writers who servilely praised Caesar, while he praises those ancient writers who obliquely blamed Caesar:[50] his preferring the latter to the former is no longer supported by "the opinion of many." At the most, one could say that he appeals tacitly from a late Roman opinion to the opinion embodied in the republican practice of ancient Rome. However this may be,[51] immediately before beginning the section on religion, he takes the extreme step of suggesting that the Rome which Romulus found was a corrupt city, i.e., that in the beginning men were not good but corrupt.

Such is the background against which Livy himself, speaking his native tongue, makes his first appearance. The first Latin quotation from Livy occurs in the chapter (I 12) in which Machiavelli attacks the opinion of "many" according to which the well-being of the Italian cities stems from the Roman Church. Against that opinion he adduces "two most powerful reasons which, according to me, suffer no denial." Yet however powerful these reasons may be according to him, he cannot take issue with the highest authority existing in his age and country without having the support of something more powerful than any reason, namely, another high authority. To take issue with the Roman Church in the section of the *Discourses* which is devoted to the religion of the ancient Romans means to question the modes and orders of the established religion with a view to the modes and orders, rediscovered by Machiavelli, of the ancient religion, or to hold up the modes and orders of the ancient religion for imitation by modern men. Whatever may be true of the introduction or restoration of civil or military modes and orders,[52] the introduction or restoration of religious modes and orders requires, as Machiavelli asserts, the support of divine authority, true or feigned, or at least, we may add, the support of authoritative historians who transmit the original authority to later ages; for religious modes and orders lack those "evident reasons" of which purely political modes and orders are capable: religious

modes and orders rest on belief.[53] Livy must take the place of
the Bible; Machiavelli's Bible permits him to uphold a teaching
opposed to the teaching of the Bible. Machiavelli makes an effort
to enter into the spirit of ancient piety: while quoting from Livy
in Latin the words "Wilt thou go to Rome?" which Roman soldiers
had addressed to the image of Juno in a Tuscan town after its
conquest, he omits Livy's remark that the question might have
been prompted by "youthful jocularity."[54] It may seem incredible that Machiavelli should have longed for the revival of the
worship of the Queen Juno. He teaches explicitly that states
which desire to keep themselves incorrupt should maintain the
established religion. This does not prevent him however from
treating the Christian Savonarola's speaking with God as an exact
parallel to the pagan Numa Pompilius' simulated converse with
a nymph: the success of Savonarola in Florence proves that the
achievement of Numa, the founder of the religion of the ancient
Romans, can be repeated now.[55] The least one would have to say
is that Machiavelli is impartial as between paganism and Christianity.
In accordance with his desire to keep a nice balance, he mentions
in the section on religion "God" seven times and "god" or "gods"
seven times.[56] Furthermore, however strongly he may have recommended that the contemporary Christian states ought to maintain the Christian religion, he believed that the Christian religion
had in fact not been maintained in its purity but had declined and
that its ruin might be near. He, as it were, applies to his own time
the words quoted by him in Latin which Livy had used about the
decline of the religion ancient in Livy's time, i.e., in the time in
which the Christian religion emerged.[57] Whatever long-range prospect this remark might suggest it is safer to leave it here at saying
that from Machiavelli's point of view the imitation of the ancient
Romans as regards religion means that one should use the Christian
religion in the manner in which, according to him, the ancient
Romans had used theirs. He conveys this lesson by retelling certain
Roman stories and by making minor changes in them. He retells
the story of how an ancient Roman, "a citizen grave and of authority," had used religion for quieting the common people. When
tacitly taking up the same matter in a later chapter, he adduces
only a Florentine example and speaks of "a man grave and of authority" who quieted the common people: the "man," as distinguished

from the "citizen," was a bishop "who is now a cardinal." According to Livy, the Roman who quieted the plebs, was a consul; Machiavelli transforms him into a citizen, a man who did not hold at the time a politico-military command; he thus prepares the transition to the bishop in Florence.[58] The lesson is obvious: the men in ancient Rome who quieted the plebs by means of religion were citizens, not necessarily priests, for in ancient Rome religion was civil religion; the imitation of ancient Rome would consist in using Christianity as a civil religion. Machiavelli also retells the story of how a Roman consul overcame the difficulty caused by the indiscretion of some hen-men, a special kind of soothsayers, by having "the prince" of the hen-men killed and by describing that dead "prince" to his army as a liar. In Livy's version no "prince" of the hen-men is mentioned, nor does Livy's consul call the hen-man in question a liar. Machiavelli stresses the hierarchic structure of the Roman order of soothsayers and injects some non-Livian venom into the consul's words. As Livy tells us, the soothsayers (*haruspices*) were aliens from Tuscany.[59] Machiavelli's changes of the Livian stories are meant to facilitate the imitation of the ancient Romans by modern men, an imitation which is compatible with the formal maintenance of the Christian religion. As he says elsewhere, "up to the coming of the Longobards, the Pontiffs did not acquire any other authority except that which was given to them on account of their manners and their doctrine. In the other things they obeyed the emperors or the kings, and were sometimes killed by them, and used by them in their actions as servants."[60] But we must not lose sight of the Latin quotations from Livy. While Machiavelli had quoted in each of the chapters 12 and 13 one Latin sentence from Livy he quotes two of them in chapter 15, the last chapter of the section. In that chapter it is shown how the Romans, led by the same consul who destroyed and discredited "the prince of the hen-men," overcame by their virtue the obstinacy which their foreign enemies had acquired by virtue of religion: Roman arms proved to be superior to Samnite religion. Machiavelli thus prepares the first repetition of the section on religion—a repetition in which he contrasts "the quiet and religious" Roman king Numa Pompilius, the founder of the ancient religion, with his successor who, "armed with prudence and arms," "recovered the reputation of Romulus."[61]

The three chapters which contain the first four Latin quotations from Livy are preceded by 11 chapters and followed by 24 chapters in which no such quotations occur. This isolation, for which there is no parallel in the book, enhances the suggestive power of the quotations discussed. Those first four quotations are separated from the next quotations by an interval of unique length. Machiavelli compensates us for the extraordinary thrift which he practices, after having whetted our appetite, by a rare act of prodigality: in the first chapter in which he begins for the second time to quote Livy in Latin—in order from then on to quote him in Latin with some degree of regularity—he gives us six Latin quotations from Livy. This density occurs in the first chapter of the *Discourses* in which he discusses with complete neutrality the policies required for saving liberty and the policies required for establishing tyranny. In order to show how a potential tyrant can be successful he studies the actions of Appius Claudius, the founder of all public and private law in Rome, who failed in his attempt to establish tyranny and whose laws retain their force despite his ruin and violent death.[62] This neutrality which to us at any rate appears in the same light in which it sometimes appears in the *Discourses,* namely, as the height of political immorality and therefore perhaps as the height of immorality simply, is a heresy comparable in gravity to the neutrality between paganism and Biblical religion. It would seem then that the Latin quotations from Livy as strands of Machiavelli's web are ominous rather than humanistic. As for the connection in Machiavelli's mind between Biblical religion and tyranny, we refer to the suggestion which he makes in *Discourses* I 26.[63]

Machiavelli begins to refer to Livy sometime before he begins to quote Livy. He begins to refer to Livy immediately after he has established the authority of Rome by proving the superiority of Rome to Sparta. In order to establish the authority of Rome and hence of Livy, he could not use Livy and he did not need Livy; the data supplied by the sixth book of the Greek Polybius, the unnamed supplier of the chief "matter" of *Discourses* I 2-6, are necessary and sufficient. The two chapters in which the first references to Livy occur (I 7-8) do not fit perfectly into what might seem to be the proper order, as Machiavelli indicates at the beginning of the 9th chapter: if he had strictly adhered to that order,

Livy would not have appeared at all prior to the section on religion. What induced or compelled Machiavelli to deviate from the apparently proper order? He begins to refer to Livy when discussing a concomitant of a democratic Roman institution, the plebeian tribunate. The tribunes of the plebs were among those who had authority to accuse people before public tribunals. The first references to Livy occur in the two chapters which are devoted to the beneficial character of public accusations requiring proof and to the pernicious character of calumnies or of sowing sinister opinions about fellow citizens among the people. Ancient Rome had adopted the right policy in regard to both accusations and calumnies. But the exact opposite is true of modern Florence. The first references to Livy occur in the two chapters in which the superiority of ancient Rome to modern Florence becomes for the first time the theme, or starting from which the intra-classical alternative 'Rome-Sparta' is superseded as it were once and for all by the alternative 'ancient republics-modern republics.' Other considerations apart, recourse to Livy becomes necessary in proportion as the quarrel between the ancients and the moderns becomes thematic or otherwise important. One is entitled to say that in the two chapters in question there is a somewhat stronger emphasis on Florence than on Rome.[64] One of the victims of the bad Florentine arrangement was "a kind of prince of the city." One may wonder whether in discussing the alternative of accusations and calumnies, which is linked up with the difference between ancient Rome and modern Florence where Savonarola had been so successful, Machiavelli was not thinking of the sermons of Savonarola, the unarmed prophet, which are "full of accusations of the worldly wise and of invectives against them." Savonarola distinguished "two armed hosts, one which fought under God and this was he and his followers, while the other fought under the devil, and this was the opponents."[65] Descriptions of one's opponents in such terms are certainly not accusations in Machiavelli's sense of the word. One may wonder, in other words, whether the difference here discussed between ancient Rome and modern Florence must not be understood in the light of the difference between civil and trans-political religion. It is true that Machiavelli does not refer only to modern Florence; despite the fact that, as he says, the previous examples are sufficient, he adds an example from ancient Tuscany. That example shows that ancient Tuscany suffered from the same bad arrangement as modern Florence. We may note in passing that Machiavelli supplies us here as it were accidentally, with that critique of ancient Tuscany which is an important step on the way from the most ancient antiquity to ancient Rome. But however this may be, ancient Tuscany too, in contradistinction to ancient Rome, was the home and center of religion. As regards ancient Rome, the example adduced by Machiavelli shows that Manlius Capitolinus, having become out of ambition a leader of the plebs and having in this capacity calumniated the nobles, suffered capital punishment through the action, not of course of the tribunes of the plebs, but of a patrician dictator, the leader of the patriciate. In modern Florence too the calumniators were "friends of the people." In modern Florence however the calumniators succeeded in driving "the great men to despair."[66] It is necessary to compare the context of the first Livy quotations with the context of the first references to Livy. The first Livy quotations occur when Machiavelli discusses the ancient religion and therewith the greatest contrast between the ancients and the moderns. The first references to Livy occur when Machiavelli explicitly discusses a much less fundamental and less general contrast between ancients and moderns. But, as may have become clear, this does not necessarily mean that the mere references to Livy do not lead the reader towards the fundamental issue. In fact, they may even lead him into a deeper stratum of the fundamental problem; the first references to Livy are very suggestive regarding the relation between the common people and religion in general, and between the common people and Biblical religion in particular. It would be dangerous to generalize from this observation regarding the difference between the first quotations from Livy and the first references to Livy. This much however can safely be said: while, as goes without saying, Livy is present everywhere in the *Discourses*, the meaning of that presence, visible or invisible, might escape the reader if Machiavelli had not isolated his first references to Livy and his first quotations from Livy and thus given us some directives.

Machiavelli was compelled to establish the authority of Rome because the superiority of the Roman modes and orders to all others, for example the Spartan, was not obvious or universally admitted. In that context he had to speak of certain alleged defects

of Rome which he did not deny but of which he asserted in effect
that they are the inevitable concomitants of the best modes and
orders. Later on, when defending the fratricide committed by the
founder of Rome, he refers again to Sparta; there he silently retracts his initial statement according to which the state and the
laws established by Lycurgus lasted for more than 800 years without corruption of those laws or without any dangerous tumult:
the Spartans had deviated from the laws of Lycurgus by the time
of King Agis, i.e., about 600 years after Lycurgus; Agis who tried
to restore the ancient laws was murdered by the ephors; Agis'
successor, who shared Agis' desire massacred "all the ephors and
anyone else who could oppose him" and yet failed to restore completely the laws of Lycurgus.[67] The stature of Rome is thus still
more enhanced than it was after the original proof of Rome's
superiority to Sparta and after the first proof of Rome's superiority
to Florence had been completed. This does not mean, of course, that
every Roman was a most excellent man: Machiavelli speaks of the
corruption of Roman royalty and of the corruption of the Roman
people which was caused by the party of Marius. In spite of this,
"the example of Rome is preferable to any other example" because
it is more instructive than any other. Above all, certainly the leading Romans under the republic, or at any rate the consuls, were
"always most excellent men." The high point in the praise of Rome
is probably reached in Machiavelli's contrasting the moderate character of the foundation of the Roman republic with the inhuman
character of the foundation of the principalities of David and of
Philip of Macedon; for the remark about David already suggests what
Machiavelli will explicitly say later about the foundation laid by
Moses in the context of the only explicit reference to the Bible
which occurs in the *Discourses*: "he who reads the Bible judiciously,
will see that Moses was forced, in order that his laws and his orders
should prosper, to massacre innumerable human beings who, moved
by nothing but envy, opposed his designs."[68] Not long after that
high point has been reached, and at the very beginning of the
second half of the First Book, more or less in the region where
Machiavelli begins to follow the Livian order even in his use of
Livy, a fundamental change makes itself felt. Rather abruptly, if
circumspectly, he begins to criticize the Roman republic as it was
in its most incorrupt period,[69] and he goes on to do so though

returning again and again to the praise of Rome. Two Roman
generals, not indeed consuls but military tribunes with consular
power, preferred the disgrace of their fatherland to a minor sacrifice
of their pride. The senate once acted contrary to the rule that one
must not postpone benefiting the people until a third power forces
one to do so.[70] While defending the Roman institution of dictatorship by means of "most evident reasons" against the opinion of
"some writer" who had not "considered the matter well" and
whose verdict "has been quite unreasonably believed," i.e., while
tracing a powerful error to its weak beginning, Machiavelli makes
it clear that that Roman institution was not superior to a different
Venetian institution which fulfilled the same purpose equally well:[71]
the modes and orders of ancient Rome are not simply the model for
the moderns. Thereafter he speaks explicitly, if with due euphemism,
of "the defect" of the Roman agrarian law. That defect was perhaps immediately caused by the dilatory policy of the senate but
it was certainly in the last analysis caused by what, without the
use of euphemism, would have to be called the avarice of the Roman
nobility. It was owing to that avarice that Rome, in contrast to
Sparta, did not comply with the basic rule that the public should
be kept rich and all citizens be kept poor. In the context of this
criticism of Rome, Machiavelli accepts the opinion of "the ancient
writers" as to the working of certain passions and, most important,
refers to Livy by name for the first time since the end of the
section on religion:[72] Livy proves to be not only the celebrator of
Rome but also her critic. Livy is no longer needed only for transmitting to modern men the counterauthority which enables Machiavelli to attack the established authority; from this point forth he
is also needed to discredit that counterauthority. In other words,
the authority is henceforth no longer the practice and the polity
of ancient Rome, but Livy, a book: only from here on is Livy
Machiavelli's Bible or his counterpart of the Bible. Just as the
authority of the Bible is admittedly not weakened but strengthened by the fact that it contains the records of how the children
of Israel were stiff-necked and went a-whoring after other gods,
the authority of Livy is not weakened but strengthened by the
fact that he enlightens us concerning the misdeeds of the Romans
and the defects of the Roman modes and orders. It is in the 39th
chapter that Machiavelli draws the decisive conclusion from his

criticism of the Romans: diligent examination of things past enables one not only to foresee what would happen in every republic in the future if the necessary remedies are not applied in time, and to apply the remedies used by the ancients, but also to discover the proper remedies in case the ancients did not use or know them. Since the Roman modes and orders have been shown to be defective in more than one respect, we are forced to conclude that, according to Machiavelli, a progress beyond the ancient modes and orders is necessary, or that modes and orders which are new, not only relatively but simply, must be sought.[73] Far be it from us to deny the genuine character of Machiavelli's admiration for ancient Rome. But there is a great difference between genuinely admiring ancient Rome and believing that ancient Rome is the peak of all possible achievements. The ancient Roman polity was a work of chance, if of chance often prudently used;[74] the ancient Romans discovered their modes and orders absent-mindedly or by accident, and they clung to them out of reverence for the ancestral. Machiavelli, however, achieves for the first time the anatomy of the Roman republic, and thus understands thoroughly the virtues and the vices of that republic. Therefore he can teach his readers how a polity similar to the Roman and better than the Roman can be deliberately constructed. What hitherto has been a lucky accident, and therefore essentially defective, can become from now on, on the new continent discovered by Machiavelli, the goal of rational desire and action. It is for this reason that the modes and orders recommended by Machiavelli, even those which he took over bodily from ancient Rome, are rightly described by him as new modes and orders. Even if the content of those modes and orders remains the same, their character is wholly new. The *Discourses* truly convey then, as Machiavelli promises at the beginning of the book, new modes and orders. Just as the *Prince*, the *Discourses* present a wholly new teaching which is shielded by a conventional or traditional exterior. But whereas the *Prince* conveys the wholly new teaching regarding the foundations of society, the *Discourses* convey in addition the wholly new teaching regarding the structure of society, i.e., of the best society.

It would be wrong to believe that Machiavelli's emphatic blame, in the next chapter, of what may seem to be the biggest blunder committed by the early Roman republic, namely, the creation of the Decemvirate, is no longer surprising. That chapter shows precisely that the creation of the Decemvirate was not a blunder from the point of view of the senate or the nobility: the Decemviri were chosen only from the nobility; they did not hurt the nobility; they were actively supported by the young nobles; the authority of the senate survived under the Decemvirate; the creation of the Decemvirate appears as a not imprudent act, by which the senate frightened the plebeians into longing for the patrician consulate which they had theretofore loathed.[75] It is therefore necessary for Machiavelli to state, or to restate, in his next remarks on the subject that the orders of Rome were perhaps not good in a certain important respect and that the Roman nobility often acted unwisely in its dealings with the plebs.[76] In the penultimate chapter of the First Book, the last chapter of the section devoted to the multitude as the home of morality and religion, Machiavelli prepares the discourses of the Second Book (the Book devoted to the Romans' foreign policy) by proving that republics are more faithful allies than princes. He refers to seven examples; none of them proves the faithfulness of the Roman republic.[77] Since the Roman republic is the primary subject of the *Discourses*, the reader cannot help being particularly concerned with the faithfulness of the Roman republic; but on the basis of the evidence adduced by Machiavelli he can do no more than believe that the Roman republic was more faithful than princes. Machiavelli trains him in believing by himself saying *credo* five times in that chapter. The five-fold *credo* pronounced by him at the end of what one might call his destruction of Rome's authority corresponds to the four-fold *credo* pronounced by him at the end of the argument by which he established Rome's authority.[78] Fourteen chapters later, when his theme is no longer the multitude as the home of faith, or of good faith, he holds up as the model for republics which aspire to greatness the fraud which the early Roman republic, i.e., the senate, habitually practiced against its very allies.[79] But, as we have seen, even by the end of the First Book Machiavelli's faith in Rome is no longer what it was at the beginning: his faith in Rome was bound to be affected by what he believed to have discerned about the Romans' faith.

At the beginning of the Second Book, a new dimension of the problem comes to sight. After having defended Rome against a certain opinion held by "many," and in particular by "a most grave writer" of antiquity who is mentioned by name, Machiavelli shows that it was in the last analysis the Roman republic which destroyed freedom for many centuries in the West. Immediately thereafter he suggests a revision of the earlier verdict on the relative merits of Rome on the one hand and of Sparta and even Athens on the other. Rome was enabled to destroy freedom in the West or to make herself mistress of the world because she liberally admitted foreigners to citizenship; Sparta and Athens, though very well-armed republics with very good laws and apparently less tumultuous than Rome, did not achieve Rome's greatness because they, and especially Sparta, were fearful lest admixture of new inhabitants corrupt their ancient customs. Rome was then enabled to destroy freedom in the Western world because she was excessively cosmopolitan or constitutionally exposed to corruption.[80] No wonder that Machiavelli takes leave of the reader of the *Discourses* with the praise of that Fabius who was deservedly called Maximus for having practically disfranchised "the new people." But Fabius' measure did not stem the tide forever. Hence it remains true that the Roman republic, the greatest republic or the most political community[81] that ever was, prepared the Western world for Asiatic obedience and for the suppression of the supremacy of political or public life. The Roman republic is on the one hand the direct opposite of the Christian republic, and on the other hand a cause of the latter, or even the model for it. This is the ultimate reason that Machiavelli's judgment on the Roman republic is ambiguous. Near the center of the Second Book, he notes that the ancient Romans once believed they could vanquish pride by humility. He continues this thought six chapters later when, after having promised to speak of both mercenary and auxiliary troops, he speaks in fact only of auxiliary troops. Auxiliary troops are soldiers sent to the help of a state by "a prince or a republic" that commands and pays those troops; in the repetition, Machiavelli drops "or a republic"; auxiliary troops are the most harmful and the most dangerous kind of troops because the state which wishes to use them has no authority whatever over them: only "the prince" who sends them has authority over them; they are so dangerous because they form a disciplined body subject to a foreign authority whereas, as Machiavelli tells us elsewhere, mercenary troops are disunited and lack fear of God.[82] Immediately thereafter he discusses the manner of controlling subjects which ancient Rome had invented. Ancient Rome did not claim to rule the towns which had become its subjects but merely bound them to certain conditions; Rome's rule was not visible and was therefore rather easily borne even though it may have imposed some hardship; since Rome did not exercise civil and criminal jurisdiction in those towns, "the prince" was much less exposed to calumny and hatred than were the municipal authorities. In other words, Rome did not exercise direct rule over her subjects. Machiavelli compares the Roman way of ruling her subject towns to the way in which Florence ruled Pistoia: the Florentines treated the Pistoians with brotherly love, or, as he says "in another discourse and for another purpose," they ruled the Pistoians by "the arts of peace," i.e., by presenting themselves as peace-makers to the quarreling groups among their subjects, thus keeping their subjects divided.[83] In the 78th chapter, i.e., almost exactly in the center of the central Book, and nowhere else, Machiavelli mentions "the authority of the Romans" in the heading of a chapter. In the body of that chapter he says that "if one has to follow authority, one ought to believe a Roman republic and many most excellent captains who were in it, rather than the one Hannibal alone." But, as he makes clear in the next chapter, in following the authority of the Romans, one does not follow the authority of the Romans: the Romans discovered their modes and orders "without any example (of others), by their prudence, through themselves."[84]

In the Third Book, there is only one chapter which can be said to be devoted to the criticism of the early Roman republic. At the beginning of the 105th chapter and nowhere else in either book, Machiavelli refers to what "some moral philosophers have written" and approves of it. The philosophers in question had understood "the virtue of necessity" or they had realized that necessity is the mother of the highest virtue. Their insight agrees with the thesis of the chapter that necessity makes men obstinate and hence excellent fighters. The wise captain or ruler will therefore use every artifice to liberate his enemies from such salutary necessity; he will deceive the enemy populace by making large promises to them and by claiming that he has no quarrel with them but only with the ambitious few in their midst. We must leave it to the readers to decide whether Machiavelli himself is a wise captain, seeing that he directs his widely audible accusations against the ambitious prelates and that he knows that the people cannot but be averse to his radical innovations. The chapter under discussion may be described as the most extreme specimen of his criticism of Rome, since it suggests a certain superiority of modern Florence to ancient Rome.[85] Before turning to Roman examples, he speaks of two Florentine examples. In discussing the first Florentine example, he exculpates Florence from what amounts to a criticism by "many"; in discussing the second Florentine example, he exhibits the cleverness of the Medici. Later he cites three examples of how the Romans rendered their enemies obstinate. The first of these examples is supplied by the Romans' conduct toward the Samnites which led to the disaster of the Caudine Forks; it would have been easy for the Romans to say, and in this particular case they would have said with perfect justice, that they had a quarrel only with the ambitious few among the Samnites; but the Romans did not avail themselves of this opportunity. In the 15th chapter, we recall, Machiavelli had retold the story of how the Romans overcame by their virtue the obstinacy which the Samnites had acquired by "virtue of religion." In the present case, the Samnites were rendered obstinate by "virtue of necessity." The second of the three Roman examples shows how a Roman commander[86] unnecessarily made the Veientes obstinate. Machiavelli does not tell us that prior to the incident retold by him, the Roman consuls had made their own soldiers obstinate by means of religion[87] or that the Romans had acted like the Samnites. The last of the three examples shows how the Romans drove the Volsci, led by Messius, into extreme obstinacy. Machiavelli quotes in Latin a part of the speech with which Messius exhorted his soldiers; in the part omitted by him, Messius says: "Do you believe that some god will protect you and carry you away from here?"[88] Here we are meant to see how an enemy of Rome was driven by necessity into "operating perfectly" precisely by his subjective certainty that he and his army will not be saved by any god.

Time and again we have become bewildered by the fact that the man who is more responsible than any other man for the break with the Great Tradition should in the very act of breaking prove to be the heir, the by no means unworthy heir, to that supreme art of writing which that tradition manifested at its peaks. The highest art has its roots, as he well knew, in the highest necessity. The perfect book or speech obeys in every respect the pure and merciless laws of what has been called logographic necessity. The perfect speech contains nothing slipshod; in it there are no loose threads; it contains no word that has been picked up at random; it is not marred by errors due to faulty memory or to any other kind of carelessness; strong passions and a powerful and fertile imagination are guided with ease by a reason which knows how to use the unexpected gift, which knows how to persuade and which knows how to forbid; it allows of no adornment which is not imposed by the gravity and the aloofness of the subject matter; the perfect writer rejects with disdain and with some impatience the demand of vulgar rhetoric that expressions must be varied since change is pleasant. The translations of Machiavelli as well as of other great writers, even if they are done with ordinary competence, are so bad because their authors read books composed according to the rules of noble rhetoric as if they had been brought forth in compliance with the rules of vulgar rhetoric. In a famous letter Machiavelli has testified to what he owed to the writers of antiquity and their creations. In the evening, when entering his study he put on regal and courtly clothes and thus properly dressed he entered into the ancient courts of the men of antiquity who received him lovingly. There he fed himself on that nourishment which alone was his and for which he was born; there he united himself wholly with the ancients, and thus did not fear poverty, forgot every anguish, and was not frightened by death. Because of his nature and his devotion he came to sur-pass Livy. The peculiar charm and the peculiar remoteness of the *Discourses* are due to the fact that a part of their teaching is transmitted not only between their lines, but as it were between the covers of the *Discourses* and those of Livy's *History*. Machiavelli draws our attention to utterances of Livy or of Livy's characters which he does not quote and to which he does not even refer, strictly and narrowly speaking. Those utterances, if read in the light of Machiavelli's suggestive context, take on a non-Livian meaning and then illumine the Machiavellian context; the thought which is transmitted in this way is not conveyed by the *Discourses* read by themselves nor by Livy's *History* read by itself. Machiavelli expects his reader less to have read Livy and other writers than to

read them in conjunction with the *Discourses* after he has read the
Discourses once or more than once.[89] He certainly expects his
reader to read Livy with more than ordinary care or, to return to
the surface, with profound reverence.[90] This reverence need not
be weakened by the changes which Machiavelli makes in the
Livian stories or in the Livian text. Not all theologians always
refrained from modifying the Biblical stories and from quoting
Scripture inexactly. Such seeming liberties taken with the sacred
books may well subserve the pious concern with applying the
Biblical message to oneself and to one's generation. The analogy
of the Bible and Livy would not be perfect if Livy were not
Machiavelli's authority in theology or its equivalent. Livy is Machiavelli's authority as regards Fortuna and her workings. It is Livy
who, according to him, through a Roman example proves at length
and with most efficacious words the power of Heaven or Fortuna
over human affairs. The Livian proof is so complete that, as Machiavelli notes, no modern examples are needed to confirm the Livian
thesis. Machiavelli reproduces the Livian proof in one of the two
chapters whose headings consist of almost literally translated Livian
statements. The Livian statement which heads the chapter containing that Livian proof is the only chapter heading in either book
which pronounces dogmatically on the power and workings of
Fortuna.[91]

Once we have taken Machiavelli's acceptance of Livy's authority as seriously as we must, we become amazed by the relative
rarity of quotations from Livy and even references to Livy. We
slowly begin to dare to ask ourselves whether Livy is after all the
highest authority for him or whether he did not regard certain
other classical writers as more important than Livy. Accordingly
we note that Livy is never mentioned in the *Prince*. Livy is an
historian, whereas Machiavelli reasons about matters of state. That
is to say, Livy supplies him with matter, with examples; the conclusions drawn from the examples (only a part of which are supplied
by Livy), or the light which illumines the matter, or the reasoning
which leads up to the causes of the events recorded by Livy and
other historians is Machiavelli's.[92] As we observe next, Machiavelli
tacitly changes Livy's stories and thus perhaps tacitly criticizes
Livy. Very slowly, very circumspectly, does he begin to attack
Livy explicitly and, after having done so, he very rarely, but all the

more impressively, returns to that attack. The first explicit attack on Livy occurs in the 58th chapter, i.e., about 20 chapters after he had begun explicitly to criticize ancient Rome. But already in the 49th chapter he openly grants that Livy's *History* may be defective in a point of some importance, namely, in a point connected with the issue of "accusations and calumnies." In the same chapter, speaking of Florence, he indicates that "true memory" of Florentine affairs is not available beyond a certain date. Could the possible defect of Livy's *History* be due to the fact that he did not have "true memory" of the event which he records in the passage referred to by Machiavelli? Certain it is that Livy himself speaks in that passage of the uncertainty regarding events which are remote in time.[93] Machiavelli then is not absolutely silent about the questionable character of Livy's stories and about Livy's own references to that questionable character. In the 16th chapter he had already spoken of the things "which are read in the memories of ancient histories": Livy's *History*, and certainly its first ten Books, consist of such memories of ancient histories.[94] But even what is known through truly historical records, i.e., through such records of past events as were set down by contemporaries of those events, is less truly known than what everyone can see now; it is an object of belief rather than of perception.[95] It is for this reason that Machiavelli can substitute his summaries of Livian stories for the Livian stories themselves by sometimes describing summaries which lack any reference to Livy as "those texts" and then suggest that "those texts" are the work of Livy and Machiavelli jointly: Machiavelli can vouch for them as well or almost as well as could Livy himself.[96] It may be for this reason that he sometimes makes trivial changes in Livy's reports: whether the early Romans waged war in a given year against one neighboring tribe, say the Aequi, and not against another, say the Volsci, is not sufficiently established by the fact that Livy says they did. Even if an historian is trustworthy regarding his facts, he is not necessarily trustworthy regarding his selection of facts; historians are inclined to regard as most worthy of being remembered that which is miraculous or spectacular. When Machiavelli retells the story of the Decemvirate, he barely refers to the Virginia incident which is told at such length by Livy, to say nothing of the fact that he does not mention that heinous crime

when speaking of Appius Claudius' mistakes.[97] It is also significant
that the first historian explicitly quoted as stating a general cause,
the cause of a kind of human conduct, is not Livy but Tacitus.[98]
Eight chapters later Machiavelli summarizes an observation of
"the ancient writers" regarding human conduct in general, and
thereafter gives a "discourse" of his own in which he states the
cause of the phenomenon observed by the ancient writers. Thereafter he indicates that the most fundamental truth regarding man
can be known more easily by the moderns than by the ancients
because that truth is most easily discerned by considering "present
and ancient things" together.[99] Long after all these preparations
have been completed does Machiavelli praise Livy for the first
time. In the chapter preceding the one in which he explicitly quotes
Livy in Latin for the first time after the central chapter of the
section on religion, i.e., in the third chapter before the one in
which he states explicitly for the first time that Livy's *History*
may be defective, he says: "Since Titus Livius most prudently
gives the reason why this arose, it does not seem to me not to be to
the purpose to state precisely his words . . . " The most prudent
reasoning of Livy includes the following two remarks: the Roman
nobility, while disapproving of the violence done by their sons
to the plebs, preferred, if the line had to be overstepped, that it
should be overstepped by their own people rather than by their
domestic enemies; and: it seems as if it were necessary either to
do wrong or to suffer wrong. It is easy to see why this Livian
reasoning should appear to Machiavelli to be "most prudent." But
the praise of this particular Livian reasoning implies that Livy
does not always reason "most prudently" about the events which
he narrates: the very praise of Livy reveals a comprehensive criticism of Livy. Moreover, Livy appears equally to accuse the nobility
and the plebs of dangerous ambition; but Machiavelli, in his own
discourse which immediately follows his restatement of Livy's
reasoning, observes complete silence regarding the ambition of the
plebs: he speaks of the ambition of individuals who exploit the
desire of the common people for protection and monetary support.
Caesar is perhaps the greatest example of such individuals. Machiavelli here quotes a sentence which Sallustius had put into Caesar's
mouth and calls that sentence "most true."[100] Why Livy's reasoning
is not "most true" is indicated in the chapter following. Retelling

a Livian story about an action of the Roman plebs, he quotes a sentence in which Livy traces that action to the dispassionate and incorrupt judgment of the then plebs. Thereafter he tacitly renders Livy's explanation more precise and thus corrects it: the plebs—any plebs at any time—has tolerably good judgment in particulars but it is easily deceived regarding generalities. After having made his point he introduces a further quotation from Livy with the remark that Livy justly wondered about that action of the plebs which, according to Livy, revealed how lofty the mind of the Roman plebs was at that particular period; Machiavelli implies that Livy justly wondered because he did not grasp clearly the character of the popular mind. Immediately thereafter, he retells a Livian story about an incident in Capua, a city in which everything, and in particular the plebs, was corrupt: the corrupt Capuan plebs did not act differently than did the incorrupt Roman plebs in a strictly parallel case. The hero of the story is a high Capuan magistrate; when reading Machiavelli's version, one receives the impression that that Capuan was a public-spirited and wise citizen; Machiavelli suppresses Livy's remark that the individual in question was "a wicked man but not altogether lost" who preferred to lord it over an intact rather than a destroyed commonwealth: the distinction between clever wickedness and moral worth is not as "true" in Machiavelli's eyes as it is in Livy's.[101] Machiavelli pursues this thought in the chapter which immediately precedes his first explicit attack on Livy. After having explicitly quoted some Livian words in Latin, he explicitly repeats Livy's words and changes them somewhat as he does so: whereas Livy himself had spoken of the plebeians having become "obedient," Machiavelli makes him speak of the plebeians having become "vile and weak."[102]

Machiavelli's subdued criticism of Livy prepares his criticism of authority as such. In the first 57 chapters of the *Discourses*, we find these further suggestions which have an immediate bearing upon the broader issue. Cicero, the most famous Latin prose writer, is mentioned three times in the *Discourses*; in the 4th chapter he is quoted with approval as a political thinker; in the 33rd chapter he is quoted as having realized a grave error committed by Pompey; in the 52nd chapter he is shown to have ruined himself and his party by a grave error of judgment which could easily have been avoided.[103] Near the beginning of the 18th chapter Machiavelli

says, quite casually as it might seem, that "it is good to reason about
everything" whereas he says in the *Prince* that "one ought not to
reason about Moses since he was a mere executor of the things which
were commanded to him by God" and that one ought not to
reason about ecclesiastical principalities, "for, since they are exalted
and maintained by God, it would be the work of a presumptuous
and temerarious man to discuss them."[104] The 18th chapter of the
Discourses begins with "I believe" whereas the preceding chapter
begins with "I judge." The distinction between "believing" and
"judging" reminds us of a passage in the first chapter of Seneca's
De vita beata: "Everyone prefers to believe rather than to judge.
One never judges but always believes regarding the things which
are vital. Error transmitted from hand to hand always turns us to
and fro and throws us down headlong, and we perish through
following examples taken from others. We shall be cured if we
were but to secede from the crowd. As it is, however, the people,
the defender of its own evil, stands firm against reason." If we
desire to understand Machiavelli's thought, we must pay great
attention to the kinship which according to Seneca exists between
"believing" and "the people."[105]

In the 58th chapter Machiavelli explicitly takes issue with Livy
and "all other historians" or, as he says shortly afterward, with
"all writers." Does he enlarge the scope of his attack as he presses
forward or as he takes breath, or does he suggest that all writers,
i.e., all writers that preceded him, are in a sense historians? He
certainly continues with these words: "I do not judge nor shall
I ever judge it to be a defect to defend any opinion with reasons,
provided one does not even wish to use in such defense either
authority or force."[106] He could not have stated more clearly and
more gently the principle that only reason, as distinguished from
authority, can command his assent. To reject authority on principle
means to reject the equation of the good with the old and hence
of the best with the oldest; it means to derogate from the reverence
for old men, the men most akin to the olden times. The First Book
of the *Discourses*, which almost opens with the praise of the most
ancient antiquity literally ends with the praise of the many Romans
who "triumphed in their earliest youth." And the Second Book
begins with a rebuke of the irrational inclination natural to men
to praise the ancient times. Machiavelli addresses his passionate

and muted call to the young—to men whose prudence has not enfeebled their youthful vigor of mind, quickness, militancy, impetuosity and audacity.[107] Reason and youth and modernity rise up against authority, old age, and antiquity. In studying the *Discourses* we become the witnesses, and we cannot help becoming the moved witnesses, of the birth of that greatest of all youth movements: modern philosophy, a phenomenon which we know through seeing, as distinguished from reading, only in its decay, its state of depravation and its dotage.

The subject concerning which Machiavelli challenges "all writers" is the wisdom and the constancy of the multitude. Opposing the whole tradition and "the common opinion," he contends that the multitude is wiser and more constant than is a prince: not without reason does one compare the voice of the people, "a universal opinion," to the voice of God. It may easily appear that Machiavelli was the first philosopher who questioned in the name of the multitude or of democracy the aristocratic prejudice or the aristocratic premise which informed classical philosophy. He preferred the more democratic Roman polity to the less democratic Spartan polity. He expressed the opinion that the purpose of the people is more honest, or more just, than the purpose of the great. It is true that he did not favor the rule of the multitude: all simple regimes are bad; every so-called democracy is in fact an oligarchy unless it verges on anarchy.[108] But his bias in favor of the multitude enabled or compelled him not to identify himself simply with the aristocratic or oligarchic republicanism of the classical tradition: the just demands of the common people may also be satisfied by a prince and even by a tyrant. This is one reason why the argument of the *Discourses* consists partly of a movement away from republics toward principalities and even toward tyrannies, why Machiavelli appears in some discourses to be completely neutral in the conflict between free states and tyrannies, or why he sometimes seems to blur the distinction among tyrannies, principalities and republics. It is no accident, I believe, that the most shocking or the most "Machiavellian" passage of the *Florentine Histories* is the speech addressed by a Florentine plebeian in the year 1378 to the Florentine plebs. The Florentine plebs had committed arson and robbery and was afraid of punishment; the plebeian leader of the plebs exhorts his audience to double the evils they had com-

mitted and to multiply the arson and the robberies, for small faults
are punished while great and grave ones are rewarded; they should
not be frightened by the ancient blood of their adversaries, for
since all men had the same beginning, all men are of equally ancient
blood or by nature all men are equal, and only poverty and wealth
make them unequal; great wealth and great power are acquired
only by fraud or by force; faithful men always serve and good
men are always poor; they should not be frightened by their conscience, for where there is fear of hunger and prison there cannot
be and ought not to be fear of hell; God and nature have so established it that the things which men desire can be acquired by
evil acts rather than by good ones. At any rate one may say that
when indicating the character of the ruling class in the *Discourses*,
Machiavelli views the ruling class from the plebeian point of
view.[109] Yet one may say with equal right that he views the plebs
to some extent from the patrician point of view.[110] At present we
must limit ourselves to a more precise consideration of the 58th
chapter of the *Discourses*, the only chapter in the very heading
of which Machiavelli asserts the superiority of the multitude to a
prince. He attacks "the common opinion" according to which the
multitude is inferior in wisdom to princes, and he contends that
the voice of the multitude, "a universal opinion," is likely to be
right. But is not "the common opinion" about the wisdom of the
multitude "a universal opinion"? And does not "universal opinion"
assert that "universal opinion" is likely to be wrong? Does not then
the oracular voice of the multitude deny wisdom to the multitude?
Must Machiavelli not question the authority of universal opinion
in order to establish the authority of universal opinion? Must he
not say that universal opinion must be wrong so that universal
opinion can be right and that universal opinion must be right so
that universal opinion can be wrong? Against this one might try
to argue as follows: "the common opinion" of "all writers" is not
"a universal opinion," i.e., an opinion of the multitude or of the
people;[111] eleven chapters earlier Machiavelli had contended that
the opinion of the people is likely to be right regarding particulars,
whereas it is likely to be wrong regarding generalities; hence even
if not only writers but the peoples themselves were to deny
wisdom to the peoples, this verdict, being a judgment on something
general, may well be wrong and yet the people may be wise in

particular matters; in the very 58th chapter Machiavelli does not go beyond contending that the multitude or the people is marvelous in foreseeing its own evil and its own good, i.e., its particular good or evil here and now. Yet in the earlier discussion he had shown how easy it was for the Roman senate to deceive the people or the plebs in regard to particulars. Granted that the multitude possesses sound judgment on particulars, such judgment is of little value if the context within which the particular comes to sight is beyond the ken of the multitude: by changing the context one will change the meaning of the particular. And the generalities regarding which the people is admittedly incompetent are an important part of that context: sound judgment regarding particulars is impossible if it is not protected by true opinion about generalities. Hence the multitude is frequently more moved by things which seem to be than by things which are. Hence Machiavelli can comfort the prince by the thought that he can easily deceive the many about his character, i.e., about a particular, and he must warn republics that the people, which is allegedly marvelous in foreseeing its own evil and good, desires frequently its own ruin because it is deceived by false appearance of good and is easily moved by grand hopes and valiant promises. In the 58th chapter itself, Machiavelli says that the people can grasp that truth which it hears. This remark means, in the light of earlier remarks, that the people cannot find the truth by itself. By itself, it is ignorant; it is in need of guidance; it must be compelled or persuaded by prudent citizens to act sensibly. The Roman senate was a body of such prudent citizens.[112] What is particularly striking in the 58th chapter is that Machiavelli compares therein the wisdom of the multitude or of the people with the wisdom of princes, i.e., of kings, emperors and tyrants, without saying a word about the wisdom of "the princes," i.e., the ruling class, in a republic. Instead, he tacitly substitutes in a considerable part of the argument of that chapter "republics" for "multitude," and thus tacitly contrasts the wisdom of princes, not with the wisdom of the multitude, the common people or the plebs, but with the wisdom of the Roman senate, and therewith renders the true issue completely invisible.[113] The true issue becomes visible once one reflects on the fact that the multitude or the plebs needs guidance. This guidance is supplied ordinarily by laws and orders which, if they are to be of any value, of necessity originate in superior minds, in the minds of founders or of princes. Of princes thus understood—and princes thus understood include the series of first rate men who were responsible for the continuous foundation of Rome—Machiavelli says in the 58th chapter that they are superior to the peoples because they alone are fit to establish new laws and orders, whereas peoples are superior to princes as regards the maintaining of modes and orders already established. In other words, "princes" are the founding or innovating or rational element in society, while the people is the preserving or conservative element: once the people begins to abhor or to love something, i.e., things of a certain status or character, it clings to that opinion for centuries. The people is the repository of the established, of the old modes and orders, of authority. Therefore one may provisionally say that the peoples are by far superior to princes in glory. But however this may be, one must say with finality that the peoples are by far superior to princes in goodness; for goodness or morality is essentially preserving or conservative, and not innovating or revolutionary, whereas the prototype of princes is Romulus the fratricide.[114] The peoples are the repository of morality. After all that has been said this does not mean that the peoples always or even mostly act morally or even that they are fundamentally moral; belief in morality is not yet morality. Machiavelli illustrates the conservative character of the people by the fact that the Roman people hated the very name of kings for many centuries. Yet in the same context he declares that "the opinion unfavorable to the peoples arises because of the peoples every one speaks without fear and freely, even while the peoples reign, but of princes one always speaks with a thousand fears and a thousand respects." The Roman people could hardly have hated the very name of kings for many centuries after the expulsion of the Roman kings, and yet always have spoken of kings with a thousand fears and a thousand respects. Considering the violent struggle between the Roman plebs and the Roman senate or the Roman "princes," the contradiction cannot be resolved unless one assumes that "princes" does not always designate monarchs or even human government in general. We suspect that Machiavelli sometimes uses "princes" in order to designate superhuman powers. And vice versa, since he sometimes uses "human beings" for designating the people, common men or the subjects,[115] there is no reason that he should not, on the proper occasion, use "the people" to designate human beings as distinguished from superhuman beings. At any rate, for the same reason for which the peoples are the repository of morality, they are also the repository of religion.[116]

We are compelled here to make an observation similar to that which we made when we considered Machiavelli's first emphatic blame of ancient Rome. The explicit and emphatic character of his disagreement with Livy's judgment on the multitude does not correspond with what we may call the reality of this disagreement. While forgoing recourse to authority, to say nothing of recourse to force, Machiavelli does not forgo recourse to guile. He does not seriously disagree with Livy's judgment on the multitude. He does disagree with Livy, and with "all writers," on the status of morality. This is not to deny that by questioning the traditional view of the status of morality he is freed to question the traditional view of aristocracy or the rule of men of moral worth. But questioning the traditional view of aristocracy is very different from adopting the extremely populist view which he seems to adopt in the 58th chapter. The traditional doctrine asserted the moral superiority of "the better people." According to Machiavelli, his dissection of the Roman republic entitles him to judge that the ruling class deserving of the name is necessarily superior to the multitude in foresight, but is most certainly not morally superior; rather it is morally inferior to its subjects. To the extent to which he ironically accepts the major premise that human excellence is moral excellence, he arrives at the conclusion that the multitude is simply superior to "princes." This does not mean that the acceptance of that major premise is arbitrary. Machiavelli is a bringer of new modes and orders. He is a revolutionary, i.e., his adversaries have on their side the laws and everything respected and honored. Compared with the powers which he attacks, he may very well appear as he describes himself, namely, a being of a low and abject condition; and, as he teaches, one rises from such a condition through fraud rather than through other means. He is "a man of the people" not only in the literal sense, and the meaning of his turning from Latin to the vulgar tongue is not exhausted by what every schoolboy is supposed to know. His plebeian leader who encourages the plebs not to be frightened by conscience, i.e., by fear of hell, is a caricature of Machiavelli, but the caricature of a man reveals something of the man himself. Still, even a plebeian leader is not simply a plebeian, and a leader of the plebs is not necessarily himself a plebeian. Yet as a rebel against everything that is respected, Machiavelli must certainly adapt himself to the taste of the vulgar, if he desires to get a posthumous hearing for his new modes and orders. This is one reason why he displays a bias in favor of the extreme and spectacular. A Fabius Maximus Cunctator is necessarily unpopular; he can never demonstrate to the populace the soundness of his opinion; his opinion is bound to appear abject.[117] Even less popular will be the man who has discerned with perfect clarity the true and natural principles on which men like the empirical Fabius act instinctively: the true opinion about the most general, the most comprehensive things can never become popular opinion; it will necessarily appear to the populace to lack glamor and even to be abject and degrading. Machiavelli cannot train his readers in discovering for themselves the lowly but true principles which he can only intimate, except by appealing on different occasions to different principles all of which are respectable or publicly defensible but which contradict one another: the contradiction between them may lead some readers to the true principles in their nakedness. Thus he mitigates his attack on the Roman Church by appealing to original Christianity. He mitigates his attack on Biblical religion by praising religion in general. He mitigates his attack on religion by praising humanity and goodness. He mitigates his analysis of the bad and inhuman conditions of goodness and humanity by cursing tyranny and by blessing liberty and its prize, the eternal prudence and generosity of a senate. He mitigates the impact of his unsparing analysis of republican virtue at its highest by paying homage to the goodness and religion of the common people and to the justice of their demands. He mitigates the impact of his unsparing analysis of the defects of the common people by his appeal to a patriotism which legitimates the policy of iron and poison pursued by a most ferocious lion and a most astute fox or which legitimates the kind of rule known traditionally as tyranny.[118]

We are now in a position to describe more adequately than was hitherto possible the relation between Machiavelli's two books. The first impression according to which the *Prince* is devoted to prin-

cipalities and the *Discourses* are devoted to republics is not misleading. The characteristic theme of the *Prince* is the prince in the
most exalted sense, the bringer of new modes and orders or the
founder. The characteristic theme of the *Discourses* is the people
as the maintainer of established modes and orders,[119] or as the repository of morality and religion. If it is true, as I believe it is, that
the Bible sets forth the demands of morality and religion in their
purest and most intransigent form, the central theme of the *Discourses* must be the analysis of the Bible. This does not mean
that the *Discourses* are silent about founders. On the contrary, the
Discourses articulate the phenomenon of the founders much more
thoroughly than does the Prince: the *Discourses* deal not only with
heroic founders like Cyrus and Theseus but likewise with the series
of "continuous founders" such as the Roman senate, and with the
founder-captain like Romulus who in the *Prince* is mentioned in
only a single chapter—to say nothing of the founder-captain Machiavelli himself. The contention that the characteristic theme of
the *Prince* is the founder as distinguished from the repositories of
morality and religion, means that the perspective of the people does
not predominate in the *Prince* in the way in which it predominates
in the *Discourses*. In the *Discourses*, even the founders themselves
are viewed in the perspective of the society already founded. Hence,
the *Discourses* make considerable use of the distinction between
kings and tyrants and they speak with proper frequency and emphasis of the common good and of the conscience; hence Machiavelli speaks in the *Discourses* sometimes of "we Christians." The
Discourses in other words come closer than the *Prince* to what is
generally or popularly accepted. But for the same reason the *Discourses* go much further than the *Prince* in the detailed analysis,
resolution or destruction of the generally accepted: the attack in
the *Discourses* on "all writers" has no parallel in the *Prince*. And
if Machiavelli had not written the *Discourses*, people would not
speak as frequently and as easily as they do of Machiavelli's "paganism." But if he had not written the *Prince*, it would not be as
manifest as it is that he transcends the standpoint of the people in
the direction of the standpoint of the founder. All this merely
confirms his suggestion that each of the two books contains everything he knows but that in the *Prince* he has condensed everything
he knows in the highest degree possible: only in the *Discourses*

does he have room and leisure for beginning with what is "first for us" and for leading up to what is "first by nature."

Furthermore, we are now in a position to defend Machiavelli to some extent against the observation of a modern critic that he completely distorts the meaning of Livy's stories and falsifies their spirit. This criticism is fully justified if it is meant to imply that Machiavelli knew what he was doing. He consciously uses Livy for his non-Livian purposes. He deliberately transforms the Roman ruling class as it was into a ruling class as, according to him, it should have been; he makes the Roman ruling class "better" than it was; he transforms a group whose best members were men of outstanding virtue and piety into a group whose best members, being perfectly free from all vulgar prejudices, were guided exclusively by Machiavellian prudence that served the insatiable desire of each for eternal glory in this world. From Machiavelli's presentation one receives the impression that prior to Numa Pompilius there was no religion in Rome: Machiavelli is silent about the Livian testimonies to the religious character of Rome's foundation by Romulus. He may well have adopted Polybius' account of the beginnings of civil societies because that account is silent about gods and religion.[120] A Livian story gives Machiavelli occasion to praise "the generosity and prudence" which the Roman senate showed in a reply it gave to Roman allies; the Livian senate referred in its reply to "the sudden wrath of the gods"; the Machiavellian senate is too "generous and prudent" or too good a knower of "the things of the world" to mention "the sudden wrath of the gods."[121] The Livian eye-witnesses to the ruin of the wicked legislator, Appius Claudius, mutter, each man to himself, that there are gods after all and that they do not neglect human things and that pride and cruelty receive their divine punishment which, though late, is nevertheless not light; the same event gives occasion to Machiavelli for the reflection that it is imprudent and useless to leap from humility to pride and from pity to cruelty without duly taking the intermediate steps.[122] According to Livy, the Roman pontiffs had a voice in the deliberations connected with Camillus' having vowed to Apollo a tithe of the booty taken in Veii; the Roman pontiffs have disappeared in Machiavelli's restatement; here as elsewhere he does everything to obliterate the

Roman pontiffs or the role that they played in the ancient Roman republic.[123] According to Livy, the Roman people acquitted Horatius Cocles from punishment for having slain his sister chiefly because they admired his steadfastness and virtue; according to Machiavelli, they acquitted him since they were moved by "the prayers of the father."[124] According to Livy, when the Gauls entered Rome after their victory at the Allia, the Roman senate resolved that the men of military age and the able-bodied senators should retire into the citadel and the Capitol together with their wives and children, for it would not have been human to prevent the wives and mothers from saving themselves although they could not contribute anything to the defense of what was left of Rome; according to Machiavelli, the women stayed in the town as prey to the Gauls because purely military considerations prevailed. According to Livy, the Romans were greatly concerned in that calamity with defending the citadel and the Capitol because those places were the dwellings of the gods, and with defending the gods themselves as well as the Vestal virgins and the sacred things belonging to the Roman people; Machiavelli does not even allude to this part of the story.[125] According to Livy, both gods and men prevented the Romans from living redeemed; Machiavelli makes him say that Fortuna did not wish that the Romans live redeemed by gold.[126] When referring to Livy's account of the self-sacrifice of the elder P. Decius Mus, Machiavelli suppresses every mention of the religious character of that act of devotion, an act meant to expiate the whole wrath of the gods, to draw upon Decius all the threats and dangers, offered by the supernal and infernal gods, or to relieve of religious fear the minds of the Romans; he merely alludes to what he had indicated elsewhere (in the section on religion) about how one might make soldiers obstinate; instead he expatiates on the order which the Romans followed in their armies and in battles, and which Livy had admittedly explained at length in the same context.[127] Quoting in the Second Book some Latin words from a Livian speech which begins with the remark that the immortal gods have made the Roman senate the master of the fate of Latium, Machiavelli leaves it open whether those words are words of Livy or of a Livian character; there can be no question that they are not the words of Machiavelli. In the whole Second

Book, Machiavelli speaks only once of gods or God; summarizing an argument of an ancient writer, he says that the Romans built more temples "to Fortuna than to any other god."[128]

By the end of the First Book of the *Discourses* the reader is supposed to have liberated himself completely from belief in any authority. The Preface to the Second Book, being a "repetition" of the Preface to the First Book, summarizes the results of the First Book insofar as they affect the problem of authority in general. The first Preface had identified the new modes and orders, discovered by Machiavelli with the ancient modes and orders, and it had appealed to the prejudice in favor of antiquity. The second and last Preface exhibits the irrational character and the causes of that prejudice. Machiavelli does not deny that in a given part of the world the men of the present may be justified in regarding themselves as inferior to their forebears with respect to virtue. But this does not mean that virtue is the preserve of antiquity and especially of classical antiquity. There is at present as much virtue in the world as there was at any time in the past, only virtue does not now reside where it resided in classical antiquity. It resides now in Northern Europe and in Turkey rather than in Greece and in Italy. This is partly due to the change in education and therefore to the change in religion. But if a contemporary Christian born, say, in Greece becomes a Turk, i.e., an infidel—a pagan or worse than a pagan—he has no reason to blame the present age or to long for antiquity. The prejudice in favor of antiquity is partly caused by the distorted accounts which we have of ancient times. Most writers are so servile as to magnify the virtues and conceal the vices of the powerful ones of their time, whereas it is possible to acquire perfect knowledge regarding "present actions." In a word, most histories are utterly unreliable. Hence the glory deriving from deeds is less solid than the glory deriving from the production of works of art: works of art can be as present to any later age as they were to the age in which they were brought forth. We had been told originally that the men most highly praised, whether rightly or wrongly, are the founders of religion: they are even more highly praised than the founders of republics or kingdoms who in their turn are more highly praised than men of letters. We are told almost immediately afterward that no glory or posthumous fame surpasses that of the founder or restorer of a city, like Romulus.

We are now given to understand that the glory of any doer is inferior to that of excellent artists or writers.[129]

In the First Book, Machiavelli had not dared openly to question Livy's judgment before the 58th chapter. In the Second Book he questions it already at the beginning of the first chapter. He disagrees with Livy on no less a subject than the power of Fortuna. Livy as well as many others held the opinion that Rome owed her empire to luck rather than to virtue. Machiavelli refuses to "confess" this in any way: he, as it were, defends the virtue of the Romans against Livy. His criticism is directed, however, less against Livy than against Plutarch, "a most weighty writer." We may note in passing that he never anywhere in the *Discourses* applies to Livy an epithet of equal force; he merely calls him "a good historian."[130] Plutarch claimed that his opinion was supported by the "confession" of the Roman people itself which had built more temples to Fortuna than to any other god. Machiavelli does not question Plutarch's contention that the Roman people ascribed its well-being to Fortuna rather than to its own virtue. Silently contradicting what he had said in the 58th chapter about the value of the voice of the people, but silently confirming what he had indicated there in regard to that subject, he attaches no importance to the opinion of the Roman people on the source of its well-being. In defending the virtue of the Roman people against its own opinion, he questions the wisdom of the Roman people. He directs his attack against Plutarch rather than against Livy because he is not quite certain that Livy shared the opinion of the Roman people regarding the power of Fortuna; it is less Livy who speaks about the power of Fortuna than Livy's Romans whom Livy "makes speak" on that subject. Livy was perhaps wiser than his Romans. Perhaps he did not "confess" everything that his Romans believed. While being the mouthpiece of pagan theology, he was perhaps also its critic.[131]

Nowhere in the First Book had Machiavelli even alluded to the problem posed by the difference between Livy and Livy's characters. Only once therein did he make an explicit distinction between an author and a character of that author: he said that Sallustius "put" a certain sentence "into the mouth of Caesar."[132] In the Second and Third Books, however, he refers 11 times to the difference between Livy and his characters by using expressions like "Livy makes someone say or do certain things" or "Livy put these

words into the mouth of someone." But this is not the only difference
between the treatment of Livy in the First Book on the one hand,
and in the Second and Third Books on the other. Only in the two
last Books do we find what we may strictly speaking call sermons
on texts,[133] i.e., discourses opening with a Latin quotation which
functions as "text" for the discourse in question. There occur
altogether 3 such discourses; only Livian texts are used in the
manner indicated. In this connection we may note that references
to a "text" occur proportionately more frequently in the Second
Book and in the corresponding parts of the Third Book than in
the First Book.[134] Finally, only in the two last Books does Machiavelli
speak of Livy as a "witness" (*testimone*) or of his "testimony"
(*testimonio*) or of his "vouching" (*fare fede*) for something.[135]
We cannot help suspecting that these peculiarities of the treatment
of Livy in the two last Books are connected with the specific themes
of these Books. The Second Book deals with foreign policy and
warfare or with the militia; the Third Book repeats the themes
of the First and Second Books. With one exception, it is only in
such chapters of the Third Book as are devoted to foreign policy
or military matters that the peculiarities of the kinds mentioned
occur; the exception is a passage dealing with Camillus, "the most
prudent of all Roman captains."[136] The reader will remember what
was stated earlier at some length regarding the ambiguity of the
themes "militia, warfare and foreign policy."

After having alluded to the difference between Livy and his
characters for the first time in the first chapter of the Second
Book, Machiavelli does not return to that subject before the 13th
chapter of the same Book. The 13th chapter forms the center of
a section the meaning of which is not obvious. The section is
immediately preceded or appropriately prefaced by the only
chapter of the *Discourses* in the very heading of which Machiavelli
explicitly attacks a "common opinion" and in the body of which
he shows that Livy expresses his disagreement with a "common
opinion" more effectively by silence than he could have done
by speech. The 13th chapter of the First Book forms the center
of the section devoted to the religion of the Romans. But neither
the 13th chapter of the Second Book nor the section to which it
belongs can be said to deal with a specifically Roman subject.
Non-Roman examples preponderate in that section. Among the 7

utterances quoted in the whole series of chapters from *Discourses* II 4 to II 18 inclusive, 6 are utterances of men who were not Romans and one is an utterance of Livy about people who were not Romans. The chapter immediately preceding the chapter under consideration is the *quaestio disputata* which opens with 7 arguments from authorities, 6 of which are of non-Roman origin, one of the latter having been taken from poetic fables. The chapter in question itself is devoted to the subject of fraud as a chief means for rising from a low to a great position. Among the individuals who are said to have risen through fraud, Cyrus, a new prince of the highest rank, a founder, is treated most extensively; for even founders and precisely founders are compelled to "color their designs." It is no accident that Machiavelli stresses the difference between authors and their characters in such a context: not the men who use fraud on a grand scale but those who write concerning such men may, under certain conditions, reveal that fraud. To reveal those conditions may be said to be the chief purpose of our chapter. As for the fraud committed by Cyrus, Machiavelli refers to Xenophon. "Xenophon in his life of Cyrus shows this need for deceit. The first expedition which he makes Cyrus make is full of fraud, and he makes him seize his kingdom with deceit and not with force . . . He makes him deceive . . . . " The evidence supplied by Xenophon's *Education of Cyrus* is then not historical. Having realized "this need for deceit" through observations made perhaps nearer home, Xenophon presents the lesson in a work of fiction the hero of which is a foreign, Asiatic ruler who, according to Machiavelli, was as much a friend of God as Moses. As for Livy, he laid bare the fraud through which Rome rose to greatness by using a victim of Roman fraud, an enemy of Rome as his mouthpiece.[137] Whereas Xenophon speaks in his own name about the fraud committed by a foreign ruler, Livy speaks through the mouth of a foreigner about the fraud committed by his own rulers. No one, it seems, speaks in his own name about the deception which is the source of the being or the well-being of his own commonwealth. Being "a good historian," Livy was not so servile as to suppress truths which were unpalatable to his own people and, being wiser than the Romans, he outwitted them. He uses a noble deception to lay bare an ignoble deception. This is not the only case in which he reveals a harsh truth about the Romans through the mouth of an enemy of Rome. In the 135th chapter of the *Discourses*, Machiavelli uses a single example in order to establish the rule that promises made by states under duress ought not to be kept; the example seems to be inadequate as appears at once if one reads Machiavelli's summary with ordinary care. If one turns therefore to Livy, one sees that the incident in question taken by itself is wholly irrelevant for supporting Machiavelli's rule. To say nothing of the fact that in the Livian story the obligatory character of promises made under duress is taken for granted by everyone, a Roman consul who had promised peace to the Samnites under duress recovers for the Romans the right to recommence war under favorable conditions by having recourse to an amazing piece of legal fiction sanctioned by sacred law. The leader of the pious Samnites, the victim of Roman piety, understandably felt that the Romans always put the appearance of justice on acts of fraud and were not ashamed to use in broad daylight mockeries of religion, mockeries of the mysterious power of the gods, as puerile cloaks for breaches of faith; for that Samnite thought that wars are just and pious by virtue of their necessity and not by virtue of religious techniques. While putting this judgment on Roman piety into the mouth of an enemy of Rome, Livy on this occasion says in his own name that in this case the Romans perhaps committed a breach of faith.[188] All the more striking is Machiavelli's reticence; he does not even refer to Livy and hence to the simple Samnite's remark about the Romans' hypocrisy. We cannot deny that there is a shocking contrast between the simple rule laid down by the irreligious Machiavelli and the complicated evasion of the opposite rule by the pious Romans. The shock may make us aware of the hidden argument which he directs against his opponents: the principles of his opponents lead to unctuous hypocrisy because those principles are at variance with the nature of things. In the 105th chapter of the *Discourses*, Machiavelli explicitly quotes with approval some words from a speech by another enemy of Rome, the Volscian Messius, and immediately thereafter explicitly ascribes to Livy a thought which is expressed, and as it is expressed, in that speech: he imputes to Livy the sentiment of a Livian character. But there is no reason why only that thought and not also other parts of Messius' speech should have to be regarded as thoughts of Livy. In that part of Messius' speech about which Machiavelli is silent, Messius says to his soldiers: "Do you believe that some god will protect you?" And he means by this that no god will protect them.[139] According to Machiavelli's rule for reading Livy as he applies it in this very passage, this denial of divine protection would have to be ascribed to Livy himself. Yet it is not Livy but a Livian character who expresses that sentiment. If one reads the statement of Messius-Livy which we have quoted, in the light of the whole chapter in which Machiavelli quotes another statement of Messius-Livy, one sees that the sentiment expressed in our quotation may well be ascribed to Machiavelli himself. It would appear then that Machiavelli stands in the same relation to Livy in which Livy stands to some of his characters: he states what he regards as the truth through sentences of Livy often unquoted but always alluded to; Machiavelli's Livy is a character of Machiavelli.

By using a variety of characters as his mouthpieces, Livy was enabled both to expound the principles on which the Romans admittedly acted or in which they believed, and to criticize them. His *History* contains the truth about pagan Rome because it contains not only what one may call the official Roman version but likewise the known or presumptive judgment on Rome by Rome's enemies, and therewith the detection of the fraud inherent in the Roman version. As for Machiavelli, he uses Livy's work first as a counter-authority or a counter-Bible; he tacitly replaces the doctrine of the Bible by the doctrine of the Romans which is transmitted by Livy, or he replaces it by the doctrine of Livy. Thereafter he explicitly questions the authority of Livy and thus draws our attention to what he had done tacitly in regard to the Bible. To mention only one example, by stating that Livy's *History* is possibly defective in an important point, he makes us aware of the possibility that the Biblical records are defective in decisive points. Livy both expounds and criticizes Roman piety and pagan theology. To the extent to which Livy expounds pagan theology, Machiavelli can use him for suggesting an alternative to Biblical theology or for sowing doubts regarding Biblical theology. To the extent to which Livy criticizes Roman theology, Machiavelli can use him as a model for his own criticism of Biblical theology. By making Livy's criticism less visible than his conformism, he presents Livy as his model or transforms him into his model and thus indicates his own procedure. For there is hardly a single passage in either the *Dis-*

courses or the *Prince* in which Machiavelli unambiguously reveals his complete break with the Biblical tradition, although there occur in each of the two books many passages which are devoid of meaning if they are not taken as allusions to that break. These passages can easily be overlooked and if they are not overlooked their bearing can easily be minimized since they are, as it were, covered over by innumerable others which are either neutral with regard to the problem posed by the Biblical tradition, or else are tolerable from the point of view of believers whose charity is greater than their perspicacity. With some exaggeration one may say that Machiavelli uses Livy as a *corpus vile* by means of which he can demonstrate how he has tacitly proceeded in regard to the *corpus nobilissimum*. This twofold use of Livy is related to the twofold character of pagan Rome which was both the enemy of the Christian Church and the model for it.

In *Discourses* II 2, Machiavelli notes that Livy's *History* is silent as to how the race of Porsenna, king of Tuscany, became extinct. He is here no longer concerned with pointing out the defective character of Livy's *History*. The remark on the extinction of Porsenna's race is the spearhead of a column of somewhat scattered observations concerning the oblivion of Tuscan things in general, and the cause of that oblivion. We hear next that the memory of most Tuscan things is lost and then that it was lost as a consequence of the destruction of Tuscan power by Rome. This fact made Machiavelli think, as he says, of the causes, and as we may add on the basis of what he does, in particular of the human causes through which the memory of ancient greatness is extinguished. These human causes are the changes of religion and the changes of language. Machiavelli develops this thought in *Discourses* II 5, where he refutes an argument allegedly proving that the world had a beginning and where he ascribes to all religions a human, not a heavenly, origin and, on the basis of this, a life span of between 1666 and 3000 years. Reflection on the policy pursued by "the Christian sect" induces him to assert that every new religion attempts to extinguish every vestige of "the old religion," and induces him to "believe" in particular that the pagan religion destroyed all vestiges of the religion preceding it. The context suggests that the religion preceding the pagan religion was the Tuscan religion. However this may be, the Romans certainly destroyed the power

of Tuscany and extinguished the customs and the language of the
Tuscans. If we read somewhat more carefully Machiavelli's remarks
concerning what the Romans did to the Tuscans, we see that the
Romans did not destroy, and did not even attempt to destroy, the
religion of the Tuscans; for instance, instead of destroying the
image of the Tuscan Juno they made it their own. Hence Machiavelli's "belief" that the pagan religion did to the preceding religion
what "the Christian sect desired to do to the pagan sect" is not
more than a stage of his argument, a provisional thought which he
discards almost immediately after he expresses it. The allegedly
universal rule inferred from the policy of Christianity, and of
Judaism, toward idolatry is a piece of fiction temporarily convenient for Machiavelli's purpose. What remains as undeniable
truth is the fact that Judaism and Christianity attempted to destroy
every vestige of the pagan religion. Here again Machiavelli
momentarily overstates the case by saying that "the Christian sect"
destroyed "every memory of that ancient theology" by which he
primarily means pagan theology.[140] A few lines later he says that
while Christianity attempted the complete destruction of every
vestige of paganism, it failed in that attempt. The two overstate-
ments perform one function. By assimilating paganism and Christianity to each other in an absurd fashion, those statements draw
our attention to the difference between paganism and Christianity.
The Romans could have destroyed every vestige of the Tuscan
religion if they had desired to do so, but they did not desire it;
persecution of "the old religion," and in particular "destruction of
images," is peculiar to the Biblical religion as distinguished from
the pagan religion. It will do no harm if the allusion to this peculi-
arity of Biblical religion reminds us of the hazardous character of
Machiavelli's campaign. On the other hand, Christianity failed in
its attempt to eradicate every vestige of paganism because it was
compelled to retain the Latin and Greek languages and hence to
preserve a considerable part of pagan literature, for instance "those
books of Livy which the malignity of the times has not intercepted."
Christianity was compelled to permit and even to encourage the
study of pagan literature. That study and the admiration for the
pagan way of life which it aroused in a few minds could thus
become the entering wedge for Machiavelli's criticism of Biblical
religion. His praise of ancient Rome is an essential element of his

wholly new teaching, but it is also, and even chiefly, a mere engine of subversion or of what one might call his immanent criticism of the Biblical tradition. Admiration for ancient Rome was the only publicly defensible base from which he could attack the Biblical religion. The properly understood remains of paganism were "the fortress of our hope and salvation," the solitary elevation which commands the enemy position and which is difficult of access to an army encumbered with baggage but not difficult for men lightly equipped. To apply to Machiavelli his own expression, not being able to blame Caesar he praised Brutus. Christianity, we must add in order to complete Machiavelli's statements, was forced to retain the Latin language because it was not, like Islam, a religion that conquered by force. Christianity was forced to preserve its enemy to some extent. It was then due to the "unarmed" character of primitive Christianity that Machiavelli was enabled to use Livy against Biblical religion. Christianity averted the dangers emanating from the relics of paganism by regarding them as unworthy of faith wherever they contradict the Biblical teaching. For instance, since the Bible is thought to teach that the world was created about 5,000 years ago, one regards the *History* of Diodorus Siculus as mendacious, "although it gives an account of 40,000 or 50,000 years." By refusing credence to the pagan historians, one arrives at the conclusion that what those historians report as regards the modes and orders of pagan Rome is not true and even is impossible and hence cannot be imitated.[141] To refute this conclusion as well as all its questionable premises, Machiavelli must first restore the credibility of the pagan historians and especially of Livy. He does this, to begin with, in an exaggerated way by establishing the authority of Livy's *History* as a kind of Bible. But he must also use such relics of paganism as stem from explicit enemies of Biblical religion, and as are therefore particularly serviceable for correcting the Biblical version of the origins. He gives a specimen of this kind of inquiry by citing in *Discourses* II 8 a sentence stemming from pagan enemies of the Jews. Livy's *History* contains both the official Roman version and its correction by the enemies of Rome because Livy used not only Romans but also enemies of Rome as his mouthpieces. The Biblical authors do not use enemies of the Biblical religion as their mouthpieces.[142] Biblical religion even attempted to suppress all vestiges of the thought of its enemies.

Hence Livy's *History* is self-sufficient in the sense that it enables its reader to arrive at an impartial judgment about Rome, whereas the critical student of the Bible must rely on potentially or actually anti-Biblical literature in order to discern the truth about the Biblical religion. While the Bible is not self-sufficient in the sense indicated, one could however say that the Biblical tradition as transmitter of pagan thought contains the judgment of its enemies within itself.

We conclude our discussion of *Discourses* II 13 with a brief survey of the principles of historical criticism indicated by Machiavelli. In order to be certain of something which one does not see or has not seen, one needs witnesses in whom one can have faith. A difficulty arises from the fact that the credibility of a witness depends to some extent on the credibility of the events to which he claims to have been a witness. What is "very remote" from "the ordinary and reasonable," or what is miraculous, is incredible. But reverence for a certain Roman historian, an "authority," induces Machiavelli to "believe" that historian's report of an event which is very remote from the reasonable. Yet to say nothing of the ambiguity of the term "belief" as used by Machiavelli, he says soon afterward of one and the same actual event which happened in ancient Greece that it was "impossible," i.e., impossible as a natural event, and that it was and is regarded by "the writers" as "rare and as it were, without example." The writers contemporary with Machiavelli will have been under no compulsion to treat the "miracles" of the pagans as more than rare natural events. This passage shows how he would have achieved the transition from his thought about the Biblical miracles to fairly candid speech about them had he been in a position to do so.[143] He demonstrates his tacit treatment of the Biblical miracles by his explicit treatment of incredible events reported by pagan historians: reports of miracles are at best exaggerated reports of rare events. Only reports of possible events are credible. One arrives at knowledge of the possible by proper generalization from the seen particular. A history does not "create faith" if the possibility of what it asserts is not borne out either by present happenings or by proper generalization from present happenings. The crucial importance of miracles in the Biblical records compels Machiavelli to adopt as a provisional canon the rule that very extraordinary events reported in the Bible for which there is no evidence stemming from men not believing in the Bible are not to be believed. He does not believe that one can doubt that there was once a flood through which almost all men perished because "all histories are full" of reports of such floods. Yet since the histories other than the Bible speak only of the destruction by floods of nearly all "inhabitants of a part of the world," Machiavelli does not believe more than the qualified reports: he tacitly rejects the Biblical report of the Flood as an exaggerated report of a big flood somewhere in Asia. He explicitly says that the survivors of great floods—i.e., we add, Noah and his family—are "all rude mountaineers who do not possess knowledge of any antiquity and therefore cannot leave such knowledge to their posterity. And if someone who did have such knowledge were to save himself, he would conceal that knowledge in order to make himself a reputation and a name and pervert that knowledge after his fashion."[144] Any tradition transmitted through Noah would then be no better than fraud, although the Bible describes Noah as a just man. Needless to say, a possible event is not necessarily the same thing as an event which has indeed happened. Machiavelli gives some indications of the difficulties which preclude certainty as to nocturnal actions in remote places.

Discourses II 14 does not properly speaking belong among the chapters in which Machiavelli draws our attention to the difficulty caused by the difference between Livy and Livy's characters. The chapter deals not with deceiving others, but with deceiving oneself. Its purpose is to show that humility is sometimes harmful or, more precisely, that "men often deceive themselves by believing that they can vanquish pride by humility." The "text" which is alleged in order to "vouch" for this is taken from the same speech by an enemy of Rome from which Machiavelli had quoted in the preceding chapter. The "text" does not speak, as the heading and the beginning lead us to expect, of the humility of the Romans but of their patience and modesty. Nor does Machiavelli himself speak of the humility of the Romans; he speaks only of their patience and, when generalizing from the Roman case, he replaces patience by fear and cowardice: the quasi-promised example of harmful humility or of self-deception regarding the power of humility is not given. The lesson of the chapter is said to be "vouched for" first by Livy and then by the Latin praetor Annius who used certain words which Machiavelli quotes and which are, of course, taken from Livy. Machiavelli's authority is then first Livy and thereafter Livy's authority, the Latin Annius. Livy's vouching for a certain truth is dependent upon Annius' vouching for it. Although Machiavelli refrains from saying so, the words used by Annius are as much put by Livy into Annius' mouth as were the words of Annius quoted in the preceding chapter. Annius as a speaker is a creation of Livy. By referring first to Livy and then to Annius, Machiavelli refers then in fact to one and the same source. What this means appears if we remember that, according to him, the Bible is of human origin, consists to a considerable extent of poetic fables, and must be read "judiciously," i.e., in the light of non-Biblical or even anti-Biblical thought. Given these premises he must raise the question "Who has spoken to a prophet?" if the prophet says that God has spoken to him, and he must answer that question in merely human terms: the words of God are words which the prophets ascribe to God or put into the mouth of God. It is not God who speaks through the mouth of the inspired speakers or writers, but the Biblical writers who speak through the mouth of God. What we believe to be reading is the word of God, but what we do read is the word of the Biblical writers. God stands in the same relation to the Biblical writers as the characters of Livy stand to Livy. In the chapter following, Machiavelli first quotes in Latin some words taken from the same speech from which the quotations used in the two preceding chapters were taken; he ascribes those words to Annius without referring to Livy; thereafter, he quotes explicitly from Livy, in translation and in direct speech, a saying of another enemy of Rome; that saying had been quoted by Livy in indirect speech, and Livy had pointed out that it might be apocryphal.[145] Machiavelli omits this qualification. Continuing the argument of the preceding chapter, Machiavelli indicates how easily the true origin of utterances can be forgotten and how easily what in the remote past was a rumor can be transformed into a fact immediately accessible to present readers however unlearned. In the chapter following, he says first that Livy "makes" the Roman and the Latin armies equal in certain respects and thereafter that Livy "says" that these armies were equal in the respects in question. By this he seems to indicate that the creativity of Livy is not limited to the speeches which occur in his *History* but may extend to the deeds which he reports.[146] In conclusion we note that all the individuals whose utterances are cited in *Discourses* II 13-18 are enemies of Rome.

We have been left in doubt as to whether, according to Machiavelli, Livy "made" his characters not only "say" what they said, but also "made" them "do" what they did according to his *History*. There is only a single passage which dispels that doubt, namely, the beginning of *Discourses* III 31. "Among the other magnificent things which our historian makes Camillus say and do in order to show what the make of an excellent man ought to be, he puts into his mouth these words. . . ." Machiavelli questions here the distinction that he had made earlier between those who reason about political life or give rules for political life or determine how princes ought to live, and those who describe the lives of princes or who are historians. By this he does not deny that precisely "the good historians" present, among other things, models of action for the instruction of posterity. For there is a fundamental difference between describing great actions or lives which can serve as models and presenting created or imaginary models like Xenophon's Cyrus.[147] Machiavelli now suggests that "our historian" is not merely an historian, a man who describes what men have done, but that he is also a man who teaches "Oughts" through making his excellent characters say and do things which excellent men ought to say and do, i.e., through acts of fiction. This remark enables us better to understand what Machiavelli had indicated earlier regarding the superiority of the best kind of writer to doers and speakers of the highest order: the writer is a creator. We also understand somewhat better how he conceived of the Biblical writers. We may try to express his thought as follows: the Biblical writers present themselves as historians, as human beings who report what God said and did, while in fact they make God say and do what in their opinion a most perfect being would say and do; the ground of what presents itself as the experience of the Biblical writers is their notion of a most perfect being; that notion is so compelling that the "Ought" comes to sight as "Is"; this connection is articulated by the ontological proof; there is no way which leads from "the things of the world" to the Biblical God; the only proof which commands respect, although it is not a genuine proof, is the ontological proof. It is hardly necessary to add that Machiavelli's explanation in merely human terms of the root of Biblical belief presupposes his denial, his destructive analysis of the phenomenon known to us as the conscience. Nor will it be surprising that the other quotations from Livy which occur in *Discourses* III 31 are ascribed to Livian characters without any reference to Livy himself.

By consciously making some Roman captains say and do what excellent captains ought to say and do, Livy magnifies the Roman republic or ascribes to it a perfection which is perhaps impossible. He "celebrates" Rome as Machiavelli says as the end of the first chapter of the *Discourses*. There is only one other occasion on which Machiavelli speaks again of Livy's "celebrating" Rome or Romans. *Discourses* III 25 deals with "the poverty of Cincinnatus and of many Roman citizens."[148] This noble poverty is "celebrated by Livy with golden words" which Machiavelli quotes in the original. Immediately afterward he quotes in translation certain words of Cincinnatus himself. The dictator Cincinnatus had relieved a Roman army, which through the fault of the consul commanding it, had become besieged by its enemies; the consul and his army had contributed to the raising of the siege and the complete defeat of the enemy. Through the words quoted by Machiavelli, Cincinnatus deprived the consular army of every share in the rich booty which the dictator's army had taken, and deprived the consul himself of his command because of his proved ignorance of how to be a consul. We are no longer concerned with the fact that we find here in Machiavelli's own text the example of a consul who did not know how to be a consul, although Machiavelli had told us earlier that the consuls elected by the Romans in the good old times were "always most excellent men." Or could a man be "a most excellent man" and at the same time a poor consul? It appears that the words of the Livian character which are not quoted in Latin are not "golden" precisely because they show the value, if not of gold, at least of what can be obtained by gold. If we turn to Livy, we see that Cincinnatus' noble poverty was not altogether freely chosen. Whether rightly or wrongly, his violent son Caeso had been accused of homicide and had been heavily fined; the fine was cruelly exacted from Cincinnatus, who had to "sell all that he had." It is for this reason that he lived on the famous small farm where he was found behind the famous plow

by the men who brought him the message that he had been named
dictator. While celebrating with golden words the noble poverty
of a great Roman, Livy also reveals those causes of his poverty
which were not golden. Because he consciously created perfect captains Livy is able to indicate the difference between the "Ought"[149]
and the "Is," between imagined perfection and "factual truth."
By merely alluding to the "factual truth" in regard to Roman
poverty and related subjects and thus to some extent concealing
that "factual truth," Machiavelli deliberately impairs the self-
sufficiency of Livy's *History*. He thus assimilates Livy's *History*
to the Bible as he conceived of it.

After having indicated that Livy makes one of his captains say
and do certain things in order to show how an excellent man ought
to act, Machiavelli owes us an answer to the question regarding
the function of this blurring of the difference between history and
political philosophy. After having shown in *Discourses* III 32 that
one can make an army obstinate against its enemy, not only "by
virtue of religion," but by some "great villainy" as well, he turns
in the next chapter to the question of how a captain can make his
army confident of victory. Among other things, the captain must conceal or minimize the things which when viewed from afar suggest
dangers. Apparently no such salutary deception is possible regarding things open to everyone's easy inspection. "The Romans used
to make their armies acquire that confidence by way of religion."
The Romans controlled what is essentially elusive and hence frightening by means of religion. One may create obstinacy by virtue
of some great villainy, but one needs religion for creating hope.
No good and wise Roman captain would ever start an action without
having used auguries and auspices, thus having convinced the
soldiers that the gods were on their side. How great an importance
the Romans attached to religion or how strongly they disapproved
of the neglect of religion is shown best by "the words which Livy
uses in the mouth of Appius Claudius." Appius Claudius had to
defend in an assembly of the people the sacred custom of treating
the auguries and auspices, i.e., the foundation of the pagan religion,
as a preserve of the patricians, or the sacred custom of keeping
the plebs at a distance from those sacred things. The defense had
become necessary on account of the machinations of domestic
enemies of the patriciate—of leaders of the laity as laity, as one might

say.[150] Among the words used by Appius Claudius there are some which he puts into the mouth of plebeians who mock religion. Those mockers regard the very foundations of religion, the things which assure men of divine help, as "little things." We do not know this from the mouths of the mockers themselves. The Roman critics of the Roman religion do not express their opinion within our hearing. Perhaps they do not dare to speak in public on this subject and therefore are condemned to failure and oblivion. Livy uses characters of one of his characters in order to inform us about Roman criticism of the Roman religion. Appius Claudius adopts the words "little things" as applied to religion and its ground; so does Livy who puts these words into Appius Claudius' mouth; so does Machiavelli who uses these words in his own name when commenting on the Livian speech. The expression or the thought migrates from the minds of the mockers through the mouths of a Livian character and of Livy himself to Machiavelli. The movement, started by nameless characters of a Livian character, reaches its end in Machiavelli. The mockers are mistaken, say Appius Claudius, Livy and Machiavelli in unison, for they are blind to the usefulness of religion: the belief of the people in "those little things" is the source of the well-being of the commonwealth. The question is whether the mockers were altogether mistaken. The leaders of certain enemies of the Romans tried to use their own soldiers' and the Romans' concern with "little things" in order to defeat the Romans. Their calculation was not altogether unreasonable; they did not put their reliance in "little things" but in other men's reliance on "little things," i.e., in a big thing. But they came to grief because they forgot that the Roman leaders did not put their trust in "little things." Machiavelli quotes some words said by Livy which the historian put into the mouth of the Roman dictator Cincinnatus addressing his master of the horse. The enemies of the Romans put their trust, says the dictator, not, as one should, in arms and courage, but in chance, or, as Machiavelli interprets this, in very minor or "weak" accidents or in things of little weight or in vain things. Both Livian characters who are introduced in this chapter as mouthpieces of Livy are patricians; the one who speaks to the people defends the little things; the other who speaks to another patrician disparages the little things. The little things mentioned by the first speaker are not the same as those which the second speaker has in mind: the former are the auguries and the auspices proper, the second are any irrelevant accidents which for very weak reasons appear to be comforting or frightening. But there is a connection between the two kinds of little things: the Roman religion served the purpose of mastering chance through the belief in gods and the worship of gods who, as perfect beings, are thought to favor the just or pious. Machiavelli here presents Livy as revealing the truth about the Roman religion by using as his mouthpieces Roman authorities addressing two different types of audience.[151]

When speaking of the Livian mouthpieces in *Discourses* III 33, Machiavelli does not say, as he ordinarily does, that the characters in question "said" what they said but that they "say" it: the chapter which is severely limited to Roman "matter" does not deal with "ancient history." The chapter ends with a brief discussion of a mode of procedure employed by Fabius in a campaign "in a new land against a new enemy"; this mode "deserves to be imitated." Not Appius Claudius nor Cincinnatus but Fabius serves as a model. But nowhere in the chapter does Machiavelli say anything against moderns who fail to imitate the Romans. Perhaps there are moderns who imitate Appius Claudius and Cincinnatus. On the other hand, when Machiavelli returns to the chief theme of the chapter in *Discourses* III 36, he stresses the inferiority of "the militia of our times" to the Roman militia. The only quotation occurring in III 36 is taken from a Livian speech, and it touches on the subject of religion. It is the only quotation occurring in the Third Book in which gods are mentioned; but "the gods" and "auguries" are preceded respectively by "men" and "the edicts of commanders." Machiavelli does not tell us to whom the speech is addressed. If we turn therefore to Livy, we see that the present case characteristically differs from the two cases discussed in *Discourses* III 33. In the present case a patrician, a dictator, defends the sanctity of religion first in an assembly of his army and then in an assembly of the people, not against nameless plebeian mockers but against another patrician, his master of the horse, Fabius himself. Fabius had waged a battle contrary to the dictator's strict orders and in the absence of favorable auspices; he had won a splendid victory. Thereupon the dictator became blinded with anger, burning with fury and athirst for the scourging and the decapitation of the offender. Yet what appeared to the dictator as holy zeal appeared to Fabius as uncontrollable cruelty, insane envy and unbearable pride, as he did not hesitate to say in a public assembly. Strongly supported by the victorious army, by the people and by the senate, Fabius was neither executed nor scourged but lives gloriously forever in Machiavelli's pages as a successful defender of liberty.[152] *Quod licet Fabio, non licet homunculis.*

According to Machiavelli, Livy revealed his judgment on Rome to some extent through judgments which he put into the mouths of his characters. In this respect, the difference between enemies of Rome and Romans, between Livian characters and characters of those characters, and among the various audiences addressed by those characters are important. We see no reason for doubting that he meant what he indicated in this respect. We judge differently of his assertion that Livy makes characters say or do things in order to teach how excellent men ought to conduct themselves. In *Discourses* III 31 he says that Livy makes one of his characters say and do certain things "in order to show what the make of an excellent man ought to be." This assertion regarding Livy's intention is not borne out by the Livian speech to which he refers. There occur only two other passages which resemble the cited Machiavellian remark. In *Discourses* III 36 he says that through Livy's testimony one can learn from certain words of a Roman leader "what the make of a good militia ought to be." In *Discourses* III 38 he says that through certain words which Livy makes one of his characters say, one can observe "what the make of a captain in whom his army can have confidence ought to be." In both cases he does not even claim that it was Livy's intention through his report or his fiction to teach an "Ought." We suggest this explanation. Machiavelli momentarily presents Livy as a conscious creator of fictitious or imaginary perfection for the reason stated above. He therewith obscures the character of Livy's *History* and thus indirectly blurs the difference between the intention of Livy the historian and his own intention. As soon as his own intention becomes Machiavelli's chief theme, as it does from *Discourses* III 35 on, he must again bring this difference to light.

Machiavelli has discovered new modes and orders which he opposes to the old and established modes and orders. He has discovered and explored territory hitherto inaccessible to men of his kind. He begins a war against the established order—a new war in a new land against a new enemy of the highest possible reputation. But he is a captain without an army. He must recruit his army. He can recruit it only by means of his books. The last section of the *Discourses* gives the necessary indications regarding his campaign and its preparation. He had told us earlier that in order to be confident of victory, an army must have confidence in the prudence of its captain. The proof of Machiavelli's prudence is the *Discourses*. The make of a captain in whom his army can have confidence is shown by Machiavelli with the words which Livy "makes" one of his characters "say" to his soldiers. In Livy, the quoted words are framed partly in indirect and partly in direct speech. The direct speech begins with the sentence "My deeds, not my words, I wish you to follow."[153] The sentence, strictly understood, applies less clearly to ordinary captains than to a captain like Machiavelli. The chapter in which this quotation occurs is as such devoted to the perfect captain simply.[154] Yet Machiavelli indicates that the chapter and a part of the preceding chapter form a single "discourse," the theme of which is less the perfect captain simply than the perfect captain with a new army facing a new enemy in a new war. Machiavelli recommends in this discourse particularly the procedure of Marius, a most prudent captain. Machiavelli chooses Marius because there does not happen to be an equally good example in the career of Fabius although it is Fabius, not Marius, who waged war against a new enemy in a new country. Before engaging in battles, Marius tried to accustom the eyes of his soldiers to the sight of a most terrifying enemy: he made them see that the new enemy which had the highest possible reputation was in fact a disorderly multitude, encumbered with baggage, with useless arms, and some of them even unarmed. For this is the way in which the established order, the venerable tradition contemporaneous with Machiavelli presented itself to him: as oblivious of the fundamental issue and therefore rent into many warring schools or factions, as encumbered with innumerable texts, treatises and discourses, and as boasting of many proofs which were no proofs. Such enemies could be depended upon, like blind Samnites, to forget to occupy "the fortress of our hope and salvation" to which he refers in the next discourse (III 39).[155] That chapter is the last in which Machiavelli refers to the difference between Livy and his characters. Of all the references to this subject in the entire book, the last reference, which contains the last explicit quotations from Livy or from any other writer, is the clearest. Machiavelli quotes first a Livian character, then he quotes Livy while explicitly distinguishing the words of the Livian character from the words said by Livy himself, and finally he quotes some words which Livy "makes" his character "say." Of the two sentences which, according to Machiavelli, Livy makes his character say, one sentence is obviously said by Livy in his own name: Machiavelli makes Livy make his characters say what Livy himself says or thinks. This clearest reference occurs in the only chapter in the book in which Machiavelli adumbrates what "science" is.[156] It is the only chapter in which he sets forth as clearly as possible both the character of his science and the character of his adumbration or figurative presentation of his science; for that figurative presentation is identical with his use of Livy. The chapter deals, not unnaturally, with the relation between war itself and hunting as an image of war, or rather with the question of how a captain can acquire the habit of finding his bearings in "new countries." Its heading says "That a captain ought to be a knower of sites" or places.[157] Machiavelli's captaincy requires, as we have seen, that he be a most excellent knower of the proper places in Livy, to say nothing of the proper places in the Bible.

We have now considered almost all 11 passages in which Machiavelli refers to the problem caused by the difference between the words of Livy and the words of Livy's characters. We are not yet prepared to discuss the two remaining passages which occur in *Discourses* II 23 and III 15, the latter being the central passage among the 11 passages under consideration. For the present we must leave it at a remark about *Discourses* II 23. That chapter is in every respect the center of the three sermons on Livian texts. Only in that chapter do we find all the features that are peculiar to Machiavelli's treatment of Livy in the Second and Third Books.[158] The chapter is of special significance because it combines the treatment of two themes, each of which is treated in isolation in one of the two other sermons. The first sermon (II 3) is the only chapter of the *Discourses* which literally begins and ends with one and the same quotation from Livy, namely, the text of the sermon. The quotation attracts our attention for two reasons. In the first place, it is the only quotation from Livy occurring in the whole division to which the chapter belongs (II 1-10). Above all, it is the first quotation from Livy as Livy that occurs after Machiavelli's open attack on Livy or his destruction of Livy's authority (I 58). In his first sermon Machiavelli comments on Livy's harsh saying "Meanwhile Rome grows by Alba's destruction." Machiavelli makes clear at the end of the chapter that the emphasis is on "two words," namely, "grows (by) destruction." His comment is to the effect that one can make a city great both by love, or charity, and by force, or by fear.[159] Livy's saying deals exclusively with force. Machiavelli's comment on that saying, however, speaks, to say the least, with equal emphasis of love. He creates the impression that he is a commentator who silently or reverently mitigates the harsh teaching of a sacred text. By this fact he draws our attention to the harshness of the text.[160] In the central sermon he indicts "the middle way" between terror and kindness or between destroying defeated enemies and reconciling them. He thus takes up the theme of the first sermon, love and fear. Both the way of love and the way of fear have their uses and, as the first sermon has shown, even the judicious combination of both ways is sensible. What cannot be tolerated is "the middle way," half measures, the weak compromise. In the very center of the central sermon Machiavelli censures a half measure once taken by Florence; he there defends a policy of harshness against a reason advanced by seemingly wise men; he says that the same reason would make impossible every harshness and every punishment. We see that Machiavelli silently passes over from the indictment of a "middle way" to the indictment of an extreme way—of a way of thinking which allows of nothing but love or charity and is therefore incompatible with the nature of things. The extreme opposite to that extreme is not the way of universal and perpetual terror, which no one even seemingly wise ever counselled, but the judicious combination of love and terror by virtue of which one either reconciles enemies after one has terrified them into submission or else destroys them if they cannot be reconciled. The first extreme, we see now, is the Christian teaching which forbids resistance to evil; the second extreme is the "natural" teaching; then the middle way between these two extremes can be presumed to be the combination of non-resistance to evil with resistance to evil—a combination which reminded Machiavelli of the policy of the Romans so severely censured by the simple Samnite.[161] Needless to say, Machiavelli knew that the Bible teaches not only love but fear as well. But from his point of view the Biblical combination of love and fear, as distinguished from the natural combination, is fundamentally vicious: the false principle of the primacy of love necessarily leads to all extremes of pious cruelty or pitiless persecution. Not without reason is the Second Book, the anti-Biblical Book par excellence, completely silent about God: it speaks only of gods.[162] It is neither desirable nor necessary to repeat here what had to be said about Machiavelli's single New Testament quotation and its implication regarding the jealous God of the Bible who demands zealous love. The central sermon contains only one quotation consisting of words which Livy is said to have put into the mouth of a character, namely, of Camillus.[163] At the beginning of the quotation, Livy-Camillus says that the gods leave the Romans perfect freedom either to destroy the Romans' enemies or to forgive them: the gods do not command their worshippers to forgive their worshippers' enemies nor do they command their worshippers to destroy their worshippers' or the gods' enemies. Paganism left human prudence free to choose the wisest course of action.

The third sermon (III 10) opens with a Livian text which gives Machiavelli occasion for censuring an error common to all or most modern men, or which legitimates such censure. The text speaks of a Roman commander who refused to entrust himself to Fortuna.[164] This gives Machiavelli occasion to speak of the moderns' entrusting to others the care of their freedom and survival, or of the moderns' trusting in someone other than themselves. When they send one of their captains on a military mission, they forbid him to engage in battle, and in so doing they believe themselves to imitate Fabius Maximus. But this is nonsense; Fabius did not avoid battle but refused to give battle on ground favorable to his terrifying enemy. The command given to the modern captains is in effect "Join battle as it suits your enemy and not as it suits you." By commanding their captains to avoid battle, they believe that they command them not to entrust themselves to Fortuna but in fact they do command them to entrust themselves to Fortuna, and they forbid them to tempt or try Fortuna. The ancients tried Fortuna; the moderns trust in Fortuna.

Machiavelli's use and non-use of Livy is the key to his questioning of the highest authority. He acquired the right to question that authority by first surrendering to it without any reserve. When he was confronted, near the beginning of the *Discourses*, with a difference of opinion between two sets of writers, he adopted the opinion of those writers who in the opinion of many are wiser than their opponents. Toward the end of the First Book, he made use of the power which had thus accumulated to attack all writers by appealing from authority as such to reason. He thus laid the foundation for what he does in the last two Books, for the intransigent and therefore reserved application of the maxim "reason versus authority." The Second Book opens with the censure of the veneration for antiquity as such, i.e., of what one might call the root of the belief in authority. The first chapter of the Second Book opens with an attack on "a most weighty writer" mentioned by name. Only in the last two Books does Machiavelli refer in chapter headings to authorities to whom a thinker as thinker could be subject: the authority of the Romans and the authority of Moses.[165] Only in the last two Books does he question "opinions" in chapter headings.[166] The center of the central Book (II 10-24) contains the most striking and most coherent, if properly dispersed, references to the issue "reason versus authority." In II 10 Machiavelli attacks a "common opinion," but after having established the truth concerning the subject matter without the assistance of any authority, he refers to Livy as the truest witness for the truth. After pointing out in the next chapter the imprudence of trusting in a prince who, perhaps because he is too far away, can help his friends less by his power than by his name, Machiavelli presents us in II 12 with his scholastic disputation in which he adduces seven reasons pro and con from authority and eight reasons pro and con from reason; he reaches his decision without having had recourse to any authority and without having referred to any author. After devoting the next three chapters to Livy and his character Annius, an enemy of the Roman people, and the following chapter to the inferiority of "all Christian armies" to the Roman armies, he attacks "the universal opinion of many" according to which ancient Rome cannot be imitated because of an alleged progress made in the meantime (II 17). This chapter too is a disputation, although less visibly so than II 12.[167] Here again

Machiavelli reaches a decision without having had recourse to any authority and without having referred to any author. In II 18, he prefers "manifest reasons" to authority as clearly as possible. On the basis of mere reason he attacks the greatest authority inimical to Rome, that authority being, as we would expect, Hannibal. Yet in order to corroborate the opinion which reason has established in opposition to the greatest authority, he refers to the authority of traditional political philosophy or to the authority of the tradition of the cultivation of reason. In order to understand this apparent recourse to authority, one would have to start from the fact that immediately afterward in the same chapter Machiavelli speaks of that sin of the Italian princes than which none is greater, namely, the sin of trusting in cavalry rather than in infantry. The examples which he adduces in order to establish the superiority of infantry to cavalry are less "true" than "beautiful." One of the examples is that of Regulus, who had the presumption to trust that he could defeat cavalry and even elephants with infantry; he was defeated, but for no other reason than that he did not have sufficient trust in his infantry: his presumption was not strong or great enough. Carmignuola, on the other hand, presumed that he could defeat infantry with cavalry; he failed, but after having dismounted his cavalry he won: he replaced the wrong presumption by the right presumption, and in accordance with this he behaved humanely toward his defeated enemies.[168] In II 19 Machiavelli asserts that a single contemporary example suffices for proving that infantry is superior to cavalry and therewith that the Roman opinion regarding the respective value of infantry and cavalry is superior to the modern opinion. With a view to this "seen" superiority, he demands that one "believe" "that all other ancient orders are true and useful"; this "belief" would have obviated all important modern sins. Lacking such salutary belief, one cannot do better than do the German cities, whose relative success depends however on the recognition by all Germans of "the authority" of the emperor—of a prince "who does not have forces" or who, as we may say, is as unarmed as Heaven has become in modern times. In II 24, which is immediately preceded by the central sermon, Machiavelli points out the imprudence of trusting in fortresses rather than in one's own virtue and prudence; while establishing this fact he refers again to "the authority of the Romans," who "were wise (also) in all their other orders." Machiavelli, we see again, does not hesitate to oppose in the proper context one authority to another authority, one notion of presumption to another notion, or one belief to another belief.[169]

While Machiavelli frequently defers to Livy's authority and sometimes questions Livy's authority, he never tries to "save" an opinion of Livy after having shown that it is not evidently correct. The only writer mentioned by name who receives such reverential treatment at his hands is Tacitus.[170] We must leave open the question whether he awards this honor to Tacitus because he regarded him as the greatest narrator of the deeds and speeches of hateful tyrants, or as the greatest historian who spoke about the origins of Judaism and Christianity, or as both. He certainly did not regard Tacitus as an authority in the strictest sense. As far as we know, the statement which he cites as a statement of Tacitus in order to "save" the opinion that it expresses was invented by Machiavelli: so far from bowing to an authority, Machiavelli treats himself as an authority.[171] Besides, his treatment of authority in the group of chapters which as it were begins with the apocryphal statement of Tacitus, and which is located near the center of the Third Book is even more outspoken than that which is found in the center of the Second Book.[172] Let us for the time being call that group of chapters (III 19-23) the Tacitean subsection. The Tacitean subsection presents itself as a unit since the chapters of which it consists are linked with each other by explicit references occurring at the end of four of its chapters. It does not form an independent section of the *Discourses*. Yet since it consists of five chapters, it reminds one of those sections of the *Discourses* which consist of five chapters: the sections on the religion of the Romans (I 11-15), on gratitude (I 28-32), on the reduction of the West to Eastern servility (II 1-5), on the difference between the conquests made by the Romans and those made by the Jews and others (II 6-10) and on the origins (II 11-15). The Tacitean subsection is immediately preceded by the chapter in which Machiavelli contrasts the ancients who believed that by ascending a nearby and fairly low elevation they could be saved for some time, and the moderns who believed in false news about a victory. It is followed by the chapters devoted to poverty and to women. The chapter on women contains the only reference to Aristotle occurring in the *Discourses;* that reference corresponds to, and thus prepares, the only reference to the Bible as Bible occurring in the *Discourses;* in the chapter in which Machiavelli refers to the Bible, he draws our attention to what Moses did on his own authority; that chapter immediately precedes the chapter in which he speaks of Livy's transforming an "Ought" into an "Is" by making Camillus say and do certain things.[173] This must suffice as regards the suggestive context of the Tacitean sub-section.

The Tacitean sub-section opens with a story according to which the cruel and rude commander Appius Claudius failed, and the kind and humane commander Quintius won a victory. From this story Machiavelli draws the tentative conclusion that in order to rule a multitude it is better to be humane and merciful than to be proud and cruel. But Tacitus arrived at the opposite conclusion. Machiavelli therefore considers how both his opinion and Tacitus' opinion can be saved. His opinion, which is based on some evidence, is threatened by the mere fact that Tacitus held the opposite opinion: so great is the authority of Tacitus. To save both opinions, Machiavelli makes a distinction. The severity recommended by Tacitus is appropriate for ruling men who are one's subjects always and in every respect. The kindness and mercy recommended by Machiavelli are appropriate for ruling one's fellow citizens in a republic. But since republics are as such superior to monarchies, the opinion of Tacitus may be said to be true regarding the inferior kind of regime whereas Machiavelli's opinion is true of the superior kind of regime: Machiavelli's opinion is truer than Tacitus' opinion. In accordance with this, the next chapter (III 20) continues the praise of gentleness and enlarges it so that it becomes almost the praise of moral virtue in general; Machiavelli praises humanity, frankness, charity, mercy, chastity, liberality and affability by using the examples of Camillus, Fabricius, Scipio, and Cyrus. A difficulty arises from the facts that Cyrus was a monarch and that Machiavelli in the preceding chapter had recommended to monarchs severity rather than kindness. But one could say that the present chapter is concerned with the question of how commanders should treat foreigners rather than their soldiers; and one could say above all, that the Cyrus there praised, being the work of Xenophon, is a fictitious being. At any rate, after having in fact restated the view of classical political philosophy, which is

represented in Machiavelli's books by Xenophon more than by
any other writer, Machiavelli shows in the next chapter (III 21)
that the opposite qualities, i.e., certain moral vices, bring fame and
victories as great as those brought by the moral virtues mentioned.
He shows this by contrasting Scipio with Hannibal. The greatness
of a captain is not dependent on morality nor reduced by immorality
but depends entirely on amoral virtue, on strength of mind, will
or temper, not to say on strength of the soul. Both morality and
immorality have their uses because both love and fear sway human
beings. But both the qualities which make a captain loved and
those which make him feared can become dangerous to him. Therefore a judicious combination of both, a sort of "middle way" is
required. We see that the central chapter of the Tacitean subsection
takes up the central theme of the central sermon. In the next chapter (III 22) Machiavelli turns from the contrast between "Hannibal and Scipio (who) accomplished the same effect, the one with
praiseworthy, the other with detestable things" to the contrast
between Manlius Torquatus and Valerius Corvinus who both used
only praiseworthy means. That is to say, he returns from the
contrast between morality and immorality to the less radical contrast between severity and humanity. Both men were equally glorious captains although Manlius was harsh and Valerius was gentle.
Manlius killed his own son; Valerius never hurt anybody. Manlius'
commands were so harsh that "Manlian commands" became by-
words. At the same time—and this is emphasized by Machiavelli—
he was full of reverence. In order to understand why Manlius was
compelled to proceed as strictly and severely as he did, one must
"consider well the nature of Manlius from the very moment when
Livy begins to mention him." The first thing which Livy mentions
of Manlius Torquatus is that he was somewhat slow of speech and
unready with his tongue. He had an imperious and inhuman father
who hated him because of his speech defect and deprived him of
every kind of decent upbringing so that he retained a rude and
rustic mind. Machiavelli also refers to Manlius' killing of "that
Gaul." As Livy tells us, that Gaul was a man of exceeding size
who had challenged the bravest Roman to single combat, who had
waited for his opponent "in stupid glee and—for the ancients have
thought even this worth mentioning—with his tongue thrust out in
derision," and who was killed by the much smaller Manlius: "To

the body of the fallen man Manlius offered no other indignity than
to despoil it of one thing, a chain which, spattered with blood, he
cast round his own neck." Manlius must have reminded Machiavelli who had read the Bible "judiciously," i.e., in the light of
what he had learned to some extent from Livy, of Moses on the
one hand and of David on the other. One difference between
Manlius and the great men of the Old Testament is noteworthy in
the present context: David cut off the head of Goliath who had
defied the armies of the living God.[174] Whatever may be true of
David, and of Moses—for of Moses, who was a mere executor of
the things which God commanded him, only a presumptuous man
would reason[175]—Manlius at any rate did what he did "compelled
first by his nature and then by the desire that the commands which
his natural appetite had induced him to give, be obeyed." Manlius
had and needed strength of mind, will or temper. Valerius however was under no compulsion "to punish the transgressors" and
could indulge his humaneness; he was humane also as a speaker.
The relation between Manlius and Valerius reminds one of the
relation between the founder and the preserver, say, between the
severe Septimius and the philosophic Marcus Aurelius.[176] In spite
of this, or because of this, but certainly in spite of what he had said
when taking issue with Tacitus, Machiavelli believes that the way
of Manlius is more praiseworthy and less dangerous than the way
of Valerius as far as the leading citizens in a republic are concerned.
For Manlius' way "is altogether in favor of the public and has
no regard at any point to private ambition, for by such a mode one
cannot acquire partisans since one shows oneself always as harsh
to everyone and loves nothing but the common good." As for
princes, the opposite is true: they must walk in the way of Valerius
or of Xenophon's Cyrus. A citizen of a republic who would imitate Valerius would in ordinary circumstances do harm not only
to his fatherland but to himself as well: he would become suspect
of striving for tyrannical or royal power. We see that Machiavelli
eventually succeeds in saving completely what he called Tacitus'
opinion: Tacitus' preference for harshness is appropriate in the
case of the preferable regime, whereas Machiavelli's initial preference
for gentleness is appropriate in the case of the inferior regime.
Tacitus' opinion is truer than Machiavelli's opinion. Machiavelli
presents to us the spectacle of his tacit conversion—of his being

converted by Tacitus to Tacitus' creed, of his being converted from his initial belief in mercy and love to the belief in harshness and terror. Tacitus does not use any reason in order to convince Machiavelli, but Tacitus' powerful presence induces Machiavelli to seek better and better reasons in favor of the belief which Tacitus, the better part of Machiavelli, had instilled into Machiavelli's mind. In the Tacitean subsection, Machiavelli makes public his tacit conversion. Whereas in the scholastic disputation the teaching of the poetic fables was true as regards the superior case,[177] in the Tacitean subsection the opinion of Tacitus is true as regards the superior case. In conclusion we note that according to Machiavelli, those who write on how a leader ought to act are in favor of gentleness whereas the historians like Livy are undecided: the historians come closer to the truth than do the teachers of "Oughts."

Among the many difficulties which the discussion just summarized presents, two seem to be particularly important: is severity incompatible with ambition, and are the harsh qualities merely opposed to the gentle ones (humanity, charity, mercy and so on)? These two questions are answered in the next chapter, the 23rd of the Third Book, which we understand more easily if we remember that the 23rd chapter of the Second Book is the central sermon. In one of the preceding chapters, M. Furius Camillus had appeared as a representative of the gentle captain. We now learn that Camillus resembled the harsh Manlius rather than the gentle Valerius. Camillus, like Manlius, benefited his fatherland and did some harm to himself since he became hated for his severity: each of the two captains did harm to his ambition. This is not to deny that ambition is best concealed by intransigent and fanatical partisanship for the common good or by zealous severity. Hence the central reason that Camillus became hated was not his severity but his creating the suspicion that out of pride he wished to become equal to a god, namely, to the Sun.[178] Yet it was less pride or ambition than its manifestation by an overt act which made Camillus hated. Camillus, "the greatest of all captains," whose deeds and speeches are to some extent fictitious, effected the transition from gentleness to severity or from love to terror, and his compelling passion was, in both states, his pride or ambition. The Tacitean subsection was opened by a reference to the cruel and rude consul Appius Claudius who, to say the least, reminds the reader of the

Decemvir Appius Claudius, Rome's legislator par excellence, who was doomed because of his attempt to establish a tyranny and whose laws retained their force despite his violent death. Appius Claudius too failed because he attempted to achieve the transition from mercy to cruelty and from humility to pride without exercising the necessary patience.[179] The fact that Appius Claudius and Camillus can be regarded as more or less successful combinations of the type Manlius and the type Valerius implies that the primary phenomenon is the opposition between these two types. Manlius is akin to Papirius Cursor who, out of extreme jealousy, thirsted for the blood of Fabius.[180] The Tacitean sub-section is silent about Fabius: Fabius is a captain of a kind entirely different from the captains mentioned in the Tacitean sub-section. The Tacitean sub-section is silent about Machiavelli's model, for Tacitus is less Machiavelli's model than his creation.[181]

The *Discourses* end with praise of Fabius: a Roman remains Machiavelli's model to the end. This fact is misleading if it is not "well considered." The *Discourses* begin with an equating of the new modes and orders discovered by Machiavelli and the ancient modes and orders. His revolt against the tradition comes to sight first as submission to "the authority of the Romans." Yet before bowing to this or that authority, one must have bowed to the principle of authority. The principle of authority finds its primary expression in the equating of the good and the ancestral. This equation implies the assumption of absolutely superior or perfect beginnings, of a golden age or of a Paradise. The ground or origin of the perfect beginning is the supremacy of the Good or of Love or, as we might also say, the rule of Providence. The origin of evil is a fall. Progress is return, betterment is restoration. To perfect oneself means to return to the beginning when men were good, to pre-historical beginnings. Especially if the pre-historical beginnings are assumed to be unknowable, one must rest satisfied with the imitation of a founder-captain who at least excels all other men, if he is not semi-divine or divine. These few words concerning the comprehensive theo-cosmological scheme implied in the principle of authority will suffice for the understanding of Machiavelli's thought. The comprehensive scheme must be rendered more precise or narrowed down in order to become salutary. Bowing to the principle of authority is sterile if it is not followed by surrender to authority itself, i.e., to this or that authority. If this step is not taken one will remain enmeshed in the religious longing or the religiosity so characteristic of our centuries, and will not be liberated by religion proper. Since Machiavelli was aware of this relation between the principle of authority and authority itself, his criticism of the authority of the Romans, of the last authority which remained for him, coincides with his criticism of authority as such. We repeat here only two of his indications: in the beginning men were not good but "corrupt," and the foundation is not a single almost superhuman act at the beginning but a continuous activity of successive rulers who are unambiguously human.[182] The most coherent discussion of authority as such occurs in the section on the founder-captain (III 1-15). Mixed bodies, i.e., states or religions, can be preserved only if they are brought back, from time to time, to their beginnings, or if they are "renewed." In their beginnings, mixed bodies must have had some goodness within them; otherwise they could not have grown: Machiavelli no longer says that in the beginning, mixed bodies, or men, were good simply. He quotes a statement of the physicians concerning the bodies of men; the parallelism of human bodies and mixed bodies shows that mixed bodies in their beginnings are necessarily imperfect. The renovation of a mixed body is a rebirth, and through the rebirth a resumption or recovery of new life and new virtue: the renewed mixed body both is and is not the mixed body in its pristine state. The renewed mixed body could be said to be the mixed body in its pristine state if the renovation consisted in the resumption of the observance of all old laws and orders. In the classic example discussed by Machiavelli, which is the rebirth of Rome after her capture by the Gauls, the Romans, while "resuming the observance of justice and religion," "renewed all orders of their ancient religion": Machiavelli does not say that the Romans renewed all their ancient orders. While the early pagan Roman republic "renewed all orders of its ancient religion," St. Francis and St. Dominic, who renewed the Christian religion, succeeded only because of the potency of "their new orders." Speaking of another kind of renovation, Machiavelli indicates in what the beneficent effect of all renovation consists. He illustrates that other kind of renovation by seven Roman examples. Five were spectacular executions of outstanding citizens, the sixth was the action of Papirius Cursor against Fabius and the seventh was the accusations against the Scipios. The renovation of mixed bodies consists of the renewal of fear in the minds of their members or of putting in men that terror and that fear which the original founders had put into their partisans. This, and not the return to the old modes and orders, is the essence of the return to the beginning. Return to the beginning means in all cases introducing new orders.[183] Therefore in particular Machiavelli's return to the ancient modes and orders means of necessity the devising of new modes and orders. Ordinary return to the beginning means return to the terror accompanying the foundation. Machiavelli's return to the beginning means return to the primeval or original terror which precedes every man-made terror, which explains why the founder must use terror and which enables him to use terror. Machiavelli's return to the beginning means return to the terror inherent in man's situation, to man's essential unprotectedness. In the beginning there was terror. In the beginning men were good, i.e., they were willing to obey because they were afraid and easily frightened. The primacy of Love must be replaced by the primacy of Terror if republics are to be established in accordance with nature and on the basis of knowledge of nature. The beginnings of men were imperfect and low. Man is exposed, and not protected, essentially and from the beginning. Therefore the perfection envisaged by both the Bible and classical philosophy is impossible. But for the same reason for which perfection, and in particular the initial as well as the ultimate Paradise is impossible, there cannot be a Hell. Man cannot rise above earthly and earthy humanity and therefore he ought not even to aspire beyond humanity. Such aspiration merely leads to the most terrible and wholly unnecessary inhumanity of man to man. The tradition which Machiavelli attacks had asserted that "the things which have a bad beginning or principle can never have a good end." But Machiavelli trusts in a "most true" Sallustian text which, after he has improved it to suit his purpose, says that "all evil examples stem from good beginnings."[184]

Through understanding what he regarded as the fundamental error of the Great Tradition, Machiavelli was compelled to seek and enabled to find fundamentally new modes and orders. Although the communication even of the new modes and orders is dangerous, Machiavelli communicates them out of concern for the common good. He wishes that they be adopted. The new modes and orders are supported by evident reasons. But those reasons cannot be made evident to the people, at least not until it is too late. On the other hand, being unarmed, Machiavelli cannot compel the people to have faith in him. Not only does he completely lack force; he does not even wish to use force. This kind of difficulty was overcome in the olden times, and could be overcome in the present time by recourse to God. Machiavelli has no moral or other objections to pious fraud. Induced not only by his lack of force but by his humanity as well, and trusting in the credulity of most men, he preserves the shadow of the established or at least of the ancient, or "retains the name" while abolishing the substance. By adapting himself to the opinion of the people, he imitates Brutus who, in order to liberate his fatherland, played the fool by speaking, seeing, and doing things against his opinion, and thus pleased the prince; for since "there is nothing in the world except the vulgar," the most powerful ruler is the people. Yet this accommodation to the opinions of the people endangers his communication; while the new modes and orders might thus be made acceptable, they will be accepted in the wrong spirit. Machiavelli therefore needs readers who are discerning enough to understand not only the new modes and orders but their ultimate ground as well. He needs readers who could act as mediators between him and the people by becoming princes. If he is an unarmed prophet, or a captain without an army who must recruit his army by means of his books, he must first recruit the highest officers directly responsible to him and commissioned by him. Owing to "the envious nature of men," he cannot expect to find his first adherents among the men of his generation. He can come into his own only after the natural death of his generation, the generation of the desert, as it were. He must appeal to the elite among the coming generations.[185]

One is tempted to describe Machiavelli's relation to the young as a potential conspiracy. That chapter of the *Discourses* which is by far the most extensive is devoted to the subject of conspiracies, i.e., of more or less violent changes of modes and orders.[186] He opens the chapter with a warning against conspiracies, i.e., against the most subtle, if not the most extreme, form of actively disobeying and opposing princes, and he re-enforces that warning by quoting a "golden sentence," not indeed of David or Paul, but of Tacitus himself. He then shows under what conditions conspiracies are bound to be not only praiseworthy but successful as well. The conspirator must fear to be betrayed by his fellows. The only protection against this danger consists in not communicating one's intention to anyone until the moment for the deed has come. You may indeed say anything to one man alone because if he accuses you to the prince, his "Yes" will have no greater weight than your "No." But "of writing everyone must beware as of a rock." Conspiracies against the fatherland or a republic are less dangerous than a conspiracy against the prince. They can be brought to a happy issue by the use of deceit and art alone. But even when conspiring against a republic, one must beware of writing as is shown by the example of the Catilinarian conspiracy. In an incorrupt republic the attempt is hopeless. One is tempted to say— and it is one of Machiavelli's *grandi prudenze* not to resist such temptations—that in an incorrupt republic the thought of conspiring against the republic cannot occur to a citizen. A few pages after saying this, he shows by the examples of Spurius Cassius and Manlius Capitolinus that the thought of conspiring against the republic does occur to citizens of an incorrupt republic. Since both Spurius Cassius and Manlius Capitolinus failed because Rome was incorrupt in their time, Machiavelli wonders whether their failure was necessary. A man may begin, he concludes, to corrupt the people of a republic, but the lifetime of one man cannot possibly suffice to corrupt a republic to the extent that he himself will derive benefit from the corruption: the work which he begins can be completed only by his successors, the young. Even if a man who begins to corrupt a republic could live long enough to finish his work, he would necessarily lack the required patience and thus be ruined. Machiavelli's argument silently shifts from more or less dangerous conspiracies against the fatherland or the common good which, if successful, benefit the conspirators, to patient long-range corruption, which is neither dangerous to the corrupter nor productive of crude benefits to him. We prefer to say that, being a teacher of conspirators, he is not himself a conspirator. It goes without saying that the man who, from the point of view of the established order, necessarily appears as a corrupter may in truth be the first discoverer of those modes and orders which are simply in accordance with nature. It also goes without saying that whether writing is dangerous or not depends to a considerable extent on whether the writing in question serves a conspiratorial purpose or merely long-range corruption. Machiavelli goes on to say that if a man desires to seize authority in a republic and to impress his evil form on a republic, he must have at his disposal a matter which little by little, from generation to generation has become disordered, or a matter which has been disordered by time; for since all things of the world, and therefore in particular mixed bodies, have a limited life span, they necessarily become disordered by the mere passing of time.[187] In order to see how near in time Machiavelli believed himself to be to those young men or potential princes or to the conspirators proper who might put into practice the new modes and orders, we must therefore consider what stage of corruption, in his opinion, his matter had reached by his time.

The matter on which Machiavelli attempts to impress his form is "the Christian republic." He is certain that despite the rebirth brought about by St. Dominic and St. Francis the Christian republic has reached an advanced stage of corruption: its end may be near. Just as Livy deplored the decay of "the ancient religion," at the time at which Christianity was emerging, Machiavelli notes the decay of Christianity at the time at which a new dispensation may be imminent. He is certain that the Christian religion will not last forever. It is "the present religion." No republic is perpetual. All religions, just as all other mixed bodies and as all simple bodies, have a life-span, ordained by heaven, beyond which they cannot live; they may die earlier. Religions or sects change two or three times in 5,000 or 6,000 years. It is difficult to say whether Machiavelli regarded as the beginning of Christianity the birth of Jesus or the Crucifixion or the reign of Constantine. Given this ambiguity, his statement implies that, as far as the life span ordained by heaven is concerned, Christianity could well last at least for another century and a half, and might last for about two more millennia. Yet its actual life span will depend decisively on what its human supporters and its human enemies will do. The outcome will depend on prudence and on chance. "Two continuous successions of virtuous princes are sufficient for conquering the world." What might happen if two virtuous Muslim princes—men comparable to Philip and his son Alexander the Great—would reign in succession? Besides, Machiavelli's silence about the Reformation need not be due to ignorance; the fact (if it is a fact) that 1517 is the date of the latest event to which he refers in the *Discourses* does not prove that the *Discourses* as we have the book was completed prior to Machiavelli's having become aware of Luther's epoch-making action. At any rate, Machiavelli saw two ways in which the ancient modes and orders might be destroyed. One was the irruption of barbarians, especially of the peoples of the North, such as the Scythians, who are at present held back by the Germans, the Hungarians, and the Poles. The other would be the rejuvenation of the West. It is the purpose of the *Discourses* to prepare this rebirth through awakening primarily the Italian-reading youth.[188]

The modes and orders which Machiavelli proposes are not simply the sound modes and orders, but new modes and orders. It is of their essence that knowledge of them is not only not coeval with man but is related negatively to Christianity or is post-Christian. The new modes and orders are brought to light by reason analyzing data partly supplied by the Christian republic. The new modes and orders, which are supported only by reason, emerge essentially in opposition to specific old modes and orders which are supported only by authority and force. Machiavelli's critique of the old modes and orders therefore takes on the character of a war waged by an unarmed man, of a spiritual war. This war can be described, with the somewhat free use of Christian terms, as a war of the Anti-Christ or of the Devil who recruits his army while fighting or through fighting against the army led by God or Christ.[189] His hope for victory is grounded on two things. His having discovered the new modes and orders and their ultimate ground merely through the use of his natural faculties makes it certain that others, if only a few, can be fully converted to the truth. Besides, the corruption of the established order makes it certain that at least his proposal of new modes and orders will receive a friendly hearing from a large audience. The corruption of a mixed body consists in its disintegration. Machiavelli is confronted less by one united mystical body than by a combination of parties which at the outset are entirely hostile to him. Yet every hostile combination can be divided "with a little art," provided one is so situated that one can sustain the first attacks. In domestic affairs one can divide one's enemies by frightening some or by corrupting some or by appealing to the love of some for the common good; the central mode, i.e., corruption, is equally applicable in war, as Machiavelli emphasizes by the order of his examples. Generally speaking, one can divide any hostile combination by bringing some sacrifice. One must certainly use every artifice which gives the composite body an opportunity to disintegrate and one must avoid every move which would put the enemies under a necessity to remain united or to recover their unity. It is this necessity to divide and thus to defeat the particular hostile combination confronting him which made Machiavelli surpass Livy and devise an entirely new strategy of spiritual warfare.[190] But his hope for the success of his teaching rests on the certainty that one of the two parties of which the Christian republic consists[191] will be attracted by his proposals. One may describe that party provisionally as the Ghibellines, as men who would have gone with Frederick the Second of Hohenstaufen. More precisely that party consists of those who "esteem the fatherland more than the soul" or who, driven and perhaps blinded by passion for the liberty of their fatherland, are more attached to their earthly fatherland than to the heavenly fatherland, or who are lukewarm Christians. They are people "of little faith," i.e., of little Christian faith who, impatient of alleged or true abuses of ecclesiastical authority, do not hesitate to attack ecclesiastical authority with more than masculine courage but become afraid once they realize the ultimate consequence of their action.[192]

We have now answered the question of how Machiavelli can hope for the success of his venture. In saying that the unarmed prophets have failed, he exaggerates in order to bring to light the difficulty with which he is faced. The example of the Roman legislator par excellence, Appius Claudius, shows that a law can survive the violent death of the legislator, not to say that it can acquire its full vigor through the violent death of the legislator. Yet Appius Claudius had been appointed by the Roman people to frame its laws. The example of Agis shows that by patiently refraining from premature action and by merely leaving writings to posterity one can bring about the desired change without any harm to oneself. Yet Agis did not desire to introduce new modes and orders but merely to restore the ancient modes and orders. By far the most important model for Machiavelli was the victory of Christianity. Christanity conquered the Roman empire without the use of force, merely by peacefully propagating its new modes and orders.

Machiavelli's hope for the success of his venture is founded on the success of Christianity. Just as Christianity defeated paganism by propaganda, he believes that he can defeat Christianity by propaganda. The *Prince*, which is dedicated to an actual prince had led up to the suggestion that Machiavelli imitates Moses, the armed prophet. The *Discourses*, which are dedicated to potential princes, lead up to the suggestion that Machiavelli imitates Jesus, the unarmed prophet. Yet Machiavelli combines the imitation of Jesus with the imitation of Fabius. Fabius, in contradistinction to Decius, judged the slow assault to be preferable and reserved his impetus for the end; choosing the safer way, he gained a more gladdening victory, remaining alive, than the victory which Decius gained by his death. For Decius, imitating his father, sacrificed himself for the expiation of the Romans.[193] Besides, whereas the victory of Christianity was ascribed to the unconquerable decree of Divine Providence, Machiavelli's hope rests on his assumption that human prudence can conquer Fortuna. Classical political philosophy had taught that the salvation of the cities depends on the coincidence of philosophy and political power which is truly a coincidence—something for which one can wish or hope but which one cannot bring about. Machiavelli is the first philosopher who believes that the coincidence of philosophy and political power can be brought about by propaganda which wins over ever larger multitudes to the new modes and orders and thus transforms the thought of one or a few into the opinion of the public and therewith into public power. Machiavelli breaks with the Great Tradition and initiates the Enlightenment. We shall have to consider whether that Enlightenment deserves its name or whether its true name is Obfuscation.

Machiavelli's Teaching

I T WOULD not be reasonable to claim, or indeed to believe, that the preceding observations suffice to elucidate every obscure passage of the *Discourses*. The utmost we can hope to have achieved is to have pointed to the way which the reader must take in studying Machiavelli's work. Books like the *Discourses* and the *Prince* do not reveal their full meaning as intended by the author unless one ponders over them "day and night" for a long time. The reader who is properly prepared is bound to come across suggestions which refuse to be stated. Pen or typewriter, to say nothing of hand and tongue, refuse their service. The reader thus comes to understand the truth that what ought not to be said cannot be said. It is fortunate for the historians of ideas, to say nothing of others, that there are not many books of this kind. Still, there are more of them than one would easily believe, for there were more great men who were stepsons of their time or out of step with the future than one would easily believe. As Faust put it to Wagner, "the few who understood something of the world and of men's heart and mind, who were foolish enough not to restrain their full heart but to reveal their feeling and their vision to the vulgar, have ever been crucified and burned"; not everyone belonging to those few failed to restrain his full heart. Goethe was the last great man who rediscovered or remembered this, especially after he had returned from the storm and stress of sentiment to the tranquillity of fullness of vision.[1] After him, social reason, sentiment and decision and whatever goes with those "dynamic forces" united in order to destroy the last vestiges of the recollection of what philosophy originally meant.

• Many writers have called Machiavelli a pagan.[2] Most of them mean by this that, "loving his fatherland more than his soul," he forgot or denied the other world, and being enamored of the worldly glory of pagan Rome, he forgot or rejected the imitation of Christ.• They mean that he forgot to think about everything which is not political in the narrow sense or that he was so self-complacent as to rest satisfied with rebelling passionately and blindly against Christian morality without giving dispassionate thought to the theological premises of that morality. They imagine that he was another Cosimo de' Medici who said among other things that states cannot be kept with paternosters and was therefore slandered as a man who loved this world more than the other world.[3] A man of this sort is not properly called a pagan. Paganism is a kind of piety and one does not find a trace of pagan piety in Machiavelli's work. He had not reverted from the worship of Christ to the worship of Apollo. On the other hand, it is not misleading to count Machiavelli among "the wise of the world." He informs us that Savonarola's sermons are full of accusations of "the wise of the world" and of invectives against them. According to Savonarola, "the wise of the world" do in fact say that a state cannot be ruled with paternosters. But they also say that they do not wish to believe anything except what rational discourse proves; they therefore regard the Biblical prophecies as "things for women"; Savonarola has heard them say in their disputations that, speaking philosophically and disregarding the supernatural, the world is eternal, God is the final and not the efficient cause of this world and there is only one soul in all men; they say that faith is nothing but opinion.[4] Those "wise of the world" who transcend the limits of political cleverness reject not only the myths of the pagans but above all revelation and the characteristic teachings of revelation on the ground indicated. They are *falāsifa* or "Averroists."

The vulgar understanding of Machiavelli is justified to some extent by his reticences. He does not often speak of theological subjects, the Bible, Biblical characters, Biblical events or Christianity. This fact does not necessarily prove indifference or ignorance. Granted that his primary theme is political, it is not obvious, and it certainly was not obvious in former times, that the Bible is mute about political conduct. But let us grant that political science is autonomous in its sphere and can be treated without any regard to the teaching of the Bible, since the Bible itself presents the non-prophet Jethro as the teacher of the prophet Moses in things political. This would explain Machiavelli's silence if there were no apparent conflict between his political science and the teaching of the Bible. But there is such an apparent conflict. To see this, it suffices that one remember simultaneously what Machiavelli says concerning the excusable character of the fratricide committed by the founder of the city of Rome and what the Bible says about the fratricide committed by the first founder of any city. Machiavelli needed much more urgently than did even Hobbes a detailed discussion revealing the harmony between his political teaching and the teaching of the Bible. Yet unlike Hobbes he failed to give such a discussion. The fact that he failed to do so and at the same time spoke so rarely about revelation cannot be explained by blindness or ignorance but only by a peculiar mixture of boldness and caution: he silently makes superficial readers oblivious of the Biblical teaching. This mixture was appropriately characterized and as it were imitated by Bacon in his 13th *Essay:* "one of the doctors of Italy, Nicholas Machiavel, had the confidence to put in writing, almost in plain terms, *That the Christian faith had given up good men in prey to those who are tyrannical and unjust.*"

The sentence to which Bacon refers occurs in the second of the three passages explicitly dealing with the essence of Christianity. We shall disregard here those innumerable passages, to say nothing of others, which in effect deal with the essence of Christianity since they deal explicitly with the contrast between the ancients and the moderns; for the ancients are primarily the pagan Romans and the moderns are primarily the Christians. In the Preface to the First Book Machiavelli expresses the "belief" that the failure to imitate the ancients in the most important matters is caused "not so much by the weakness into which the present religion has led the world or by that evil which ambitious leisure has done to many Christian countries and cities, but by the lack of true knowledge of the histories." If we surrender to the drift of the sentence, we are led to "believe" that the failure to imitate the ancients properly is in no way due to Christianity. But if we follow that drift without surrendering to it and if we assume that the present religion is the Christian religion, and not merely the Christian religion in its alleged present state of decay, we see that according to Machiavelli Christianity has led the world into weakness, and the failure to imitate the ancients properly is due to some extent to Christianity. This induces us to reflect on the connection between the prevailing weakness and the prevailing unwillingness or inability properly to imitate the ancients, and thus to realize that according to Machiavelli the decisive reason for the failure to imitate the ancients properly is precisely Christianity, i.e., a phenomenon which he apparently regarded only as a secondary reason.[5] Apart from this, Machiavelli speaks frequently about pagan Rome without contrasting pagan Rome with Christianity or modernity; even in those cases, we are not permitted to forget his general thesis that the present religion has led the world into weakness. While "the present religion has led the world into weakness," "the world triumphed" under the pagan emperors from Nerva to Marcus Aurelius as distinguished not only from the later emperors but from the earlier ones as well: the world did not triumph in the reign of Augustus, during which Jesus was born; that reign, so far from being "the fullness of time" and thoroughly just, was a period of utter corruption; Augustus has the primary responsibility for the Roman people becoming unarmed.[6] Nor can one say that Christianity compensated for the weakness into which it led the world by making the world more God-fearing: "there was never for centuries so great fear of God as there was in that republic," i.e., the Roman republic. It is true that if "that religion had been maintained in the princes of the Christian republic in accordance with what the giver of the same had ordained, the Christian states and republics would be more united and much more happy than they are"; but this does not mean that, given this condition, the Christian states and republics would equal the Roman republic in union, happiness and virtue. Whereas the Roman Church is the greatest enemy of the well-being of Italy, the pagan auguries were the cause of "the well-being of the Roman Republic."[7]

In the central statement on the essence of Christianity Machiavelli speaks, not indeed of Christianity nor yet of "the present religion," but of "our religion." That statement contains the only density of "we's" in the sense of "we Christians" which occurs in the *Discourses*.[8] Machiavelli again expresses a belief. Yet whereas the first statement had opened with one *Credo*, the second statement opens with two *Credos* and ends with one *Credo*. While he now speaks with unique frequency of "we Christians," he does not express what "we (Christians)" believe but only what he himself believes.[9] He now raises the question of why the peoples were greater lovers of freedom in ancient times than in the present, and he answers it by expressing the belief that the cause is the same as the cause that men are now less strong than they were in ancient times; that cause, he believes, is the difference between "our" education and ancient education, which difference is founded on the difference between "our" religion and the ancient religion. Up to this point he merely restates, although with greater force and clarity, what he had already said in the first statement. He goes on to explain why, or by virtue of what, Christianity has led the world into weakness. By showing the truth and the true way, Christianity has lowered the esteem for "the honor of the world," whereas the pagans regarded that honor as the highest good and were therefore more ferocious or less weak in their actions. Machiavelli seems to say that awareness of the truth and the true way is destructive of the strength of the world. Does he mean to say that the strength-giving esteem for worldly honor is based on error or delusion, and therewith that his own political teaching which favors the strength of the world is based on the open rejection of the truth and the true way? Yet he is undoubtedly concerned with teaching the truth and the true way. To quote the strongest statement regarding truth which he ever makes, "It is truer than every other truth that where men are not soldiers this is due to a fault of the prince."[10] He admits then that there is a truth which is truer than the truth of Christianity. In accordance with this, he traces the religious establishment of pagan Rome to heavenly inspiration. The truth of Christianity then depends on whether Christianity is in agreement and sympathy with the most perfect truth mentioned. That most perfect truth upholds the demand for the strength of the world. Hence if Christianity has led the world into weakness, it cannot be true. There is essential harmony between truth and worldly strength: "all those modes

and those opinions deviating from the truth arise from the weakness
of him who is lord."[11] What has been said about the truth, applies
to the true way. The true way—the way shown by experience to
be true—is the way of a warlike republic like the Roman.[12] When
Machiavelli says that Christianity has shown the truth and the
true way, he lets us see that he is aware of the claim of Christianity
and that he has come to grips with that claim. What characterizes
Christianity according to him is not its alleged truth but its lowering the esteem for worldly glory or, as he says in the sequel, its
regarding humility, abjectness and contempt for things human as
the highest good. The ancient religion, he had originally said,
regarded worldly honor as the highest good. He now says that the
ancient religion regarded greatness of mind, strength of the body
and all other things which are apt to make men very strong, as
the highest good. He thus suggests a corresponding improvement
of his statement concerning the highest good as understood by
Christianity: the highest good is God who assumed humility and
weakness and thus consecrated humility and weakness. "Hence
our religion . . . demands that you be fit to suffer rather than to
do something strong." The unarmed heaven demands an unarmed
earth, an unarmed emperor and an unarmed heart.[13] The belief in
the Passion fosters passivity or the life of humility or contemplation
rather than the active life. "This mode of life then appears to have
rendered the world weak and given it up in prey to criminal men
who can manage the world with safety seeing that the large
majority, in order to enter Paradise, think more of bearing their
beatings than of avenging them." After having traced the present
weakness of the world to its ground, Machiavelli says that the
present effeminacy of the world is due not to Christianity but to
a false interpretation of Christianity: since Christianity permits the
exaltation and defense of the fatherland, it demands that Christians
be strong. He concludes the statement by saying that the decline
of love of freedom is due, as he believes, less to Christianity than
to the destruction by the Roman empire of all republics. Yet in
making these amazingly bold retractions, he does not retract what
he had said about the superiority of worldly glory to humility,
about the ground of the preference generally given to humility,
and about the weakness and servility prevailing in the Christian
world.[14] And in saying that Christianity "permits" the defense

and even the exaltation of the fatherland, he is not oblivious of the fact that Christianity subordinates the earthly fatherland to the heavenly fatherland and thus subordinates the power temporal to the power spiritual.[15]

The third statement occurs in the first chapter of the Third Book. Machiavelli there discusses the need for periodic renovations of republics, sects, and kingdoms. He illustrates the renovation of sects "by the example of our religion" which had been renewed and thus preserved by the new orders of St. Francis and St. Dominic. Through poverty and the example of the life of Christ they restored Christianity in the minds of men from which it had already vanished. Their new modes and orders prevented the immorality of the prelates and of the heads of religion from ruining the religion. "They give the peoples to understand that it is evil to speak evil of evil and it is good to live in obedience to them and, if they err, to let God chastise them; and thus they do the worst they can for they do not fear that punishment which they do not see and in which they do not believe." Shortly afterwards, when he speaks no longer of sects, Machiavelli shows that the neglect of law enforcement, of human punishment, leads to the consequence that either the evils will be eventually corrected with non-legal violence or else that society will perish. In the last statement, Machiavelli finds the root of the prevailing weakness in the prohibition against speaking evil of evil or, more generally and more clearly, in the prohibition or counsel against resisting evil. Non-resistance to evil would secure for ever the undisturbed rule of evil men. Resistance to evil is natural to man as well as to any other living being. The counsel against resisting evil can therefore lead only to evasion of that counsel.[16]

Machiavelli himself has indicated the difficulty to which his thesis is exposed. In the only chapter explicitly devoted to criminal rulers, he explicitly contrasts a single ancient and a single modern example. The ancient criminal Agathocles ruled "securely for a long time in his fatherland," whereas the modern criminal Liverotto was destroyed one year after he had come to power. Yet Liverotto was destroyed by Cesare Borgia, and one might say that Cesare himself was a criminal ruler. Still, Cesare was not as successful as the criminal pagan emperor Severus who succeeded in being "revered by everyone." Machiavelli probably meant that since

Cesare was only the tool of his father, Pope Alexander VI, the destruction of the criminal Liverotto was the work of another modern criminal ruler who, at any rate by virtue of his sacred office, was revered, not to say worshipped, by everyone. If one objected that the pagan emperors received even divine honors, Machiavelli would perhaps reply that the worship of the pagan emperors did not preclude the assassination of many of them. He certainly shows in both books at considerable length how insecurely those pagan emperors lived who lacked virtue.[17]

To overcome easily the obvious difficulty to which Machiavelli's thesis is exposed, one merely has to assume that that thesis expresses in an exaggerated manner what he seriously means: not the world has been rendered weak by Christianity but Italy has been rendered weak by the Roman Church. He frequently praises the strength shown by Christian nations like the French, the Germans, and the Swiss. Besides, he can maintain his thesis regarding the weakness of the moderns only by being almost silent about the modern conquest of the ocean.[18] Furthermore, he cannot deny that in two of the three branches of the army the moderns are superior to the ancients. If we had not learned something about Machiavelli's art, we might have the presumption to say that it is almost pitiful to see how he struggles to minimize the significance of artillery and cavalry in order to save the superiority of the ancient Romans. In the chapter on artillery he tries to show that if artillery had been known to the Romans as well as to their enemies, the Romans would nevertheless have succeeded in acquiring their empire; he does not come to grips with the fact that the inventors of the legion were unaware of artillery, a source of considerable strength especially with regard to the reduction of fortresses. In the chapter on cavalry he tries to show that the Romans were right in regarding infantry, and not cavalry, as the queen of battles; he is silent there about the superiority of modern cavalry to Roman cavalry and the superiority of cavalry to infantry in terrain of a certain kind, e.g. in some parts of Asia; he merely alludes to these facts by his examples, not all of which are apt or appear in the proper places.[19] One cannot do justice to Machiavelli's argument if one does not remember the following points: he did not deny the possibility of progress beyond the Romans; his discussion of infantry, artillery and cavalry in the three central chapters of the central Book of the *Discourses* does not merely deal with the three inseparable parts of a modern army in the literal sense; his argument proceeds on more than one level. However highly he regarded the French, the Germans and the Swiss, he left no doubt about their inferiority to the Romans. The French know nothing of politics; a French king has acted against the greatest truth by disarming his peoples; while less corrupt than Italy, France is more corrupt than Germany. Machiavelli especially praises the German cities. Yet these cities control only small territories and they are subject to the German emperor though he has reputation rather than force. They cannot be compared to the Swiss who are not only, like the German cities, free to the highest degree but besides armed to the highest degree. The Swiss can be compared to the ancient Tuscans. But they cannot be compared to the ancient Romans. The modes and orders of ancient Rome, as distinguished from those of ancient Tuscany or modern Switzerland, enable a state to acquire a large empire. When Machiavelli speaks of the weakness of the modern world, he thinks in the first place of the fact that after the destruction of the Roman empire, no lasting and ecumenical empire emerged. As builders of empires, the Muslims appeared to him to come closer to the Romans than did the Christians. He seems to have been struck by the contrast between the Crusades and the conquest of the East by the Romans and by Alexander the Great.[20] The two classical empires owed their being directly or indirectly to classical republics and the superiority of the latter to the monarchic East. When Machiavelli speaks of the weakness of the modern world, he has chiefly in mind the weakness of the modern republics. In classical antiquity as long as it was incorrupt, the West was predominantly republican, whereas the modern West, the Christian republic, is predominantly monarchic. Machiavelli thinks of Athens and Sparta, of Rome and the republic which bred Hannibal, and even of Tyre which withstood Alexander "after he had already conquered the whole Orient." He does not think of Jerusalem.[21]

It was impossible to analyze the outer layer of what Machiavelli means by the weakness of the world without at the same time indicating what he means by making Christianity responsible for that weakness. Christianity stems from the servile East which is habitually subject to princes who are destroyers of countries and squanderers of everything reminiscent of civilization. It stems more particularly from a weak Eastern nation which had a very defective polity. Machiavelli expects the readers who have been trained by him, to read the Bible "judiciously"; he limits himself to giving a few indications. Regarding the exodus from Egypt, he suggests that the Jews were unwilling to live any longer as slaves in Egypt, a well-ordered, fertile, most pleasant country of great military power, and therefore had to flee from Egypt; they were not strong enough to conquer Palestine but had to accommodate themselves to some extent to the natives whom they were unable to dislodge. By leading the Jews out of Egypt, Moses "redeemed his land" and "ennobled his fatherland." The inappropriateness or ambiguity of the term "fatherland" in this context draws our attention to the long periods of oppression or exile in which the Jewish people only longed for the land that had belonged to their fathers and was promised to them, rather than possessed it; this longing foreshadows the Christians' longing for the heavenly fatherland or the Christian dualism of the heavenly and the earthly fatherland; the true Christian is an exile on earth who lives in faith and hope and who arouses these passions in others. Machiavelli explicitly contrasts the greatest Jewish king, David, with his successors who were "weak princes." He tacitly contrasts the succession of the two virtuous princes, Philip who "from a little king became a prince of Greece" and Alexander the Great, with the succession of David who "vanquished and beat all his neighbors" and Solomon. The former succession, Machiavelli notes, culminated in the conquest of the world; the latter succession, as he refrains from saying, culminated in the building of the temple in Jerusalem. Certainly David's successors were "little kings." Machiavelli gives us no reason for believing that he excepted the kings of Israel and Judah from his verdict about "the oriental princes" who in his eyes were barbarians. He says of David that he "was undoubtedly a man most excellent in arms, in learning, in judgment" whereas he says of Savonarola that "his writings show the learning, the prudence and the virtue of his spirit or mind" and that "his life, his learning and the subject which he took up were sufficient to make men believe in him": whereas David had arms, and even his own arms, Savonarola was unarmed; whereas one must live in a certain manner in order to find belief, one does not need prudence and judgment for that purpose; whereas the writings of Savonarola do not show the excellent character of his learning nor of his judgment, the life of David was not such as to make him worthy to be believed, for "one comes from a low to a high position through fraud rather than through force." Regarding the defective character of the Biblical polity, it suffices to compare the Biblical modes and orders with the Roman modes and orders praised by Machiavelli. To mention only one example, one must compare the legal and the trans-legal context of Moses' severities with that of the severities of his Roman parallels, Manlius and Papirius. Thanks to their institutions and their spirit, the Romans could lawfully prevent, or at any rate lawfully disapprove of, severities of their dictators which they regarded as excessive, to say nothing of the fact that their dictators had extremely short tenures of office. There is an immediate connection between this difference and the presence or absence of proper safeguards for distinguishing between accusations and calumnies.[22]

It is particularly necessary to compare the status of priests and augurs in the Roman polity with that of priests and prophets in the Biblical polity. In Machiavelli's presentation the Roman polity as the model is characterized by the unqualified supremacy of political authority proper as distinguished from any religious authority. He indicates his reason for that preference by saying that good arms are the necessary and sufficient condition for good laws. Priests and prophets are not as such warriors. The natures, the habits, the training, the function, and the tastes of the two types of men differ radically. Machiavelli shows the difference between the ways of life of the ruler-warrior and the priest most forcefully by presenting his Castruccio as confronted with a choice between them; the reader is reminded of young Heracles at the crossroads who has to choose between pleasure or vice and virtue. If the fundamental alternative is that of rule of priests or rule of armed men, then we understand why Machiavelli suggested that the truth "where men are not soldiers, this is due to a fault of the prince" is the greatest truth. Priests as priests cannot defend their subjects against people who are not frightened by maledictions or appearances. Ecclesiastical principalities may be secure and happy; they are not powerful and respected because they are not armed. They are, or tend to become, a kind of Capua in which even ancient Romans would forget the fatherland.[23] In his judg-

ment on the rule or supremacy of priests Machiavelli merely follows the classical tradition. Plato's rule of philosophers is meant to
replace the Egyptian rule of priests. According to Aristotle, priestly
functions ought to be assigned to distinguished citizens who are
too old in body or mind to fulfill political functions proper. The
concern with divine things is in one sense the first concern of
the city but in a more important sense it comes after the arts, arms
and wealth, to say nothing of the deliberative-judicial function.[24]
Machiavelli would have been the first to admit that there may be
warlike and armed prophets and priests. As regards armed priests,
he points out that it was Pope Alexander VI through whose efforts the Church became armed; the first armed Pontiff conspicuously lacked goodness. The chief reason why Machiavelli opposed
the direct or indirect rule of priests was that he regarded it as
essentially tyrannical and even, in principle, more tyrannical than
any other regime. Commands which are alleged to be derived from
divine authority or given by virtue of divine authority are in no
way subject to approval by the citizen body however wise and
virtuous. Priestly government cannot be responsible to the citizen
body however excellent. Hence, ecclesiastical principalities more
than any others can be acquired and maintained without virtue. If
a government is based on divine authority, resistance is in principle
impossible; the rulers have nothing to fear. On the other hand,
if a government is based on arms and if the citizen body is armed
and virtuous, misgovernment can easily be prevented.[25]

By saying that Christianity has rendered the world weak Machiavelli does not deny that Christianity wields very great power.
We must try to show how he could have accounted on the basis
of his principles for the victory of Christianity. According to him,
Christianity acquired its power through a particular constellation
of circumstances, or "the quality of the times." Rome had destroyed freedom and the spirit of freedom in the only part of the
world in which freedom ever existed. Rome itself had become
corrupt. The Romans had lost their political virtue. Roman men
and especially Roman women became fascinated by foreign cults.
Christianity originated among people who completely lacked political power and therefore could afford to have a simple belief in
morality. The severe morality preached and practiced by the early
Christians created respect and awe especially in those subjects of

the Roman empire who equally lacked political power. By de-
manding humility, Christianity appealed to the humble and gave
them strength. It thus was enabled to inherit the Roman empire
and whatever remained of the classical arts and sciences. In this
shape it confronted and over-awed the young and vigorous if rude
nations which conquered the Roman empire. It succeeded in putting its stamp on those nations so deeply that the Roman modes
and orders have not yet been restored, not to say surpassed.

Machiavelli appears to judge Christianity with exclusive regard
to an end which is not specifically religious, namely, political happiness, i.e. strength and freedom combined. He is so confident of
the propriety of such judgment that he can indicate that, by
making the Italians thoroughly irreligious, the Roman Church has
harmed Italy less than by keeping Italy divided.[26] He begs the
decisive question unless one would say that a divinely established
order is of necessity good also with a view to political happiness or
that according to the Bible itself its political arrangements are
perfect and not essentially punitive. To enter a deeper layer of
Machiavelli's argument, we start from the observation that he
applies almost the same expression to both Philip of Macedon and
Ferdinand of Aragon.[27] It looks as though he had known or foreseen that, just as Philip was succeeded by Alexander the Great,
Ferdinand was or would be succeeded by Charles V, the ruler of
an empire on which the sun never sets. We must then consider how
in his opinion the strength compatible with the Biblical teaching
differs from the strength of the ancient Romans. Whereas Philip
used most cruel means which were inimical not only to the Christian way of life but to the humane one as well, Ferdinand always
used religion as a cloak, and turning to pious cruelty, hunted the
Marranos from his kingdom and deprived it of them. "A certain
present-day prince, whom it is not good to name, never preaches
anything but peace and faith and is the greatest enemy of the one
and of the other, and one as well as the other if he had observed
them, would many times have taken from him either his reputation
or his state." Through using both pious cruelty and faithlessness
Ferdinand became out of a weak king the first king of the Christians in fame and in glory. His fame and glory is then not comparable to that of the good Roman emperors under whom the
world was filled with peace and justice, not to say with peace and

faith, and whose times were the golden times when everyone could hold and defend every opinion he wished. Ferdinand is a good example of a fox; he is not, like the criminal Roman emperor Severus, a good example of both a fox and a lion. The outstanding contemporary Christian prince is inferior in goodness to the good Roman emperors and inferior in badness to the bad Roman emperors: he does not "know how to be altogether bad or altogether good."[28] Through his arrangement of subject matter and his choice of examples in the *Prince* as well as through the "repetition" in the *Discourses*, Machiavelli suggests that the moderns are not inferior to the ancients in faithlessness, are inferior to them in cruelty,[29] and are superior to them in pious cruelty. Ferdinand's expulsion of the Marranos was "a rare example" but hardly "a grand enterprise." It was an act of pious cruelty; Machiavelli does not say that it was an act of cruelty well used.[30] He has much to say in favor of cruelty. Certainly a new prince cannot avoid acquiring a reputation for cruelty.[31] The most important remarks on cruelty occur in the Tacitean subsection of the *Discourses*. Hannibal's cruelty, not to say inhuman cruelty, was justified by the fact that he was the captain of an army which consisted of men of many races. Could it be that the government of an ethnically heterogeneous mixed body, of a society embracing members of many nations, not to say all nations, requires a degree of severity which would not be needed for the good government of a homogeneous society? Certainly only a being "born of man" can be expected to have those feelings of humanity which lead to revulsion against tyranny. According to Machiavelli, even in a homogeneous society like the early Roman republic, cruelty or extreme severity of leading citizens is most useful or desirable. It makes a man thought to be a lover of nothing except the fatherland or the common good, or to be thoroughly just, and to be completely indifferent to his or others' private good.[32] The Biblical expression for love of the common good is love of the neighbor whom one is commanded to love as oneself. According to the Biblical teaching, love of the neighbor is inseparable from love of God whom one is commanded to love with all his heart, with all his soul, and with all his might. From Machiavelli's point of view, the Biblical teaching regarding man's destiny appeared to lead to a more than Manlian severity, to pious cruelty, as a duty. We must try to understand what he meant by indicating that the Biblical God is a tyrant.[33] The Biblical command is revealed; its acceptance is based not on reason but on authority; authority will not be accepted in the long run and by many people if it cannot use compulsion "in order to keep firm those who already believe and in order to make the unbelievers believe"; for not only actions but beliefs are demanded. To demand belief is to stamp as criminal or sinful thoughts of a certain kind which man cannot help thinking precisely because of the unevident character of what man is commanded to believe; it means to induce men to confess with their tongues what they do not believe in their hearts; it is destructive of generosity. The Biblical command is very difficult to fulfill, and it is a most true rule that when difficult things are commanded, harshness, and not sweetness, is needed in order to bring about obedience.[34] The Biblical command cannot be fulfilled: all men are sinners; the universality of this proposition proves that all men are necessarily sinners; this necessity must derive from a disproportion between the command and man's nature or original constitution. Man is so placed that he is capable of deserving infinite punishment but not infinite reward; while he is punished as a matter of right, his reward is entirely a matter of grace. The Biblical command given to man out of love for man implies as command that man can rebel against God or hate God or that man can be an enemy of God. Disobedience to God and estrangement from God is in itself absolute misery. Those who neither adhere to God nor rebel against God may deserve infinite contempt; those guilty of rebellion deserve infinite pity because they cannot have understood what they did. Yet that rebellion is in addition a crime which must be punished. Punishment must fit the crime. Eternal and infinite punishment—punishment which excludes the possibility of repentance or forgiveness—is needed. The punishment meted out or threatened by God becomes the model for man's punitive justice. The God of Love is necessarily an angry God who "revengeth and is furious" and "reserveth wrath for his enemies," a consuming fire, who has created Hell before he created man, and the fire of Hell is reflected in the fire with which the enemies of God are burned at the stake by faithful men.[35] Machiavelli tacitly rejects the very notion of divine punishment. Whereas according to his understanding of the Christian teaching one should obey evil rulers and let God chastise them, he prefers to follow provisionally the golden sentence of the historian Tacitus according to which one should obey evil rulers; shortly afterward, he quotes two verses in which it is said that few tyrants "descend to the son-in-law of Ceres without murder and wounds":[36] Pluto is not the Devil, Hades is not Hell, to say nothing of the fact that it is fit for poets to use "poetic fables." Machiavelli teaches that man's nature is not bad, originally or as a consequence of sin; men are often corrupt; yet this corruption can be counteracted only by "the virtue of a man who is alive at that time"; corrupt men can only be restrained by a practically regal power and this means of course by the power of a human king; any other way of attempting to make them good would be either a most cruel enterprise or else altogether impossible.[37] On the basis of the Biblical teaching, love of God becomes fervent zeal for the glory of God; it becomes a passion which in Machiavelli's eyes is not distinguishable from the passion of partisanship or fanatical loyalty to a leader whose cause is not identical with the common good of a particular state. From this Machiavelli can understand why Christian nations as Christians can rear good soldiers. Whereas the ancient Romans were good and faithful soldiers because they fought for their own glory, Christians may be good and faithful soldiers because they fight for the glory of God.[38]

When Machiavelli teaches that Christianity has rendered the world weak by commanding men not to glory in their virtue and power, he means also that Christianity has lowered the stature of man by rejecting the seeking of one's own honor and one's own glory as such. The distrust of the concern with one's own honor and glory goes hand in hand with the distrust of one's own virtue: one ought to put one's trust less in flesh and blood, in men's will, and ultimately in one's own arms, virtue and prudence than in prayer and in God. If one were to follow the Bible, one could not count Moses among those new princes who acquired their power by their own arms and their own virtue. One would have to say that he deserves admiration "only with regard to that grace which made him worthy to speak with God." God desires that the glory be given to him while he leaves us "part of that glory which belongs to us," whereas the leading Romans who trusted in their own arms and courage desired that "the glory should belong wholly" to the victorious consuls. According to Machia-

velli, man will not reach his highest stature if he himself does not
demand the highest from himself without relying on support
from powers outside of him, and if he cannot find his satisfaction
in his achievement as his own achievement. Not trust in God and
self-denial but self-reliance and self-love is the root of human
strength and greatness. Trust in one's own virtue enables one to
have trust in the virtue of other men.[39] Consciousness of excellence
on the part of excellent men must take the place of consciousness
of guilt or sin. That man is mortal does not mean that he should
regard himself as dust and ashes; it means in the case of the best
men that they seek immortal glory. The truth in the assertion that
all men are sinners is that all men however excellent are imperfect.
No one can possess all perfections. A man's excellence will necessarily be accompanied by specific shortcomings, for the various
kinds of excellence cannot co-exist in the same individual, at least
not on their highest level. Certain excellences are denied to men
by the very nature which enables and compels them to acquire
other excellences. To say nothing of the fact that the nature of
man, of human society, nay of fame and infamy itself implies that
the large majority of men will be neither famous nor infamous.
Machiavelli goes further. Man is by nature compelled to sin. Subjects are compelled to be disloyal to a prince who, without any
fault of his own, is unable to protect them. "Our nature does not
consent" to any man remaining on "the true way," "the way of
the mean." Some men are compelled by their natures to be cruel
or arrogant or irascible so that their efforts to be gentle or humble
or meek are tantamount to attempts to change their natures, and
the results will be indistinguishable from more or less successful
dissimulation. For instance, Pope Julius II was incapable of proceeding with humility and meekness and compelled by his nature
to proceed with ferocity and fury.[40] Machiavelli is willing to
compare his admired Roman nobility to small birds of prey whose
natural greed makes them unaware of the big bird which is about
to swoop upon them; he is then willing to grant even more than
was meant by the saying that the virtues of the Romans were
resplendent vices; yet this does not prevent him from holding up
as models the qualities and achievements of the Roman nobility,
although those very achievements prepared the ruin of the Roman
nobility and of the Roman republic by the big bird Caesar. For

such is the nature of human life that actions prompted by un-
Christian and even inhuman passions can redound to the lasting,
although never perpetual, benefits of society and even of Christianity, nay, may be required by the needs of society or of the Church;
to expect perpetual benefits is unreasonable since no mixed body
can be perpetual. The sins which ruin states are military rather
than moral sins. On the other hand, faith, goodness, humility and
patience may be the road to ruin, as everyone understanding anything of the things of the world will admit. There is no pious
work which may not be the origin of tyranny and therefore in
fact be cruel. Pious bequests for the benefit of the poor and the
sick will lead sooner or later to the accumulation of very great
wealth in the hands of pious administrators; this wealth is bound
to have its natural effects on the administrators and the people who
look up to them, regardless of the quality of their intentions. Despite the necessary connection between good and evil, or virtues
and vices, a crude and simple political virtue can be instilled into
the minds of the citizens and can be made dominant in a city.
Corruption in the politically relevant sense is destructive of this
kind of virtue. But corruption thus understood is caused, not by
sin but by temptations which the large majority of men cannot
possibly resist; those temptations are caused by such things as
intercourse with foreigners and gross inequality. Given the in-
stability of human things, states cannot choose the true way or
the right mean which consists in keeping what one has and in not
taking away from others what belongs to them; one is forced to
choose one of the extremes: either to allow the others to take
away from one what one has or else to take away from others
what belongs to them; honor, worldly honor, dictates the choice
of the latter. Yet it is not always and not fundamentally honor
which dictates that choice. Should Heaven be so kind to men that
they should never be compelled to go to war, they would become
effeminate or else engage in civil strife. Thanks to Heaven's deficient kindness, nations sometimes wage war because the alternative
is to perish through famine. This kind of war is much more cruel
than the one caused by love of honor and glory because in wars
of survival the survival of every member is at stake.[41] The warriors
fight for the very life of their neighbors, their fathers, their children and their womenfolk. In this case, the fulfillment of the divine

command to multiply reduces large multitudes to the necessity of massacring large multitudes or else of committing the sin of suicide. Since the attacked nation is in the same danger as the attacking one, the war is just on both sides. One cannot say that this difficulty is limited to states; it suffices to think of the two shipwrecked men on a raft. It is hard to say that the famine is a punishment for sin. For a punishment for sin which compels men to sin still more, or at any rate to behave with the utmost savagery, does not appear to be wise. It is then ultimately the nature of man and of man's situation which accounts for the necessity to sin.

Once one realizes the power of that necessity which is the natural necessity to sin, and therewith the inseparable connection between sinning and everything noble and high, one will cease to deplore that necessity or to wish it away. Nor will one disingenuously conceal it from oneself, for instance by presenting acts of savagery or of astuteness prompted by necessity or even by the desire for honor or glory as acts of love or piety. Knowing that all men seek wealth or honor, one will be certain that the desire for distinction and all its noble and base companions affect even those who are reputed to be saints. One will recognize the desire for dominion in what presents itself as charity and one will recognize in religion a kind of "the arts of peace" not morally different from the art of war. Gratitude is the root or support of all profound obligation. By his virtue and merits Scipio had deserved the gratitude of all Romans. Yet by his very virtue and merits he had become a menace to Roman freedom. It was Cato, the reputed saint, who stood up for Rome's freedom and was not ashamed to act, or to appear to act, ungratefully. Tutored by Machiavelli, we must assume that Cato's good conscience in acting as he did is indistinguishable from his envy of Scipio's fame.[42] Awareness of the necessity mentioned will secure "knowers of the world" who are fortunate enough to be born with the right kind of temper, against both pride or arrogance and humility or abjectness. The most excellent men will have a proper estimate of their worth and of the conduct becoming to them, and they will not be shaken in their opinion and their conduct by the whims of fortune. They will live in an even temper without hope and without fear or trembling. They may have regrets but they will feel no need for repentance or redemption, unless it be the redemption of their fatherland from foreign or tyrannical domination. Imitating nature, they will be filled with both gravity and levity but they will be free from fanaticism. They will not expect to find perfection or immortality anywhere except in works of art. They will regard as the virtue opposite to pride or arrogance, not humility, but humanity or generosity.[43]

This is the place to survey Machiavelli's teaching regarding the conscience. He does not often speak of the conscience. In the *Florentine Histories*, which are almost as long as the *Prince* and the *Discourses* taken together, there occur five mentions of the conscience; four mentions occur in speeches by Machiavelli's characters; the fifth and last mention occurs in Machiavelli's description of Piero de'Medici who was inferior in virtue of the mind and of the body to his father Cosimo and his son Lorenzo.[44] In the *Discourses*, he speaks of the conscience on four occasions. Baglioni did not abstain from killing or otherwise hurting the Pope and all cardinals "for reasons of either goodness or conscience, for into the breast of a criminal man who kept his sister, who had killed his cousins and nephews in order to reign, no pious or compassionate respect could descend." Machiavelli clearly distinguishes here between "goodness" and "conscience" as two different sources of restraint. We are inclined to believe that whereas Baglioni's lack of goodness or compassion showed itself in his murders, his lack of conscience or piety showed itself in his incest. When Machiavelli speaks later on of a sin similar to incest, namely, sodomy— he does this shortly after having referred to the *ius gentium* which, to say the least, reminds one of the natural law—he says of a youth who refused to comply with the desire of a man merely that that youth was "averse to things of this kind"; the crime of the older man consisted in using force in order to satisfy his desire.[45] The second mention of conscience likewise occurs within a Christian context. Machiavelli compares or contrasts two similar cases which show "the goodness and religion" of the common people in incorrupt cities; one example is Roman, the other is Christian; only in the Christian example does he mention the conscience. When the German cities levy a property tax, each citizen takes an oath that he will pay the proper amount and then throws into a public chest the sum of money which "according to conscience he believes he ought to pay; of this payment no one is

witness except him who pays."[46] By virtue of the conscience, a
man judges by himself and in solitude as to what he ought to do.
But the conscience also pronounces a man's own and solitary judgment on whether he did what he ought to have done. The conscience of a man is the witness within him; this witness is in many
cases the only witness to what he does and, so to speak, in all cases
the only witness to what he believes. The goodness and religion
of the Christians is connected with the belief that everything a
man does or believes is witnessed not only by the man himself but
by God as well. As one would expect, Machiavelli is silent about
God's witnessing or the relation between the conscience and God.
We are led to wonder what Machiavelli thought about the status
of the conscience: Does it belong to man's natural constitution or
to the natural constitution of men of a certain type or is it the
work of society, if not of societies of a certain kind? With a view
to what does the conscience decide on what a man ought to do?
What is the relevance of a man's condemnation by his conscience?
To answer these questions, one would have to summarize Machiavelli's analysis of morality. At present we note that he does not
speak of pangs of conscience whereas he speaks of the pangs of
ingratitude suffered or injustice suffered. He does this while showing that the vice of ingratitude is the effect of a natural necessity.[47]
If man is compelled to sin, there is no reason why he should have
a bad conscience for sinning. If human goodness and the conscience
belong to two different orders, there may be badness undisturbed
by conscience. This conclusion is confirmed by Machiavelli's numerous and detailed stories of famous and otherwise contented
criminals. The satisfaction of a good conscience is not in all cases
as gratifying as the sweetness of triumph or of revenge. The third
mention of *coscienza* occurs in a context which is no longer obviously Christian. The Latins had secretly prepared a revolt against
the Romans. The Romans became aware of this and asked the Latins
to send a certain number of Latin citizens to Rome for consulta-
tion. Thereupon, the Latins knew that the Romans knew of the
conspiracy. The Latins knew—or, more literally, had awareness
(*coscienza*)—of many things which they had done against the will
of the Romans. Originally, only the Latins knew of their preparations for revolt; thereafter, the Romans shared this knowledge
with the Latins without the Latins knowing that their knowledge

was shared by the Romans; finally, the Latins shared with the Romans the knowledge that the Romans knew of the Latin conspiracy. Only because the Latins and the Romans "knew together" that both knew the secret of the Latins, could the Latins have had a bad conscience. But in fact the Latins were not afraid. They were fearless not because the Romans had been most unjust to them or because they trusted in the justice of their cause, but because they had awareness (*conscientia*) of their power on the one hand and of the power of the Romans on the other. The event showed indeed that they had not "measured well their forces"[48] and therewith that they ought to have a bad conscience, because they knew that the Romans had come to know their intentions. Could the conscience in Machiavelli's opinion be based on true knowledge of the relation of the power of man to the power of God? In that case, the conscience would be prudence modified by the knowledge of the overwhelming power of God who punishes every action done against his will. Certainly one of Machiavelli's characters identifies the conscience with the fear of hell.[49] The last mention of conscience occurs in the chapter on conspiracies. Despite the Christian command and the Tacitean counsel not to conspire against princes, even if they are evil, "many attempt" such conspiracies. Machiavelli desires to buttress the command and the counsel and thus to achieve what neither the command nor the counsel had ever achieved by showing that ordinary prudence strongly dissuades from conspiracies against princes. Conspiracies against princes, as distinguished from conspiracies against the fatherland for instance, are by far the most dangerous enterprises. This does not mean that all conspiracies against princes are doomed to failure and that if they succeed the reward is disproportionate to the toil and anguish of the conspirator. Conspiracies may be said to be distinguished from all other crimes by the fact that if they fully succeed, their very notoriety contributes to the extinction of their criminality and they may carry with them rewards surpassing by far the rewards to be hoped for from any other action. Successful conspiracies may therefore be said to shake the common notions regarding penal justice. In addition, conspiracies are enterprises in which human beings share, or "know together," a punishable secret or in which there are necessarily *conscii*. Machiavelli speaks of the conscience explicitly in that part of the chapter which deals with the dangers run during the execution of the conspiracy. In the first example, he mentions a conspirator who was willing to kill a Medici but not to kill him in church; it would seem, although Machiavelli does not say so, that that man was restrained by his conscience; his conscience spoke against sacrilege but not against homicide. Machiavelli then turns to those dangers run during the execution which are caused by failure of courage and lack of prudence. Failure of courage may be caused by rever·ence or by cowardice; or, as Machiavelli shows by his example, reverence may make a man vile; in cases of this kind men do not know what stopped them; for what stopped them was an uncanny mixture of power and graciousness. One cannot say that the failure was due either to lack of courage or to lack of prudence but one can say definitely that it was due to "a confusion of the brain." After having turned to another part of the argument, Machiavelli speaks of his own reverence for a historian called Herodian whose authority induces him to believe something which he would never otherwise have believed to be possible. Returning to the earlier part of the argument Machiavelli speaks of the dangers to the execution which are caused by "false imaginations." Those who conspired against Caesar were tempted to murder him at the wrong time because they had "a false imagination": they wrongly believed that Caesar knew of their conspiracy. The false imagination consisted in a wrong interpretation of an accident. It was caused by the "stained conscience" of the conspirators, i.e. by their belief that there might be a disapproving witness of their secret.[50] Was the bad conscience of these ancient Romans caused by the suspicion that they did wrong or by fear of detection by human beings? Machiavelli forces us to raise this question but does not answer it. For the time being we suggest that Machiavelli tried to replace the conscience, or religion, by a kind of prudence which is frequently indistinguishable from mere calculation of worldly gain: "the true way" consists, not in obeying God's invariable law, but in acting according to the times.[51]

It is impossible to excuse the inadequacy of Machiavelli's argument by referring to the things he had seen in contemporary Rome and Florence. For he knew that the notorious facts which allowed him to speak of the corruption of Italy proved at the same time the corruption of Christianity in Italy. It is somewhat worthier but still insufficient to excuse the inadequacy of Machiavelli's argument by the indescribable misuse of the Biblical teaching of which believers in all ages have been guilty. At any rate, many present-day readers who have some understanding of the Bible are likely to be less shocked than amazed by Machiavelli's suggestions. They have become accustomed, not only to distinguish between the core and the periphery of the Biblical teaching, but to abandon that periphery as unnecessary or mythical. Machiavelli was unaware of the legitimacy of this distinction.[52] Recent theology has become inclined to deny that divine punishment is more than the misery which is the natural or necessary consequence of the estrangement from God or of the oblivion of God, or than the emptiness, the vanity, the repulsive or resplendent misery, or the despair of a life which is not adherence to God and trust in God. The same theology tends to solve the difficulty inherent in the relation between omnipotence and omniscience on the one hand and human freedom on the other by reducing providence to God's enabling man to work out his destiny without any further divine intervention except God's waiting for man's response to his call. Machiavelli's indications regarding providence are concerned with that notion of providence according to which God literally governs the world as a just king governs his kingdom. He does not pay any attention to the fact that the prosperity of the wicked and the afflictions of the just were always regarded by thinking believers as an essential part of the mystery of the providential order. We almost see him as he hears the saying "all they that take the sword shall perish by the sword" and answers "but they who do not take the sword shall also perish by the sword": he does not stop to consider that only the first, by appealing to the sword, submit entirely to the judgment of the sword and therefore are self-condemned, seeing that no mixed body is perpetual.

Machiavelli's characters in his *Florentine Histories* speak as a matter of course explicitly of God's justice as the cause of their actual or hoped for successes against their enemies as well as of their own misfortunes, and of their successes as proofs of the justice of their cause.[53] In the same work, which is dedicated to the Medici Pope Clement VII, Machiavelli in his own name twice speaks explicitly and without qualifying expressions like "it seems," of God's taking care of men insofar as God's providence relates to justice. The first remark occurs in an excursus which is preceded by an account of the consequences of the capture of Constantinople by the Turks and of the victory of the Christians over the Turks at Belgrade. These two events may be said to have been the greatest exhibitions of the power of human arms which are mentioned in the work. At that time when, owing to the Turkish danger, men had laid down arms in Italy, God seemed to wish to take them up. An awful storm and whirlwind in which superior forces, "natural or supernatural," were at work, terrified Tuscany so that everyone judged that the end of the world had come; very great harm was done to the country, houses and temples were ruined, but not many people were killed. "Undoubtedly God wished to threaten rather than chastise Tuscany." He wished that "this little example should suffice for refreshing among men the memory of his power." The second remark occurs in Machiavelli's account of the events of the year 1480. Not only the Florentine people, "subtle interpreters of all things," but the leading men too asserted that Florence had never been in so great a danger of losing her liberty. The Medici were in particular danger. "But God who always in similar extremities has had particular care of (Florence), made an unexpected accident arise" which caused the Pope and the other enemies of Florence to turn to something else. The unexpected accident through which God saved Florence from the Pope and his allies was the landing of the Turks at Otranto, their sacking of that town, their killing all its inhabitants and their "good cavalry" devastating the countryside. God's special care for Florence showed itself in his threatening his vicar with the power of the infidels. The Pope became meek and willing after the example of the highest Redeemer to embrace the Florentines with the utmost compassion.[54]

But let us return to the *Prince* and the *Discourses* in which Machiavelli sets forth "everything he knows." His doctrine regarding providence[55] may be summarized as follows. Since man is by natural necessity compelled to be ungrateful to man, he has no reason to be grateful to God. For if there is a natural necessity to sin, one is compelled to ascribe to God the origin of evil; one cannot speak of God as pure goodness or as the highest good which does not contain any evil within itself. Man cannot be expected to be grateful to God for undeserved blessings since he receives with equal abundance sufferings which he does not deserve. Necessity rather than God or necessity governing God or necessity in God, not to say chance, and not human merit or demerit, is the cause of those blessings or sufferings which are not due to man's own prudence or folly. We find just retribution only where just men rule. Every other just government is imaginary. The effective rule of just men depends on good arms, on human prudence and on some measure of good luck. There is no shred of evidence supporting the assertion that chance favors the just more than the unjust. God is not a judge or even an arbiter but a neutral. If it is true that extreme injustice arouses men's hatred, resistance and desire for revenge, it is also true that perfect justice would paralyze the hands of government; states can only be governed by a judicious mixture of justice and injustice. God is with the strongest battalions, which does not mean that he is with the largest number of battalions. Virtue, i.e. man's own virtue, and chance take the place of providence.

In the last chapter of the *Prince* Machiavelli speaks of what God has done in order to help the Italians to redeem their country. He mentions there some extraordinary events without example which resemble miracles performed on the way from Egypt to the promised land. Yet there is this decisive difference between the Biblical miracles and Machiavelli's extraordinary events. The Biblical miracles evidently protected the children of Israel against their enemies, against their losing their way in the desert, against thirst and against hunger and thus contributed to their safely reaching the promised land. Machiavelli's extraordinary events have no evident relation to the needs of the Italians; they appear to be entirely useless. Of ecclesiastical principalities, Machiavelli says that while they are undefended, they are not taken away from their rulers because they are exalted and maintained by God; somewhat later he says that without having arms of its own, no principality is secure but it is entirely dependent upon chance since it lacks virtue which would defend it faithfully in adversity; immediately afterward he quotes a Tacitean sentence which deals with the weakness of such a reputation for power as is not based on force; Tacitus speaks only of the reputation of mortals; Machiavelli changes the text so that the text speaks by implication of the reputation of immortals as well.[56] In the chapter on principalities acquired by crime, by the breach of human and divine law, Machiavelli describes what one is tempted to call the speedy punishment of the parricide Liverotto; yet that speedy punishment proved to be possible only because of Liverotto's "simplicity" or Cesare Borgia's superiority in crime. Answering a doubt with his creed, Machiavelli says in the same context that Agathocles could live securely for a long time in his fatherland after he had committed innumerable treacheries and cruel deeds because he used his cruelty judiciously; God opposed his designs as little as he did those of Cesare Borgia.[57] All conspiracies against the Roman emperors which were undertaken by men who had been made great by the emperors in question had "the end which the ingratitude of the conspirators deserved," i.e. a bad end. But a similar conspiracy in more recent times had a good end. Is retribution for ingratitude less effective now than it was under the pagan emperors? Another modern conspiracy of the same kind "ought to have had a good end" because the conditions were highly favorable to its success: Machiavelli has learned through the comparison of the ancients and the moderns that there is no correspondence between success and justice but only a correspondence between success and prudence in the crude sense.[58] Considerations of crude prudence would be affected by expectations of punishment after death or, more generally, by belief in the immortality of the soul. Machiavelli reveals his opinion on this subject clearly enough by refusing to use, in the *Prince* and the *Discourses*, as distinguished from his other writings, the terms "soul,"[59] "the other life" or "the other world." Two ways are open to founders, the way of kingship and the way of tyranny: "one which makes them live securely and renders them glorious after death; the other makes them live in continuous anguish and makes them leave, after death, an infamy which lasts always."[60] "Life" means here only "this life"; after life, there is no longer either security or anguish, continuous or discontinuous, but fame or infamy of which the dead are not aware. In opposing the imagined republics and principalities which are based on the assumption that man can act as he ought to act, Machiavelli states that by acting as one ought to act, one is likely to bring about one's ruin:[61] he does not even allude to the danger of eternal ruin which may be run by those who do not act as they ought to act. The dangers run in a conspiracy, i.e. the dangers of torture

and death, "surpass by far every other kind of danger" and therefore, we must add, the danger of damnation.[62] Or did Machiavelli
believe that the danger of damnation can be averted by repentance
and perhaps even by repentance on the deathbed? "Penitence," he
says in his *Exhortation to Penitence*, "is the sole remedy which can
wipe out all evils, all errors of men." He does not even allude to
this possibility in the *Prince* and the *Discourses*.

If all men's being sinners would have to be understood as a
consequence of sin, man must have been radically different prior
to his original sin from what he is now; his passions must have
been different; this would require, as matters stand, that man was
created in the image of God and that man, and the world as a
whole, had a beginning in time: there was a first man not born
of man. "In the beginning of the world, the inhabitants being
scarce, men lived for some time dispersed in similitude to the
beasts."[63] If we assume that in considering this sentence Machiavelli remembered the fact that there are gregarious beasts, he would
be making two suggestions by means of the sentence quoted: in the
beginning of the world men lived both dispersed and in similitude
to the beasts. In addition, the Bible denies that in the beginning
of the world men—Adam and Eve—lived dispersed. Certainly,
Machiavelli's notion of the beginning of the world is not the
Biblical but rather the "Epicurean" notion which presupposes the
eternity of "matter"; by assuming that matter is uncreated, one
could admit the necessity of evil or of sin without derogating from
God's goodness.[64] Certain scholars believe that every difficulty
vanishes once one assumes that in the passage quoted Machiavelli
merely copies Polybius. Apart from the fact, which we regard as
most important, that Machiavelli does not deign to mention Polybius, Polybius does not say that men lived in the beginning of
the world dispersed like beasts. He implies that in the beginning
there were only few men, and he says that only at a later date
they formed herds as do other animals. Above all, he makes it
quite clear that he does not speak of the beginning of the world
but of the beginning of the world's present epoch which began
after an almost complete destruction of the human race; and he
teaches explicitly that such destructions have occurred and will
occur many times. If Machiavelli had referred us to Polybius,
we would be inclined to believe that he wished here to indicate

that "the beginning of the world" is in fact only the beginning of the present epoch of civilized life on earth which is preceded by other such epochs. In the first of three parallel statements he declares that there has been no change in the motion, the order, and the power of heaven, the sun, the elements, and man since antiquity. In the second statement he declares that men always were born, lived and died under the same order. In the third statement he declares that in all cities and in all nations there are, and there always will be the same desires and the same humors. Twenty-six chapters later he silently expresses his view on the creation of the world by refuting an argument advanced against the most famous alternative thesis which affirms the eternity of the visible universe. At the beginning of the 136th chapter he indicates, while referring to a saying of the prudent, that men always had and will have the same passions and that therefore there always have been and will be the same consequences of the passions, i.e., the same human actions, unless the actions are modified to some extent by education.[65] "I judge that the world has always been in the same manner and there has been (always) as much good as there has been evil."[66]

Almost all statements just referred to express mere judgments, i.e., mere conclusions without the reasoning supporting them. The only exception is Machiavelli's summary refutation of an argument in favor of creation. "To those philosophers who have meant that the world has been eternal, I believe, one could reply that if so great an antiquity were true, it would be reasonable that there should be memory of more than 5000 years—if it were not visible how those memories of the times are extinguished by various causes."[67] The weakness of a single argument in favor of the beginning of the world is not a sufficient ground for rejecting the Biblical account. Machiavelli draws our attention to "those philosophers" who taught that the world is eternal, or, in other words, that there is no efficient cause of the world. Savonarola mentions contemporary "worldly wise" men who assert that God is not the efficient but the final cause of the world as well as that there is only one soul in all men, i.e., that there is no immortality of individual souls. The men who held these views were the Averroists.[68] The fundamental tenets of Averroism were as well known to intelligent men of Machiavelli's age as the fundamental tenets of, say,

Marxism are in the present age. We must turn to the books of the "Averroists" in order to complete Machiavelli's intimations and to fill the gaps between the seemingly unconnected denials without which his political teaching as a whole would be baseless. The most important of those books are not easier of access than are Machiavelli's books.

At first glance, Machiavelli seems merely to attempt to show that the Biblical teaching contradicts experience or contradicts itself. He does not refer to the possibility that human assertions regarding God and divine things are necessarily self-contradictory nor does he consider the limitations of experience as he understood experience. A "first man," a "man not born of man" is essentially inaccessible to our experience, and yet the Epicureans in former times and today even people who do not believe in the truth of the Bible admit, on the basis of reasonings which start from experience, that there were "first men," men not generated by men. Machiavelli goes beyond the ways of reasoning mentioned by suggesting that there is no evidence supporting the Biblical teaching. He may be said to exclude dogmatically all evidence which is not ultimately derived from phenomena that are at all times open to everyone's inspection in broad daylight. Or, to elaborate a suggestion which he makes, whereas Isaac judged rightly by hearing but falsely by touching, Machiavelli holds that one judges falsely not only by hearing but even by seeing and that the few who are able to judge, judge well by touching: in order not to be deceived, one must be close to the deceptive things and immune to false imaginations.[69] By complying with his canon of criticism, he is led to think that the beginnings of revealed religion, as all other beginnings, are not only necessarily imperfect or of deficient goodness but also imperfectly known. The study of the Roman commonwealth led him to the insight that there was not a single founder but a continuous series of founders; this insight must be applied to the other mixed bodies.[70] We would go too far were we to assert that Machiavelli has never heard the Call nor sensed the Presence, for we would contradict his remarks referring to the conscience. But he certainly refuses to heed experiences of this kind. If we consider the case of the man whose conscience spoke against sacrilege but not against homicide, we become inclined to believe that, according to Machiavelli, every articulation of the dictate of the conscience needs a support different from the conscience itself. In accordance with this, traditional theology had a proper regard for the objective evidence concerning the beginnings of revealed religion.

Whereas Machiavelli does not explicitly discuss the beginnings of Christianity, he explicitly discusses what one may call the beginnings of Judaism. He opens that discussion by saying that one ought not to reason about Moses since he was merely an executor of the things which God commanded him, and that only a presumptuous and temerarious man would discuss ecclestiastical principalities since they are ruled by higher causes than the human mind can reach. Even the increase of the temporal power of the Church is discussed by Machiavelli only with a view to the possibility that someone might ask him about the subject.[71] Although one cannot reason about Moses, "yet he ought to be admired solely on account of that grace which made him worthy to speak with God." Does God give his grace without any regard to the previous worthiness of the individual concerned? Did Moses lack virtue of his own? Machiavelli settles these questions by counting Moses among those who became princes by their own virtue and their own arms. He goes on to say that if one considers the actions and "the particular institutions" of men like Cyrus, one will not find them discrepant from those of Moses "who had so great a teacher," namely, God and not "Chiron." Whereas the Bible asserts that there is a fundamental difference between Moses and other founders like Cyrus and Romulus, reason does not find such a difference: the Mosaic foundation was as purely human as all other foundations.[72] As Machiavelli suggests shortly thereafter, states are natural things:[73] no state, not even the state founded by Moses, has a supernatural basis. In the lives of the founders one finds much to admire but one does not find miracles. "The actions and the life" of Moses and Cyrus show that God was not more a friend to them than he is to the house of the Medici who have been encouraged by extraordinary events without examples, but not by miracles. Or if one insists on finding miracles in the life of Moses, one must also admit the miracles told in the lives of other founders. According to the order of a cruel king, the new-born Moses was to be thrown into a river and yet he was saved; according to the order of a cruel king, the new-born Romulus was to be thrown into a river and yet he was miraculously saved. Hiero of Syracuse, who can be compared to founders like Romulus and Moses, was exposed as an infant and saved miraculously by bees which fed him; other portents distinguished him in his later life.[74] The Biblical miracles and revelations are as credible as the miracles and revelations of the pagans. If Moses and Savonarola speak with God, Numa speaks with a nymph. Machiavelli does not believe that there are nymphs nor that one can speak with God: one does not hear the words of God but only the words of men. He says therefore that Numa pretended he spoke with a nymph, and he implies that Savonarola and Moses deceived themselves in believing that they spoke with God. Moses and Savonarola did what they did on their own authority. There is no essential difference between the decay of paganism and the decay of Christianity. Religion belongs to the desires and humors which are always the same in all nations.[75] We find *padri* in pagan Rome as well as in Christianity. As Machiavelli makes us realize by both treating Demetrius and Pompey as parallels and yet being silent as to a point concerning Demetrius, as to which he is not silent regarding Pompey, and by thus inducing us to look up his source, the people of Athens decreed that Demetrius be given the appellation "Saviour-god." According to Livy, Alexander of Epirus went to Italy because he wished to escape the doom threatened by an oracle of Jupiter; Machiavelli makes him go to Italy because he was deceived by exiles: there is no fundamental difference between people who, being full of faith and full of hope of returning to their fatherland, promise that fatherland to anyone likely to help them, on the one hand, and ancient oracles on the other.[76]

According to Machiavelli, Biblical religion and pagan religion have this in common, that they are both of merely human origin. As for the essential difference between them, he is primarily concerned with its political aspects. The independent Old Testament priests and prophets and the independent Christian clergy have no parallel in the Roman republic but they correspond in certain respects to the "third" force, different from the prince and the people, which existed under the Roman emperors, i.e., to the soldiers. The contrast between priests and soldiers indicates the essential difference. The preponderance of "arms and the man" in pagan Rome explains why the Romans were less in need of "others" for their defense or why they were less dependent on fortresses and consolations or why they were less exposed to Fortuna than the moderns. To repeat Machiavelli's primary contention, whereas the pagan religion was conducive to the triumph of the world, Christianity has rendered the world weak.[77] Since the character of a society is determined by the character of its ruling element or of its "princes," the difference between paganism, or at any rate Roman paganism, and Christianity must be traced to the fact that in Rome a warlike nobility predominated whereas Christianity was originally a popular and not war-like movement. For Machiavelli it is not an accident that the Church favored the popular element in the Italian cities against the nobles. The Roman counterpart to Savonarola was the plebeian leader Virginius; but as long as Rome remained incorrupt, men like Virginius could never play the role which Savonarola played in Florence; the senate was there to undeceive the people. The difference between paganism and Christianity would then seem to be rooted in the fundamental difference of political "humors," the "humor" of the great and that of the people. Machiavelli is willing to praise the intention of the populist Gracchi but he cannot praise their prudence, for, to say nothing of their peculiar mistake, the preponderance of the great and exalted over the weak and humble is essential to the strength of society.[78] If it is true, as Machiavelli contends, that unarmed prophets necessarily fail, one would have to say that Christianity was originally a populist movement which failed and that Christianity took on its purely religious character by virtue of the attempt to interpret that failure as a victory. "All histories," nay, "all writers" accuse the multitude of inconstancy. Livy gives the example of Manlius Capitolinus whom the plebs originally supported, then condemned to death, and for whom finally, after his execution, the plebs most passionately longed. Machiavelli defends the Roman common people, as distinguished from other common peoples, against this accusation: the Roman people condemned Manlius for his seditious activity and it longed for his virtues. "If amidst so great a longing Manlius had been resurrected, the Roman people would have passed on him the same sentence" as before. If we turn to Livy, we find that the plebs had almost made Manlius a god, the equal of Jupiter, and that the plebs traced a plague which occurred after Manlius' execution to the pollution of the Capitol by "the blood of its saviour."[79]

Although Machiavelli admitted that the Biblical religion cannot be understood in purely political terms, he did not reject the view that it can be characterized with regard to its political implications. Even the most obvious difference between Biblical and pagan religion, the monotheism of the former and the polytheism of the latter, offers itself to a political characterization. The pantheon of the pagans resembles a republic or the rulers of a republic, whereas the Biblical God resembles an absolute monarch. Certain observations of Machiavelli regarding the difference between republics and absolute principalities lend themselves to being understood as keys to his judgment regarding the difference between paganism and Biblical religion. Paganism is characterized by satisfaction with the present, with the world and its glory, and therefore by despair regarding the future, the ultimate future, of the individual as well as of the mixed body to which it dedicates itself; the utmost the pagan expects is temporary security to be found on a low and nearby elevation on earth; for since the memory of every human work is extinguished sooner or later, there can be no eternal glory strictly speaking. Biblical religion is characterized by dissatisfaction with the present, by the conviction that the present, the world, is a valley of misery and sin, by longing for perfect purity, hence by such a noble scorn for the world and its ways as to pagans was bound to appear as hatred for the human race, and by a hope which derives from the promise or certainty of ultimate victory. The poetic fable of the pagans regarding Anteus, the son of Earth, agrees with Machiavelli's judgment: if man has his heart armed, he cannot do better than to take his stand firmly on earth and to oppose the efforts of the Egyptian Heracles and his like to lift him high; man ought to tempt or to try Fortuna, the goddess of man's world, but he ought not to try to conquer the kingdom of heaven.[80]

The peculiar difficulty to which Machiavelli's criticism of the Bible is exposed is concentrated in his attempt to replace humility by humanity. He rejects humility because he believes that it lowers the stature of man. But humanity as he understands it implies the desire to prevent man from transcending humanity or to lower man's goal. As for the other elements of his criticism of the Bible, it would be useless to deny that they were implicit in the teaching of Aristotle and developed by those intransigent Aristotelians who knew the Bible. The Aristotelian God cannot be called just; he does not rule by commanding but only by being the end; his rule consists in knowing, in his knowing himself. Aristotle tacitly denies cognitive value to what is nowadays called religious experience. There is no place for piety in his ethics. According to him, humility is a vice. On the other hand, he identifies the virtue opposed to humility not as humanity but as magnanimity.

In order to bring out more clearly the difference between Machiavelli and Aristotle, we must consider Machiavelli's doctrine regarding God and his attributes. Let us consider first the explicit references to God which occur in the *Discourses*. The first references of this class occur in the section on the Roman religion (I 11-15). In the Roman republic there was great "fear of God"; that fear was related to "the power of God," and it resided in the general run of citizens rather than in the leading men. It appears from the context that the pagans feared not "God" but their "gods." Lycurgus, who according to Machiavelli had recourse to God, had in fact recourse to Apollo. Numa was in need of the authority of God; he therefore pretended to be familiar with a nymph. The pagans feared the gods because they believed that the gods could grant them good and evil; and they believed this because they believed that the gods could predict people's future good or evil. The Roman plebs could easily be induced to believe that the gods were angry and had to be placated. On a certain occasion "Apollo and certain other responses" gave a counsel of eminent political benefit: what the Romans heard was a response said to be Apollo's, but not Apollo himself. The auguries were the cause of the well-being of the Roman republic. As the context shows, they were also the cause of great embarrassments: unfavorable omens frightened the soldiers. To counteract this bad effect, the ancient captains either showed the cause, i.e., the natural cause, of the frightening event or else gave the event a favorable interpretation. On the whole Machiavelli teaches in the section on the Roman religion that fear of God's or the gods' power and wrath can be very useful; he is silent as to whether God and the gods are powerful or exist. He can hardly be said to break that silence in the only other reference to God which occurs in the First Book: "not without cause does one liken the voice of the people to that of God; for a universal opinion visibly produces marvellous effects in its prognostications, so much so that it seems as if the people foresees its evil and its good by an occult virtue." In the Second Book he mentions God or gods only once; he does this when stating the opinion of a pagan writer concerning the belief of the Roman people. In the Third Book he mentions God once, the gods twice, Apollo thrice and the Sun-God once; all mentions occur in his statements of other people's opinions.[81]

Whereas the *Discourses* are then in the decisive respect silent about God, they make significant assertions regarding heaven. Following the "astrologers" or "scientists" of his age, and perhaps even going beyond them, Machiavelli replaces God by "heaven."[82] "Heaven, the sun, the elements, and men" have always the same "motion, order and power." This does not contradict the fact that "heaven" is not always kind; for plagues, famines and great floods are somehow caused by "heaven." Accordingly one can say that some men are "more loved by heaven" than others. "Heaven" establishes for "all things of the world," i.e., for all terrestrial beings, specific life spans; whether they live out their time or not does not depend on "heaven" but on what these beings themselves do and on chance. "Heaven" is the summit which human fame can reach.[83] None of these remarks necessarily implies that "heaven" is a thinking and willing being. There occurs only one passage in the *Discourses* where "heaven" is described as a thinking and willing being, and in that passage "heaven" (*il cielo*) is used interchangeably with the Biblical "the heavens" (*i cieli*). Of "the heavens" Machiavelli says that they give men occasion for acquiring glory, that they form judgments, that they inspired the Roman senate, that they have purposes and act in accordance with them. Now, in the passage in which Machiavelli tacitly identifies "heaven" with "the heavens," he tacitly identifies both with Fortuna.[84] Fortuna is not the same as heaven or the all-comprising vault. Fortuna can be said to be the goddess which rules the little world of man in regard to extrinsic accidents.[85] We shall then say that Machiavelli replaces God, not by heaven, but by Fortuna.

Machiavelli has explicitly devoted two chapters of the *Discourses* to what one may call theology as distinguished from re-

ligion.[86] In I 56 he teaches that accidents of public importance are
always preceded by "heavenly signs" such as divinations, revelations, and prodigies. The accidents in question appear to be public
disasters such as foreign invasions and deaths of princes. Machiavelli gives three examples of recent Florentine disasters and then
one example of an ancient Roman disaster, all of which were preceded by heavenly signs; heavenly signs are obviously not a preserve of revealed religion proper. One of the Florentine disasters
was preceded by two heavenly signs, while each of the others
was preceded by one heavenly sign. In speaking of the recent
heavenly signs, Machiavelli says three times that "everyone knows"
of their having happened. The fact that important accidents are
preceded by heavenly signs is then undeniable. The difficulty concerns the cause of the heavenly signs. In order to discover the
cause, one would have to possess knowledge of things natural and
supernatural, a knowledge "which *we* do not possess."[87] Machiavelli does not exclude the possibility that other men might possess,
or might have possessed, such knowledge. He regards the explanation given by "some philosopher" as a possible explanation without
either accepting or rejecting it. According to that philosopher, the
air is "full of intelligences which through their natural powers
(*virtù*) foresee future things and, having compassion for men,
warn them with such signs so that they can prepare themselves
for defense."[88] This philosopher does not regard the heavenly signs
as miracles or as acts of God. Nor does Machiavelli give any indication that he himself thinks that God causes the heavenly signs.
The intelligences in the air which may be the cause of the heavenly
signs are neither gods nor heaven. The gods, including Fortuna,
which are thought to foresee evil, are also thought to cause evil,
and heaven causes evil without foreseeing it.[89] The intelligences in
the air, on the other hand, do not cause the disasters of which they
warn men nor can they prevent those disasters; they merely foresee them. Machiavelli does not even remotely suggest that the
heavenly signs are marvellous effects of God's prescience. According to our nameless philosopher, the heavenly signs are not signs
of the wrath of God or of the gods. The intelligences which give
the signs are moved, not by wrath but by compassion. They do
not punish men nor do they announce punishment. Accordingly,
the heavenly signs do not prove the existence of angry gods. The

possible explanation of the heavenly signs which Machiavelli reports is in entire agreement with the intention of his whole work —with the intention sufficiently revealed by his silence in both books regarding devil and hell, as distinguished from God and heaven, and by his silence regarding divine punishment.[90] Yet we must not for one moment forget that Machiavelli does not assert the existence of those intelligences in the air; the only superhuman intelligent and willing being whose existence he asserts in the *Discourses* is Fortuna. This however does not dispense us from the duty to wonder why he refers to those intelligences as a possible cause of the heavenly signs. The answer is revealed by the practical consequence of the tentative explanation. Man does not have to fear the intelligences in the air, for they are compassionate and not cruel, but man need fear only the accidents which they announce; the signs given by the intelligences are meant to induce men not to repentance but to vigilance. The suggested explanation is then conducive to making men not weak but strong. The suggested explanation may not be true; it is certainly salutary. The question arises as to why the heavenly signs are frequently interpreted, e.g., by Livy or his Romans, as indicating the wrath of the gods or of God. Machiavelli gives his answer through the context. The chapter on heavenly signs is preceded by one of the two chapters in which he mentions the Christian conscience, the silent witness within the individual; it is succeeded by the chapter which deals with the fundamental difference between the plebeian individual by himself and the plebs as an acting whole: whereas Livy had said of the individual that he is obedient, Machiavelli says that he is vile and weak.[91] Weakness is not only the effect but the very cause of the belief in angry gods.

The explanation of the heavenly signs which is reported by Machiavelli as not inadequate does not fit all kinds of heavenly signs in which men believed or believe. It does not fit favorable auguries or prophecies. It would seem that favorable and at the same time true auguries are not as well attested to as unfavorable ones. The philosophic explanation of heavenly signs does not even fit equally well all five examples which Machiavelli mentions. The intelligences in the air are said to warn men through heavenly signs so that they can prepare themselves for defense. According to the central example, the death of the elder Lorenzo de'Medici was preceded by "a heavenly arrow" striking the cathedral and damaging the building severely. If what happened to the cathedral announced the death of Lorenzo, it is hard to see how that heavenly sign could have been a warning to Lorenzo or to the Florentines to avert Lorenzo's death. The uneasiness would seem to be strengthened by the next example. Soderini's downfall was preceded by lightning striking the palace; Soderini could indeed have taken this heavenly sign as a warning addressed to him to be on his guard; yet according to Machiavelli's analysis, Soderini would have lacked the astuteness and ruthlessness required for his salvation; the warning would have been useless. One might say, however, that the heavenly sign preceding Lorenzo's death was a warning addressed to the Florentines to be on their guard against the evil consequences of Lorenzo's death. Still, we wonder whether all five heavenly signs mentioned by Machiavelli as undeniable facts possess the same status. Machiavelli speaks of three heavenly signs which announced the invasion of Italy by the modern French or the ancient Gauls. One of them was a fight of armed men in the air above Arezzo, a fight vouched for by what was said, not in Arezzo in particular but everywhere in Tuscany. The only heavenly sign mentioned as reported by Livy was vouched for by a plebeian who had heard a superhuman voice in the middle of the night while he was alone. The only example of heavenly signs mentioned by Machiavelli which both is certainly authentic and easily fits the tentative explanation of heavenly signs is that of Savonarola's predicting the invasion of Italy by the French.[92] Yet precisely this example shows the difficulty of discerning the meaning of heavenly signs or of distinguishing between heavenly signs and mere accidents. Savonarola's prediction was not unconnected with his belief that the sins of Italy deserve extraordinary punishment; by virtue of this belief he could not draw the proper conclusion, i.e., the military or political conclusion, from what he foresaw or expected or guessed.[93] At any rate, heavenly signs announcing foreign invasions appear to be the clearest case of warnings addressed to men to prepare themselves for defense. Heavenly signs thus understood announce terrors stemming, not from heaven however understood, but from other men. The only proper way of heeding heavenly signs would then be political and military preparation: good arms are the one thing needful. Machiavelli draws our at-

tention to the difficulties mentioned by expressing himself differently on the subject under discussion in the heading and the beginning of the chapter on the one hand, and at its end on the
other. He draws our attention, in other words, to the movement of
thought which underlies the chapter or finds expression in it. The
first statement is to the effect that grave accidents which occur in
a city or in a country are always preceded by heavenly signs. The
repetition is to the effect that extraordinary and new things which
happen to countries, are always preceded by "such accidents," i.e.,
human predictions, lightning striking temples or palaces, or nocturnal or diurnal apparitions. In the repetition he replaces "city
or country" by "country": the foreign invasions mentioned were
invasions of Italy, whereas the death or downfall of princes mentioned affected primarily the city of Florence. In the repetition
Machiavelli replaces "grave accidents" by "extraordinary and new
things." Grave accidents are distinguished from extraordinary ones
by the fact that the former cannot possibly be handled without
the use of extraordinary powers whereas this is not true of extraordinary accidents.[94] The death of a prince is not necessarily a
grave event. Above all, in the repetition Machiavelli replaces
"heavenly signs" by "accidents." We shall have to consider the
relation between those "accidents" which come to sight primarily
as "heavenly signs" and the workings of Fortuna.

Whereas I 56 leads up to a merely hypothetical suggestion
belonging to quasi-theology, II 29 promises by its very heading to
contain Machiavelli's assertoric quasi-theology: "Fortuna blinds the
minds of men when she does not wish them to oppose her designs."[95] This sentence is taken almost literally from Livy; it em-
bodies Livy's "conclusion" from certain events which he had
stated prior to drawing his conclusion; Livy has thus "demonstrated" fully and effectively the power of Fortuna over human
things: whereas the existence of the intelligences in the air remains a mere possibility, the existence of Fortuna has been demonstrated. By ascending from the phenomena to their causes we
finally come to realize the existence of Fortuna rather than of God.
Livy has established to Machiavelli's entire satisfaction that Fortuna is a willing and thinking being. To leave no room for the
slightest doubt, he quotes literally Livy's conclusion in the body
of the chapter and alters it in the Italian statement in the heading:

whereas Livy speaks of "Fortuna's might," Machiavelli speaks of "Fortuna's designs." Fortuna is not only one god among many; as Machiavelli indicates by using in this chapter "Fortuna" and "heaven" synonymously, Fortuna takes the place of all gods. Not only is the existence of Fortuna more certain than that of the intelligences in the air; she is also more powerful than they might be. Fortuna did not wish the Romans to prepare themselves for defense against the Gauls; according to the philosophic explanation of the heavenly signs, the intelligences in the air warned the Romans at that time to prepare themselves for defense against the Gauls; the intelligences were overruled by Fortuna just as in Machiavelli's time, as he says in the *Prince*, someone apparently chosen by God was rejected by Fortuna.[96] It appears that Fortuna is distinguished from the hypothetical intelligences in the air also by the fact that whereas the latter are benevolent, Fortuna is malevolent. Both Machiavelli and Cesare Borgia suffered from the malignity of Fortuna. "Human appetites owe it to nature that they can long and that they wish to long for everything, and they owe it to Fortuna that they can attain only a few of those things": whereas Nature wishes to grant, Fortuna denies.[97] This notion of Fortuna is however somewhat modified in our chapter. Fortuna inflicted indeed many evils on the Romans; but she did this, not out of malevolence, but because she wished the Romans to recognize her power, and she wished this with a view to a further or an ultimate end: she wished to make Rome great because she had elected Rome. In the preceding chapter Machiavelli had said that the disasters of the Gallic War befell the Romans "only because the Romans had not observed justice." Must we then say that Fortuna had originally elected the Roman people because of its justice and that Fortuna is the guardian or source of justice? Certain it is that Fortuna blinds cities or countries less the more they are filled with virtue, religion and order. Fortuna reminds one in some respects of the Biblical God. She takes the place of the Biblical God. She is indeed not a creator and she concentrates entirely on the government of men: Machiavelli does not mention in our chapter a single "heavenly sign"; the workings of Fortuna as described here show themselves exclusively in human actions or sufferings. But to return to the question of Fortuna's justice, Fortuna caused the Fabii, the ambassadors whom the Romans had sent to the

Gauls, to commit a sin against the law of nations and thus to bring on the war with the Gauls. "Fabius" seems to be an enemy, not only of the Gauls, but of Fortuna herself. Fortuna as it were hardened the heart of the Fabii. It does not appear however that the sin of the Fabii was caused or predestined by Fortuna as a punishment for preceding sins. Besides, the sin of the Fabii was avenged, not by Fortuna, but by the Romans.[98] Above all, Machiavelli would hardly have traced his own misfortune to Fortuna in the Epistle Dedicatory of the *Prince* if he had thought that Fortuna is just. We must then leave it at saying that Fortuna mysteriously elects some men or nations for glory and others for ruin or infamy. She certainly is not always malevolent. She certainly is, if not all powerful, at least so powerful that men cannot oppose her designs. The practical consequence is not quietism. As we have seen, the end which Fortuna pursues is unknown, and so are her ways toward that end. Hence, Machiavelli concludes, men ought always to hope, men ought never to give up, no matter what the condition into which Fortuna may have brought them. We need not discuss whether Machiavelli is consistent in drawing this sanguine conclusion from his quasi-theology. His conclusion from his assertion regarding Fortuna is certainly consistent with the conclusion which follows from his assumption regarding the intelligences in the air: man has no reason to fear superhuman beings. But whereas in the earlier chapter he had left it to the reader to draw the conclusion, he now explicitly urges all readers to hope, i.e., to abandon themselves to the passion opposite to fear.

It suffices to remember what was said earlier concerning the primacy of terror, in order to see that the reasoning of *Discourses* II 29 cannot be Machiavelli's last word on Fortuna. He indicates the difficulty to which that reasoning is exposed by making a mistake in the center of the chapter. He says that Livy states the "conclusion" regarding the power of Fortuna after having narrated the mistakes which the Romans had made prior to the war with the Gauls and at the beginning of that war. If we turn therefore to Livy, we see that his "conclusion" precedes rather than follows his narrative of the Romans' mistakes or that the "conclusion" precedes the establishment of the premises: the events narrated by Livy do not justify his conclusion.[99] Accordingly, the immediately following chapter which touches upon the theme of the *quaestio disputata* and refers to "an imagined danger" and "unarmed heart" leads up to a practical conclusion entirely different from that of II 29. Fortuna is changeable, and her power shows itself in unexpected political changes or victories and defeats; Machiavelli continues to be silent about heavenly signs. Fortuna shows her power the less, the more men possess virtue. Hence, a man of supreme virtue, of ancient virtue, should and can "regulate" Fortuna so that she has no cause to show her power all the time. Fortuna is changeable and hence unreliable: to trust in her and to put one's hopes in her is madness. She is so far from possessing superhuman power that man cannot only tempt or try her without having to fear her, but can even "regulate" her. Or to quote from the *Prince*, "Fortuna is a woman, and if one wishes to keep her down, it is necessary to beat her and to pound her." Fortuna can be vanquished by the right kind of man.[100] The fact that man's well-being depends on his vanquishing Fortuna shows that the initial suspicion was right: Fortuna is the enemy. Lacking superhuman power, she is not likely to be a superhuman being, a being which is more powerful than man and which wills and thinks. When speaking in *Discourses* II 29 of Fortuna's "judging" that she must beat Rome in order to make Rome great, Machiavelli says that he will discuss this "at length in the beginning of the following Book." He had used the story of the Gallic War in II 29 in order to show the power of Fortuna. He uses the same story in III 1 in order to show that mixed bodies must frequently be restored to their beginnings. Such restoration can take place in the case of republics[101] through "intrinsic prudence" or through "extrinsic accident." The restoration or rebirth of Rome at the time of the Gallic War was caused by "extrinsic accident." Every mixed body has a natural tendency to decay or to become corrupt. This tendency can be arrested by unexpected disasters which compel the mixed body or its rulers to restore order and virtue. Not Fortuna had then blinded the Romans at that time, but the Romans had degenerated by a natural process or they had become careless and vile; therefore they made disastrous mistakes; but their disasters brought them to their senses. When discussing his subject "at length," Machiavelli replaces the figurative expression "Fortuna judged" by the proper expression "extrinsic accident caused."[102]

By sometimes identifying Fortuna and heaven, Machiavelli is enabled to present Fortuna not merely as the only superhuman being which thinks and wills, or as the only god, but likewise as the all comprehensive order which does not think and will, or as nature. What then is the relation between Fortuna and nature? According to one passage, "human appetites owe it to nature that they can long and can wish to long for everything, and they owe it to Fortuna that they can attain only a few of these things." This remark serves the provisional purpose of presenting Fortuna as a thinking and willing being which is malevolent. Machiavelli expresses himself differently in another passage: "Nature has so created men that they can long for everything and cannot attain everything"; this gives rise to their being discontented and to conflict among them, and hence to the varying of their fortunes.[108] The power of Fortuna is based on the primary action of nature. Nature somehow comprises Fortuna. Fortuna is a part, and not the ruling part, of the whole. The whole is ruled by heaven. Heaven establishes for all earthly beings specific life spans beyond which they cannot live. Heaven does not determine, however, that each earthly being should live out its time, for heaven is the cause of plagues, famines, and similar disasters. Heaven leaves room for human causation, for action, for prudence and for art. Fortuna belongs to the same domain to which art and prudence belong.[104] Fortuna is thought to be the cause of men's good or ill fortunes. But if one looks more closely, one sees that in the most important cases "the cause of (good) fortune" is not Fortuna but human virtue and good institutions, i.e., the work of prudence or art. Rome owed her greatness decisively to her virtue and not to Fortuna. Rome, as distinguished from Sparta, rose to greatness, not through the prudence of her founder, but through chance or accidents; these accidents however arose from the discord between the nobles and the plebs; that discord in its turn arose from the opposition between the humor of the great and that of the people, from an opposition which is essential to every republic; the alternative to that discord is the oppression of the people; the accidents which made Rome great must then be traced, not to chance, but to the prudence or generosity of her nobles and the virility of her plebs.[105] Conversely, the cause of misfortune is frequently not Fortuna, but lack of virtue and art—a lack which can be traced to determinate causes and which therefore can be remedied to some extent. Still, a complete control of chance is impossible. If Lorenzo de'Medici had not died in his 44th year from a disease of his stomach, the ruin of Italy would have been averted.[106] This is not to deny that the dependence of a country on the life of a single man is the consequence of a fundamental defect of the moral and political constitution of that country. The good or ill fortune of captains or princes like Fabius Maximus, Pope Julius II and Machiavelli himself is caused by the agreement or disagreement between their specific natural qualities and the characters of their times; for different types of human beings agree with different times; the agreement between the nature of an individual and his times, and hence his good fortune, is caused by Fortuna, by chance.[107] A man, like Machiavelli, who was born in the wrong time, may achieve posthumous success through his writings, but this depends on the survival of his writings, i.e., on something which is essentially exposed to chance. Since the success or failure at any rate of individuals depends then ultimately on unconquerable chance, the rule "Conquer Fortuna" is insufficient. Excellent men will rise above chance. Chance will have no power over them, over their minds. While their fortune varies, they will always remain the same. The dignity of man consists, not in conquering chance, but in independence. This freedom, this dignity, this genuine "good fortune" can arise only from a man's having knowledge of "the world," i.e., in particular of the place and significance of accidents. Contrary to what Machiavelli had indicated in his chapter on heavenly signs, such knowledge is available to him. Inner freedom from chance, an ultimate superiority to every fear and every hope, presupposes recognition of the true power of chance, of the natural necessities by virtue of which chance rules supreme within certain limits. The alternatives to that freedom are either faith or vulgar worship of success.[108]

The most important errors arise from false notions regarding chance. They consist in assigning to chance a much greater power than it possesses and in obscuring the nature of chance. In order to prepare the discussion of this subject, Machiavelli replaces "chance" by "accidents," either by "extrinsic accidents" or by "trivial accidents."[109] By substituting "accidents" for "chance," he deliberately blurs the distinction between nature and chance in order to indicate the common origin of both belief in gods and knowledge of nature. For that purpose, accidents may be defined as events which are not foreseen by every human being of common understanding.[110] An event which a man intentionally brings about is therefore not an accident for him. Accidents are either foreseen or not foreseen; they are not foreseen either because they cannot be foreseen or because the people to whom they occur lack foresight. Accidents are either important or unimportant. Men can cope, if sometimes only by resignation, with the ordinary and familiar. They therefore attempt to understand the new in the light of the old, or they tacitly identify the natural with the common or ordinary. If they once lost a battle at a certain place, they are afraid to wage another battle at the same place; lacking knowledge of the causes, they mistake the merely accidental but very striking for the cause; they mistake an unimportant accident for an important accident. They understand the new in the light of the old because, owing to the primacy of terror, they are upset and frightened by the new, unforeseen or extraordinary. They are therefore anxious to foresee what is unforeseeable either in itself or for them. For this purpose they as it were postulate beings of superhuman perfection which can predict to them the future; once they believe that there are gods who can predict to them their future good and evil, they readily believe that those gods cause their good and evil. They thus arrive at making foreseeable the unforeseeable and at transforming the simply unintended into something intended. Being frightened by the extraordinary or new as such, they identify the extraordinary with the grave. By virtue of this effect of the new on the minds of unwise and undisciplined men, the new as such becomes important. Accidents may therefore be grave though they are in themselves trivial or "weak." An unimportant but striking accident may be connected with an intrinsically grave accident by mere accident, e.g., because it happens in or near the same place or at the same time as a grave accident or shortly before a grave accident. Thus, striking accidents will be regarded in retrospect as signs of grave accidents. This will give rise to the belief that striking accidents always portend grave accidents. An event brought about intentionally is an accident for those men who did not intend it or foresee it. Let us now call "new accidents" such accidents as are not in themselves grave. New accidents happen not only by accident; they can also be fabricated, e.g., for the purpose of upsetting an enemy. In the chapter on new accidents (III 14) Machiavelli gives five examples, three of which were fabricated accidents. New accidents may be perceived by seeing or by hearing. Machiavelli speaks only of such fabricated new accidents as were seen; he leaves it to the reader to discover whether voices or words can be fabricated as well. But he makes clear that if one fabricates new accidents, one must prevent the people who are to be deceived from coming close to those accidents. He seems to pay a compliment to the human race by choosing as his examples three fabricated accidents of which two failed to deceive; yet these three accidents were all seen and not heard. However this may be, it would seem that the prudent use of genuine new accidents is safer than the fabrication of new accidents. That prudent use consists either in revealing the true cause of the accident in question or else in interpreting it as a favorable sign, i.e., in not questioning its being a sign. In the latter case one must prevent the people who are to be deceived from coming close to the accident, i.e., from discovering its true cause.[111] What the wise captain does regarding the particular accident which upsets his army, Machiavelli does regarding all accidents: he either does not question their being signs or heavenly signs but interprets them as warnings sent by friendly spirits, or else he indicates their natural causes.

In the *Prince*, in which Machiavelli never speaks of "we Christians," he never mentions the gods or heaven. Similarly, while he asserts in the *Prince* the existence both of God and of Fortuna as a willing and thinking being, he never refers there to any demonstration of the existence or power of Fortuna. The first reference to Fortuna as a thinking and willing being occurs in the third part of the book, some time after the beginning of the descent. Especially when she wishes to make a new prince great, Fortuna causes enemies to rise against him and causes him to act against them so that he has occasion to overcome them and thus to acquire reputation. Therefore "many" judge that a wise prince ought to nourish some enmity against himself in order to increase his reputation by suppressing the enemy whom he created.[112] "Many judge" then that a wise prince ought to imitate Fortuna or that Fortuna is the model for wise princes. But the phenomenon which

Machiavelli here traces to Fortuna was traced by him, in the central chapter of the first part, to the nature of things: against a new prince many enemies rise of necessity. Machiavelli takes up the opinions of the many regarding Fortuna in the 25th chapter, which is explicitly devoted to the question of the power of Fortuna. "Many have had and have the opinion" that the things of the world are governed by Fortuna and by God in such a way that human prudence is powerless. They believe then that Fortuna and God are not only to be imitated but also that they are so powerful that they cannot be imitated unless Fortuna and God decree or cause such imitation. Yet such power of Fortuna and of God, or such exercise of their power, is incompatible with human freedom. Machiavelli therefore judges that one half of our actions is determined by Fortuna whereas the other half, or about the other half, is left to our own determination. The popular error consists in assigning to Fortuna a much greater power than she possesses. Machiavelli is silent now about the causality of God. Instead he explains that Fortuna is like one of those ruinous rivers which "when they become angry," destroy everything men have built and are simply irresistible. Fortuna is the enemy of man. Fortuna exercises her power only when she is angry, when the times are turbulent or difficult; the half ruled by Fortuna is the difficult times, whereas the half ruled by man is the peaceful times. Yet if men are virtuous and prudent, Fortuna leaves them alone at all times; Fortuna favors virtue and prudence in the sense that she has a healthy respect for them. Machiavelli makes it clear that he could have said more regarding the resistance to Fortuna, or the war against Fortuna, in general, had he wished to do so. He hardly sheds further light on Fortuna, or on chance, by saying at the end of the chapter that Fortuna is like a woman who can be vanquished by the right kind of man. For if Fortuna can be vanquished, man would seem to be able to become the master of the universe. Certainly Machiavelli does not recommend that Fortuna be worshipped: she ought to be beaten and pounded.

We have stated the reasons which may induce one to think that Machiavelli's cosmological premises were Aristotelian.[113] Yet there is no place in his cosmology for a ruling Mind. This by itself does not prove that he consciously broke away from Aristotle's doctrine of God, for that doctrine has been understood in greatly different ways.[114] Machiavelli indicates his fundamental disagreement with Aristotle's doctrine of the whole by substituting "chance" (*caso*) for "nature" in the only context in which he speaks of "the beginning of the world." Polybius had called the cyclical change of regimes a change which takes place "according to nature"; Machiavelli says that that cyclical change occurs "by chance." By this he does not mean that the changes of regimes occur without any order or regularity, at random or haphazardly, for he shows that they occur with necessity and in an unalterable sequence. He understands "chance" in opposition to "prudence":[115] the cyclical change of regimes does not occur because it has been planned by any being or because it serves an end. The substitution of "chance" for "nature," or the understanding of nature as chance was imputed to Democritus in particular. Among "the philosophic family" surrounding Aristotle in Dante's Limbo we find "Democritus who ascribes the world to chance." From the point of view of Aristotle, or of Plato, every doctrine which understands the world as the work of soulless bodies not tending towards ends in fact identifies nature and chance.[116] By substituting chance for nature when mentioning "the beginning of the world," Machiavelli indicates that he has abandoned the teleological understanding of nature and natural necessity for the alternative understanding. He speaks very frequently of "accidents" but never of "substances." Just as he never mentions souls in the *Prince* and the *Discourses*, he speaks in those books not of "substances" but of "bodies." In the first mention of this subject, he distinguishes between "simple" and "mixed" bodies, understanding by simple bodies living beings. In the repetition he distinguishes between "mixed bodies" and "the bodies of men," having fallen silent about simple bodies. He thus forces us to wonder whether the bodies of living beings can properly be called simple bodies and therewith whether simple bodies have to be conceived in the Aristotelian or in the Democritean-Epicurean or in some other manner.[117] In both books he rather frequently uses the terms "form" and "matter" but he never speaks of the form of a natural being and he speaks only once of matter while having in mind natural beings.[118] It is reasonable to assume that Machiavelli favored a cosmology which is in accordance with his analysis of morality. His analysis of morality will prove to be incompatible with a teleological cosmology. We conclude that the movement of fundamental thought which finds expression in both books consists in a movement from God to Fortuna and then from Fortuna via accidents, and accidents occurring to bodies or accidents of bodies, to chance understood as a non-teleological necessity which leaves room for choice and prudence and therefore for chance understood as the cause of simply unforeseeable accidents.

Machiavelli has indicated his fundamental thought also in his *Life of Castruccio Castracani*. The *Castruccio* presents itself as a biography. Machiavelli dedicated it to two friends, one of whom was one of the addressees of the *Discourses*. In considering the *Castruccio*, one must be mindful of the distance between the two books in which Machiavelli expresses "everything he knows" and all his other utterances. Castruccio appears to be the greatest man of post-classical times: he would have surpassed Philip, the father of Alexander, and Scipio had he been born in antiquity. He lived 44 years, like Philip and Scipio, and, we may add, Lorenzo the Magnificent. He surpassed Philip and Scipio because he rose to greatness from "a low and obscure beginning and birth." He resembled the men of the first rank who were all either exposed to wild beasts or else who had fathers so contemptible that they made themselves sons of Jupiter or of some other god. Having been found as a baby by the sister of a priest in her garden he was raised by her and her brother and destined for the priesthood. But as soon as he was 14 years old, he left the ecclesiastical books and turned to arms. He found favor in the eyes of the most distinguished man of his city, a Ghibelline condottiere, who took him into his house and educated him as a soldier. In the shortest time Castruccio became a perfect gentleman, distinguishing himself by his prudence, his grace and his courage. When on the point of dying, his master made him the tutor of his young son and the guardian of his property. Castruccio had no choice but to make himself ruler of his city. He won brilliant victories, rose to be the leader of the Tuscan and Lombard Ghibellines, and eventually became almost prince of Tuscany. He never married lest love of his children prevent him from showing due gratitude to the blood of his benefactor. After having described Castruccio's beginning, life and death, Machiavelli devotes half a page to a description of his character or manners and thereafter more than three pages to a

collection of witty remarks made by Castruccio or listened to by
him. These sayings reveal to us Castruccio's mind. There are altogether 34 such sayings. Almost all—31—can be traced to Diogenes
Laertius' *Lives of the Famous Philosophers.* This fact is all the
more remarkable since Machiavelli refers so rarely to philosophy
and philosophers: in the *Prince* and the *Discourses* taken together
there occurs only one reference to Aristotle and one reference to
Plato. Whenever it is appropriate, Machiavelli changes the sayings
of the ancient philosophers to make them fit Castruccio. For instance, when the ancient philosopher speaks of "the festivals of
the gods," Castruccio is made to speak of "the festivals of our
saints"; whereas the ancient philosopher said he would wish to
die like Socrates, Castruccio is made to say that he would wish
to die like Caesar; the ancient philosopher, noticing a certain inscription at the door of a rascally eunuch, made a remark which
Castruccio is said to have made when noticing a similar inscription
in Latin letters. A single saying (no. 19) stems from Aristotle. The
Aristotelian saying is surrounded on each side by two sayings of a
certain Bion. Bion was a pupil of the notorious atheist Theodorus
and was himself a man of many wiles, a sophist of many colors,
and so shameless as to behave like an atheist in the company of his
fellows. Yet when he fell ill, he was persuaded, people said, to wear
an amulet and to repent his offenses against the divine. The five
central sayings (nos. 17-21) are surrounded on one side by 15
sayings of the Cyrenaic Aristippus and on the other by 11 sayings
of the Cynic Diogenes. Aristippus and Diogenes shared an extreme
contempt for convention as opposed to nature. One or two of
the three sayings to which Castruccio listened are transmitted
by Diogenes Laertius as sayings of Aristippus to which the tyrant
Dionysius listened: Castruccio takes the place not only of Aristotle,
Diogenes, Bion and Aristippus, but also of the tyrant Dionysius.
One saying of Castruccio (no. 33) stems from "a black devil" in
Dante's *Inferno.*[119] What we learn from Diogenes Laertius concerning Bion's sick-bed repentance draws our attention to what
Castruccio had said when he had fallen mortally ill. Castruccio,
who speaks in his witty sayings and elsewhere of God, mentions
Fortuna in his dying speech five times, but never God. Castruccio,
who in his witty sayings speaks of the soul, of hell and of paradise,
mentions this world once in his dying speech and the next, never.

Similarly, when expressing his own thought, Machiavelli mentions this world once in the *Castruccio* and never the next; and he mentions fortuna eight times and God never. However these things will be understood, the mind of Machiavelli's exemplary prince, as revealed by that prince's sayings, reminds most strongly of such unsung and undignified philosophers as Aristippus and Diogenes and hardly at all of Aristotle. It would not be prudent to forget this ironical but not misleading expression of Machiavelli's innermost thought. That expression is not misleading since it points to a thought at the core of which Aristotle is kept in bounds or overwhelmed by Bion and the periphery of which consists of a shocking moral teaching.

Machiavelli uses the term "religion" in two senses. He uses "religion" synonymously with "sect" and understands by it a mixed body, or a society of a certain kind. "Sect" is used also in the sense of "party," i.e., an association whose end is not identical with the common good of a particular state. Parties are not necessarily parts of an individual state but may, like the Guelphs and the Ghibellines, permeate many states, not to say all states. In accordance with this, the religion of the ancient Romans was the religion not only of the Romans but of the Gentiles in general, just as the religion of the modern Romans is Christianity. Machiavelli also understands by "religion" a part of virtue or one of the virtues. He may have conceived of the relation between religion as a virtue and religion as a society as parallel to the relation between justice and the other virtues on the one hand and civil society on the other. The acts of religion appear to be worship of gods, fear of gods and trust in gods. "Observance of religion" can therefore be used synonymously with "observance of religious ceremonies." Yet religious ceremonies are not the foundation of religion. The foundation of religion is in the last analysis a belief, the belief in the power and intelligence of gods. Therefore the vice opposed to religion is incredulity. Religion is of human, not divine, origin. For instance, heaven inspired the Roman senate to elect as king the future founder of the Roman religion; heaven did not inspire the founder of that religion himself; that founder merely pretended to converse with a nymph. Generally stated, the belief which is the foundation of religion is not true belief, i.e. not belief based on firm or reliable experience but belief caused by self-deception and to some extent even by deception. With a view to the facts that religion is to some extent intentionally created by men and, whatever its origins may be, can be used intentionally by men, it can be called an art. It belongs to the arts of peace as distinguished from the art of war. Certainly at first glance religion and arms are the highest powers of man; these powers, while in a sense opposed to each other, supplement each other.[120]

Machiavelli was not the first man to assert that religion is both untrue and salutary. Religion is a part of virtue or is a virtue. Among all men who are praised, the heads and founders of religions occupy the highest place. Machiavelli "believes" that Rome owed more to Numa, the founder of her religion, than to Romulus, her founder simply who gave her arms; for where there is religion, arms can easily be introduced, but where there are arms and no religion, religion can only with difficulty be introduced. Rome was corrupt under Romulus; Numa made Rome religious and hence good or incorrupt. Religion was the cause of the well-being of the Roman republic.[121] After having made these suggestions, i.e. after having adopted certain opinions which were generally received or akin to the generally received, Machiavelli goes on to question his first statements. Let us first recall the further fate of Numa in Machiavelli's pages. At first glance, Rome seemed to owe more to Numa than to Romulus because the work of Numa was more difficult than that of Romulus. Some lines later, Machiavelli states that Numa could achieve his work with great ease because of the rudeness of the early Romans: the obstacle to the introduction of religion is not arms but civilization or sophistication. Given the essential character of the multitude, the condition for the introduction of religion is fulfilled always and everywhere. Numa was not only not superior to Romulus, he even proves inferior to him. In his second statement, Machiavelli contrasts Romulus, as an excellent prince, with "the quiet and religious" Numa who was a weak prince. Numa's characteristic policy made the Romans effeminate and slothful or, in other words, Numa made Rome entirely dependent on chance. He was then inferior to Romulus in prudence. He was inferior in virtue and prudence not only to his predecessor but also to his successor, Tullus Hostilius. In order to bring out the fundamental defect of Numa's policy, Machiavelli goes so far as for a moment to call Tullus "a most prudent man," although the only action of Tullus which he discusses was in fact extremely imprudent: even this most imprudent action of Tullus was more prudent, as a matter of principle, than Numa's whole policy. Machiavelli had prepared this disclosure, before he began the discussion of the Roman religion, by saying first that the founders of religions are the men most highly praised, and shortly thereafter that no glory surpasses that of the founder of a city, such as Romulus.[122]

If religion stems from weakness of mind and will and fosters such weakness, it cannot be simply necessary for the well-being of society. After having said that the observance of divine worship causes the greatness of republics, Machiavelli says that a kingdom in which fear of God is lacking will either be ruined or will have to be maintained by the fear of a prince who makes up for the lack of religion. Religion is indeed indispensable for the well-being of a republic but not for that of a principality ruled by a prince of outstanding virtue. In accordance with this remark, Machiavelli praises the religiosity of the unsophisticated Roman republic, but when he points out the virtues of the reigns of the five good emperors from Nerva to the philosopher Marcus Aurelius, he mentions, not religion but perfect freedom of opinion. The substitution of the fear of a virtuous prince for the fear of God might not seem to be satisfactory, for, as Dante wisely says, virtue rarely descends from father to son, as God wills so that men must pray to him for virtue as his gift. For Machiavelli however the unreliability of hereditary succession is not a reason for prayer but a reason against hereditary succession: a virtuous prince will so order his state that it can maintain itself after his death, i.e. he will follow the example of the good Roman emperors by appointing as his successor an adopted son.[123] Machiavelli may be said to foreshadow the extreme form of "enlightened despotism." In his usage, a virtuous prince is not so much a prince possessing moral virtue as a prince of strong mind and will who prudently uses his moral virtue and vice according to the requirements of the situation. A virtuous prince in this sense cannot be religious. In other words, a prince need not be religious and ought not to be religious, but it is most important for him to appear to be religious. Machiavelli does not resist the temptation to say on one occasion that the appearance of religion is more important for the prince than anything else. On the other hand, it seems to be highly desirable that his soldiers should possess fear of God.[124]

Republics on the other hand stand or fall by religion. We are inclined to understand this assertion to mean that political freedom requires, or consists in, dedication to the common good or free subjection to serving the whole or one's neighbors, and that such dedication or subjection is achieved by means of religion and only of religion. By maintaining the foundations of their religion, the rulers can keep their republic "religious and hence good." Yet religion or serving gods is not invariably followed by goodness or serving men. Machiavelli reminds us through the mouth of Livy of a pirate who was as religious as any Roman.[125] But "goodness" does not necessarily have the broad meaning indicated. It may mean merely obedience to the ruler or the rulers.[126] Accordingly, the effect of religion on a republic would consist in making the citizens obedient to their rulers. The fact that the Roman republic was filled with fear of God facilitated every enterprise on which the senate and the leading men embarked. More simply, the rulers of the Roman republic used religion for the control of the plebs. Hence Machiavelli is silent about religion in the section in which he analyzes the character of the Roman nobility (I 33-45), while he speaks of religion in the section in which he analyzes the character of the Roman multitude (I 46-59). In the central chapter of the section on the religion of the Romans (I 13), he makes a distinction regarding the uses to which the Roman nobility put religion. Religion proved to be very helpful for certain limited purposes, but it proved to be indispensable for stopping the agitation by the tribune of the plebs, Terentillus, in favor of a law which would have destroyed the pre-eminence of the nobility forever. Machiavelli refers in I 13 to a later discussion of the Terentillian law. From that later discussion (I 39) it appears that the use of religion by the nobility was neither sufficient nor necessary to overcome the serious danger caused by Terentillus' bill. The success of the Roman nobility depended decisively on the use, not of religion but of purely political means. Furthermore, the Roman republic owed its well-being to "the religion of the Gentiles," i.e. to a religion which was not peculiar to the Romans; that that religion did not cause the well-being of the other pagan republics is shown by the fact that they were subjugated by the Romans;

hence not that religion as such but its "good use" by the Romans, that prudent use of religion by the Roman nobility which included the prudent disregard of religion, accounts for the well-being of the Roman republic. The Samnites for instance were no less religious than the Romans, but they did not use religion well. Desirous to continue their war with the Romans after their cause had already become hopeless, the Samnites tried to make their soldiers obstinate by having recourse to an ancient and awesome rite. But, as the Roman commander opposing them pointed out to his soldiers, by making this use of religion the Samnites increased the fear which their soldiers had felt before; they added the fear of the gods to the fear of the enemy. In fact, Roman virtue proved to be superior to whatever obstinacy the Samnites might have acquired through "the virtue of religion." Machiavelli makes it clear at the beginning of this reasoned narrative that religion is not the best means for making soldiers obstinate. As he notes on a later occasion, Manlius' killing his son and Decius' killing himself made the Roman army more obstinate than the equally strong and good Latin army and thus brought about the victory of the Romans. Or, as he shows by two non-Roman examples, there is "no truer nor more reliable" means for making soldiers obstinate against an enemy than to make them commit a grave crime against that enemy: fear of human beings may have the same effect as the fear of gods. But the truest and best means for making one's soldiers obstinate is to impose upon them a manifest necessity to fight and to conquer, or to make them fully aware of the fact that only their virtue, and no god, can save them. Even a Samnite appealed to such necessity on the eve of the greatest Samnite victory over the Romans.[127] Besides, it would be wrong to say that religion is necessary to protect society against tyranny; for religion can be used for the establishment and preservation of tyranny. Finally, it is obvious that religion is indispensable to the extent to which oaths are indispensable. At the beginning of the section on the religion of the Romans, Machiavelli adduces two examples of how Roman patricians compelled fellow citizens at sword's point to swear that they would act in a certain way, and how the people who had sworn under duress kept their oaths: having a higher regard for the power of God than for the power of men, the citizens of Rome were in greater fear of breaking an oath than of breaking the laws. In the sequel Machiavelli draws our attention to the facts that since the purport of oaths is not always clear, there is need for authoritative interpretations, and that, if oaths have a higher status than laws, it is hard to see how the political government can hand down such interpretations; this difficulty throws light on the connection between religion as virtue and religion as sect. On the other hand, the procedure followed by the German cities in levying taxes shows the great convenience afforded by oaths. But as is shown by a parallel example taken from the history of the Roman republic regarding the payment of a tithe, the same desirable result can be achieved without resort to oaths, provided the populace is simply honest.[128]

Observations like those just mentioned make one wonder whether Machiavelli was convinced that religion fulfills an important function. They make one wonder whether according to him religion is more than a necessary consequence or product of the mind of "the vulgar"—an enormous rock which cannot be removed or split, which is useless and with which one must reckon. This doubt however goes too far. Since according to Machiavelli the locus of religion is the multitude, one must consider his opinion of the multitude or the people. The people, in contradistinction to the great, make very modest demands on their rulers; they merely desire that their lives, their small properties and the honor of their women be respected. Yet as human beings they are necessarily dissatisfied with what they possess more or less securely. Being by nature compelled to crave a satisfaction which is impossible, they will be fundamentally in a situation no less desperate than that in which the Samnites were when they longed for independence after having suffered many disastrous defeats. The great no less crave a satisfaction which is impossible, but wealth, pre-eminence and glory give many comforts of which the many are necessarily deprived. Society would be in a state of perpetual unrest, or else in a state of constant and ubiquitous repression, if men were not made incorrupt by religion, i.e. if they were not both appeased by religious hopes and frightened by religious fears. Only if their desires are thus limited can the many become satisfied with making those small demands which can in principle be fulfilled by political means. Religion as reverence for the gods breeds deference to the ruling class as a group of men especially favored by the gods and reminiscent of the gods. And vice versa, unqualified unbelief will dispose the people not to believe in what they are told by venerable men. The ruling class will not be able in the long run to elicit this kind of deference if it does not contain men, and especially old men, who are venerable by virtue of their piety. The venerable old men are not necessarily identical with the prudent old men, the repositories of political wisdom.[129]

We have devoted what at first glance seems to be a disproportionately large space to Machiavelli's thought concerning religion. This impression is due to a common misunderstanding of the intention, not only of Machiavelli but also of a whole series of political thinkers who succeeded him. We no longer understand that in spite of great disagreements among those thinkers, they were united by the fact that they all fought one and the same power—the kingdom of darkness, as Hobbes called it; that fight was more important to them than any merely political issue. This will become clearer to us the more we learn again to understand those thinkers as they understood themselves and the more familiar we become with the art of allusive and elusive writing which all of them employ, although to different degrees. The series of those thinkers will then come to sight as a line of warriors who occasionally interrupt their fight against their common enemy to engage in a more or less heated but never hostile disputation among themselves. The conditions of political thought were radically changed by the French Revolution. To begin with, we cannot help reading earlier thinkers in the light afforded by the changed condition or the novel situation of political thought. All serious errors in the interpretation of the thinkers in question can be traced to a failure to grasp the parochial character of the 19th and 20th century outlook which inevitably pretends to be wider than that of any earlier age.

We are entitled to make a distinction between Machiavelli's teaching regarding religion and his teaching regarding morality since he himself makes a distinction between religion and justice or between religion and goodness.[130] His discussion of morality has fundamentally the same character as his discussion of religion. In both cases there is a foreground of "first statements" which reproduce accepted opinions and a background of "second statements" which are more or less at variance with accepted opinions.

But the explicit discussion of religion occupies much less space than the explicit discussion of morality. There is a much greater number of statements which visibly agree or disagree with accepted opinions on morality than of statements which visibly agree or disagree with accepted opinions on religion. Machiavelli is less reticent regarding morality than regarding religion. The integration of morality into religion or the subordination of morality to religion leads to the consequence that morality appears to be less comprehensive and hence less fundamental than religion.

If one desires not to lose one's way, one must start from Machiavelli's claim, raised at the beginning of the *Discourses* and in the middle of the *Prince*, that his teaching which is comprehensive or concerns the foundations is new. The claim to novelty is obviously raised on behalf of the teaching concerning politics and morality, as distinguished from the teaching concerning religion; and in fact it is only his teaching concerning morality and politics which can be considered wholly new. In his teaching concerning morality and politics Machiavelli challenges not only the religious teaching but the whole philosophic tradition as well. This novelty is compatible with the fact that the teaching in question contains many elements which were known before him to all men or some men; for Machiavelli integrates those elements into a new whole or understands them in the light of a new principle. Even if it were true that that whole or that principle were known to certain earlier thinkers but not set forth by them coherently or explicitly, or in other words, if it were true that Machiavelli differed from those predecessors only by his boldness, his claim would be wholly justified: that boldness as considered boldness would presuppose a wholly new estimate of what can be publicly proposed, hence a wholly new estimate of the public and hence a wholly new estimate of man. Machiavelli has indicated his new principle by opposing it to the principle underlying classical political philosophy. Traditional political philosophy took its bearings by how one ought to live or what one ought to do or by "the good man"; it thus arrived at the description of republics or principalities which are imagined but "have never been seen and known to be truly" or which exist only in speech. The traditional teaching is therefore useless. Being concerned with usefulness, Machiavelli is more concerned with "the factual truth," with how men are seen to live or with what men are seen to do than with imagined things and with what exists only in speech but not in deed. Accordingly, he derives greater benefit from historians, from writers who describe how men in fact acted, than from the authors of e.g. mirrors of princes. At first glance, it seems as if Machiavelli's revolt against classical political philosophy merely gives expression to that contempt for classical political philosophy which many practitioners of politics must have felt at all times—a contempt of the men of deeds for the men of words, not to say of book learning. Such contempt somehow lives on in Machiavelli's teaching. But his perspective is not identical with that of the practicing politician. He is concerned with reasoning about matters of state and he very frequently addresses men of action, be they princes or conspirators against princes; but he is also concerned with "reasoning about everything," with such reasoning about everything as does not permit recourse to authority or force, and he also addresses readers who merely try to understand "the things of the world."[131] The teaching of the *Prince* and the *Discourses* is based not only on extensive practice or experience of contemporary things but on continuous readings of ancient things as well. That teaching combines "general knowledge" with "particular knowledge" or "practice," for no science can be possessed perfectly without practice. The proper order is ascent from particular knowledge, the knowledge inherent in practice, to general knowledge. Practice supplies detailed knowledge of the individual society here and now within which the practitioner operates; general knowledge or "firm science" of the "nature" of society or of the "nature" of the things of the world is arrived at by recognizing the universal in the particular; the general knowledge thus acquired can thereafter be applied to any other society, even "from afar."[132] It is no longer necessary to show that this scheme must be modified with a view to the fact that practice within a corrupt society must be combined with readings regarding incorrupt societies in order to supply one with a sufficient basis for generalization. "The firm science" or the "general knowledge" which is meant to be useful is for this reason at least partly preceptive or normative. Machiavelli does not oppose to the normative political philosophy of the classics a merely descriptive or analytical political science; he rather opposes to a wrong normative teaching the true normative teaching. From his point of view, a true analysis of political "facts" is not possible without the light supplied by knowledge of what constitutes a well-ordered commonwealth.[133]

Before he can show the uselessness or wrongness of classical political philosophy, Machiavelli must show that he has understood classical political philosophy. Classical political philosophy claims to be in fundamental agreement with what is generally said about goodness. Machiavelli must therefore reproduce the outlines of what is generally said about goodness. He knows that these generally held opinions are not entirely baseless. They contain elements which he can preserve. Besides, by reproducing those opinions he furnishes himself with the indispensable "first statements." As he shows in his very attack on the principle of classical political philosophy, he does not deny that there are good men and he agrees with his opponents as to what is a good man. He knows that the generally held opinions regarding goodness have an evidence of their own and are not arbitrary. "I know that everyone will confess that it would be most praiseworthy for a prince to possess all the above-mentioned qualities which are held to be good," i.e. liberality, mercy, fidelity, courage, chastity, sincerity, religion, and so on. There exists "knowledge of honest and good things" as well as of justice. All men understand by goodness and badness the same things and they know that goodness deserves praise and badness deserves blame. This does not prevent them from acting badly in many cases, so much so that, as is universally admitted, the legislators must assume all men to be bad.[134] Goodness in the wider sense is identical with virtue, i.e. moral virtue. To act virtuously means to act as one ought to act. Virtue embraces many virtues or praiseworthy qualities which are the opposite of vices, i.e., of blameworthy and detestable qualities. "One cannot call it virtue to murder one's fellow citizens, to betray one's friends, to be without faith, without mercy, without religion." Machiavelli can use "virtue" as the synonym of Dante's "probity." "Goodness" can also designate one of the moral virtues. A good man is an unselfish man, a man who avoids hurting others and who thinks more of benefiting others than of benefiting himself; he is therefore in particular a law-abiding man; if he is a prince, he will never kill a subject except by due process of law.[135] Goodness is the habit of choosing good means for the good end. The good end is the common or public good. Good means are means other than fraud and lawless force. Goodness or virtue is both praiseworthy for its own sake and useful as regards its effects. It is followed by honor and glory, and it preserves and makes great kingdoms and republics. For instance, a republic will increase its well-being by treating its neighbors as brothers and not as enemies, and the most important concern of the prince is to benefit his subjects. On this basis one can easily make a distinction between the prince and the tyrant: the prince in the strict sense is informed by virtue and dedicates himself to the common good, whereas the tyrant is prompted by ambition and greed and is concerned only with his own good; the prince, being loved by his subjects, lives in much greater security than the tyrant, who is hated by them. What moral demands are to be made on the prince appears from Machiavelli's remark that the prince has to contend with the ambition of the great and the insolence of the people, and in some cases also with the cruelty and avarice of the soldiers. However this may be, the common good is taken care of only in republics, so much so that one can equate the common good with public liberty. In other words, republics are to be preferred to princes because they are morally superior to the latter: they are less given to ingratitude and bad faith than are princes.[136] Goodness as the habit of benefiting others includes honesty as the habit not to hurt others or not to deprive them of the good things which they possess. From this it follows that the demands of the common people are more honest than the demands of the great: the common people merely desire to keep the few good things which they possess or not to be oppressed whereas the great desire to oppress. Goodness is primarily respect for possession: he who possesses nothing in the first place or has not been deprived of anything by others cannot in decency complain; nothing remains to him except to ask for favors. The man who receives favors or benefits is obliged to be grateful. On the other hand, he who is merely left in possession of what he has or who is not hurt feels no obligation. If goodness consists in dedication to the common good, the good man will be satisfied with having little of his own: the good republic will keep its citizens poor and the commonwealth rich.[137] The virtuous man is guided by considerations not only of the honest but of the honorable as well. The honorable is that which gives a man distinction or which makes him great and resplendent. Hence extraordinary virtue rather than ordinary virtue is honorable. To possess extraordinary virtue and to be aware of one's possessing it is more honorable than merely to possess it. To have a sense of one's superior worth and to act in accordance with that sense is honorable. Hence it is honorable to rely on oneself and to be frank when frankness is dangerous. To show signs of weakness or to refuse a fight is dishonorable. To make open war against a prince is more honorable than to conspire against him. To lose by fighting is more honorable than to lose in any other way. To die fighting is more honorable than to perish through famine. Noble birth is honorable. A young nobleman of extraordinary virtue is more readily honored than an older nobleman of the same degree of virtue.[138] The implicit distinction between the honest and the honorable reminds us of the distinction between justice and magnanimity, the two peaks of Aristotle's ethics. It is noteworthy that Machiavelli avoids mentioning justice in the most striking passages. For instance, he does not mention justice in his most comprehensive enumeration of the praiseworthy qualities.[139]

After having referred to the fact that all men agree in praising goodness or virtue and in blaming badness or vice, and hence in praising the virtuous rulers and in blaming tyrants, Machiavelli notes that the writers, and hence the unwary readers, praise the tyrant Caesar most highly. One could dispose of this difficulty by suggesting that while men have a clear grasp of first principles, of what is general, they are easily deceived regarding the application of those principles or regarding what is particular. But according to Machiavelli just the opposite is true: men err more easily regarding what is general than regarding what is particular. The fact that men agree in praising goodness or virtue does not then settle the question regarding the status of goodness or virtue. What men generally say is identical with what most men say most of the time or with what is said publicly. The common opinions regarding goodness or virtue are then most effective in states in which the most important decisions are made by public assemblies, by the assembled people, on the basis of public deliberation. Hence only a fool would dismiss these opinions as mere words and still believe that he can understand political things. Even granted that the substance of the virtues and vices is "names" so that what counts is not that one is virtuous but that one has the name of a virtuous man, such names convey good or bad reputation and hence power or impotence. Yet public deliberations are in many ways prepared and influenced by private deliberations in which the power of the generally held and publicly defensible opinions is weaker than in public deliberations.[140] The generally held opinions thus appear to be a surface phenomenon. Therefore the question arises as to how one can proceed in an orderly and convincing manner from the primarily given, from what can be known by everybody in broad daylight, to the hidden center. While all men praise goodness, most men act badly. It seems that the error contained in what is generally and publicly said can be recognized by simply confronting the manifest speeches with the equally manifest deeds. But the deeds which contradict the speeches praising goodness do not prove that those speeches are untrue, i.e. that men ought not to act virtuously; the deeds by themselves prove merely that most men do not in fact act virtuously. Yet the way in which men mostly act is also expressed by speech, by laudatory speech. Hence the laudatory speeches contradict each other. Machiavelli's analysis of morality will therefore begin with the observation of the self-contradictions inherent in what men generally and publicly praise. The order of that analysis must be distinguished from the order in which its results are presented. Towards the end of his work, he indicates his procedure by the following sentence: "Although to use fraud in any action is detestable, yet in the conduct of war it is praiseworthy and glorious." Common opinion on the one hand unqualifiedly condemns fraud and on the other hand praises fraud when committed in certain circumstances. Common opinion, we may say, hesitatingly and inconsistently takes a middle course between unqualified blame of fraud and unqualified praise of it. It is no accident that the chapter which opens with the sentence just quoted, the 133d chapter of the *Discourses*, ends with the last of the seven references, occurring in the book, to "the middle course."[141]

The common understanding of virtue had found its classic expression in Aristotle's assertion that virtue, being the opposite of vice, is the middle or mean between two faulty extremes (a too little and a too much) which are opposed to each other. Machiavelli occasionally bears witness to the truth of this analysis. A prince must proceed in such a way that too much confidence does not make him incautious and too much diffidence (or too little confidence) does not make him unbearable. The Roman people kept its place honorably by neither ruling arrogantly nor serving abjectly. Liberty is the mean between principality or tyranny and license. On the other hand, however, people condemn "the middle course" (*la via del mezzo*) as harmful. Mercy and justice despise the undecided, the lukewarm, those who are neither for nor against God. Furthermore, we may add in accordance with what Aristotle has said, justice is not a mean between two vices but is opposed only to one vice; in the case of some other virtues, Aristotle's view is not supported by usage: the alleged mean or one of the two alleged opposite vices has not received a name, perhaps because they are not generally regarded as virtues or vices. At any rate Machiavelli tacitly rejects the view that virtue is a mean between two vices. In his most comprehensive enumeration of virtues and vices, each virtue appears as the opposite of a single vice. Elsewhere he contrasts the equanimity of the excellent or great man with a single opposite vice of weak men; that vice consists of two "defects," conceit or arrogance on the one hand and vileness or humility on the other. What he means to convey can be stated as follows. The two opposite defects are merely two aspects of one and the same vice which comes to sight in opposite forms in opposite circumstances; one does not understand either defect if one does not see in each the co-presence of the other. The virtue in question on the other hand comes to sight as one and the same in all situations; it is stable and unchanging, for it is based on "knowledge of the world."[142]

Machiavelli opens his most comprehensive enumeration of virtues and vices by making a distinction between the virtue of liberality and the virtue of giving. The distinction is connected with Tuscan usage. The Tuscan tongue distinguishes somehow between stinginess and rapacity. If stinginess and rapacity are two different vices, and if each vice is the opposite of one virtue and vice versa, there must be two virtues which correspond to stinginess and rapacity respectively. The stingy man abstains "too much" from using his own; the rapacious man desires to acquire by rapine what belongs to others. Since stinginess is an excess ("too much"), it seems to demand a corresponding defect ("too little"), i.e. prodigality;

Machiavelli tacitly denies this by assigning to liberality only one opposite vice, namely, stinginess. Whereas stinginess is the only vice concerning the use of property, rapacity seems to be the only vice concerning acquisition. To our surprise Machiavelli identifies the virtue opposed to rapacity as the virtue of giving: he tacitly substitutes the virtue of giving for justice. He alludes to the fact that liberality has two opposite vices and he alludes to justice which is thought to have only one opposite vice. He explains the meaning of these allusions partly in the following chapter. That chapter is entitled "Of liberality and parsimony." It seems then to be devoted to the virtues dealing with use and preservation of property rather than with its acquisition. A prince, Machiavelli says, who desires to be regarded as liberal must exhibit every sign of sumptuousness. By doing this he is eventually compelled to become stingy: the virtue of liberality necessarily turns into the vice and the infamy of stinginess. What is true of liberality is even truer of prodigality; this is the reason why the difference between liberality and prodigality is irrelevant. The prince ought to practice parsimony; by being parsimonious, he will be enabled to be liberal in the sense that he will not be compelled to rob his subjects or to become rapacious. In the sequel Machiavelli retracts his distinction between liberality and the virtue of giving: not liberality and the virtue of giving but liberality and justice ought to be distinguished from each other. Parsimony necessarily comes to sight as the vice of stinginess but this vice is preferable to the virtue of liberality.[143] Machiavelli's conclusion seems to be unnecessarily shocking; he could have limited himself to replacing the virtue of liberality by the virtue of parsimony. More precisely, since parsimony is praised because it prevents men from becoming rapacious and hence unjust, he could have contented himself with saying that the virtue of justice requires the sacrifice of the virtue of liberality. Only by considering his indications regarding justice can we understand why he denies that the virtuous mean is possible.

Machiavelli raises the question of whether it is better for a republic to devote itself to acquisition, i.e. to the acquisition of what belongs to others, or to the preservation of what it possesses, i.e. to forgo ambition. At first glance the second way seems to be preferable. It is the middle course between taking away from

others what belongs to them and losing to others what one possesses.
Yet since all human things are in a flux, one cannot always do what
reason suggests but must sometimes do what necessity demands:
a consistent policy limited to preservation is impossible. One must
choose between losing to others what one possesses or taking away
from others what they possess. But the latter course is more
honorable than the former. One cannot leave it then at sacrificing
the virtue of giving; one must choose the vice of rapacity. Or, if
one prefers, one may say that true liberality or the virtue of giving
consists in giving away what one has taken from strangers or
enemies; the virtue of liberality is grounded on the vice of rapacity:
the model prince Cyrus was liberal only in this sense.[144] Justice
as the stable mean between self-denial or giving away what one
has on the one hand and injustice on the other is impossible; a bias
in favor of the latter is necessary and honorable.[145] Machiavelli
discusses the same difficulty also in the following form. Men have
the choice between the way of good and the way of evil but "they
take certain middle courses which are most harmful, for men do
not know how to be altogether evil nor how to be altogether good,
as will be shown in the following chapter by an example."[146] We
pass over the fact that Machiavelli here calls "certain middle courses,"
and not the evil course, "most harmful." The promised example
shows that a tyrant who lacked both goodness and conscience did
not dare to commit a certain evil deed: he took a most harmful
middle course because he did not know how to be altogether evil.
But Machiavelli calls the evil deed which the tyrant did not dare
to commit—a deed which by its greatness would have overcome
every infamy—"honorably evil"; the tyrant's previous deeds were
unqualifiedly evil, altogether evil; the deed which he failed to
commit could therefore be described as a mean between good and
evil; precisely by committing the honorably evil deed he would
not have remained altogether evil. Not all middle courses but only
"certain middle courses" are most harmful. Let us replace the
tyrant by a virtuous prince whose previous deeds had been altogether good; if that prince out of his goodness or virtue had refrained from committing the honorably evil deed in question, he
would have been as blameworthy as the tyrant referred to: he
would have been blameworthy for remaining altogether good instead
of taking a middle course between good and evil. It would seem

then that the right way, at any rate for a prince, is indeed a mean—
yet not the mean between two opposite vices but the mean between
virtue and vice. As we have seen earlier, according to Machiavelli
the right course regarding fraud is the middle course between the
unqualified rejection of fraud and its unqualified approval. Humanity
is praiseworthy and makes a man loved whereas cruelty is detestable
and makes a man hated; yet "the true way" consists in not desiring
"too much" to be loved and therefore in not being too humane;
it consists in a certain combination of humanity and cruelty: "the
true way" is "the middle course." "The middle course" cannot
be kept strictly because our nature does not permit it, but it ought
to be kept as much as possible. A prince must know how to use the
nature of man and the nature of the beast: he must follow a middle
course between humanity and inhumanity, for humanity and goodness are appropriate for one kind of circumstances whereas the
opposite vices are appropriate for the opposite kind of circumstances; since "the times change," the change from virtue to vice
or vice versa, the movement between the one and the other, is the
right course.[147] One may therefore speak of a similarity of virtue
and vice: unqualified virtue and unqualified vice are faulty extremes. The true way is the way which imitates nature. But
nature is variable, and not stable like virtue. The true way consists
therefore in the alternation between virtue and vice: between
gravity (or full devotion to great things) and levity, constancy and
inconstancy, chastity and lasciviousness, and so on. Thus the great
Lorenzo de'Medici led both a voluptuous and a grave life; it
seemed therefore that in him "two different persons" were united
in an apparently impossible union; yet precisely this union agreed
with nature.[148] That the alternation between virtue and vice somehow occurs in all men is generally admitted; what is controversial
is the interpretation of this phenomenon: the alternation which
Machiavelli calls natural is understood by the tradition which he
attacks as the alternation between sin and repentance. The alternation which he praises as agreeing with nature does not consist
however in being pushed or pulled now in one direction and then
in the opposite direction; it consists in choosing virtue or vice with
a view to what is appropriate "for whom, toward whom, when and
where." For instance, the alternation in question will be different
in the case of a prince and in the case of a man like Machiavelli.

That alternation is a movement guided by prudence and sustained by strength of mind, will or temper. Prudence and that strength are then always required: whereas in the case of the moral virtues it suffices for the prince to possess the appearance of them, in the case of prudence and strength of mind or will he needs the substance.[149] In other words, prudence (judgment) and strength of mind, will or temper are the only generally recognized virtues which truly possess the generally recognized character of virtue in general: they are themselves always salutary. Whereas the moral virtues and vices (e.g. religion and cruelty) can be well and badly used because their use must be regulated by prudence, prudence cannot be badly or imprudently used.[150] We must emphasize the fact, which Machiavelli has deliberately obscured by his usage, that his doctrine of "virtue" preserves the relevance, the truth, the reality of the generally recognized opposition between (moral) virtue and (moral) vice. This fact affords perhaps the strongest proof of both the diabolical character and the sobriety of his thought. This is not to deny but rather to affirm that in his doctrine of "virtue" the opposition between moral virtue and moral vice becomes subordinate to the opposition between another kind of excellence and worthlessness. Machiavelli expresses the difference between moral virtue and certain other kinds of excellence most simply by distinguishing between goodness (i.e. moral virtue) and virtue or by denying to moral virtue the name of virtue. In fact in most cases he uses "virtue" in a sense different from that of moral virtue. He draws our attention to the deliberate character of his usage most forcefully by in one breath denying and ascribing virtue to the criminal Agathocles.[151] In accordance with this usage characteristic of him, one would have to say that the alternation between goodness and wickedness must be guided by prudence and sustained by virtue.

In his most emphatic references to "the middle course" Machiavelli questions the desirability or possibility of "the middle course." If one examines his remarks on this subject more carefully, one sees that he favors a "certain middle course" rather than the extremes in question.[152] We still have to consider whether the apparently unqualified rejection of the middle course does not convey an important message. Machiavelli is an extremist in the sense that he challenges the whole religious and philosophical tradition. Yet for the reason set forth earlier he is compelled to conceal the full extent of his innovation and to suggest frequently what is in fact a compromise between his view and traditional views. The indictment of the middle course as such is necessary to counteract Machiavelli's own accommodations.[153] The willingness to rest content with compromises has its root in man's strong desire to eat his cake and to have it. Men long for a perfectly good combination of all good things which has all the advantages of its elements and is free from their defects. They see for instance that both monarchies and republics have their virtues and their defects; they wish therefore for a mixed state which combines the advantages of the monarchy and the republic and is free from the defects of either; they overlook the fact that the mixture or mean is inferior to these extremes because it is less stable than they.[154] Generally stated, there is no good, simple or combined, without its accompanying evil, so much so that all choice can be said to be a choice among evils. If a certain institution appears to be altogether salutary, one can be certain that it will prove to carry with itself an unsuspected evil so that one will be compelled sooner or later to modify or to abolish that institution: one will always be in need of new modes and orders.[155] The best regime and happiness, as classical philosophy understood them, are impossible. There cannot be a political order which satisfies all reasonable demands nor a state of the individual which satisfies all reasonable desires. Still, Machiavelli seems to admit a *summum bonum;* he praises the pagans for having seen the highest good in worldly honor or, more precisely, in "greatness of mind, strength of the body and all other things which are apt to make men most strong."[156] To understand this passage, we must return to Machiavelli's remarks on Agathocles. Agathocles was of outstanding greatness of mind and strength of body but he conspicuously lacked moral virtue; thus he could acquire empire but not glory; he cannot be judged inferior to any most excellent captain but his vices and crimes do not permit that he be counted among the most excellent men.[157] It would seem that "the other things which are apt to make men most strong" are the moral virtues and therefore that, according to the pagans whom Machiavelli praises, the highest good consists in virtue in the most comprehensive sense, i.e. in that quality which makes one not only a most excellent captain but a most excellent man. The most excellent man would then be good without having any defect—contrary to Machiavelli's assertion that every good is accompanied by its own evil. Yet every man, however good, has his specific limitations, or no man partakes of all excellences which can ennoble man: no man is complete; a "universal man" is an imagined being. The most perfect prince or ruler cannot possibly possess the specific excellence of which the people is capable, an excellence not inferior to the excellence of the prince.[158] The excellence of a man who is the teacher of both princes and peoples, of the thinker who has discovered the modes and orders which are in accordance with nature, can be said to be the highest excellence of which man is capable. Yet this highest freedom cannot become effective if the thinker does not undergo what to him must be the most degrading of all servitudes. Or if, prompted by levity, he would derive enjoyment from undergoing that servitude, he would lose the respect of his fellow men. The conclusion that excellence, and every kind or degree of excellence, necessarily carries with it its peculiar defect or evil is strengthened if excellence consists in an alternation between moral virtue and moral vice. To sum up, Machiavelli rejects the mean to the extent to which the notion of the mean is linked up with the notions of a perfect happiness that excludes all evil and of the simply perfect human being or of the "universal man," and therefore with the notion of a most perfect being simply which possesses all perfections most eminently and hence cannot be the cause of evil.[159]

The common understanding of goodness had found its classic expression in Aristotle's assertion that virtue is the habit of choosing well and that choosing well or ill as well as the habits of choosing well or ill (the virtues or vices) are voluntary: man is responsible for having become and for becoming virtuous or vicious. Man can choose the good or the bad; he possesses a free will. This freedom is compatible with the "natural and absolute necessity" through which man is inclined towards the perfect good or true happiness; it is also compatible with that necessity through which means or particular good or evil things are linked to ends or the end: by choosing the means without which he cannot possibly achieve his end or achieve it well, man chooses freely. But freedom of the will is incompatible with the necessity of compulsion through which a man is literally compelled by other agents to act against his natural inclination. Machiavelli seems to adopt this view. In accordance with the fact that he teaches throughout his two books what man ought to do, he explicitly rejects the opinion of "many" who hold that chance and God govern all things of the world: that opinion is incompatible with the recognition of free will and therewith of prudence and virtue. Chance, he declares, rules half of our actions whereas "our free will" or "we" rule the other half. "Our free will" or "we" seem to be limited only by chance; there seems to be no room for nature or necessity. Chance is irresistible to everything except virtue or the wise use of our freedom; virtue can limit, if not break, the power of chance; virtue can subjugate chance, i.e. it can put chance into its service. Man can be the master of his fate. Yet chance presupposes nature and necessity.[160] Therefore, the question concerns less the relation of freedom and chance than the relation of freedom on the one hand and nature and necessity on the other: can virtue control nature and necessity as it can control chance?

If the core of virtue is freedom of the will, the acts of virtue consist in freely choosing the right means for the right end or in freely choosing to do what, as reason or prudence shows, ought to be done. Actions prompted by virtue are fundamentally different from actions prompted by necessity; only the former deserve praise. For instance, to relieve the burden of the common people out of liberality is radically different from doing the same action because necessity compels one to it or because one has no choice but to do it. To act virtuously means to follow reason and in so doing not to be subject to necessity. Yet it is not always possible to follow reason (e.g. to be liberal or to be just). Men are compelled by necessity to do many things of which reason disapproves. In such cases acting virtuously consists in submitting to necessity[161] —and even to the necessity to sin. Necessity makes it impossible for men always to obey what we would call the moral law.[162] Since people ascribe to man a much greater freedom than he possesses, or since they ignore the power of necessity, they frequently blame men for actions which those men were compelled to commit. They believe for instance that it was Caesar's wickedness that was responsible for the fall of the Roman republic: he was free to live in his fatherland like Scipio before him; they do not see that the Roman republic fell because of its corruption which antedated

Caesar and which was caused by the strife connected with the agrarian law and by the prolongation of military commands, to say nothing of the inevitable ruinous consequences of Rome's glorious conquests and also to say nothing of the fact that Caesar's action was excused by the ingratitude which the Roman republic had exhibited toward him.[163]

The question whether man can control nature and necessity is identical with the question regarding the precise character of man's ability to control chance. Whether a man's chance or luck is good or bad depends to a considerable extent on whether his mode of action agrees or does not agree with "the quality of the times" in which he lives. Since he cannot change the times and has no influence on its changes, he cannot control chance unless he is able to change his mode of action in accordance with the changing times or to adapt his mode of action to the given "matter": only a perfectly prudent man, a man who would be prudence incarnate or rather disembodied prudence, could control chance. But there are limits to a man's ability to change his modes of action, and this is ultimately due to the fact that each man has a natural inclination to act in a specific manner, an inclination which he cannot completely change. The specific nature of a man so far from being determined by him, by his choice or free will, determines him, his choice or free will. E.g., Fabius Maximus was cautious not by choice but by nature; "nature forced" him or his "humor" forced him to proceed with caution. What is true of Fabius' caution is true of Soderini's patience and humility, Pope Julius II's opposite qualities, Manlius Capitolinus' "evil nature," Appius Claudius' "innate arrogance," Remirro's "bitter nature," Scipio's kindness and Manlius Torquatus' severity, and indeed of the corresponding qualities of all men: "we cannot change ourselves." Machiavelli knows that what is called a man's nature is frequently that nature modified by habit, and if he says that we cannot change ourselves he means that we cannot significantly modify those qualities which stem partly from nature or inheritance and partly from education and habit. Still, innate qualities are of decisive importance. Virtue in the highest sense, "extraordinary virtue," grandeur of mind and will, the pre-moral or trans-moral quality which distinguishes the great men from the rest of mankind, is a gift of nature. Such virtue, which is not chosen, compels a man to set himself high goals, and since such virtue is inseparable from the highest prudence, to set himself the wisest goal possible in the circumstances. In spite of the fact that such virtue is not chosen by its possessor but given by nature, it is more highly praised than any other kind of virtue. In the case of men of extraordinary virtue or prudence, "Is" and "Ought" coincide: they cannot do what they ought not to do and they must do what they ought to do; in their case the dictates of prudence have compulsory power. Conversely, the majority of men are compelled by their native lack of understanding to act unwisely, although everyone is expected to act morally and this means according to the traditional view prudently. Hence, precepts are much less useful than is believed by those who give rules to men in general and to princes in particular: all precepts must be prudently applied, and prudence is given only to a few. Machiavelli indicates the difficulty by saying "And above all, a prince ought to contrive to make himself famous by every action of his as a great man and one of excellent mind."[164]

"As has been written by some moral philosophers, men's hands and tongue, two most noble instruments for ennobling him, would not have done their work perfectly nor would they have carried the works of men to the height to which they are seen to have been carried, if they had not been driven on by necessity." Man's doing his work in the best manner—the fullest exercise of his virtue—is due to necessity and not to choice and still less to chance. Yet are not men's failures also due to necessity? Man's nature is such that necessity compels him to be virtuous or good as well as to be vicious or bad. Machiavelli's praise of necessity must then refer to a particular kind of necessity. In the chapter from the beginning of which we have just quoted, he gives some indications of what he understands by "such necessity" as make soldiers operate perfectly. To speak here only of Machiavelli's primary examples, soldiers fighting against a superior enemy operate perfectly if they have no choice except to die or to fight; they cease to operate perfectly if they can achieve safety by flight or surrender. To be driven by necessity means here to have no choice except to die or to fight; for to have this choice means to have no choice at all since men are compelled by nature to try to avoid death; fighting is chosen because it is the only way in which in the circumstances certain and imminent death could possibly be avoided: the choice of fighting is imposed by necessity. If the soldiers can save their lives by flight or surrender, they choose flight or surrender as offering a greater prospect of avoiding death and as requiring a much smaller effort or as being easier. Fighting as well as flight or surrender aim at the same end, namely, the preservation of one's life; this end is imposed, as we may tentatively say, by an absolute and natural necessity. If the enemy makes impossible flight or surrender, fighting is imposed on the soldiers in question as the only possible means to achieve the end mentioned. On the other hand, if the enemy gives them an opportunity to flee or surrender, flight or surrender is imposed on them as the better or easier means to achieve that end. Yet in the latter case, we do not speak of necessity prompting them because flight or surrender are easier than fighting, i.e., because they go less against the soldiers' natural inclination. We shall then say that the necessity which makes soldiers fighting against a superior enemy operate well is the necessity, rooted in fear of death, to act against their natural inclination but within their ability. Generalizing from this, we may say that it is fear, the fundamental fear, which makes men operate well.[165]

Machiavelli elucidates the necessity which makes men operate well also in the following manner. He distinguishes two kinds of war, wars caused by necessity and wars caused by choice or ambition; almost all wars waged by the Romans were wars of choice. Wars of choice or ambition serve the purpose of acquisition or aggrandizement; wars of necessity are waged by whole peoples which are compelled by hunger or a lost war to leave their homeland and conquer another land in which to live. In the most important cases, the necessity to conquer other peoples' lands and to massacre all their inhabitants is caused by hunger due to overpopulation. If just wars are wars waged by those for whom war is necessary, the wars caused by hunger are the justest of all wars: everyone is compelled to fight for the sake of mere life and there can be no doubt that this necessity is not derived from previous guilt. Wars which are freely chosen are then, to say the least, less just than wars of necessity. Furthermore, hunger and poverty, people say, make men industrious. Again we see that the kind of necessity which makes men operate well—in this case induces them to be just and industrious—is the necessity rooted in the concern

for mere life. Necessity thus understood is related to choice as
hunger is to ambition: no one is compelled by ambition in the
way in which he is compelled by hunger. The satisfaction of the
need for food or, generally, for the preservation of life cannot be
postponed in the way in which the satisfaction of ambition can be
postponed. It is precisely necessity in the sense of the most urgent
need or the corresponding fear which as a rule suppresses ambition. Fighting from necessity precedes fighting from ambition:
man's primary condition is one of scarcity.[166] The compulsion
proceeding from hunger precedes all compulsion caused by men.
There is a necessary connection between the primary need and the
means of satisfying it ("things useful"), and between the latter
and property. Property, we may say, is self-preservation which
has taken on flesh. Thus life and property are more "necessary"
than honor and glory. In accordance with this, when life and
property are at stake, as distinguished from when honor is at
stake, men are not altogether insane. Men are more concerned with
property than with honor; even the Roman nobles, although they
were great lovers of honor and glory, were still greater lovers of
property. Even Rome's wars of ambition were not unconnected
with concern with property; those wars made Rome and the
Romans wealthy.[167] Considering the connection between property
and money, we are not surprised to learn that while virtue is indeed much more important for winning wars than is money, yet
money is necessary in the second place.[168]

Necessity makes men not only virtuous but good as well. Men
in general have no natural inclination toward goodness. Therefore
they can be made good and kept good only by necessity. Such
necessity is brought upon men originally by non-human nature,
by the original terror. But the quasi-original goodness is inseparable
from defenselessness and want. Men are therefore compelled to
form societies in order to live in peace and security. The security
afforded by society would remove the necessity to be good if the
primary necessity to be good were not replaced by a necessity to
be good which stems from laws, i.e., from punishment or threat
of punishment—by a necessity originating in men. Men living in
society can be made good and kept good only by such compulsion causing fear as originates in other men.[169]

Of the men who originate compulsion or impose necessities,

those operate well who choose the right time and other right circumstances to apply compulsion; they act freely. The modes and
orders by which leaders are trained, enabled and compelled to
apply compulsion properly, i.e., to operate well, originate in virtuous legislators or founders. The virtuous founders operate well
because they are prompted by their natural desire for the common
good, by the pleasing prospect that they will make their fatherland happy and that they themselves will become happy through
earning "the glory of the world" for their work: the virtuous
founders do not operate well because they are compelled by other
men or by the harsh necessity that they will perish from hunger
or from the sword of the enemy if they do not do their work
well. Thus the necessity to operate well which originates in men
appears to be derivative from choice. It is then ultimately choice
and not necessity which makes men operate well. Choice belongs
together with ambition which is hard to distinguish from the desire
for honor or glory, whereas necessity belongs together with the
concern for mere life or the fear of death or of punishment. It
was not necessity thus understood but love of glory which, in the
opinion of the Romans, makes captains operate well. The Roman
nobility was compelled to give the plebs a great share in political
power because it wished to use the plebs in its glorious enterprises;
the necessity prompting the Roman nobility was derivative from
its love of glory, from its choice. A man need not be compelled
by others to be good and to remain good; he himself can make
arrangements which compel him to be good and to remain good;
the necessity which makes and keeps him good may originate in
his choice. The necessity to be ungrateful or unjust can be avoided;
hence one's being compelled by the necessity to be ungrateful or
unjust is due to primary wrong choice. A republic which wages
war only when necessity compels it to do so will be less in need
of excellent men than a republic like Rome which was constantly
engaged in wars of choice; it will therefore operate less perfectly
than Rome. Wars of choice or ambition may be less just than wars
of necessity or survival; they are however much less savage or inhuman than the latter. Necessity and choice are related to each
other as the low and the high. Choice, wise or honorable choice,
is the prerogative of the prudent and the strong, of individuals
and societies which are animated by ambition or love of glory.

For since there is no perfect good, to choose means at best to choose a good mixed with evil. To choose means therefore in all important cases to take a risk and to trust in one's power to keep under control the evil which goes with the good chosen. The weak lack that trust; they never choose well unless other men compel them to choose well.[170] Not the strong but only the weak operate well by virtue of that necessity which stems from compulsion, fear or hunger.

Machiavelli's praise of necessity, which surpasses in emphasis everything he says in praise of choice, would be untenable if he had not seen his way toward conceiving of ambition or the desire for honor or glory, and especially of the desire of the founder for supreme glory, as a form of that necessity which makes men operate well. In the first place, ambition—the desire to acquire, to have more than one needs, not to be inferior to others, to be superior to others, to be outstanding—arises with necessity as soon as the primary wants are satisfied and exerts a compulsory power. But ambition does not necessarily make men operate well. Not all men know how to satisfy "the natural and ordinary desire for acquisition." The most outstanding example used by Machiavelli to illustrate this is Manlius Capitolinus, who sought supreme glory without considering the "matter" with which he had to deal; his unwise cupidity to reign, his blindness of mind led to his failure. Only men of supreme virtue or prudence are compelled by their desire for glory to operate in the most perfect manner. What they recognize as wise or honorable acts on them with the same compulsory power with which only fear of great, manifest and imminent evils acts on most men. One of the necessities which compelled Hannibal to fight at Zama was the fact that it is more glorious to go down fighting than to lose everything without fighting. While the desire for glory in its highest form acts with compulsory power, it can be identified with choice or freedom for the following reasons. The compulsion stemming from the desire for glory cannot be imposed on a man as can be the compulsion stemming from fear; the former compulsion arises entirely from within. The man driven by the desire for glory is guided by a pleasing prospect rather than compelled by a harsh present; he is not hemmed in by darkness and misery but a broad sunlit field is open to his view. The necessities, with a view to which men of supreme prudence as such necessarily act, are not so much present as foreseen necessities. The two kinds of necessity which make men of the two kinds operate well are naked necessities, necessities known as such. The soldiers led by Messius would not have fought well if Messius had not enlightened them as to the necessity to fight well by shouting to them "Do you believe that some god will protect you and carry you off from here?"[171] Only the known necessity compels men to make the supreme effort, not to trust in Fortuna but to try to subjugate her. If men do not know the necessity in question or are under the spell of false opinions denying it, that necessity is counteracted by the compulsory power of ignorance or false opinion; this composite necessity—a wrong kind of "middle course"—prevents them from operating well.

A man who is by nature supremely virtuous and is as such subject to specific necessities cannot mould his matter as he sees fit, or cannot be the master of his fate and the fate of his people, or cannot operate in the most perfect manner possible to men, if he lacks the occasion or opportunity for so operating. In the highest case, the case of the founder, this opportunity consists in the necessity inherent in his matter, i.e., his people, to exert itself to the utmost, to be open to a complete change of modes and orders and to submit to the compulsion required for effecting such change. In other cases the opportunity for a man of supreme virtue to operate perfectly consists in the availability of good or incorrupt matter, i.e., of a people which has become virtuous through the application of compulsion of a certain kind during many generations, and in the presence of great public challenges of a pressing character, i.e., domestic or foreign dangers which are felt by everyone and therefore are "necessities." The man of supreme virtue lacks opportunity in easy times, in times in which men can permit themselves a great variety of "free choices" without themselves encountering serious dangers and in which therefore they do not operate well. The highest achievement requires that the necessity to operate well which is effective in the giver of the "form" and the necessity to operate well which is effective in the "matter" should meet. But there is no necessity that the two supplementary necessities should meet; their meeting is a matter of chance. Still, the man of supreme virtue can create his opportunity to some extent. Contrary to Aristotle's view according to which multitudes have a natural fitness either for being subject to a despot or for a life of political freedom, fitness for either form of life can be artificially produced if a man of a rare "brain" applies the required degree of force to the multitude in question; compulsion can bring about a "change of nature." No "defect of nature" can account for the unwarlike character of a nation; a prince of sufficient ability can transform any nation however pampered by climate into a race of warriors.[172] We may express Machiavelli's thought by saying that Aristotle did not see that the relation of the founder to his human matter is not fundamentally different from the relation of a smith to his iron or his inanimate matter: Aristotle did not realize to what extent man is malleable, and in particular malleable by man. Still, that malleability is limited and therefore it remains true that the highest achievement depends on chance. Conversely, chance may favor the enterprises of founders or captains who lack prudence. This would not make their achievement admirable except for vulgar minds. Machiavelli is far from being a worshipper of success: not the success but the wisdom of an enterprise deserves praise and admiration. The man who has discovered the modes and orders which are in accordance with nature is much less dependent on chance than is any man of action since his discovery need not bear fruit during his lifetime. He too however depends on chance as is shown by the fact that he needs for the actualization of his modes and orders the cooperation of unreliable allies, i.e., of men whose action in the decisive moment cannot possibly be foreseen. Besides, there is no guarantee whatever that future opportunities for introducing the new modes and orders will not be spoiled or missed. In spite of all this, his discovery will always be vindicated by the failure of all modes and orders which differ from those he has discovered: "if your advice is not taken and through the advice of others disaster follows, you will reap from this very great glory."[173] Only he subjugates chance or is master of his fate who has discovered the fundamental necessities governing human life and therewith also the necessity of chance and the range of chance. Man is then subject to nature and necessity in such a way that by virtue of nature's gift of "brain" and through knowledge of nature and necessity he is enabled to use necessity and to transform matter.

The common understanding of goodness had found its classic

expression in Aristotle's assertions that virtuous activity is the core of happiness for both individuals and societies, that virtue or the perfection of human nature preserves society, and that political society exists for the sake of the good life, i.e., of the virtuous activity of its members. In order to fulfill its natural function in the best way, the city must have a certain order, a certain regime: the best regime. The best regime, the regime according to nature, is the rule of gentlemen or perhaps the mixed regime. Under certain conditions the best regime may be kingship which is the best regime simply. Its opposite is tyranny, the simply worst regime: whereas the king finds his chief support in the gentlemen, the tyrant finds his chief support in the common people. Apart from its depraved character and depraving effect, tyranny is particularly short-lived; its being against nature shows itself in the fact that tyranny is not viable in the long run. On the other hand, the best regime strictly understood exists very rarely, if it has ever existed, although it is of its essence to be possible. From Machiavelli's point of view this means that the best regime, as Aristotle as well as Plato conceived of it, is an imagined republic or an imagined principality. Imagined states are based on the premise that rulers can or must exercise the moral virtues and avoid the moral vices even in the acts of ruling. According to Machiavelli this premise is based on the more fundamental premise that most men are good; for if most men are bad, the ruler cannot possibly rule his subjects if he does not adapt himself in a considerable measure to their badness. As will appear later, Machiavelli has indicated precisely the root of his disagreement with the classics by pointing to the fact of human badness. But every indication is insufficient and may even be wrong if taken literally. For Aristotle teaches as clearly as Machiavelli himself that most men are bad as well as that all men desire wealth and honor. Yet this very fact leads the classics to the conclusion that the best men, to be rewarded with outstanding honors, ought to rule the many bad by coercing them; they must indeed know thoroughly the bad and their ways; but such knowledge is perfectly compatible with immunity to badness.[174]

Yet according to Aristotle, man is the worst of all living beings if he is without law and right, and law and right depend upon political society. In other words, men become virtuous by habituation; such habituation requires laws, customs, examples and exhortations, and is therefore properly possible only within and through political society. In the words of Machiavelli, good examples arise from good education, good education arises from good laws, and good laws arise from most shocking things. For if virtue presupposes political society, political society is preceded by pre-moral or sub-moral men and indeed founded by such men. There cannot be a moral law of unconditional validity; the moral law cannot possibly find listeners and hence addressees before men have become members of civil society, or have become civilized. Morality is possible only after its condition has been created, and this condition cannot be created morally: morality rests on what to moral men must appear to be immorality. One can avoid this conclusion only by making one of the two following assumptions. Either one must assume that men are good, not only at the beginning of republics but at the beginning simply; in that case they would not need civil society for becoming good. Or one must assume that civil society is founded by men of heroic virtue—of a kind of moral virtue which is not derived from habituation. To make this assumption means from Machiavelli's point of view to have an unwarranted belief in the goodness of which man's nature is capable and in the power of that goodness. Not semi-divine or divinely inspired benefactors of the human race but men like Cesare Borgia and especially the criminal emperor Severus reveal to us the true features of the first founders of society.[175] The situation in which the foundation took place recurs whenever society as a whole is in grave danger from within or without. In all such situations, the modes used by the original founder must be used again if there is to be society and its offspring, morality. Morality can exist only on an island created or at any rate protected by immorality.

The primary badness which is severely limited by civil society and especially by the good civil society affects civil society however good. Reason may dictate the practice of moral virtue; necessity renders such practice impossible in important areas. Therefore the best regime of the classics is merely imaginary. The classics demand that the end of civil society be the practice of moral virtue. But even the sober Aristotle is compelled to admit that no state which has "ever been seen and known to be truly" makes moral virtue its end: to the extent to which actual states have any single and supreme end, that end is lording it over their neighbors without any regard to right or wrong. These states admit that virtue is necessary and they praise and honor virtue; but they conceive of virtue as a means for obtaining external goods, i.e., wealth and honor or glory. But if no state regards moral virtue as its end, how can one say that the natural end of the state is the promotion of virtue? Can something which is contradicted by the universal practice of mankind be natural to man? Classical political philosophy culminates in the description of imagined states and thus is useless because it does not accept as authoritative the end which all or the most respectable states pursue. That end is the common good conceived of as consisting of freedom from foreign domination and from despotic rule, rule of law, security of the lives, the property and the honor of every citizen, ever increasing wealth and power, and last but not least glory or empire. The common good as pursued by states which are "seen and known to be truly" does not include virtue, but a certain kind of virtue is required for the sake of that common good. In accordance with how men live one must then start from the fact that virtue, far from being the end of civil society, is a means for achieving the common good in the amoral sense. Virtue in the true sense is patriotism, full dedication to the well-being of one's society, a dedication which extinguishes or absorbs all private ambition in favor of the ambition of the republic. The common good is the end only of republics.[176] Hence, the virtue which is truly virtue can best be described as republican virtue. Republican virtue has some affinity to moral virtue, so much so that republics come to view as morally superior to principalities. Republics are less given to ingratitude and faithlessness, and they possess greater goodness and humanity than do princes. Political freedom is incompatible with corruptness of the people. This does not mean however that republics are to be preferred in the last analysis on moral grounds. They are to be preferred with a view to the common good in the amoral sense. Republics can adapt themselves better to the change of times than can monarchies because their government consists of men of different natures, and different natures are required in different kinds of times. Republics do not depend upon the hazards of hereditary succession. They are incompatible with absolute power of any individual. In republics there is more life and therefore greater dedication to the common good than in monarchies. The moral superiority of republics is to some extent an accidental result of the republican structure. A republic can afford to be more grateful than a prince because, if it is properly constructed, it has a sufficient supply of able captains who mutually supervise and check one another so that no harm will come to the republic from the gratitude by which it encourages its victorious captains. Republics keep better faith than princes because of the cumbersome character of republican proceedings, which do not permit sudden and secret switches from one policy to another.[177]

One of the reasons why Machiavelli distinguishes between virtue and goodness is his desire to indicate the difference between republican virtue and moral virtue. Goodness is not always compatible with the common good, whereas virtue is always required for it. Acts of kindness, however well-intentioned, may lead to the building up of private power to the detriment of the public power. A most important means for making a republic great is to keep the public rich and the citizens poor. To permit the citizens to become rich means to permit some citizens to become rich and hence to make possible the dependence of citizens on private citizens or the destruction of civic equality. At the same time it means to introduce luxury and therewith effeminacy into the city. To keep the citizens poor, the republic must honor poverty; it must prevent the preponderance of trade and the mingling with foreigners. Austerity and severity are the clearest signs of republican virtue. The leading men in a republic ought to be harsh rather than gentle, cruel rather than humane, hated rather than beloved, lest the people adhere to them rather than to the republic. By becoming humane, a republic runs the danger of becoming abject. This is not to deny that humane conduct towards enemies may sometimes be more conducive to conquest than force itself. In the chapter which is devoted to proving this proposition, Machiavelli retells the story of how Scipio acquired high reputation in Spain by his chastity: he returned a young and beautiful wife to her husband without having touched her; it was not his chastity, which in the circumstances would have been a politically irrelevant virtue, but his generosity which redounded to the benefit of Rome.[178] The substitution of republican virtue for moral virtue implies a criticism of moral virtue which can be stated as follows.

From the point of view of society at any rate, the moral virtue which comprises all other moral virtues is justice. In order to bring to light the nature of justice, Plato wrote the *Republic* in which he demanded among other things that the guardians of the city be savage toward strangers. Aristotle, the classic exponent of moral virtue, i.e., of the highest kind of that virtue which is not knowledge, reproves Plato for having made that demand: one ought to be gentle toward everyone, one ought not to be savage toward anyone except toward those who act unjustly. Aristotle assumes that it is always possible and safe to distinguish between foreigners and unjust enemies. He certainly refrains from reproving Plato for having purified the luxurious city without having forced it to restore the land which it had taken from its neighbors in order to lead a life of luxury. Cruelty towards strangers cannot be avoided by the best of citizens as citizens.[179] Justice which is the habit of not taking away what belongs to others while defending what belongs to oneself rests on the firm ground of the selfishness of society. "The factual truth" of moral virtue is republican virtue.

If the common good in the sense stated is the ultimate end, every means, regardless of whether it is morally good or not, is good if it is conducive to that end. The killing of innocent men, even of one's own brother, will be good if it is needed for that most just and laudable end. It can only be for lack of a suitable example that Machiavelli did not apply to parricide what he teaches regarding fratricide. The example of Junius Brutus enables him to say that those who wish to maintain a newly established republic must kill the sons of Brutus, i.e., those disaffected with the republic. Those who say that the killing of innocent men for the good end sets a bad example forget that terrible things manifestly done for the salvation of the fatherland cannot be used to excuse the doing of terrible things which have no connection whatever with the salvation of the fatherland. This is to say nothing of the fact that only known or professed misdeeds can be used by others as examples. For if deception is laudable and glorious when practiced against foreign enemies, there is no reason that it should not be permissible against actual or potential domestic enemies of the fatherland, i.e., of the republic—for where there is no republic there is no fatherland—and not merely after the outbreak of a civil war or when it may be too late. When the existence of the fatherland is at stake, one ought not to be concerned with justice or injustice, with compassion or cruelty, with the laudable or the infamous. There cannot be republics where there is no equality; such equality is abhorred by the feudal nobility or gentry, i.e., by a certain kind of men who live in abundance without having to work; such men must be destroyed if there is to be a republic. All laws favorable to public liberty arise from civic discord, from the liberty-loving people venting its ambition, its anger, its malignant humors against fellow citizens in tumults or riots; since the effect is good, the causes—discord, disorder, the passions—must be declared to be very good if it is true that the principal cause is of higher rank than its effects. The multitude does not desire public liberty in all cases; in case it does not, to use fraud and force against the multitude itself for the sake of public liberty is unobjectionable. If every mode of action and every quality deserves praise or blame only with a view to its being conducive or harmful to the common good, able governors or captains degraded by vices however unnatural which do no harm to the republic and do not become publicly known are infinitely to be preferred to saintly rulers who lack political and military ability. To use the words of a historian who is well-known for his strict adherence to moral principle, "a weak man may be deemed more mischievous to the state over which he presides than a wicked one." The common good may be endangered by the legal use of public power; in such cases it is unobjectionable, if appeals to the patriotism of the power-holder are useless, to bribe him for the sake of the public good. One may summarize Machiavelli's thought on this point by saying that moral modes of action are the ordinary modes, the modes appropriate in most cases, whereas the immoral modes are the extraordinary ones, the modes required only in extraordinary cases. One may object to Machiavelli's view of the relation between moral virtue and the common good by saying that it abolishes the essential difference between civil societies and bands of robbers, since robbers too use ordinary modes among themselves whenever possible. Machiavelli is not deterred by this consideration. He compares the Roman patricians, the most respectable ruling class that ever was, to small birds of prey, and he quotes Livy's observation that a certain chief of pirates equalled the Romans in piety.[180]

The common good claims to be the good of everyone. But

since the common good requires that innocent individuals be sacrificed for its sake, the common good is rather the good of the large majority, perhaps even the good of the common people as distinguished from the good of the nobles or of the great. This does not mean that the majority ought to rule in order to take care of the good of the majority. The majority cannot rule. In all republics, however well ordered, only a tiny minority ever arrives at exercising functions of ruling. For the multitude is ignorant, lacks judgment, and is easily deceived; it is helpless without leaders who persuade or force it to act prudently. There exists in every republic an antagonism between the people and the great, the people desiring not to be oppressed by the great and the great desiring to lord it over the people. It is in the best interest of the people that it be confronted and led by a virtuous and warlike nobility with which it shares political power in due proportion. Only if political power is shared by the great and the people in due proportion, or in other words if there is a proper proportion between the force of the great and the force of the people, will there be public liberty and proper consideration for the common good. What that proper proportion is depends decisively on whether the republic in question wishes to found an empire or is content with preserving itself. A republic dedicated to aggrandizement or acquisition needs the voluntary cooperation of its armed plebs; an armed and virile plebs will naturally demand a considerable share in political power and in the fruits of conquest, and will not hesitate to support those demands with indecorous, disorderly and even illegal actions; republican greatness and perfect order are incompatible; an imperial republic must give its plebs a greater share in political power than a non-imperial republic. In fact, republics are not free to choose between a policy of aggrandizement or one of mere preservation. Every republic may be compelled by circumstances to engage in a policy of aggrandizement and must therefore prepare itself for such contingencies by enlisting the fervent cooperation of the common people. It would be more precise to say that "the desire for acquisition is very natural and ordinary, and when men who are able to acquire do acquire, they will always be praised and not blamed." Accordingly one of the ends of every republic is to make acquisitions.[181] An intelligent policy of imperialism as it was practiced by the Romans requires that the republic permit the strengthening of its plebs by liberally admitting foreigners to citizenship; the republic is thus compelled to permit a considerable degree not only of domestic turbulence but above all of corruption of manners. The common good then requires the sacrifice not only of moral virtue but to some extent even of republican austerity and severity. A non-imperial republic can afford "equal poverty" of all its citizens. An imperial republic will necessarily develop a great inequality of wealth, for aggrandizement means also enrichment, and the enrichment of the state will lead to the enrichment of its citizens. The maxim that the public should be rich and the citizens should be poor will have to give way to the maxim that the public should be rich and the common people not become spoiled and effeminate by becoming too wealthy. One must go beyond this and say that in a flourishing republic everyone strives to acquire wealth, i.e., private wealth, because property and its acquisition is secure thanks to the rule of law, and not only public wealth but also private wealth increases marvellously. If it is true that poverty brings better fruits than wealth, one must say that these better fruits must be sacrificed on the altar of the common good and that this sacrifice will hardly be noticed by the happy citizens who enrich the public by enriching themselves. In the long run, the disastrous effects of great and excessive private wealth will make themselves felt. In addition, once the imperial republic has reached a state of unchallengeable supremacy, salutary necessity ceases to operate and decline inevitably follows. Finally, the imperial republic destroys the freedom of all other republics and rules over them much more oppressively than any non-barbarous prince would. These facts force one to reconsider the assumption that imperialism in the Roman style is the wisest policy or even simply necessary, i.e., to reconsider a tentative assumption which allowed Machiavelli to make clear that even republican austerity is not a quasi-unconditional demand. Confederacies of equal republics can be sufficiently strong for mutual defense, and at the same time they are prevented by their structure from engaging in a policy of large scale aggrandizement. Republics of this character would seem to be able to preserve their republican austerity. On the other hand they are not under the same necessity as the Roman republic to give their common people a share in political power. It seems as if republics would have to choose between oppressing foreigners and oppressing their own plebs. Besides, as the examples of the modern Swiss and the ancient Aetolians show, confederacies of warlike republics tend to become notorious for their avarice and their faithlessness towards the foreign states which hire them to serve in their wars. To sum up, there is no good without its accompanying evil, and this is true even of republican virtue.[182]

Machiavelli elucidates the difference between the imperial republic and the confederacy of equal republics by using the examples of ancient Rome and ancient Tuscany. His remarks on this subject are meant both to reveal the nature of human things and to indicate political possibilities for contemporary Italy. The imitation of the Romans being difficult, especially the modern Tuscans ought to imitate the ancient Tuscans; for modern Tuscany too is unusually rich in states eager to preserve or to recover their republican liberty. But a new Tuscan league would only be the second best solution. No country was ever united or happy if it was not ruled by a single republic or a single prince like France and Spain. The most satisfactory solution to the Italian problem would be the union of all Italy under a hegemonial republic like ancient Rome as it was prior to its making conquests outside of Italy. Ancient Rome prior to the First Punic War was wholly incorrupt; it had not yet reduced its allied republics to the status of subjects, at least not fully and openly; and it was still compelled and able to use its whole citizenry in frequent wars. The successful imitation by modern Italians of the early Roman republic would necessarily be accompanied by a peculiar evil: an Italy unified by a republic or a prince would no longer abound in independent republics and thus would be less likely to abound in excellent men.[183]

It is not sufficient to say that Machiavelli in effect makes a distinction between republican virtue and moral virtue, and sees in republican virtue "the factual truth" of moral virtue. Republican virtue as dedication to the common good includes all habits which are conducive to the common good and in particular it includes opposite habits (e.g., severity and gentleness) to the extent to which each is conducive to the common good. The common good includes all things which both can be produced or preserved by common action and are good for almost all members of society, be they great or commoners.[184] Since the ruling class and the common people have different functions, each of these two parts must also possess a peculiar kind of virtue. Machiavelli illustrates this difference of virtues chiefly by examples taken from the Roman senate and the Roman plebs. The characteristic virtues of the senate were prudence and a calculated liberality dispensing sparingly such goods as had been taken from enemies; also, dignity and venerability; and finally, patience and artfulness. The characteristic virtues of the plebs were goodness, contempt for the seemingly or truly vile, and religion. Goodness is then at home with the people. This is the reason that public deliberations, deliberations in popular assemblies, are unlikely to favor proposals which seem to be cowardly or which suggest open breaches of faith. Machiavelli has set forth his view of the innocence of the perfect plebs and the lack of innocence of the perfect patricians in a manner on which it is impossible to improve. According to his version of a Livian story, the angry plebs demanded, after the downfall of the Decemviri, full criminal jurisdiction and the surrender of the Decemviri, whom it desired to burn alive; the two most decent patricians replied to this effect: your first demand is laudable but the last is impious; besides, it is sufficient to ask a man for his weapons, and superfluous to go on to tell him "I want to kill you with them," for once you have his weapons in your hand, you can satisfy your desire. The goodness of the people consists less in its inability to commit impious or atrocious actions—Machiavelli's *Florentine Histories* are full of accounts of atrocious actions of the Florentine plebs—than in its inability to color its wicked actions: it does not understand the things of the world. In spite or because of this, the perfect plebs is impressed by the dignity and the lofty bearing of the most venerable members of the ruling class; on this basis it believes in the goodness and liberality of the ruling class.[185] One is tempted to say that the goodness of the plebs consists in its belief in the goodness of the ruling class, or that goodness exists only in men's thoughts about other men. But this would be an unbearable exaggeration. What Machiavelli means to say is that the natural home of goodness is the people because the people lacks responsibility for the common good and can therefore afford to be good or to abide by those rules of conduct with which the citizens must generally comply if there is to be society. Machiavelli does not mean to say that the people is by nature good: men must be made good and kept good by laws, by speedy, spectacular and equal law enforcement, and by rewards. "Goodness" or "incorruptness" may therefore come to mean no more than fear-bred obedience to the government and even vileness. On the other hand, the people has a very great interest in a somewhat different goodness of its rulers: it longs for kindness, liberality, gentleness, humanity and compassion in the great men, and not the least if the great men are their foreign conquerors. The people wishes to be certain that its rulers are fully dedicated to the common good and in no way prompted by ambition, to say nothing of avarice. Manlian severity is therefore more laudable in republican leaders than humanity; such severity appears to be incompatible with private ambition. The strongest argument which Thucydides' Nicias used, in order to be believed and trusted by the people when he attempted to dissuade the Athenians from the Sicilian expedition, was the consideration that that enterprise would redound to the satisfaction of his ambition, since he would be the chief commander. And yet it was obvious that his ambition could not be satisfied by an enterprise of which he was certain that it was fraught with disaster. There was in fact perfect harmony between his public proposal and his private ambition. The people are then guided by a false notion of virtue. "True virtue," "the true way," consists not in the extirpation of ambition but in ambition guided by prudence. Lacking prudence, the people identifies human excellence with goodness or with unselfish devotion to the well-being of others. Therefore it can be said that "the many good ones," whom one may call slaves, make their leader or leaders good.[186] The many are good, or they can be good and ought to be good, because, being more or less downtrodden, they are satisfied with little, each of them is frequently in need of the help of others, and what each of them desires can generally speaking be reconciled easily with what every other one of them desires. In order to rule them, the great men must somehow conform to the people's notion of goodness: they must appear to be free from selfish desires. Machiavelli is far from denying that man's dependence on man compels most members of a society in their intercourse with one another to comply with certain simple and crude rules of conduct (the prohibitions against murder, fraud, theft and so on) and to cherish such qualities as gratitude, kindness, faithfulness and gentleness; but he contends that the same needs which make man dependent on other men compel him to form political societies the very preservation of which requires the transgression of those simple rules no less than their observation, as well as the practice of those virtues no less than that of their opposites. He is far from denying that the divorce of those simple rules of conduct from their selfish end is wise, for the selfish end can sometimes be served by secret transgression of those rules; but he contends that those rules cannot be understood if one accepts their wise interpretation. He is far from denying that all or most men by nature have compassion for the sufferings of other men, not only when they see those sufferings but even when they merely read of them; but he contends that many of those sufferings were inflicted by men. He is far from denying that there are some men who are genuinely kind and humane, not from fear or calculation but by nature; yet he contends that such men when entrusted with high office can become a public menace.[187] It would seem that, according to him, virtue and goodness are praiseworthy only with regard to their social and political utility. Goodness is the sum of habits which the majority of men living together must possess in order not to be disturbed by one another and by their government in the enjoyment of life, liberty and property. Virtue as it has hitherto come to sight is the sum of habits which the rulers must possess in order to protect themselves and the good subjects against the bad subjects as well as against foreign enemies; the army, i.e., the citizenry, must partake of this virtue to some extent.

If there is no good which is not accompanied by its peculiar evil, we have to keep watch for the peculiar defects of even the best republic. If it is true that the common good is the end only of republics and that the common good is the ground of virtue, the defective character of republics will prove the defective character of the common good and of virtue. Here the question arises whether the defects of republics are not of such a character as to suggest a certain superiority of principalities. At any rate, every consideration favorable to principalities implies a questioning of the common good and of virtue. Machiavelli believed that princely rule is defensible to some extent. Otherwise he could hardly have taken a position of neutrality with respect to the issue "republic or principality," and he could not have blurred the difference between republics and principalities as he frequently does in the *Discourses*. In this explicitly republican book he is indeed slow to introduce the subjects "kingdoms" or "principalities," as a glance at the headings of the first ten chapters will have shown. In the first chapter in the heading of which he uses the term "prince," (I 16) he deals with the question of how to secure not only newly established republics but newly established principalities as well; but in that place he still almost apologizes for treating the latter subject, whereas later on he deals with principalities as a matter of course. One might say that in order to deal properly with one opposite he must deal with the other opposite as well, or that one cannot set forth the art of the keeper without setting forth the art of the thief. Still, we must note that the detachment or the generosity with which he gives advice to both republics and destroyers of republics is amazing. For instance, he discusses with perfect impartiality the mistakes which the Roman people made in trying to preserve its freedom and the mistakes which Appius Claudius made in trying to destroy it; and he gives the best advice possible both to conspirators against princes and to conspirators against the fatherland.[188] To understand this ambiguity, we start from the following considerations. If a country like Italy, France or Spain cannot be happy unless it is subject to a single government, and an imperial republic is necessarily more oppressive of all other cities in the country than a non-barbarous prince would be, then the common good of the country as a whole, as distinct from the common good of the ruling city, would be better served by a national monarchy. Besides, it would be wrong to believe that principalities are as such inferior in military virtue to republics. Furthermore, the mirror of republican virtue provided that no philosopher be received in Rome, whereas in the golden times under the Roman emperors, everyone could hold and defend every opinion he wished; for the fear of God which is indispensable in republics can be replaced by the fear of a prince. It would seem to follow that freedom to hold and defend every opinion one wishes, while a great good for some men, is incompatible with the common good.[189]

Above all, republics are not always possible. They are not possible at the beginning and they are not possible if the people is corrupt. There is a connection between these two conditions.

Since it is only government, laws and other institutions which make men good, men are bad or corrupt prior to the foundation of society; in that state they cannot yet have acquired habits of sociability through social discipline. Only after they had undergone training in such habits, through the application of regal power for a considerable time, can they have become good or incorrupt. This is one reason that the founders of republics must be princes. The Romans with whom Romulus had to deal were corrupt in spite of, or because of, their being simple, i.e., they were rude and crude, while by the time of the expulsion of the kings they had become incorrupt, i.e., capable of living as citizens of a republic. There is however another kind of corruption, namely, late rottenness, the corruption of Rome at the time not of Romulus but of Caesar. Initial corruption, we may say, is the state of mind which necessarily follows from the absence of law and government; late corruption is the state of mind which necessarily follows from gross inequality in respect of power and wealth among the members temporal and spiritual of a society. The former kind of corruption allows of a republican future; the latter kind of corruption precludes a republican future. Contemporary examples of the latter kind of corruption are supplied by Milan and Naples, states which cannot possibly be transformed into republics but are compelled forever to live under princes. But living under princes unfits the people for freedom. Hence, the transformation of any corruption into incorruption or of any principality into a republic, and in particular the emergence of Roman freedom, seems to be a miracle. One could suggest, as Machiavelli does, that Rome was a republic from the very beginning insofar as its founder shared his power with the senate or the assembly of elders and the senate elected Romulus' successors; but this suggestion does not dispose of the difficulty created by the fact that it is precisely regal power that is required to make the people incorrupt or fit for the life of freedom and that it is precisely living under regal power which makes the people unfit for a life of freedom. Machiavelli therefore revises his first statement and asserts that not only the initial corruption but even the late corruption can be removed by the proper application of regal power, of the power of a human being who is alive at that time: even Milan and Naples could be transformed into republics by a man of rare brain and authority who in a rare way combines goodness and badness. Still, it is doubtful whether there is a single example of a restorer, of a founder confronted with late rottenness, who succeeded in making a corrupt people fit for a life of freedom. It is doubtful, in other words, whether there ever was a late founder of rare brain. Yet given the almost infinite malleability of "matter" and the almost infinite power of "brain," the possibility of a late founder or of a restorer cannot be denied. It is therefore insufficient to say that republics are not always possible.[190] The difficulty concerning the transformation of a principality into a republic consists rather in the unwillingness of the prince to effect such transformation, and this unwillingness is not altogether reprehensible. In order to make a given corrupt matter incorrupt and thus to make possible freedom and the common good, it is necessary to commit innumerable acts of murder, treachery and robbery or to display an extreme cruelty. A humane prince will shrink from such a course, especially since the future realization of the common good is of necessity uncertain, and will instead prefer to tolerate the prevailing corruption and thus perpetuate it. In order to rule the corrupt multitude with some degree of humanity, the prince is compelled to satisfy its corrupt desires and he cannot afford to perform good deeds. Yet a prince does not have to be humane to make this choice so agreeable to humanity. Princes prefer to keep princely power for ever in their families. The self-interest of the prince is therefore as salutary as his humanity could be, and since most men are bad, one would have to say that the self-interest of the prince affords a greater guarantee for his conduct being agreeable to humanity than would a humaneness for which one could merely wish. Even if principalities are incompatible with the common good in the full sense, they are compatible with some kind of common good, as has just appeared. The common good possible under a prince will in the best case be "security"; i.e., it is not impossible that a prince protect his subjects in regard to their lives, their property and the honor of their women against bad subjects as well as against foreign enemies; but the common good under a prince cannot include freedom of the subjects. The prince on the other hand cannot perform his function if he does not possess freedom, power, and outstanding honor in addition to security.[191] This freedom is not necessarily in harmony with the security of all his subjects. It is as necessary for him to be concerned with his security and freedom as it is for a republic to be concerned with its security and freedom; the distinction between the common good and the private good is less pronounced in the case of the prince than in that of a republican magistrate; for the prince "to maintain the state" means "to maintain himself." The prince is justified in committing all kinds of terrible deeds provided they are necessary for his security and the security of his power and provided he uses his power afterward for benefiting his subjects. In order to benefit his subjects or to make his fatherland most happy, it is not necessary that he be dedicated to the common good or possess goodness and conscience. It is sufficient if he realizes that his power cannot be secure and his ambition cannot be satisfied unless he benefits his subjects, if he has a clear grasp of what constitutes the well-being of his subjects, and if he acts vigorously in accordance with this knowledge. Exclusive concern with his own well-being, i.e., with his security and glory, so long as that concern is guided by intelligence and sustained by strength of will or temper, is sufficient to make a prince a good prince and even to earn him eternal glory. He certainly need not possess and exercise moral virtue proper, although the reputation for possessing some of the moral virtues is indispensable for him. The prince need not even possess virtue in the sense of such dedication to the common good as excludes ambition. But he must possess that virtue which consists of "brain," or "greatness of mind," and manliness combined—the kind of virtue praised by Callicles in Plato's *Gorgias* and possessed by the criminals Agathocles and Severus. This is the most obvious message of the *Prince* as a whole. Whereas moral virtue and republican virtue are the effects of habituation and hence of society, this kind of virtue which we have now encountered is natural. Its ground is not the common good but the natural desire of each to acquire wealth and glory: men are praised or blamed also with a view to their being good or bad at acquiring.[192] Goodness at acquiring is praised because it is rare, difficult to practice, and salutary to its possessor; it requires at least as much toil and sacrifice of ease as does moral virtue itself.

If we look back to Machiavelli's analysis of republics, we see at once that there is no essential difference between the motives of the prince and the motives of the ruling class. The excellent ruling class as exemplified by the Roman senate is not dedicated to the common good as the common good is primarily understood. It identifies the common interest with its own particular interest and is shrewd enough to realize that it serves its own interest best by restraining its desire to command and by making judicious concessions to the plebs. The virtue of the senate and of the individuals belonging to it is not different from the virtue of the excellent prince. If the modes of action of the senate differed from those of excellent princes, the whole reason is the difference between the structure of republican and monarchic governments, and not a difference in morality. Republican virtue requires that the citizens be free from ambition and be poor, but the Roman nobility was moved by great ambition and still greater avarice; its poverty in the early times was due not to virtue nor even to law but to circumstances. What made the Roman nobility tolerably humane towards the plebs was fear of the plebs and of potential tyrants on the one hand, and the calculation of the profitable character of cooperation with the plebs at the expense of foreign cities on the other. The tribunes of the plebs were useful for preserving or restoring unity among the nobility: they fulfilled the function of an enemy. As for that model of a leader in a republic, Manlius Torquatus, whose mode of proceeding had no relation whatever to private ambition and who showed himself at all times to be a man who loved only the common good, he was compelled by his nature to proceed in this severe manner which was so useful to the public and he was prompted to his actions by the desire that his severe commands, which his natural appetite had made him give, were observed.[193] What the classics called aristocracy, we may say, is an imagined republic; the factual truth of aristocracies which are known to exist or to have existed is oligarchy. This is not to deny that generally speaking a republic is more advantageous than any principality for the large majority of the people and the majority of the great, at any rate in cities. But this is not universally true.

If the great in a republic go too far in oppressing the people, it may be better for the people to turn for their protection to an ambitious man of sufficient intelligence and courage, and to help him in setting up and preserving a tyranny. According to Aristotle, the fact that the tyrant is supported by the people as distinguished from the gentlemen is an argument against tyranny; according to Machiavelli, it is the strongest argument in favor of tyranny, for the end of the people is more just—or, as Machiavelli, choosing his words carefully, prefers to say, more decent or more respectable —than the end of the great. The common good may well appear to be identical with the good of the many. And just as free states may be established by means of violence, tyranny may be established by consent. For the proper conduct of tyrannical government, it is necessary to remember that while the end of the many is most respectable, the many themselves are not. They are unable to rule themselves or others. Those whose cause is most just are least capable of defending it; it must be defended by men whose end is, to say the least, less just; justice depends on injustice. At any rate, the common good consists in a precarious harmony between the good of the many and the good of the great; whenever this harmony has ceased to exist, the good of the many takes precedence over the good of the few in accordance with the same principle according to which the common good takes precedence over any particular or sectional interest. Needless to say, the maxim "the end justifies the means" applies to the establishment and the preservation of tyranny thus justified as well as to that of republics: the tyrant is justified in securing himself by cutting to pieces the great and their irreconcilable brood. Cleomenes of Sparta "conspired against his fatherland" because he desired to be helpful to the many whose good was opposed by the few; he had all his opponents massacred; but for an accident he would have acquired the fame of Lycurgus himself. If one says that the tyrant must use fraud in order to rise to power, Machiavelli replies to him that the model king Cyrus and the model republic Rome rose to greatness in no other way. Still, not all tyrannies are defensible. It makes a difference whether an ambitious individual, commanding armed men, murders the great and makes himself master of the people who had lived in harmony with the great, or whether the man in question enters the scene after civil war has broken out or is imminent. The latter too is compelled to cut the great to pieces and to pay due regard to the demands of the common people for security, and he too is moved to all his actions by private ambition; but he is excused by the occasion or opportunity whereas the criminal tyrant is not. As for the contention that tyrannies are unstable, it is bound up with an arbitrary definition of tyranny. Tarquinius Priscus and Servius Tullius are remembered as Roman kings although they were usurpers or had taken possession of their kingdom by extraordinary means. Tyrants who have succeeded in founding a principality which lasts for centuries are remembered as princes by a grateful, if hypocritical, posterity. What name or title is more glorious than "Caesar," and Caesar was the first tyrant in Rome. As a typical tyrant, he based his power on the common people who avenged his murder. He usurped his power because he was prompted by ambition; but one could say with equal right that he took by force and out of just anger what ingratitude had denied him. In spite or because of this, he was the first emperor; he laid the foundation for the late Roman monarchy, prepared the peaceful reign of Augustus and the golden times of the good Roman emperors. Considerations like these induce Machiavelli frequently to use "prince" and "tyrant" as synonyms, regardless of whether he speaks of criminal or non-criminal tyrants.[194] It therefore becomes necessary to reconsider the distinction between criminal and non-criminal tyrants. It is not sufficient to say that the criminal tyrant lacked opportunity, since without opportunity he could never have become a tyrant. The classic example of a potential tyrant who lacked opportunity and therefore failed was Manlius Capitolinus. Capitolinus was induced to strive for tyranny by the envy he felt for the honor and glory which his contemporary Camillus, the most prudent of the Roman captains, had earned; he believed himself to be Camillus' equal. He knew then that he was not the first man in Rome. In his second statement Machiavelli traces Capitolinus' abortive conspiracy against his fatherland to "either envy or his evil nature"; it is no longer certain that envy offers a sufficient explanation, and Capitolinus' envy is not a sign of an evil nature: envy as such is a passion which arises with necessity in all men under certain conditions for which they are not responsible. In his last statement Machiavelli finds the origin of Capitolinus' action in his envy, which blinded his mind so far that he did not examine whether the available matter permitted the establishment of tyranny; his "evil nature," it appears, consisted in the excessive power of a passion which more than any other makes men operate well, for the root of envy proves to be love of glory; but his love of glory was stronger than his understanding: his evil nature consisted in his lack of understanding; he was "full of every virtue and had done publicly and privately very many laudable works," but he lacked that prudence which lets a man see that one must seek glory by different ways in a corrupt city than in a city which still leads a republican life; oppositely to Camillus, Capitolinus chose badly or had a natural inclination which did not agree with the times; in a corrupt city he would have been a rare and memorable man. His error was not fundamentally different from that of Fabius Maximus, who tried to continue a cautious strategy when a bold strategy had become possible and hence necessary. Machiavelli draws the conclusion that the citizens who in a republic engage in an enterprise either in favor of liberty or in favor of tyranny, must consider the available matter: the neutrality of his advice corresponds to the moral neutrality of the problem, namely, of the problem as to how to seek glory or to "acquire."[195] It is likewise not sufficient to say that a criminal tyrant, while not lacking opportunity, lacked justification, for where there are opportunities of this magnitude, justification will not fail to be forthcoming. A potential tyrant of extraordinary gifts may think, not without reason, that after having successfully conspired against the republic, he could defend the city or the country against foreign enemies and take care of the good of the many in a much better way than any of his rivals; it is impossible to say after he has succeeded whether the republican leaders would have been capable of the same outstanding achievements. There is then no essential difference between the public-spirited founder of a republic and the selfish founder of a tyranny: both have to commit crimes and both have to pay due regard to that part of society the cause of which is most just. As for the difference between their intentions, one may say with Aristotle that the intentions are hidden. In the last analysis farsighted patriotism and farsighted selfishness lead to the same results. In other words, regardless of whether we start from the premise of justice or from the premise of injustice, we arrive at the same conclusion: in order to achieve its goal, justice must use injustice and injustice must use justice; for both, a judicious mixture of justice and injustice, a certain middle course between justice and injustice, is required.

However this may be, the tyrant as well as any other new prince must arm his subjects. Yet he cannot arm all his subjects. It is therefore sufficient if he benefits those whom he has armed.

In other words, just as the tyrant comes to power by exploiting the division between the great and the people, he maintains himself in power by creating a division within the people. In some cases he does not have to create such a division; he can arm the peasantry, perhaps a cruelly oppressed peasantry, and with its help keep down the urban populace. Since his first duty is to maintain himself and his position, he may also have to seek his support in a previously oppressed neighboring people or for that matter in mercenaries in whose loyalty he can have a greater trust than in that of the people who indeed helped him to come to power but who are distracted by memories of a republican freedom which they did not have the wits to preserve and of which they therefore were not worthy. That a regime based on a soldiers' caste is possible and that under such a regime no consideration to speak of need be paid to the people is shown by the Roman emperors, the Turk and the Sultan: the emperor Severus who, in order to satisfy the soldiers, oppressed the people in every way, "always reigned happily," was "revered by everyone" and had "a very high reputation." After all, what the soldiers do to the people is not different from what the people do, if they can, to other peoples. We may summarize Machiavelli's argument as follows. Either one questions the principles on which republics act: one arrives at imagined republics; or one accepts those principles: one cannot radically condemn tyranny. There is no other way in which one can account for the fact that Machiavelli offers his advice to tyrants with equal alacrity as to republics. To mention only one further example, the would-be tyrant Appius Claudius acted imprudently by turning suddenly from appearing as a friend of the people into its enemy, for in this way he lost his old friends before he had acquired new friends: he ought to have effected his change from humility and kindness to pride and cruelty in stages.[196] It goes without saying that this advice, as well as other advice of the same kind, is innocent of any consideration of the common good.

If Machiavelli can give advice to actual or potential tyrants with exclusive regard to their security or glory, there is no reason why he should not give advice of the same character to men who do not aspire beyond the status of subjects or of private citizens or to all men as acting with a view to their private advantage. He concludes the first chapter of the Third Book of the *Discourses*

with the remark that that Book will deal with the actions of
"particular men" as distinguished especially from the actions of
political society, and, as far as the Roman kings are concerned,
he will discuss only such things as they did with a view to their
private advantage. He begins the discussion with Brutus, the father
of Roman freedom. Did Brutus too act with a view to his private
advantage? According to Machiavelli, Livy explained Brutus' simulating stupidity by Brutus' desire to live securely and to preserve
his patrimony under the oppressive rule of a king. Machiavelli
however thinks that Brutus was moved to his course of action
also by his desire to liberate his fatherland. Machiavelli claims
then that he makes Brutus more public-spirited than Livy had
made him. Certainly Livy's Brutus deliberately committed an act
which according to the plausible interpretation of an oracle would
have made him the king of Rome. Could the father of the Roman
republic have had the desire to reign as king? Machiavelli himself
notes a few pages later that the desire to reign as king is so great
that it enters even into the hearts of those who can never become
kings strictly speaking. After having opened, with the support
of Livy's authority, the question of the selfish motive of the most
famous patriot, Machiavelli draws this lesson from Brutus' conduct:
the enemy of a prince ought to live in familiarity with the prince
because this affords him security and permits him to enjoy the
amenities of court life. The patient and good Soderini did not
know how to resemble Brutus and so he "lost, together with his
fatherland, his power and his reputation"; to say the least, Machiavelli puts as great a stress on Soderini's private loss as on his fatherland's public loss. He thereafter devotes two chapters (III 4-5) to
the three last Roman kings; while he does not there discuss explicitly
how those kings acted wisely or foolishly with regard to their
private advantage, and while he even refers there to such public
spirited princes as Timoleon and Aratus, we are not permitted to
forget that the theme of these chapters is private advantage. The
chapter on conspiracies which follows immediately thereafter is
meant to warn both princes and private men: conspiracies are
dangerous for both princes, the intended victims, and private men,
the would-be murderers of princes. It appears that it is not difficult
to kill a prince but extremely difficult to kill the prince and to
survive; Machiavelli's chief concern is with advising conspirators

as to their self-preservation. Acting in the same spirit, he next teaches citizens how to seek glory and reputation in both corrupt and incorrupt cities. When in the sequel he teaches captains important rules of strategy and tactics, he draws our attention to the fact that in so doing he teaches them how each can earn glory for himself. He shows in particular how a captain can earn glory for himself in spite of having lost a campaign: the captain may show that the defeat was not due to his fault. When contrasting the modes of the severe and the gentle captains, he is careful to distinguish how those modes affected the fatherland on the one hand and the individual in question on the other; he pays equal regard to public advantage and to private advantage. In a dangerous situation, the colleagues of Camillus ceded to him the supreme command for the sake of the salvation of the fatherland; each of his colleagues saw his own danger, postponed for this reason his ambition, mastered his envy and hastened gladly to obey the man who, he believed, could with his virtue save him. A man counseling measures conducive to the common good may expose himself to great danger; Machiavelli therefore considers how the fulfillment of public duty can be reconciled with private safety; by not standing forth as the sole and passionate promoter of a bold scheme, the counselor will earn less glory but greater safety; on the other hand, if his advice is not taken because of his cautious procedure and disaster follows, he will earn "very great glory; and although the glory which is earned through evils which befall your city or your prince cannot be enjoyed, yet it counts for something."[197] While advice with regard to the private advantage of private men becomes conspicuous only in the Third Book of the *Discourses*, it is not absent from the other parts of Machiavelli's work. In the center of the section on gratitude, a virtue which is no less insinuated by calculation than it is commanded by duty, he raises the question as to the proper use of gratitude and its opposite by a prince who does not lead his army but sends out a captain in his stead. He gives precepts not to the prince, for every prince knows by himself what to do in such a case, but to the captain. Under certain conditions the captain ought to be "altogether bad," i.e. punish the prince for his anticipated ingratitude by rebelling against the prince, i.e. by committing an action which because of its boldness and grandeur cannot but be honorable. Here Machiavelli does not limit himself to giving advice to a man who is already desirous of becoming a tyrant but suggests the thought of tyranny to a previously innocent man. In the heading of the chapter he promises that he will also discuss what the citizen of a republic ought to do in order not to suffer from the ingratitude of his fatherland; he does not keep that promise since he had said in the preceding chapter that Caesar took by force what ingratitude had denied him. Machiavelli stands in the same relation to the innocent captain who is subject to princely or republican government in which the two decent Roman patricians stood to the Roman plebs after the fall of the Decemviri. Machiavelli goes beyond this. The "style" of Piero Soderini, a man distinguished by goodness, humanity, humility and patience, the official guardian of Florentine liberty, was to favor the common people; the enemies of Piero—Machiavelli does not tire of speaking of "Piero" in this context—made the mistake of not using the same style; Piero, as it seems at first glance, made the mistake of not using the style of his enemies which was to favor the Medici and thus to betray the liberty of the fatherland. Machiavelli is on the verge, as it were, of posthumously suggesting to Piero that he commit an atrocious treachery. Yet he "excuses" Piero for not having committed that treachery by the consideration that by favoring the Medici he would have lost his good reputation whereas by remaining loyal he only lost his reputation, together with his power and his fatherland. But this consideration is insufficient for a reason which even Machiavelli shudders to state in this context. He goes on to say that Piero could not have effected the switch from favoring the common people to favoring the Medici "in secret and at one stroke." He thus excuses Soderini for not having betrayed his trust by the consideration that such betrayal was not feasible in the circumstances. He draws the conclusion that one ought not to choose a course of action the danger of which outweighs its advantage. We read in the *Prince* that the minister of a prince ought never to think of himself but only of the prince; the minister must possess goodness. But since men are bad the prince must make his minister good and keep him good by honoring him and by making him rich. The minister does not have to think of his advantage if he can be certain that his prince thinks of it. Yet there are honors above honors and riches beyond riches. The prince must therefore watch his minister carefully. If he has the intelligence and the assiduity required for this, the minister will always be good.[198]

Let us survey the movement of thought which leads from unselfish patriotism to criminal tyranny. The republic of the character exemplified by the early Roman republic is the best regime because it fulfills the natural function of political society. Men who originally live like beasts establish government in order to escape insecurity; the function of political society is to make men secure. Security, equally desired by all potential members of a political society, can be achieved only by the union of them all; it is a common good since it must be shared in order to be enjoyed. Political society fulfills its function through political power, and political power is apt to threaten the very security for the sake of which it was established. To avoid this danger, the majority must have a share, commensurate with its capacity, in public power. But men cannot be sure of their security without having acquired superiority to their potential enemies. Besides, they are necessarily dissatisfied with security as soon as they possess it; they no longer appreciate it; they subordinate it to superiority to others in wealth and honor. Constant vigilance and periodic return to the beginnings, i.e. periodic terror, do not suffice. Society cannot be kept united if it is not threatened by war, and this threat will soon lose its salutary character if it is not followed from time to time by war itself. War at any rate leads to oppression of the vanquished, even if oppression should not have occurred within the society on account of the desire of some of its members to lord it over their fellows.[199] Oppression, or injustice, is then coeval with political society. Criminal tyranny is the state which is characterized by extreme oppression. There is then in the decisive respect only a difference of degree between the best republic and the worst tyranny. This difference of degree is of the utmost practical importance, as no one knew better than Machiavelli. But a difference of degree is not a difference of kind. One can meet Machiavelli's argument either by appealing to a higher principle which legitimates the oppression exercised by decent societies while condemning tyrannical oppression, or by pointing to political societies in which oppression has been abolished. Oppression exists wherever there is not equal protection, by enforced laws, of everyone in his life, freedom, property and honor except of those who have been convicted by fair judges of crimes against the life, the freedom, the property or the honor of anyone or of all. But oppression perhaps exists also where extreme inequality of wealth causes an extreme dependence of the poor on the rich.

Oppression is coeval with society, or with man, because man is by nature compelled to oppress or because men are bad. It is man's nature to be envious, ambitious, suspicious, ungrateful, discontented and predatory. Only through necessity, and in particular through compulsion exercised by other men and therefore especially through laws, do men become good. To be bad is the same as to be untied or unchained. Man's becoming good requires that violence be done to him because goodness goes against his grain or against his nature. One would have to say that man is by nature bad if, to quote Hobbes, this could be said without impiety. At any rate, men do not possess a natural inclination toward the good. They are more inclined toward evil than toward the good and therefore they can be corrupted more easily than they can be made incorrupt. Yet since they can be made good, they are not radically evil: they suffer from curable ills. Only very rarely do they know how to be altogether evil. This is indeed due to the fact that they do not have the courage to be altogether evil or that they are vile; they are cowardly, unstable in evil as well as in good, and simple or easily deceived. Yet this description does not fit all men. Therefore one has to say that most men are by nature bad or that there are various kinds of badness belonging to various kinds of men. Yet even this does not suffice. Machiavelli takes issue with those who explain the bad conduct of men by their bad nature: men are by nature malleable rather than either bad or good; goodness and badness are not natural qualities but the outcome of habituation.[200] We have seen that in attacking "the middle course" Machiavelli in fact attacks only a certain kind of middle course and yet his attack on the middle course as such conveys a lesson which is not identical with the rejection of a certain kind of middle course. Similarly, in suggesting that man is by nature bad, Machiavelli does not indicate merely that man is not by nature directed toward the good or that most men, or the vulgar, are contemptible. The assertion that man is by nature bad means above all that man is by nature selfish or prompted by self-love alone. The only natural good is the private good. Since this is so, it is absurd to

call men bad with a view to the fact that they are selfish. Even
those who appear to be wholly dedicated to the common good or to
forget themselves completely in the service of others are driven
to such conduct by their peculiar natures and their natural desire
to see themselves obeyed or to acquire reputation or to be pleased
by pleasing. Camillus, who had always administered the highest
offices of the republic with exclusive regard to the public interest,
appeared to desire to become equal to the highest god. Man's
selfishness is badness as long as it is not molded with a view to the
needs of living together; it becomes goodness through such molding;
but it always remains selfishness. For the same reason for which
men are not by nature directed toward the good, they are not
by nature directed toward society. Man does not possess a natural
end proper, i.e. he does not have a natural inclination toward the
perfection of the nature peculiar to him, the nature of the rational
and social animal. Man is not by nature a social or political animal.
Men are indeed by nature in need of each other, but they are also
by nature no less antagonistic to each other; one cannot say that
one of these two opposed necessities is more natural than the other.
In adopting Polybius' account of the origin of political society,
Machiavelli omits even Polybius' extremely brief references to the
union of men and women and the generation of children as well
as to man's natural rationality, to say nothing of the fact that
whereas Polybius speaks in this context of "nature," Machiavelli
speaks of "chance." Machiavelli, who occasionally speaks of the
"natural affection" of subjects for their prince, does not deny that
there is natural affection of parents for their children and vice
versa; but he contends that the natural affection of the children
for their parents' property is no less strong than their affection
for their parents, and that a mother's desire for revenge may be
stronger than her maternal love. The various kinds of natural affection for human beings do not have a status different from that of
the various forms of natural affection for wealth and honor or of
natural hostility toward human beings; they all are equally passions,
self-regarding passions.[201]

While everyone is by nature concerned only with his own
well-being—with his preservation, his security, his ease, his pleasures,
his reputation, his honor, his glory—he must be concerned with the
well-being of his society on which his own well-being appears

to depend. The society which is most conducive to the well-being of the large majority of the people and of the great is the good republic. Although the reasoning which leads to the demand that one ought to dedicate oneself to the common good starts from the premise of selfishness, that reasoning is less powerful than the passions. Men need additional selfish incentives in order to comply with the result of that reasoning. The task of the political art consists therefore in so directing the passions and even the malignant humors that they cannot be satisfied without their satisfaction contributing to the common good or even serving it. There is no need for a change of heart or of the intention. What is needed is the kind of institutions which make actions detrimental to the common good utterly unprofitable and which encourage in every way such actions as are conducive to the common good. The link between the private good and the public good is then punishments and rewards or, in other words, fear of the government and love of the government. To some extent, the government must try to gain the love of the governed by paying a price, i.e. by acts of liberality and gentleness; this love coincides with the obligation of gratitude; but the bond of obligation is felt as a burden and therefore it is broken on every occasion on which it restrains the self-interest of the obliged. The government must then be at least equally concerned with being feared while it must avoid arousing hatred. It is impossible to preserve the perfect combination of being loved and being feared, but deviations from that "middle course" are unimportant if the governors are men of great virtue, i.e. of greatness and nobility of mind, and therefore revered as good at protecting the good and the friends, and at harming the bad and the enemies. The task of the political art consists in providing not only that the most able men can rise to the highest positions but above all that they be kept good while they occupy such positions. The Romans achieved the first by making the most important offices the reward of excellence rather than of birth or wealth, or by the judicious handling of free elections. They achieved the second by devising a scheme which permitted the inoffensive supervision, by their rivals, of the consuls' conduct of their office and which at the same time did not stifle the consuls' initiative. They relied most of all on the leading men's love of glory. Judging that the love of glory is a sufficient "restraint and rule" for making a commander operate well, they provided that the glory of victory be "entirely his." The desire for glory as the desire for eternal glory liberates man from the concern with life and property, with goods which may have to be sacrificed for the common good; and yet glory is a man's own good. It is therefore possible and even proper to present the whole political teaching as advice addressed to individuals as to how they can achieve the highest glory for themselves. To the extent to which Machiavelli's two books are meant for immediate prudent use rather than for rendering secure the basis of prudence, their broad purpose is to show the need for reckoning with the selfish desires of the rulers and the ruled as the only natural basis of politics, and therefore for trusting, not in men's good will, nor in mercenaries, fortresses, money, or chance but in one's own virtue (if one possesses it) as the ability to acquire for oneself the highest glory and hence to acquire for one's state whatever makes it strong, prosperous, and respected. The wise rulers who act with a view to their own benefit will enlist the cooperation of the ruled, who likewise act with a view to their own benefit, in such activities as cannot but be detrimental to others. Since the many can never acquire the eternal glory which the great individuals can achieve, they must be induced to bring the greatest sacrifices by the judiciously fostered belief in eternity of another kind.[202]

Machiavelli's book on principalities and his book on republics are both republican: the praise of republics which is expressed in the book on republics is never contradicted by a praise of principalities in either book. All the more striking is the seemingly inhuman detachment with which Machiavelli acts as the teacher, and hence as the benefactor, of tyrants as well as of republics. How can we respect someone who remains undecided between good and evil or who, while benefiting us, benefits at the same time and by the same action our worst enemies? We called Machiavelli's detachment or neutrality inhuman, for, as he says, by nature men take sides wherever there is a division which concerns them. Even if someone is unconcerned with honors and profit and therefore tries to stay aloof, the others will not permit him to do so. Or could such unconcern explain Machiavelli's neutrality? He has written the *Prince* in order to be useful to him who understands. In the *Discourses* he expresses himself somewhat more clearly. He has written the *Discourses* because he was moved "by that natural desire which was always in (him), to do, regardless of any other consideration, those things which, as (he) believe(s), bring about the common benefit of everyone." Machiavelli's work brings benefits to both republics and tyrants. This benefit is common because identically the same counsels or rules of action or rules regarding causes and effects are beneficial equally to republics and to tyrants. For instance, by learning which conduct is beneficial to republics, we learn at the same time which conduct is conducive to the destruction of republics. Machiavelli's apparent neutrality in the conflict between republics and tyrants is defensible if the common good as intended by republics is not the common good strictly speaking: the only good which is unqualifiedly the common good for all men is the truth, and in particular the truth about man and society. Knowledge of that truth, it would seem, is incompatible with unqualifiedly preferring republics to tyrannies, not because "value judgments" are not rational but because they are rational: while a strong case can be made for republics, a not altogether negligible case can be made for tyranny. We have seen that Machiavelli's apparent rejection of "the neutral course" is in fact a recommendation of discriminating impartiality and therefore of what one might call the highest form of neutrality. In accordance with this, he does not judge it to be a defect to defend with reasons any opinion, and therefore in particular both the opinion favorable to republics and the opinion favorable to tyranny. This difficulty, however, remains. Machiavelli claims to serve the common benefit of everyone by communicating to all the new modes and orders which he has discovered. Yet, as he points out, the new modes and orders cannot benefit those who benefit from the old modes and orders. There are two ways of solving this difficulty. Either one must say that the defenders of the old modes and orders who profit from the untruth profit from it in so far as their subjects believe in the untruth and they themselves do not act on the untruth; they too are benefited by Machiavelli since they learn from him the full truth on which they must act, and the public communication of which they must prevent at all costs; they are benefited by Machiavelli since he gives them a good conscience in doing what they hitherto did with a more or less uneasy conscience; they learn from him to think like Cesare Borgia who also benefited from the old modes and orders but renewed the old orders by means of new modes or of a new spirit. Or else one must say—and this is what Machiavelli in fact says—that there is no good however great which is unqualifiedly good.[203]

The common good in the political sense is defective not only because it is inferior *qua* common good to the common good simply, which is the truth. The good things of which the political common good consists or which it protects or procures are incompatible with other good things which are even less common than the political common good but which give a satisfaction no less pleasing, resplendent and intense, yet more within the reach of some men than glory. This supplement to the common good which exists on the same level as the common good, i.e., on a level lower than the truth, is the theme of Machiavelli's comedy *La Mandragola*. The *canzone* which introduces the play praises the retired life, the unpolitical life, of nymphs and shepherds. The hero of the play, Callimaco, leads an unpolitical life. Being a Florentine by birth, he had been sent to Paris as a boy and there had spent many years in the greatest happiness and tranquillity, helping everyone and trying to offend no one; his well-being did not depend on the well-being of his fatherland. For the chief reason that he stayed so long in Paris was the ruin of Italy and the insecurity prevailing in Italy, which were the effect of the invasion of Italy by the king of France. He returned to his fatherland not because it was his fatherland or because it needed his help but because Florence was the home of the most desirable woman, as he had learned from a certain Cammillo. His desire to see that woman and to win her favors was so strong that he could no longer think of either the wars in Italy or the peace of Italy: not the concern with the common good nor the desire for glory but the desire for a woman made him cease worrying about his own security. Lucrezia is married and of exemplary virtue and piety; she appears to be utterly incorruptible. The hero is near despair. He must choose between death and doing anything, however criminal, which might gain him the possession of Lucrezia. He saves himself by means of a series of deceptions. Lucrezia's husband, a foolish lawyer whose name reminds us of a most virtuous and pious general, is deceived into wishing that she should lie with another man. This of course is not sufficient to overcome

Lucrezia's resistance. Needed, therefore, is the help of a priest who is won over to the cause of the hero by being confronted with the choice between persuading a virtuous woman to commit an action most unbecoming a virtuous woman or not receiving money for alms: the good of the many is preferable to the good of one. The priest persuades Lucrezia by pointing to the example of Lot's daughters who were with child by their father because of the apparent necessity to secure the survival of the human race: what is required for the common good takes precedence over the moral law. The appeals to the common good are made in order to secure the private good of the hero. The case of Lucrezia's lover is strictly parallel to that of the tyrant. The triumph of forbidden love which is celebrated in the *Mandragola* is strictly parallel to the triumph of the forbidden desire to oppress or to rule. In both cases it is an intense pleasure divorced from its natural end (procreation or the common good respectively) which is desired. In both cases it is necessity which makes men "operate well," i.e., to acquire by prudence and strength of will that for which they long. The difference between matters of state and matters of love corresponds to the difference between gravity and levity, between the two opposed qualities, the alternation between which, or rather the union of which, constitutes the life according to nature. The union of gravity and levity, we suspect, is achieved, according to Machiavelli, by the quest for the truth, or for that good than which none is more common and none is more private.[204] If our information is correct, it is universally admitted that Machiavelli questions the supremacy of morality with a view to the requirements of the common good or of the fatherland. This is no accident. The reason is not that Machiavelli obviously points out the tension between the requirements of morality and those of the fatherland, for there are other elements of his teaching which are no less obvious and yet are not universally admitted. The reason is rather that the questioning of morality in the name of patriotism may go together with gravity, whereas the questioning of morality on other grounds is publicly indefensible.

Some people will think that the obscurities which we were compelled to imitate can be avoided if one simply disregards the *Mandragola* as an extraneous work which belongs to a department wholly unconnected with the department of serious thought, and if one limits oneself strictly to the two books each of which contains in its way everything Machiavelli knows. The reader will have observed that we have laid a proper foundation for the use of the comedy which, however unseemly it is, is not more improper than the *Prince* and the *Discourses*. The action of the comedy agrees with Machiavelli's claim that he was always moved by the natural desire to work for the benefit of everyone. Yet if the desire to work for the common good is natural in Machiavelli, one should expect that it is by nature effective, if in different degrees, in all men. This expectation is not borne out by his teaching. What then is "the factual truth" of Machiavelli's natural desire? As the desire to work for the common good is meant to bring benefit to everyone, it must also be directed toward Machiavelli's own good. He hopes to be rewarded for his achievement. The reward would consist in nothing but praise. The praise for which he could hope is necessarily much smaller than the praise which men bestow on the founders of religions and the founders of kingdoms or republics. Praise is akin to honor and to glory. Of these three things glory is the highest or the end. From this we can see how Machiavelli must have answered a question which is crucial on a certain level of his argument. If men must be made good and kept good by laws, and if it is the function of laws to make men good and to keep them good, the original lawgivers or founders must have been bad men who were passionately concerned with compelling their fellows and innumerable generations of their descendants to become good and to remain good. The only selfish desire which can induce men to be passionately concerned with the well-being of remote posterity is the desire for perpetual or immortal glory. The desire for such glory is the link between badness and goodness, since while it is selfish in itself it cannot be satisfied except by the greatest possible service to others. The desire for immortal glory is the highest desire since it is the necessary accompaniment of the greatest natural virtue. It is the only desire of men of the greatest natural virtue. It liberates men from the desire for petty things—comfort, riches and honors—as well as from fear of death. Yet since the glorious deed requires a long preparation, the man desirous of the highest glory must be concerned with his safety, his sustenance, and his quiet while the preparation is carried on. The desire for glory is not always distinguishable from the desire for the useful. Thus Machiavelli can occasionally use "force" and "glory" synonymously. The useful coincides with the honorable in the case of the powerful as powerful: the honorable is that which is good for him who possesses force, prudence, and courage. Since no one is absolutely powerful, conflicts between honor or glory and interest are inevitable. In case of such conflict, generous or proud natures tend to prefer the former, but so do those who regard themselves as free men without being free men. Prudence dictates to princes and republics that interest should take precedence of honor or glory, or true generosity demands that one swallow one's pride. Even if a prudent captain in a desperate situation prefers to lose gloriously rather than to flee, he is guided by the consideration that by some stroke of good luck he might win the battle. Consideration of glory alone may be said to be decisive in the case of the counselor of a state who is mindful that his advice might not be accepted, with the consequence that his prince or his fatherland is ruined; he thus acquires "very great glory" and nothing else.[205] Could pure glory be the privilege of the powerless? Men bestow the highest glory on those to whom they believe they owe the greatest benefits and whom therefore they regard as outstanding in wisdom and goodness. Yet glory is bestowed not only on benefactors. Since all men strive for wealth or glory, men are praised if they are good at acquiring wealth or glory, regardless of whether this success is beneficial or harmful to those who praise it; since all men are by nature concerned with "acquisition," they are by nature sensitive to goodness and badness at acquiring, or to virtue and weakness, and they cannot help somehow expressing what they sense. But the large majority are poor judges of virtue, especially in its higher forms. They judge by success and they admire men who merely had good luck or low cunning. They are overawed by power. They are moved by appearance rather than reality. They are more impressed by the spectacular than by the solid: they are not concerned with the wisdom of their favorites. For instance, they are more impressed by Manlius Torquatus' killing his own son than by Brutus' wisdom in simulating folly. The vulgar delusions regarding glory find their most important expressions in the vulgar reverence for the single founder, i.e., in the vulgar blindness to the fact that in every flourishing society foundation is so to speak continuous. The highest glory goes to men of the remote past who are vulgarly thought to be the greatest benefactors of mankind, who in fact are at best the originators of the most influential and the gravest errors and who may well be only the reputed originators of the errors in question. Genuine immortal glory requires that the man who claims such glory or on whose behalf it is claimed himself be present to posterity: genuine immortal glory is reserved for most excellent artists or writers.[206] The highest glory goes to the discoverer of the all-important truth, of the truth regarding man and society, of the new modes and orders which are in accordance with nature. He can justly claim to be superior in virtue to all men and to be the greatest benefactor of all men. He can justly claim the glory generally given to more or less mythical founders. He looks at society not theoretically but, being the teacher of founders, in the perspective of founders. The desire for the highest glory, which is the factual truth of the natural desire for the common good and which animates the quest for the truth, demands that the detachment from human things be subordinated to a specific attachment or be replaced by that attachment. The perspective of the teacher of founders comprises the perspectives of both the tyrant and the republic. But since the founder in the highest sense, who will deserve the admiration of the many as well as of the discerning few, is as such concerned with preparing the establishment of the most stable, the most happy and the most glorious society, and since a society of this description is necessarily republican, he necessarily has a bias in favor of republics. He realizes that, as a matter of principle and if one disregards what is required in more or less unfavorable circumstances, precisely the men of the greatest gifts can find, as leading men in republics, the highest glory accessible to political men; although Camillus was exiled for some time by the plebs, "he was through all times of his life worshipped as prince."[207]

The manner in which Machiavelli achieves the transition from neutrality in the conflict between the tyranny and the republic to republicanism, from selfishness to devotion to the common good, or from badness to goodness reminds one of the action of Plato's *Republic*. In the first book of the *Republic* Thrasymachus questions justice, i.e., he raises the question as to whether justice is good. Glauco and Adeimantus are perplexed by the argument, at least to the extent that they are thoroughly displeased with Socrates' apparent refutation of Thrasymachus' contention. After Glauco and Adeimantus have restated Thrasymachus' thesis, Socrates does not immediately turn to refuting it directly. Instead he begins to found a city in speech or to help Glauco and Adeimantus to found a city in speech. Within that speech he takes for granted the goodness of justice which had become thoroughly questionable. What does he mean by this? The assertion that injustice is good means that the life of the tyrant is the best life for the best men because the pleasure deriving from authority or honor is the highest or the all-comprehensive pleasure. By suggesting to his young companions that they should together found a city, Socrates appeals from the petty end of the tyrant to the grand end of the founder: the honor attending the tyrant who merely uses a city already in existence is petty in comparison with the glory attending the founder and especially the founder of the best city. The founder however must devote himself entirely to the well-being of his city; he is forced to be concerned with the common good or to be just. Desire for glory appears to be that passion which, if its scope is broadened, transforms the lover of tyranny, to say nothing of the lover of bodily pleasures, into a lover of justice. In Plato's *Republic* this transformation proves to be only the preparation for the true conversion from badness to goodness, the true conversion being the transition to philosophy, if not philosophy itself; this conversion is effected by the understanding of the essential limitations of everything political. In Machiavelli the transformation of man through the desire for glory seems to be the only conversion; the second and higher conversion seems to have been forgotten. This conclusion however is not compatible with Machiavelli's clear awareness of the delusions of glory and of the limitations of the political. Immortal glory is impossible, and what is called immortal glory depends on chance. Hence to see the highest good in glory means to deny the possibility of happiness. This is the reason that Machiavelli finds the good life or the life according to nature in the alternation between gravity and levity: between the expectation of a satisfaction or a pleasure which is always and essentially in the future and the enjoyment of present pleasure. But, as was indicated before, he rises above the plane on which the political good and the erotic good supplement each other while conflicting with each other. The most excellent man, as distinguished from the most excellent captain, or soldier of war or of love, acquires full satisfaction and immunity to the power of chance through knowledge of "the world."[208] To the extent to which this knowledge permeates a man, it engenders in him a humanity which goes together with a certain contempt for most men. Since republics are as such more conducive to humanity than are principalities, it engenders in him a bias in favor of republics. If it remains true that even on the highest level the alternation between gravity and levity is according to nature, one must say that whereas gravity belongs with knowledge of the truth, levity comes into play in the communication of the truth. The same man who is the teacher of founders or princes and who discovers the true character of "the world" communicates this truth to the young. In the former capacity he is half-man half-beast or alternates between humanity and inhumanity. In the latter capacity he alternates between gravity and levity. For in the latter capacity he is the bringer of a light which illumines things that cannot be illumined by the sun. The unity of knowledge and communication of knowledge can also be compared to the combination of man and horse, although not to a centaur.

Machiavelli claims to have taken a way not yet trodden by anyone and thus to have discovered new modes and orders. His discovery is implied in the principle that one must take one's bearings by how men live as distinguished from how they ought to live, or that one must pay proper regard to man's badness, i.e., to the roots, the pre-political or sub-political roots, of society or to the phenomena indicated by the expression "the wholly new prince in a wholly new state": not the one end by nature common to all which is visible in the sky—a pattern laid out in heaven—but the roots hidden in the earth reveal the true character of man or society. The teaching which derives from this principle is obviously opposed to that of classical political philosophy or of the Socratic tradition. Machiavelli's almost complete silence about Plato, Aristotle, and the political philosopher Cicero, to say nothing of scholasticism, expresses adequately this state of things. Near the beginning of the *Discourses* he almost copies a philosophic passage from the historian Polybius; but to say nothing of the facts that he nowhere mentions Polybius and that he makes radical changes in Polybius' statement,[209] he who reserves the full power of his attack rather for the end is not likely to reveal the scope of his deviation from the most revered tradition at the beginning of a book. For him the representative par excellence of classical political philosophy is Xenophon, whose writings he mentions more frequently than those of Plato, Aristotle, and Cicero taken together or those of any other writer with the exception of Livy. Xenophon's *Education of Cyrus* is for him the classic presentation of the imagined prince.[210] At the same time Xenophon is that writer who for Machiavelli has come closest to preparing his questioning of the imagined prince. Xenophon's *Hiero* is the classic defense of tyranny by a wise man, and the *Education of Cyrus* describes how an aristocracy can be transformed by the lowering of the moral standards into an absolute monarchy ruling a large empire. We add the observation that Xenophon's *Oeconomicus*, which starts from the view that the management rather than the increase of one's landed estate, to say nothing of the pursuit of crafts and trade, befits the gentleman, leads up to the proposal of such a compromise between the noble and the profitable as consists in a certain kind of trading in landed estates; Xenophon appears to be much more tolerant of that "natural and ordinary desire to acquire" than any other classic. But Machiavelli refers only to the *Hiero* and the *Education of Cyrus*, not to the *Oeconomicus* or to any other of Xenophon's Socratic writings. Xenophon's thought and work has two foci, Cyrus and Socrates. While Machiavelli is greatly concerned with Cyrus, he forgets Socrates.

Machiavelli's claim that he has taken a road not yet trodden by anyone implies that in breaking with the Socratic tradition he did not return to an anti-Socratic tradition, although he could not help agreeing in numerous points with the Socratic tradition on the one hand and the anti-Socratic tradition on the other. We have indicated the kinship of his thought with hedonism. But he agrees with classical political philosophy against classical hedonism in admitting the high dignity of political life. For classical hedonism, honor and glory are contemptible; for Machiavelli the pleasure deriving from honor and glory is genuine and perhaps the highest pleasure. Classical hedonism, we may say, is insufficiently attentive to the conditions and the context of the highest pleasure, which it sees to be dependent on philosophy. Since philosophy consists in

ascending from opinion to knowledge, and opinion is primarily
political opinion, philosophy is essentially related to the city; as
transcending the city, it presupposes the city; philosophy must
therefore be concerned with the city or be politically responsible.
In this important respect Machiavelli agrees with classical political
philosophy over against classical hedonism.[211] As for Epicureanism
in particular, it teaches that happiness presupposes moral virtue as
opposed to moral vice, and it is as distrustful of "acquiring" as is
classical political philosophy. Machiavelli's teaching is said to be
reminiscent of the teaching of "the sophists." To turn from modern hypotheses to the facts vouched for by Aristotle, sophistic
political science was either identical with rhetoric or subordinate
to it, and somehow concerned with teaching the art of legislation
by collecting renowned laws.[212] As for teachings like those which
Plato put into the mouths of Thrasymachus and Callicles, it suffices here to say that those Platonic characters stop where both
Socrates and Machiavelli begin; the originators of such teachings
have not even grasped the essential connection between ruling and
service or between private vice and public benefit because they
look at political things in the perspective of the exploiter of the
city and not in the perspective of its founder. Other contemporary
readers are reminded by Machiavelli's teaching of Thucydides;
they find in both authors the same "realism," i.e., the same denial
of the power of the gods or of justice and the same sensitivity to
harsh necessity and elusive chance. Yet Thucydides never calls in
question the intrinsic superiority of nobility to baseness,[213] a
superiority that shines forth particularly when the noble is destroyed by the base. Therefore Thucydides' *History* arouses in
the reader a sadness which is never aroused by Machiavelli's books.
In Machiavelli we find comedies, parodies, and satires but nothing
reminding of tragedy. One half of humanity remains outside of
his thought. There is no tragedy in Machiavelli because he has no
sense of the sacredness of "the common." The fate of neither Cesare
Borgia nor Manlius Capitolinus is tragic or understood by Machiavelli as tragic; they failed because they had chance or the times
against them. As regards chance in general, it can be conquered;
man is the master.

The modern historian disposes of an immense apparatus supplying him with information which can be easily appropriated

because it is superficial; he is therefore tempted to try to be wiser than the great men of the past whose work he studies. This is true particularly of his efforts to judge of their positions with respect to their predecessors. We repeat therefore that Machiavelli points to Xenophon more strongly than to any other thinker. He may be said to start from certain observations or suggestions made by Xenophon and to think them through while abandoning the whole of which they form a part. The novel teaching which he thus develops cannot be characterized as the first political teaching which gives its due to foreign policy or which recognizes the primacy of foreign policy. He has stated the case for imperialism or for "power politics" more clearly than any earlier or later thinker. But the principle which enabled him to do so applies equally to domestic policy; according to him the fundamental human fact is acquisitiveness or competition.[214] We also cannot accept the assertion that he was the first to realize what some people call the narrowness of the traditional condemnation of tyranny. This assertion is indeed confirmed rather than refuted by the fact that Machiavelli sometimes takes up what Aristotle said about the means for preserving tyranny; for, as soon as we consider the context, we see that Aristotle treats tyranny as a monstrosity whereas Machiavelli rather deals with tyranny as essential to the foundation of society itself. In this point, as well as in others of the same character, Machiavelli is closer to Plato than to Aristotle. Plato does not hesitate to make his founder of a good society, the wise legislator, demand that he be supported by a tyrant. Yet, to disregard the facts that Plato makes a nameless stranger state this demand and that even this nameless stranger makes this demand primarily in the name of an absent and nameless legislator, Plato demands the tyrant merely as a helper or a tool for the wise and virtuous legislator. In other words, Plato states with great caution the case for a tyrant preparing a republic in which moral virtue can be practiced. Machiavelli however may be said to argue for a tyrant preparing a republic in which republican virtue is indispensable.[215] He even argues for tyranny pure and simple. Yet what enables him to do so is not a more thoroughgoing or comprehensive analysis of political phenomena as such than that given by the classics but his destructive analysis of moral virtue or what one may call his emancipation of acquisitiveness. Machiavelli's most

emphatic attack on "all writers" is directed, not against the traditional condemnation of tyranny but against the traditional contempt
for the multitude.[216] This may incline us to believe that he was the
philosopher who originated the democratic tradition; the undeni-
ably non-democratic character of classical political philosophy
might thus seem to some extent to justify Machiavelli's revolt
which, through Spinoza and Rousseau, led to democratic theory
proper. But just as in the case of tyranny, we must note here
that the change in judgment is only a part of a comprehensive
argument meant to lay bare the essential dependence of morality
on society: the unmasking of the alleged aristocracy of the classics
as oligarchy leads necessarily to a somewhat more favorable judgment on the common people, and the unmasking of the rule of
men of moral worth is part of the destructive analysis of moral
virtue. The result of that analysis can be stated as follows. Moral
virtue, wished for by society and required by it, is dependent on
society and therefore subject to the primary needs of society. It
does not consist in the proper order of the soul. It has no other
source than the needs of society; it has no second and higher
source in the needs of the mind. Through an irony beyond Machiavelli's irony, his silence about the soul is a perfect expression of
the soulless character of his teaching: he is silent about the soul because he has forgotten the soul, just as he has forgotten tragedy
and Socrates. It is ironical in the same way in which his half
silence about philosophy is ironical.

To avoid the error of denying the presence of philosophy in
Machiavelli's thought, it suffices to remember what he indicates
regarding the relation between the superiority of "the most excellent man" to fate and that man's knowledge of "the world."[217]
Still, as our presentation could not help showing, one is entitled to
say that philosophy and its status is obfuscated not only in Machiavelli's teaching but in his thought as well. That moral virtue is a
qualified requirement of society is infinitely clearer to him than
that it is a requirement of philosophy or of the life of the mind.
As a consequence he is unable to give a clear account of his own
doing. What is greatest in him cannot be properly appreciated on
the basis of his own narrow view of the nature of man. Even the
union of gravity and levity of which he speaks appears to be a
dim reflection of what Plato says about the union of seriousness

and play. Machiavelli has two great themes, glory and the pleasures of love; the classic comic poet Aristophanes has three great themes, justice, the pleasures of love and the wise man (e.g., Euripides and Socrates): wisdom is not a great theme for Machiavelli because justice is not a great theme for him. He does not give an account of how the stability of excellence, or the firmness of knowledge of "the world," of equanimity, of strength of will and of prudence is compatible with the variability of all human things and of nature; his argument would seem to require a movement from excellence to vileness as well as a movement from moral virtue to moral vice. The fact that humanity and inhumanity are required for the well-being of society proves to him that humanity is not more "according to nature" than its opposite: he denies that there is an order of the soul, and therefore a hierarchy of ways of life or of goods. Hence his assertion that there is no good without its peculiar evil amounts to the absurdity that God cannot be the most perfect being because he lacks the specific excellences of which created beings as such are capable.[218] While the supra-political is everywhere and always present and effective in Machiavelli's thought, he analyses the political as if it were not ordered toward the supra-political or as if the supra-political did not exist. The consequence is an enormous simplification and, above all, the appearance of the discovery of a hitherto wholly unsuspected whole continent. In fact, however, Machiavelli does not bring to light a single political phenomenon of any fundamental importance which was not fully known to the classics. His seeming discovery is only the reverse side of the oblivion of the most important: all things necessarily appear in a new light if they are seen for the first time in a specifically dimmed light. A stupendous contraction of the horizon appears to Machiavelli and his successors as a wondrous enlargement of the horizon.

Instead of saying that the status of philosophy becomes obscured in Machiavelli's thought, it is perhaps better to say that in his thought the meaning of philosophy is undergoing a change. The classics understood the moral-political phenomena in the light of man's highest virtue or perfection, the life of the philosopher or the contemplative life. The superiority of peace to war or of leisure to business is a reflection of the superiority of thinking to doing or making. Solutions of the political problem which are altogether satisfactory to the good citizen prove to be inadequate solely because they make men oblivious of man's highest perfection. This is the reason why the best regime is so lofty that its actualization is very improbable or why its actualization so much depends on chance. Philosophy transcends the city, and the worth of the city depends ultimately on its openness, or deference, to philosophy. Yet the city cannot fulfill its function if it is not closed to philosophy as well as open to it; the city is necessarily the cave. The city understood in its closedness to philosophy is the *demos* in the philosophic sense, i.e., the totality of the citizens who are incapable or unwilling to defer to philosophy. The philosophers and the *demos* in the sense indicated are separated by a gulf; their ends differ radically. The gulf can be bridged only by a noble rhetoric, by a certain kind of noble rhetoric which we may call for the time being accusatory or punitive rhetoric. Philosophy is incapable of supplying this kind of rhetoric. It cannot do more than to sketch its outlines. The execution must be left to orators or poets.[219] Machiavelli's philosophizing on the other hand remains on the whole within the limits set by the city qua closed to philosophy. Accepting the ends of the *demos* as beyond appeal, he seeks for the best means conducive to those ends.[220] Through his effort philosophy becomes salutary in the sense in which the *demos* understands, or may understand, the salutary. He achieves the decisive turn toward that notion of philosophy according to which its purpose is to relieve man's estate or to increase man's power or to guide man toward the rational society, the bond and the end of which is enlightened self-interest or the comfortable self-preservation of each of its members. The cave becomes "the substance." By supplying all men with the goods which they desire, by being the obvious benefactress of all men, philosophy (or science) ceases to be suspect or alien. It ceases to be in need of rhetoric, except insofar as the goods which it procures must still be advertised in order to be sold; for men cannot desire what they do not know of. To return to that manifestation of the new notion of philosophy which appears clearly in Machiavelli's books, the new philosophy takes its bearings by how men live as distinguished from how they ought to live; it despises the concern with imagined republics and imagined principalities. The standard which it recognizes is "low but solid." Its symbol is the Beast Man as opposed to the God

Man: it understands man in the light of the sub-human rather than of the super-human. The scheme of a good society which it projects is therefore in principle likely to be actualized by men's efforts or its actualization depends much less on chance than does the classical "utopia": chance is to be conquered, not by abandoning the passionate concern with the goods of chance and the goods of the body but through giving free rein to it. The good society in the new sense is possible always and everywhere since men of sufficient brain can transform the most corrupt people, the most corrupt matter, into an incorrupt one by the judicious application of the necessary force. Since man is not by nature ordered toward fixed ends, he is as it were infinitely malleable. This view becomes a settled conviction long before philosophers begin to think of "evolution." Since man is not by nature ordered toward goodness, or since men can become good and remain good only through compulsion, civilization or the activity which makes men good is man's revolt against nature; the human in man is implicitly understood to reside in an Archimedean point outside of nature. The "idealistic" philosophy of freedom supplements and ennobles the "materialistic" philosophy which it presupposes in the very act of negating it. The brain which can transform the political matter soon learns to think of the transformation of every matter or of the conquest of nature. The charm of competence bewitches completely first a few great men and then whole nations and indeed as it were the whole human race. Yet before that grand revolt or emancipation can get under way, the hold which the old modes and orders have over the minds of almost all men must be broken. It cannot be broken by frontal assault, for there does not yet exist an army which has sworn to the new modes and orders. Therefore a most subtle rhetoric is still needed for recruiting the highest officers or the general staff of the new army. The new philosophy lives from the outset in the hope which approaches or equals certainty, of future conquest or of conquest of the future—in the anticipation of an epoch in which the truth will reign, if not in the minds of all men, at any rate in the institutions which mold them. Propaganda is to guarantee the coincidence of philosophy and political power. Philosophy is to fulfill the function of both philosophy and religion. The discovery of the Archimedean point outside of everything given, or the discovery of a radical freedom, promises the conquest of everything given and thus destroys the natural basis of the radical distinction between philosophers and non-philosophers.[221] Yet in looking forward to the extreme consequences of Machiavelli's action, we must not forget the fact that for Machiavelli himself the domination of necessity remains the indispensable condition of every great achievement and in particular of his own: the transition or the jump from the realm of necessity into the realm of freedom will be the inglorious death of the very possibility of human excellence.

The necessity which spurred on Machiavelli and his great successors spent itself some time ago. What remains of their effort no longer possesses the evidence which it possessed while their adversary was powerful; it must now be judged entirely on its intrinsic merits. Modern man as little as pre-modern man can escape imitating nature as he understands nature. Imitating an expanding universe, modern man has ever more expanded and thus become ever more shallow. Confronted by this amazing process, we cannot cease wondering as to what essential defect of classical political philosophy could possibly have given rise to the modern venture as an enterprise that was meant to be reasonable. We disregard the many answers which assume the truth of the modern premises. The classics were for almost all practical purposes what now are called conservatives. In contradistinction to many present day conservatives however, they knew that one cannot be distrustful of political or social change without being distrustful of technological change. Therefore they did not favor the encouragement of inventions, except perhaps in tyrannies, i.e., in regimes the change of which is manifestly desirable. They demanded the strict moral-political supervision of inventions; the good and wise city will determine which inventions are to be made use of and which are to be suppressed. Yet they were forced to make one crucial exception. They had to admit the necessity of encouraging inventions pertaining to the art of war. They had to bow to the necessity of defense or of resistance. This means however that they had to admit that the moral-political supervision of inventions by the good and wise city is necessarily limited by the need of adaptation to the practices of morally inferior cities which scorn such supervision because their end is acquisition or ease. They had to admit in other words that in an important respect the good city has to take its bearings by the practice of bad cities or that the bad impose their law on the good. Only in this point does Machiavelli's contention that the good cannot be good because there are so many bad ones prove to possess a foundation. We recognize the consideration which we have sketched in his overstatement that good arms are the necessary and sufficient condition of good laws or in his eventual identification of the most excellent man with the most excellent captain. The difficulty implied in the admission that inventions pertaining to the art of war must be encouraged is the only one which supplies a basis for Machiavelli's criticism of classical political philosophy. One could say however that it is not inventions as such but the use of science for such inventions which renders impossible the good city in the classical sense. From the point of view of the classics, such use of science is excluded by the nature of science as a theoretical pursuit. Besides, the opinion that there occur periodic cataclysms in fact took care of any apprehension regarding an excessive development of technology or regarding the danger that man's inventions might become his masters and his destroyers. Viewed in this light, the natural cataclysms appear as a manifestation of the beneficence of nature. Machiavelli himself expresses this opinion of the natural cataclysms which has been rendered incredible by the experiences of the last centuries.[222] It would seem that the notion of the beneficence of nature or of the primacy of the Good must be restored by being rethought through a return to the fundamental experiences from which it is derived. For while "philosophy must beware of wishing to be edifying," it is of necessity edifying.

Notes

[*In references to Machiavelli texts numbers in parentheses indicate the pages of the Italian edition of Machiavelli's* Opere, *edited by F. Flora and C. Cordié (Milan: Arnoldo Mondado, 1949-50).*]—EDS.

Introduction

1. *Prince* chs. 17 (Dido) and 18 (Chiron).

2. Bacon, *Essays* (*Of Atheism*).

3. *Rights of Man*, Part the Second, Introduction.

4. Cf. Henry Adams, *The First Administration of Thomas Jefferson*, II (New York 1898), 56, 71-73, 254.

Chapter I

1. *Prince* chs. 1 beginning, 2 beginning and 8 beginning.

2. *Discourses* I 17, 49, 55 (211), II 2 beginning. Numbers in parentheses indicate the pages of the edition of Machiavelli's *Opere* edited by F. Flora and C. Cordié (Arnoldo Mondadori, 1949-50 Milan).

3. In the *Discourses* there are only 2 chapters of 142 which contain only modern examples (I 27 and 54) whereas in the *Prince* there are 8 chapters of 26 which contain only modern examples. Conversely there is no chapter in the *Prince* which contains only ancient examples whereas there are at least 60 chapters in the *Discourses* which contain only ancient examples.

4. *Discourses* I pr., 55 (213), II 4 towards the end, 15 end, 33 end.

5. *Discourses* I pr. Cf., apart from the numerous chapter headings in which both republics and princes are mentioned, especially I 16 (138-139), II 24 (300-301), III 1 towards the end, 3-4.

6. *Prince* chs. 3, 5, 9 (31), 10 (35), 12, 13 towards the end, 17 (54), 21 (71-72).

7. *La Mandragola* III 2; *Prince* ch. 25 (heading and beginning); *Discourses* I 38 towards the end, 56, II 5, III 1 beginning, 6 (346), 30 (410), 31 (413).

8. *Florentine Histories* VII 6.

9. *Prince* chs. 3 (6), 10 (35-36); *Discourses* I 12, 57, 58, III 8, 36 near the beginning. "Nature" is mentioned in only one chapter heading in the two books, in *Discourses* III 43, which is the 136th chapter of the book.—At the beginning of the first chapter of the *Prince* Machiavelli gives a divi-

sion of "all states, all dominions" into principalities and republics. "All states, all dominions" comprise more than the principalities and republics "of which there exists memory"—ch. 4 (13)—; they include also the imaginary principalities and republics of which he speaks in ch. 15: the proof of their essentially imaginary character is in fact a most important part of the argument of the *Prince*.

10. *Prince* chs. 3 (8-9), 7 (20), 25 beginning; *Discourses* I pr., II pr. (228), 5, III 1 beginning, 43 beginning.

11. *Discourses* III 35 beginning.

12. E.g., I 40, III 6, 8. Cf. note 5 above.

13. *Prince* chs. 6 and 13.

14. Cf. *Discourses* II pr. (230) with I 9.

15. Cf. note 3 above.

16. *Discourses* I 58 end; *Prince* ch. 18 toward the end.

17. In the Epistle Dedicatory to the *Discourses* Machiavelli substitutes "long practice" for "long experience" which he had used in the Epistle Dedicatory to the *Prince*: Machiavelli's practice was "republican"; experience could have been acquired by an onlooker. In the Epistle Dedicatory to the *Prince* Machiavelli merely alludes to his practice: he refers to the many discomforts and perils under which he had acquired his experience.

18. *Discourses* II 18 (281).—As for "rules" and "general rules," cf. *Prince* chs. 3 (11, 13), 9 (33) and 23 towards the end, with *Discourses* I 9 (119), 18 near the beginning, III 22 (393), Cf. *Art of War* I (463) and VII (612).

19. Cf. *Discourses* I 4, 12, 41, II 10, 17, III 3, 4.

20. *Discourses* I 8 (117), 11 (127), 45 (192), 53 (206), II 5 (247), III 27 (404), 29 end, 30 (410), 43 (436).

21. *Discourses* I 44 (190), 46 (193), II 16 (271-272), 18 (280).

22. Cf. the letter to Vettori of December 10, 1513 with *Prince* chs. 6 and 14 (the greatest examples or the most exalted examples are ancient examples). Cf. the reference to "ancients and moderns" in the Epistle Dedicatory to the *Prince*.

23. *Prince* ch. 19 end; *Discourses* I 9 (120), 58 (220). Cf. *Florentine Histories* III 6.

24. Cf. *Prince* ch. 2 and the remark about the virtue of the hereditary right of Marcus Aurelius and Commodus in ch. 19 with *Discourses* I 2 (99), 10 (123), 19-20.

25. Cf. *Prince* ch. 19 and *Discourses* I 10: see especially in *Prince* ch. 19 the characteristic phrase *Voglio mi basti* near the beginning of the discussion of the Roman emperors: Machiavelli draws our attention to the arbitrary character of his selecting these particular emperors.

26. Cf. Nabis in *Prince* ch. 9 and *Discourses* I 10, 40; Petrucci in *Prince* ch. 20 and *Discourses* III 6; Caesar in *Prince* ch. 16 and *Discourses* I 10, 37; King David in *Prince* ch. 13 and *Discourses* I 25-26. As for Agathocles, cf. *Prince* ch. 8 with Justinus XXII 1. In describing Agathocles and Liverotto in the *Prince* (ch. 8), Machiavelli tacitly describes them in the way in which Aristotle explicitly describes tyrants: Machiavelli only tacitly describes them as tyrants.

27. *Discourses* I 40, III 6, 8.

28. Cf. especially *Prince* ch. 26 beginning, with the parallel in *Discourses* III 34 (420).

29. *Prince* chs. 8, 9, 19; *Discourses* III 6 (345); Justinus XXIII 2.—In the first chapter of the *Prince* he mentions as examples only Milan and Naples; in ch. 23 Milan and Naples prove to be the outstanding examples of principalities lost in Machiavelli's time.

30. Cf. *Prince* ch. 19 (59-60) where Machiavelli speaks of a conspiracy which happened "within the memory of our fathers" with *Discourses* III 6 (343) where he speaks of the con-

spiracy of the Pazzi which took place "in our times." Cf. likewise the praise in the *Prince*, loc. cit., of the French kingdom with the blame of all modern monarchies in the *Art of War* I (458-459).

31. *Prince* ch. 5 end; *Discourses* III 6 (345, 351-352); *Florentine Histories* VII 33.

32. *Prince* chs. 6 (19) and 18; *Discourses* III 35 beginning; *Florentine Histories* VI 17. Cf. *Prince* ch. 3 (a remark made by Machiavelli to a French Cardinal) and ch. 7 (a remark made by Cesare Borgia to Machiavelli) with *Discourses* II 16 (a remark made only in Machiavelli's presence).

33. *Discourses* II 10. Machiavelli could have quoted an explicit statement of Livy (IX 40. 6) in support of his opinion about money. If someone would object that this statement is made, not by Livy, but by a Livian character, I would refer him to *Discourses* III 12 toward the end, where Machiavelli ascribes to Livy an expression used by a Livian character.

34. In ch. 7 of the *Prince* Cesare Borgia had come to sight as the model of a new prince; in ch. 11 he is revealed to have been a mere tool of Pope Alexander VI, his father (cf. *Discourses* III 29).

35. *Florentine Histories* V 1: letters and philosophy belong to "decent leisure." This "decent leisure" whose beneficiaries while giving occasion to persecution, abhor persecution, seems to be the pagan counterpart of the "ambitious leisure" characteristic, according to Machiavelli, of "many Christian countries and states" (*Discourses* I pr.).

36. Consider in this connection the similar phrasing of the charge against Caesar in *Discourses* I 10 (124) and of the charge against the Church in I 12 (130): the "obligations" which Italy has against Caesar and against the Church.

37. *Discourses* II pr. (227), 23 (298),

III 2.

38. *Discourses* I pr., II 2 (238), III 35 (421-422); *Prince* ch. 6 (19).

39. *Discourses* II 29: "Fortuna sometimes *blinds the minds of men*"; the expression used in III 48 "the desire to conquer *blinds the minds of men*" might by itself remind the reader of II 29 where Machiavelli gives a contradictory explanation of the same event as in III 48. (III 48 is the 52nd chapter of the series of chapters which begins after II 29).

40. Letter to Vettori of April 29, 1513 (beginning). Cf. *Art of War* V (564-565) and VII (606-607).

41. Letter to Guicciardini of May 17, 1521. Cf. *Discourses* II 13 end with III 40-42.

42. Machiavelli indicates the difficulty by saying in I 28: "he then, who will consider as much as has been said," (i.e., he who disregards, among other things, the Decemvirate) will agree with Machiavelli's explanation.

43. *Discourses* I 2 (100) and 5 (105-106).—In *Discourses* I 20 Machiavelli says that since the Roman consuls owed their office to free votes, "they were always most excellent men." This is again a temporary overstatement of the goodness of the Roman republic; it is tacitly contradicted later on (cf. I 24 end, 50, 53, III 17, to say nothing of I 35 beginning).— Cf. the first sentence of III 40.

44. *Discourses* I 18 (143), 20, 25-26, 58 (217), II pr. (228).

45. Cf. note 19 above.

46. Cf. letter to Vettori of January 13, 1514 with *Florentine Histories* VIII 36.

47. Nietzsche, *Froehliche Wissenschaft*, aph. 1.

48. These remarks are, of course, quite insufficient for the full interpretation of *Discourses* III 18. Since we do not intend to give a full interpretation of this chapter or of any other chapter (for considering the interdependence of all chapters,

this could only be done in a commentary consisting of many volumes), we merely note that the parallelism of the four examples (twice an ancient example is followed by a modern example) conceals the fact that the fourth example is in a class by itself, since no error whatsoever was committed in the event with which it deals. Of the first three examples, two are pagan and one is Christian, the latter being in the center. In the Roman examples, the Romans erroneously believed that they had been defeated (in the first example, the Romans despair of their salvation but in the third example the Romans while erroneously believing that they had lost, believe correctly that by withdrawing to very nearby hills they will be temporarily secure); the moderns, on the other hand, believe erroneously in victory or even in false news about victory. In the second and fourth examples, the alleged victory is explicitly stated to have been announced either orally or in writing.

49. Plato, *Rivals* 133 d8-e1 (cf. 134c 1-5).

50. As regards the pre-history of this view, cf. Strauss, *Persecution and the Art of Writing*, 13.

51. *Discourses* II 12 (262): *le ragioni* are distinguished from *le cose dette*; the arguments from authority were called *ragioni* near the beginning of the chapter. The argument taken from the poetic fables is followed immediately by an argument taken from "modern judgments."

52. This step is prepared by II 16 (271) where Machiavelli refers twice to "Tuscan" equivalents of Latin expressions.

53. *Discourses* II 8 (253). Cf. *Opere* II 517.

54. See the very favorable judgment on Caesar in *Discourses* I 52 and in *Prince* ch. 14 (Caesar "an excellent man"). Cf. the analysis of Manlius' policy in the light of the distinction between corrupt and un-

corrupt cities (*Discourses* III 8) with the different analysis in *Discourses* I 8.

55. Cf. *Discourses* I 49 and III 49.

56. Cf. also *Discourses* II 29 (Fortuna) with the repetition in III 1 (extrinsic accident); also cf. I 58 (the people are wiser than a prince) with the explicit re-examination of the thesis of that chapter in III 34 (the important qualification "when peoples can be advised as princes are advised").—What is true of the discussion of founders in *Discourses* I, applies also to the other chief subject of that Book, namely, religion (cf. I 9 beginning). Religion is discussed explicitly in I 11-15; it is taken up in a more or less disguised way first in I 19-24, then in I 28-32, and finally in I 46-59, the section devoted to the multitude or plebs; for, according to Machiavelli, the multitude as distinguished from "princes" is the home of religion (cf. *Prince* ch. 18 toward the end). The primary subject of I 19-24 is Tullus Hostilius who is the counterpart of the religious Numa Pompilius and who is described, in contrast with the "weak king" Numa, as a man of outstanding virtue and as "most prudent." After having overstated the prudence of Tullus in order to underline the contrast with Numa, he reduces this praise to reasonable proportions in I 22-24. The primary subject of I 28-32 is gratitude; as regards the relation of gratitude and religion, cf. Machiavelli's *Esortazione alla penitenza* (*Opere* II 801-804).

57. *Discourses* II 28 (313); cf. III 20 (388) and 21 (390).

58. Toward the end of the eighth chapter of the *Prince* Machiavelli speaks of "cruelty well used" and excuses himself for employing this expression; at the beginning of ch. 17 he speaks of "the bad use of mercy" without excusing himself any further. Toward the end of ch. 6, he speaks of Hiero's dissolving the old militia; in ch. 13, he tells us that Hiero had

these soldiers cut to pieces. At the end of ch. 18 he does not yet dare to mention the name of Ferdinand of Aragon; at the beginning of ch. 21 he does dare to do so. In ch. 3 (7), he speaks first of the necessity of extinguishing the "line" of a prince, and thereafter of the necessity of extinguishing his "blood." Cf. also ch. 4 (15) where he replaces "memory" by "blood." "Blood" is a very delicate matter; hence it occurs only once in a chapter heading (*Discourses* III 7) and there only in the expression "without blood."

59. Cf. note 25 above.

60. Cf. page 32 above.

61. In this connection we may note that Machiavelli distinguishes in *Prince* ch. 3 (12) between "someone" raising a certain objection and "some others" raising another objection; the first objection is political, the second one is moral.

62. *Prince* ch. 19 (61, 62, 65, 66) and 20 (67); cf. *Discourses* I 10 (123) and 40 (187) as well as *Art of War* I (*Opere* I 476). The connection between that chapter of the *Prince* which deals explicitly with crime as a way to princely power (ch. 8) and ch. 19 is indicated by the fact that both chapters, and no other chapter, begin with the words *Ma perché*. Incidentally, there are four chapters of the *Prince* which begin with *Ma* (But) whereas no chapter of the *Discourses* begins with that word. The equivalent within the *Discourses* is the beginning with *Ancora che* (Although) of which we likewise find four cases (*Discourses* I pr., 32, 55, III 40): the tempo of the two books is very different. In order to see the special significance of the discussion of Severus, one should also compare Machiavelli's judgment on his apparent hero Cesare Borgia with his judgment on Severus; cf. ch. 7 (24) with ch. 19 (62-63).

63. *Prince* chs. 8 (28), 11 end, 16 beginning, 17 (54).

64. Cf. *Discourses* I 46-47 whose chapter headings begin with "Human beings."

65. *Discourses* I 56.

66. Cf. e.g., I 10, II 1, 8-9, 30 (317), III 6, 24-25. Our attention is drawn to the number of chapters of the *Discourses* by the following striking irregularity: Whereas Books I and II have a preface, Book III does not; the effect or the cause of this irregularity is that the *Discourses* consist of 142 chapters. It was common knowledge that Livy's *History* consisted of 142 books; cf. Petrarca, *Epistolae de rebus familiaribus*, liber 24. epistola 8., and *Rerum memorandarum* liber 1. paragraph 18. (I am obliged for this information to Mr. A. H. Mc Donald of Clare College, Cambridge.)

67. I Kings 3. 14; Luke I. 53. Cf. Luke 1. 51-52 with Aristotle, *Politics* 1314 a 1-29 (*apud tyrannos autem adulatores honorati sunt quia humiliter colloquuntur* etc.)

68. *Prince* chs. 6 and 18; *Discourses* III 30 (409). Machiavelli has incorporated into his books infinitely more of such "judicious readings" of the Bible than is immediately visible. This assertion is not contradicted by the fact that he refers explicitly to the Bible only once. He also refers explicitly to Aristotle only once, and it would be unintelligent to infer from this that he has not given careful consideration to Aristotle's doctrine. Each of the two most authoritative "texts," the Bible and Aristotle, is indeed mentioned only once *eo nomine*. Aristotle is mentioned in *Discourses* III 26 (the only mention of Aristotle is followed by the only quotation from a contemporary prose writer—Biondo—in III 27) and the Bible is mentioned in III 30 (the only mention of the Bible is preceded by the only quotation from a contemporary poet—Lorenzo de' Medici—in III 29). Of Savonarola Machiavelli says that his writings show his learning,

his prudence, and the virtue of his mind; of King David he says that he was a man most excellent in arms, in learning and in judgment, and besides of outstanding virtue: he does not refer to David's writings; cf. *Discourses* I 19 (147) and 45 (192). (Cf. the similarly phrased judgment on Dante in the *Discorso o Dialogo intorno alla lingua nostra, Opere* II 808.)

69. *Discourses* III 12 beginning.
70. *Discourses* I 10.
71. *Discourses* II 3, 23, III 10.
72. Cf. note 54 above.

Chapter II

1. Letter to Vettori, December 10, 1513.

2. Of the 142 chapter headings of the *Discourses*, 39 contain proper names.

3. *Discourses* II 1 (234), III 19 and 42; cf. II 20 beginning.

4. Cf. *Prince*, ch. 15 beginning.

5. See page 23 above.

6. Cf. the Epistle Dedicatory of the *Prince*.

7. We are thus not unprepared to find that the most extraordinary conqueror, Alexander (the Great), is mentioned twice in the heading of the following chapter.

8. *Discourses*, I pr.

9. The tacit emphasis on ancient examples in ch. 9 has a special reason. It draws our attention to the impropriety of discussing in the *Prince* the most important modern example of civil principalities i.e., the rule of the Medici. Machiavelli leaves it at discussing the ancient counterpart: Nabis of Sparta. Cf. ch. 21 (73).

10. Compare also the chief example of ch. 10 (the German cities which are free to the highest degree) with the remark about the Swiss in ch. 12 (the Swiss are armed to the highest degree and free to the highest). This distinction is developed somewhat more fully in *Discourses* II 19 (286-287).

11. Chs. 12 (41) and 13 (43, 44). Cf. the letter to Piero Soderini of January 1512.

12. Chs. 17 (52) and 18 (55). In the only intervening reference to literature—ch. 17 (54)—Machiavelli attacks "the writers" and no longer merely as he did at the beginning of ch. 15, "many" writers. Incidentally, "many writers" are attacked in the *Discourses* as early as the tenth chapter; the break with the tradition becomes explicit in the *Discourses* proportionately much earlier than in the *Prince*.

13. Cf. the relation of princes and ministers as it appears in ch. 22 with the relation of Cesare Borgia and his minister as presented in ch. 7 (24).

14. Chs. 20, 22 and 23 contain only modern examples. The explicit emphasis on modern examples in ch. 18 (How princes should keep faith) has a special reason just as had the tacit emphasis on ancient examples in ch. 9: Machiavelli draws our attention to the modern form of faithlessness or hypocrisy which strikingly differs from the Roman form (cf. *Discourses* II 13 end). There is a connection between this thought and the reference to "pious cruelty" in ch. 21. Machiavelli indicates that the argument of ch. 18 requires a special act of daring (56).

15. Ch. 19 is the center not only of the third part but of the whole section of the *Prince* which follows the discussion of the various kinds of principality, i.e., of that whole section which in the light of the beginning

of the *Prince* comes as a surprise (cf. ch. 1 where the theme "the various kinds of principality" is announced with the beginnings of chs. 12, 15 and 24). Whereas the first, second, and fourth parts of the *Prince* each contain one Latin quotation, the third part contains two of them.—Compare the beginning of ch. 6 with the beginnings of chs. 21-23 in the light of the observation made in the text.

16. Cf. pages 46-47 above.

17. Ch. 20 (67-68). The opinion described there as held by "our ancients" is described in *Discourses* III 27 (403) as a modern opinion held by "the sages of our city sometime ago."

18. Shortly before, Machiavelli mentions "natural affection" for a prince. He had not used that expression since early in ch. 4. But there he had spoken of the natural affection of the subjects for the French barons, their lords from time immemorial; now he speaks of natural affection for a new prince. The transition is partly effected by what he says in ch. 19 (60) about the hatred, founded in fear, of the French people against the French magnates.

19. Ch. 21 (72). Cf. ch. 3 end.

20. The most unqualified attack in the *Prince* on ancient writers in general ("the writers")—ch. 17 (54)—occurs within the context of a praise of ancient statesmen or captains.—The fourth part of the *Prince* contains one Latin quotation and the only Italian quotation occurring in the book.

21. *Prince* chs. 6 (18) and 11 (36).

22. To "treat" something means to "reason" about it (*Prince*, ch. 2 beginning and ch. 8 beginning). Machiavelli calls his discourse on the Decemvirate, which includes an extensive summary of Livy's account of the Decemvirate and therefore in particular of the actions of the would-be tyrant Appius Claudius, the "above written treatise" (*Discourses* I 43), whereas he calls his discourse on the

liberality of the senate "the above written discourse" (*Discourses* I 52 beginning). In *Discourses* II 32 (323) *trattato* means "conspiracy." He calls Xenophon's *Hiero* a "treatise" on tyranny (II 2) while he calls Dante's *Monarchia* a "discourse" (I 53). In *Florentine Histories* II 2, he calls the First Book of that work *nostro trattato universale*.

23. Compare also the end of ch. 13 with ch. 25.—In the first chapter Machiavelli indicates 13 subjects whose treatment might seem to require 13 chapters, and he indicates in the fifteenth chapter 11 subjects whose treatment might seem to require 11 chapters.

24. Chs. 26 and 4 of the *Prince* begin with practically the same word.

25. Cf. *Discourses* I 23 (153).

26. Only at the end of ch. 4 does Machiavelli allude to Italy by mentioning the failure of Pyrrhus, i.e., his failure to keep his conquests in Italy.

27. *Prince* ch. 7 (23-25); cf. *Opere* I 637. Consider Machiavelli's statement on the pernicious character of the feudal nobility in *Discourses* I 55.

28. The term "fatherland" which occurs in chs. 6, 8 and 9 is avoided in ch. 7, the chapter devoted to Cesare Borgia.

29. The subject-matter of ch. 5 is slightly concealed (see the unobtrusive transition from states in general to cities i.e., republics, near the beginning: *volerli . . . ruinarle*). It almost goes without saying that almost all examples in this chapter are ancient. All the more striking is Machiavelli's silence about the Roman mode of ruling republican cities by making them allies; see *Discourses* II 24 (303) and 19 (285); he tacitly rejects this mode in the *Prince* because it is impracticable for a prince who is to become prince of a united Italy.— When discussing the badness of mercenary armies, Machiavelli uses almost exclusively examples which show that

mercenary armies have ruined or endangered republics. He thus shows in effect that mercenaries can be eminently good for a leader of mercenary armies, like Sforza who by being armed became a new prince; compare ch. 12 with chs. 7 (21) and 14 (36). As we learn from Livy (XXXVII 27.15), Nabis of Sparta whom Machiavelli praises, placed the greatest confidence in his mercenary troops. (This report of Livy precedes almost immediately his account of Philopoemen which Machiavelli uses in *Prince* ch. 14). These remarks taken together with those about the soldiers of the Roman emperors in ch. 19 and about the impossibility of arming all able-bodied Italian subjects in ch. 20 (67) reveal a possibility which deserves attention. In this connection one should also consider what Machiavelli says toward the end of the ninth chapter, immediately after having praised (the tyrant) Nabis of Sparta, about the superiority of absolute principalities, i.e., about the kind of principality which was traditionally called tyranny (*Discourses* I 25 end), and compare it with the confrontation of the Turkish and the French monarchies in *Prince* ch. 4 (14).

30. Compare ch. 25 (79) with chs. 18 end and 21 beginning, as well as *Discourses* I 12 (130).

31. Compare *Discourses* I 26 with *Prince* chs. 7 (24), 8 (30), 13 end, 17 and 21 beginning. Just as Philip became "from a little king, prince of Greece" by the use of the most cruel means, Ferdinand of Aragon became "from a weak king, the first king of the Christians" by the use of "pious cruelty."

32. *Prince* chs. 3 (11-13), 7 (23,26), 11 (37-38); cf. *Discourses* III 29. We note in passing that in the *Prince* ch. 16 (50-51) Machiavelli holds up "the present king of France," "the present king of Spain," and Pope Julius II but not the present Pope, Leo

X, who possesses "goodness and infinite other virtues," (ch. 11 end) as models of prudent stinginess which is the indispensable condition for "doing great things." Cf. Ranke, *Die Roemischen Paepste*, ed. by F. Baethgen, I, 273 on Leo X's extravagance.— In the *Prince* Machiavelli tells two stories about private conversations which he had had (chs. 3 and 7). According to the first story Machiavelli once told a French cardinal that the French know nothing of politics, for otherwise they would not have permitted the Church to become so great (through the exploits of Cesare Borgia). The second story deals with what Cesare told Machiavelli on the day on which Pope Julius II was elected, i.e., on which Cesare's hopes were dashed through his insufficient control of the Church: Cesare had in fact committed the same mistake as the French, but he had the excuse that he had no choice. In *Florentine Histories* I 23, Machiavelli alludes to the possibility that the papacy might become hereditary. Could he have played with the thought that a new Cesare Borgia might redeem Italy after having himself become Pope and the founder of a papal dynasty?

33. *Discourses* I 12. Cf. the letter to Vettori of April 26, 1513.

34. *Discourses* I 27; *Opere* I 683.

35. Machiavelli prepares for the silence about Romulus in ch. 26 in the following manner: in ch. 6 he enumerates the four heroic founders three times and in the final enumeration he relegates Romulus to the end. Cf. *Florentine Histories* VI 29.

36. *Prince* chs. 1, 6 (17-19), 8 (29-30), 14 (48), 19 (66), 20 (67) and 24 (77); cf. *Art of War* VII (616-617).

37. Cf. *Prince* ch. 22.

38. Ch. 7 (21-22). Cf. pages 22-23 above.

39. Letter to [Ricciardo Bechi], March 8, 1497.

40. The shift in *Prince* ch. 26 from

Lorenzo to his family can be understood to some extent from the point of view indicated in the text. As for the unreliability of promises stemming from passion, cf. *Discourses* II 31; as for the popularity of grand hopes and valiant promises, cf. *Discourses* I 53.

41. This is not to deny the fact that the miracles attested to by Machiavelli are without example insofar as their sequence differs from the sequence of the Mosaic miracles.

42. *Prince* chs. 3 (13), 12 (39,41), 18 (56-57) and 25 (80-81); cf. *Discourses* I 27. One can express the progress of the argument in the last part of the *Prince* as follows: 1) everything depends on virtue (ch. 24); 2) very much depends on chance but chance can be kept down by the right kind of man (ch. 25); 3) chance has done the most difficult part of the work required for liberating Italy, only the rest needs to be done by means of virtue (ch. 26).

43. The 7 real defeats must be taken together with the 4 invented miracles if one wants to grasp Machiavelli's intimation.

44. *Discourses* II 30 end.

45. In the "highest" part of the *Prince* Machiavelli speaks of "us Florentines," (chs. 15 and 20) while in the other parts of the book he speaks of "us Italians" (chs. 2, 12, 13 and 24).—The tyrant Nabis had destroyed the freedom of many Greek cities (Justinus XXXI, 1); by his assassination that freedom was restored. Cf. note 9 above.

46. *Prince* chs. 9 (32), 18 (57), 19 (58-59), 20 (68-69) and 23 (76-77). In each of the two chapters, 20 and 21, Machiavelli gives five rules to princes; the fourth rule in ch. 20 concerns the employment of men who were suspect at the beginning of the reign of a new prince; in the fourth rule given in ch. 21 the prince is urged to honor those who are excellent in any art.

47. *Discourses* III 2 end and 35 (422-423).

48. Compare *Discourses* I 30 (163) with 29 (160-161).

49. Apart from the Epistle Dedicatory and ch. 26 where Machiavelli, speaking of Lorenzo to Lorenzo uses the plural of reverence, he uses the second person plural only in connection with verbs like "seeing," "finding," "considering," and "understanding." There are, I believe, 11 cases of the latter kind in the *Prince* while in the *Discourses*, if I remember well, there are only 2 (I 58 [221] and II 30 [317]): in the *Discourses* which are addressed to potential princes, the need to distinguish between doers and thinkers does not arise to the same extent as it does in the *Prince*. Consider *Discourses* II pr. (230). In the chapter of the *Prince* on flatterers—ch. 23 (75)—Machiavelli uses Thou when speaking of the prince to the prince, while he uses the third person when speaking of the prudent prince: he is not a flatterer. Ch. 3 (10-11) beautifully illustrates how Machiavelli the teacher works together with his readers in examining certain things as well as how his contribution differs from that of his readers.

50. *Prince* chs. 18 (55) and 19 (62).

51. Swift's Houyhnhnms, being reasonable horses, are centaurs if a centaur is a being which combines the perfection of a horse with the perfection of man. In order to understand what the recommendation to imitate these beast-men means in *Gulliver's Travels*, one would have to start from the facts that the relation between Lilliput and Brobdingnag imitates the relation between the moderns and the ancients, and that the same relation is imitated again on a different plane in the last two parts of the work.

52. Compare *Prince* ch. 14 end with *Discourses* II 13.

53. Machiavelli does not even sug-

gest that Cesare Borgia, the model, was animated by patriotism or concerned with the common good. It is true that he contrasts Cesare with the criminal Agathocles by not calling Cesare a criminal. But if one looks at the actions of the two men, the contrast vanishes: in describing Agathocles as a criminal, he provisionally adopts the traditional judgment on that man, whereas there does not yet exist a traditional judgment on Cesare. The traditional condemnation of Agathocles was partly based on the fact that he had risen to princely power from "a base and abject condition." Machiavelli refers to a similar consideration when explaining the failure of Maximinus—*Prince* ch. 19 (64-65)—but it is irrelevant for his own judgment as can be seen from *Discourses* II 13, to say nothing of the Epistle Dedicatory to the *Prince* where he describes himself as "a man of low and base state." The main reason why Machiavelli had to speak of a criminal ruler was that he was compelled to indicate that he was questioning the traditional distinction between the criminal and the non-criminal as far as founders are concerned. He thus presents Agathocles as the classical example of the criminal ruler, as a breaker of all divine and human laws, a murderer and a traitor, a man without faith, mercy and religion; Agathocles possessed indeed greatness of mind; although a most excellent captain, he cannot be counted among the most excellent men; his actions could acquire for him empire but not glory; he benefited indeed his subjects, or rather the common people, but he did this of course entirely for selfish reasons. In the sequel Machiavelli retracts everything he had said in connection with Agathocles about the difference between an able criminal ruler and an able non-criminal ruler. The first step is the praise of Nabis whom he calls a prince in the *Prince* while he

calls him in the *Discourses* a tyrant: Nabis' policy was fundamentally the same as that of Agathocles (compare *Prince* chs. 9 [33] and 19 [58] with *Discourses* I 10 [122] and ch. 40 [187]). The second step is the questioning of the difference between "most excellent captain" and "most excellent man": good arms are the necessary and sufficient condition of good laws, and Agathocles had good arms; Cyrus, the excellent man most emphatically praised, is not said to have possessed faith, mercy and religion, but he is distinguished by greatness of mind, i.e., by a quality which Agathocles also possessed. One reason why Agathocles cannot be counted among the most excellent men is his savage cruelty and inhumanity; but Hannibal who is likewise characterized by inhuman cruelty is a most excellent man. (Compare *Prince* chs. 12 [38-39], 14 [47-48], 17 [54], 26 [81] with *Discourses* II 18 [280] and III 21 end). The last step is to show that glory can be acquired by crime or in spite of crime. This is shown most clearly by the case of Severus (see pages 46-47 above), but hardly less clearly by *Prince* ch. 18 toward the end, to say nothing of Machiavelli's observations regarding Giovampagolo Baglioni in *Discourses* I 27.

54. *Prince* chs. 6 (18), 8 (27,29,30), 9 (31,33), 26 (84).

55. *Prince* ch. 26 (83); *Discourses* II 4 toward the end and III 43; *Art of War*, at the end; compare *Discourses* I 1 end with Livy I 34. 12-35. 12, also Livy V 15. Cf. note 45 above.

56. Cf. *Art of War* II (489).

57. Cf. *Discourses* I 53.

58. *Prince* ch. 5; *Discourses* II 2 (239-240). In the preceding chapter of the *Discourses* (234) there occurs one of the few references to the *Prince*; the reference is to the third chapter i.e., to the section which deals with conquest.

59. *Prince* ch. 21 (71-73).

60. *Prince* chs. 12 (38-39) and 19 (58); *Discourses* I 4 (103); *Opere* II 473.

61. *Prince* chs. 3 (6), 6 (19), 9 (31,32), 10 (35-36), 17 (53), 18 (57), 23 (75), 24 (78); *Discourses* I 57 and 58 (217-219). In the *Prince* chs. 7 (22) and 8 (28) he applies expressions to Cesare Borgia and to Agathocles which he had applied to himself in the Epistle Dedicatory.

62. Cf. *Discourses* Epistle Dedicatory and the letter to Vettori of December 10, 1513.

63. The 11 pairs of moral qualities mentioned in ch. 15 and the 11 rules of conduct discussed in chs. 20-21 prove on examination to be 10.— Compare Hobbes' re-writing of the decalogue in *Leviathan*, ch. 30.

64. W. K. Jordan, *Men of Substance* (Chicago: The University of Chicago Press, 1942), p. 82.

65. Compare *Discourses* III 35 beginning with *Prince* ch. 6 (19).

Chapter III

1. *Discourses* I pr., II 2 (237-238), 19 (285) and III 27 (403-404); cf. III 30 (410) and 31 (413).

2. *Discourses* I pr., II 5 and III 30 (410). Cf. *La Mandragola*.

3. *Discourses*, Ep. Ded. and I pr. Cf. II 22 (293) and III 1 toward the end.

4. See especially *Discourses* II 2.

5. *Discourses* III 17 and 25.

6. *Discourses* I 20. Cf. II 19 (285, 288), 21 beginning and 32 (324). The date suggested in the last mentioned passage almost coincides with the date at which the first decade of Livy ends. Cf. *Opere* I 683.

7. I 26, 30, II 31, III 32, 35, 40, 43 and 44. Cf. ch. I, note 3 above.

8. The shortest chapter (I 48) has an unusually long chapter heading (34 words); there are only two other chapters (I 31 and 34) whose headings are of equal length.

9. *Prediche sopra Ezechiele*, X. Cf. *Discourses* II 5.

10. I 1 (95), 58 (217), II pr. (228) and 5 (247). *Opere* II 711.

11. *Discourses* II 2 (235) and 4-5. Cf. Livy V 1.6 with *Discourses* II 4 end: while the power and glory of the ancient Tuscans was destroyed by Rome, the same cannot be said of their religion.

12. I 1 (94-95), 2 (100-101) and 9 (120). Cf. *Prince*, chs. 6 (18) and 13 (43). In *Discourses* I 1, the chapter on the building of cities, Machiavelli mentions repeatedly Alexander the Great, who appears from I 19 and 26 as a parallel to King Solomon, but he does not mention Solomon in that chapter, although he too was a builder of cities (I Kings 9.17-19).

13. *Discourses* I 2, 4 and 6. Cf. III 12 (372-373).

14. *Discourses* I 2 (101-102), 3 beginning and 4. By speaking of classical political philosophy, I remain closer to Machiavelli than do those interpreters who speak of Polybius: Machiavelli does not mention Polybius. Cf. also I 2 (98) where he expresses his opinion about the classical doctrine by imputing to it an inferior rhetoric (*facilmente, con facilità, sanza difficultà*).—As for Machiavelli's praise of discord, cf. Plutarch, *Agesilaus* 5. 3-4.

15. *Discourses* I 5-6.

16. *Discourses* II 31 (cf. Livy VIII 24.18). Neither II 26 nor I 26 contain modern examples while each of these chapters contains an Asiatic example. III 26 also does not contain modern examples.—I 3 beginning, 39 beginning and II 16 (270).

17. *Discourses* I 1 end, II pr. end
and III 1 end. Cf. I 15 end.

18. I 13 (referring to I 39); I 29
(referring to II); I 47 end (referring
to III 28); II 22 (referring to III 16);
II 23 end (referring to III 41-42); II
26 (referring to III 6, the chapter on
conspiracies; cf. the somewhat different reference to the same chapter
in II 20). The connection between
the themes of II 24 and 25 is established by the fact that both themes
were mentioned in a single Florentine
maxim, as appears from III 27 (403)
and *Prince*, ch. 20 (67); starting from
this maxim, Machiavelli looks out for
Livian passages which he can use as
pegs on which to hang his discussion
of the themes; the passages in question occur in widely separated parts
of Livy. (II 25 is the chapter containing the unique reference to what had
been said on the same subject in another chapter and "for another purpose.") Near the beginning of III 13,
Machiavelli speaks of what Livy says
about a certain "place," i.e. topic (*locus*) as distinguished from a "place"
in Livy; see on the other hand the reference to "many places of (Livy's)
history" a few lines afterwards, and
to "many places" in Livy near the
beginning of III 14. Note in III 26 the
contrast between the reference to
"this [Livian] text" and the reference
to "the chapter in which *we* treat of
conspiracies." Cf. also the use of "in
its place" in the chapter on conspiracies—III 6 (339)—for referring to
other places within that chapter; that
chapter is a regular treatise by itself
and its plan is of course entirely Machiavelli's.

19. III 6 (342). Some discourses
immediately following one another
are explicitly connected with a view
to the fact that they are discourses
occasioned by the same Livian text;
see I 40-43, 53-54, and III 26-27.

20. I 9 beginning and 15 end (cf. I
1 end).

21. By references to Livy, I understand both Latin quotations from
Livy regardless of whether or not
they are introduced as statements
from Livy, and summaries or indications of Livian passages introduced by
expressions like "Livy says,' "our historian says," "the history shows," "the
text says," "the history of Horatius
Cocles," "one reads" etc.: the use of
a Livian passage does not yet constitute a reference to Livy. For establishing the sequence of references to
Livy, I take into account only the
first reference, if more than one
reference occurs in a given chapter
(I do not regard as a reference to
Livy the formula of the *Senatus
consultum ultimum*, which is quoted
in I 34.)—The references to Livy in
I 1-15 lead us in a very irregular way
from Livy II to Livy X; if one considers what has been indicated in ch.
I note 56 above, one may understand
why the references to Livy in I 16-
60 do no longer lead up to the end of
Livy X.

22. The expression "in the following chapter(s)" occurs 26 times at
or near the end of the chapter. (Only
in 17 cases can the expression possibly have the function of indicating
the beginning or the end of a section.) In this connection we may note
that 13 chapters of the *Discourses*
begin with the first person of the
personal pronoun.

23. Statius, *Silvae* I 1 v. 22.

24. Every reader of the *Discourses*
can see that I 11-15, 16-18, 19-24, 25-
27 and 28-32 form separate sections.
(This does not contradict our remark
that there is no manifest plan in I
16-60: a clear division into sections
does not by itself reveal a plan, since
such a division does not necessarily
reveal the reason for the sequence
of the sections.) We observe that
the expression "in the following chap-
ter(s)" occurs at or near the end of
I 14, 16, 22, 25, 26 and 28; the expression as used at the end of I 22
links that chapter with the two fol-

lowing chapters; hence the expression in question links the last chapters or the first chapters of a section. Since the expression occurs again at the ends of I 47 and of I 58, we tentatively assume that either I 47 is the beginning of a section or I 48 is the end of a section, and that I 59 is the end of another section. Expressions to the effect that the subject to be discussed in the immediate sequel is "not foreign to (my) purpose" occur at the beginning of I 13, the central chapter of a section, and at the beginning of I 18, the last chapter of a section. Since such expressions occur again near the beginnings of I 46 and of I 55 and at the end of I 58, and since the expression as used at the end of I 58 refers to the subject matter of I 59, we tentatively assume that I 46 and I 59 are ends of sections while abstaining for the time being from trying to guess what the use of that expression means in I 55. We note however in passing that such expressions occur only three times at the end of a chapter: at the end of I 58, the second chapter before the last in I, at the end of II 31, the second chapter before the last in II, and at the end of III 5 where it helps to introduce the chapter on conspiracies which is the 99th chapter of the *Discourses*. Another hint regarding the plan of I is provided by the quotations from Dante and his guide Virgil. Each poet is quoted twice in I; first they are quoted in widely separated chapters, Dante in I 11 and Virgil in I 21; the second quotations occur in two subsequent chapters which immediately precede I 55: Dante is quoted in I 53 and Virgil in I 54; the sections within which these quotations occur (I 11-15, 19-24, and 46-59) deal with fundamentally the same theme. Furthermore, we mention here the expression "everyone knows," which first occurs densely in I 56 and whose occurrence in other passages—I 21, 23, 24, 29—helps us to discern the meaning of the contexts in question. Finally, considering the special significance which the number 13 has in Machiavelli's work, we are not ashamed to note that the 13th and the 26th chapter are unquestionably centers of sections; we assume therefore tentatively that I 39 and I 52 are centers of sections. But, to repeat, the decision regarding assumptions suggested by hints, depends in the last resort on the consideration of the subject matter alone. On the basis of such consideration, we contend that this is the plan of I: 1) origin of cities (the most ancient antiquity): I 1; 2) the polity: I 2-8; 3) founders: I 9-10; 4) religion: I 11-15; six further sections dealing alternately with founders and religion (I 16-18, 19-24, 25-27, 28-32, 33-45, 46-59); 11) earliest youth: I 60. The division indicated at the beginning of I 9 (founders, religion, militia) will then refer to the subject matter of 51 chapters of I (founders and religion) and to that of II (militia). Cf. pages 43-44 above.

25. In I the beginning in question ends with the 15th chapter, in II it ends with the 10th chapter at the latest. Cf. the explicit remark about Machiavelli's plan in I 9 beginning, with the equivalent in II 6 beginning. The status of the Livy references in II 1-10 is underlined by the unusual, though not unique, frequency of references to authors other than Livy in that group of chapters.

26. The number of Latin quotations from Livy in I is 17; in II it is 21; and in III it is 31. The number of chapters containing Latin quotations from Livy in I is 9; the number of such chapters in II is 14, and in III it is 20. In the first 39 chapters of I, there are only 3 chapters which contain Latin Livy quotations; i.e. on the average one chapter in every group of 13 chapters contains a Latin Livy quotation; in the rest of I (40-60) there occur 13 Latin Livy quotations.

27. Thus he indicates that II 7-10 belong to a different section than II 1-5, and that new sections begin with II 11, 19, 23, with or before 28, and with 33. The only parallel to this procedure in I is the sequence of Livy references in I 15 and 16.

28. II 1, 4, 11, 16, 19, and 31.

29. II 17 beginning, 31 beginning and end. The purport of the expression as used in II 31 beginning has been explained on pages 96-97 above.

30. Cf. the density of this expression in II 21 (292) with the only other case of this kind, viz. I 56; also II 12 (261).—There are no explicit references to Dante in the Second Book which consists of 33 chapters.

31. At the beginning of II 8, and nowhere else in the book, Machiavelli uses the expression "not alien to the matter." "Matter" occurs in no chapter more frequently than three times. The term occurs three times in II 8, I 58, and in I 17 (the density of "matter" in I 17 is underlined by the fact that in I 18 "matter" is used once and is twice replaced by "subject.") The density of the term "matter" in the *Prince* occurs in chs. 19-20.

32. Cf. I 28 end, 29 beginning and 42 beginning.

33. I 1 end and 9 beginning, II pr. end.

34. II 2 (238). The expression "unarmed heaven" reminds one of "the unarmed prophet" alluded to in *Prince* ch. 6. In *Discourses* II 18, when discussing "the sins of Italian princes" (a subject connected with "the unarmed prophet" Savonarola), Machiavelli calls these princes "unarmed." Cf. also the reference to "unarmed" modern peoples and to "the unarmed heart" as distinguished from "the well armed heart" in II 30. At the end of II 15, Machiavelli refers back to I 38 where he had called the Florentines "unarmed." Cf. also the difference between "the true way" as shown by "our religion" and "the true way

of making a republic great": II 2 (237) and 19 (286). II 15, where Machiavelli makes a distinction between a certain "matter" and a certain historical event, is devoted, according to its heading, to "weak states."

35. The central chapter of II as well as the chapter preceding it (16 and 17) are the only chapters of the *Discourses* the headings of which refer to "our times" or "the present times." (Cf. the heading of II 17 with the beginning of the chapter.) The soldiers who are called in the heading of II 16 "soldiers of our times" are called in the body of that chapter "all Christian armies" and "our armies" (272). Cf. the reference to "weak states" in the heading of II 15. "Weak" also occurs in the headings of I 19, 38 and 57; the distance between II 16 and I 57 equals the distance between I 57 and 38 and the distance between I 38 and 19: "our times" are "weak times." Cf. II 15 end ("our republic," i.e. Florence), 18 end ("modern princes"), 19 beginning ("our corrupt ages") and the density of "Pope" and "Church" in II 22.—Cf. Pierre Bayle, *Pensées Diverses* Sect. 51: "les Anciens et les Modernes, les Païens et les Chrétiens." See also Strauss, *Natural Right and History*, 266.

36. By considering Machiavelli's indications as well as the subject matter, we discern the following plan of *Discourses* II: 1) II 1-5 (the Roman conquests and their consequences, viz. the reduction of the West to Eastern servility); 2) II 6-10 (Roman warfare in contradistinction to the kinds of warfare waged by the conquerors of the Roman Empire, by the Jews and by the moderns); 3) II 11-15 (the origins); 4) II 16-18 (the fundamental triad: infantry, artillery, cavalry); 5) II 19-22 (the false opinions—cf. II 19 beginning and 22 end); 6) II 23-25 (the reasons—cf. II 23 [297], 25, 27 [309]); 7) II 26-32 (the

passions); 8) II 33 (the Ciminian Forest). The provisional headings given to these sections will be replaced by the final formulations as soon as the necessary preparations have been completed. At present we merely add these three remarks. The first ten chapters of II deal with "the causes" of modernity while ostensibly dealing only with the Roman procedures in regard to aggrandizement and warfare; cf. the references to "causes" in the headings of II 1, 8, 9, and the density of "cause" at the beginning of II 9. The key to the plan of II is II 19-22, just as the key to the plan of I was I 19-24; for the understanding of II 19-22 one has to contrast the discussion of the German cities in II 19 with the parallel in I 55, and one has to consider the parallels between II 21 and I 56. The last section of II corresponds to the last section of I as is indicated by the fact that they are the only sections of the *Discourses* which consist of one chapter only; the purport of these sections is revealed, to the extent to which it is revealed, by the last section of III; the correspondence of the end of II and the end of I is indicated by the following features: the second person plural of the personal pronoun occurs in the *Discourses* only in I 58 (221) and in II 30 (317), apart from the Ep. Ded.; Machiavelli speaks of "occult virtue" in the *Discourses* only in I 58 (219) and in II 32 (323); cf. also the reference to *ciascuno dì* in I 59 beginning, II 31 beginning, and III 49 beginning (cf. I 49 end), as well as the use of the expression "not foreign to (my) purpose" in I 58 end and in II 31 end.

37. *Discourses* III begins like I with a series of explicitly connected chapters, the meaning of which in Machiavelli's own plan is clear, at least as regards the first 8 chapters of III (cf. the density of "in the next chapter" occurring at the ends of chapters in III 3-10 with the only other case of this kind, i.e. with I 2-8); hence the Livy references occurring in this group of chapters do not follow the Livian order; see especially the flagrant disregard of the Livian order in the announcement of the first subject of the Third Book in III 1 end. (In the other series of connected chapters in III—19-23—the Livian order is likewise disregarded.) III resembles I also by containing a large group of chapters in which Machiavelli's plan is obscure and at the same time the Livian order is strictly adhered to as far as the Livy references are concerned: III 25-44 leads us in a straight way from Livy III to Livy X. Furthermore, Machiavelli uses the sequence of his Livy references for indicating his own plan as little in III as he did in I. On the other hand, III contains proportionately the same number of Livy quotations in Latin and of chapters containing Livy quotations in Latin as does II. (But III contains a proportionately smaller number of chapters containing Livy references than does II: out of the 49 chapters of III, 26 contain Livy references.)

38. According to the suggestions of the chapter headings, approximately the same number of chapters in III 12-49 are devoted to domestic affairs as to foreign affairs. As for the alternation mentioned, cf. e.g. III 42 (foreign), 43 (domestic), 44 (ambiguous), 45 (foreign), 46-47 (domestic), 48 (foreign), 49 (domestic). Cf. III 11 where the relation of the one senate to the many tribunes is used as an exact parallel to the relation between one state and a hostile alliance.

39. I 1 end, II pr. end, III 1 end. The reference to III 16 in II 20 (a certain subject will be discussed "in its place in this part") suggests that II and III form a single "part"; it still leaves it open whether "this part" is the last part; the reference also underlines the particularly close connection

between II and III.

40. III 3, 21, 22, 23, 25 and 49. Altogether 8 names of individual human beings are mentioned in chapter headings of the *Discourses*, the names of 7 Romans and of the most famous enemy of the Romans who was known to the Romans while they were still incorrupted. Consider also the use of expressions referring to human individuals like *uno capitano*, *uno cittadino, uno e non molti, uno* (i.e. someone) in chapter headings of III (10, 12, 13, 15, 17, 18, 30, 34, 38, 39, 47) with the absence of such expressions from headings in II and their great rarity in I (48, 50, 52, 54). (For an obvious reason I disregard the use of *uno principe* in chapter headings.)

41. *Discourses* I 37; Livy II 44.5 and 54.2-10. Cf. *Discourses* I 52 (204) about the difference between "public deliberations" of a populist intention and "secret" actions of an anti-democratic character as well as I 59 about Themistocles' private and dishonest counsel and its repudiation by the honest Aristides and by the Athenian people.

42. Cf. the reference to Romulus in III 1 (328) with that to Rome's "first legislator" in II 1 (231). Cf. also the reference to Timoleon in III 5 with its only parallels in I 10 and I 17, and also the kinship of the argument of III 11 with that of I 37 ff. Both III 8 and I 8 are devoted to Manlius Capitolinus (cf. the reference in both chapters to the *Padri;* that expression also occurs in III 5 and I 49; it is meant to remind us of a certain kinship between the aristocracy of pagan Rome and the hierarchy of Christian Rome).

43. Cf. I 1 end and 15 end.

44. A founder captain in the full sense of the term is a man or a god who, after having founded a society and after having died, still protects it and therefore in a sense rules it; an example is Romulus (cf. Livy III

17.6 and I 16.3-8).

45. Cf. the usage in I 58-59. Cf. the reference to Nicias in III 16 with the only other reference to him, which occurs in I 53.

46. The parallel in Boccaccio's context is the contrast between Lambertuccio and Leonetto in the 66th story of the *Decamerón*.

47. Some of the lessons stated in the last section (III 35-49) had been stated in earlier parts of the book with sufficient clarity, and all the lessons stated there together with their Livian pegs could easily have been distributed among various earlier sections. The only link between the chapters of the section might seem to be the Livian order. Closer inspection shows that even there Machiavelli impresses his form on the Livian matter. After having indicated the theme in III 35, he turns to the "French" who combine courage and cowardice in an astonishing way (36) or who lost a war because they were disturbed by "something of little importance" (37); he returns to the "French" in 43 ff. The intervening chapters deal with "feigned battles" as distinguished from a "true fight" (38), with "an image of war" as distinguished from war itself (39) and with "fraud" (40-42); i.e. they deal with various kinds of useful untruth as distinguished from the truth: III 39, the 132d chapter of the *Discourses*, is the only chapter of either book which speaks with considerable emphasis of "knowledge" and of "science." The remaining seven chapters deal with two related subjects: the "French" who now reveal themselves as people "of little faith" (43) or as people who are equally capable of being frightened and not being frightened by the Pope (44) or as people who are erroneously afraid (48) on the one hand, and "Fabius," prudence incarnate, on the other (45-47 and 49). The French represent Machiavelli's unreliable allies. "Fabius" however

"judged the slow attack to be more useful and reserved his impetus for the end" and "moved by love of his fatherland" expressed his feelings not by speech but by "silence and in many other ways."

48. As regards the connection between the end of I and the end of II, see note 36 above. The connection between the last section of II and that of III is indicated by the fact that the last reference to Livy in II and the last reference to Livy in III guide us towards immediately neighboring passages in Livy (II 33 toward Livy IX 35-36, and III 46 toward Livy IX 33-34).

49. Livy IX 36.14 and 36.1-6. Cf. note 47 above. As for the relation between the different Fabii, cf. *Discourses* III 46.

50. It is because of the phenomena of servility and of obliqueness that the histories of the Roman emperors have to be "well considered": I 10 (123).

51. Machiavelli mentions principalities in the heading of I 10; in the heading of the preceding chapters only republics had been mentioned. This step too serves to prepare the introduction of the first Livy quotation in Latin: Machiavelli's use of Livy is misunderstood if republics or republicanism are taken to be the sole or even the chief theme of the *Discourses*. In I 12 he refers to "the Christian republic." He thus indicates that "republic" does not necessarily mean a kind of merely political society. To the extent to which he is critical of "the Christian republic," he is not necessarily committed to the ancient Roman republic: he praises certain Muslim principalities as highly as the ancient Roman republic (II pr.). The issue posed for him by "the Christian republic" transcends the issue posed for him by the alternative of purely political republics and purely political principalities (consider the first sentence of the *Prince*).

52. The restoration of something which has been disestablished for a long time is no less revolutionary or shocking than the introduction of something wholly new; cf. *Discourses* I 9 (119, 120-121), 37, III 8 (362).

53. I 11 (126); *Prince* ch. 6. Cf. Marsilius of Padua, *Defensor Pacis*, I, cap. 5. sect. 10.-11. *Discourses* I 11-15 is the only section in which the headings of all chapters contain proper names.

54. Livy V 22.5.

55. *Discourses* I 11-12. Cf. the remark in I 11 that "Lycurgus, Solon and many others" had recourse to God in order to give authority to their laws, with the reference to "Moses, Lycurgus, Solon and other founders" in I 9. Observe the manner in which Machiavelli, as it were, trains his reader in thinking as a pagan: "the gods who predicted thee thy future good or thy future evil . . ." (I 12).

56. He also mentions Jupiter, Juno and Apollo once in that section. The monotheistic expression occurs, as one would expect, in the first chapter of the section, while the polytheistic expressions occur in the following chapters.

57. I 12 (129-130) and 13 (133).

58. I 13 (cf. Livy III 17.1-8) and 54. Machiavelli also changes the name of P. Valerius (the consul) into P. Ruberius; one is tempted to transform the latter name into Italian. While I 11 and 12 contain both ancient and modern examples, I 13 and 14 contain only ancient examples: one of the ancient examples in each of these chapters serves as a substitute for the modern example which is required by the drift of the argument.

59. *Discourses* I 14; Livy X 40, V 15.1 and I 34.9 (cf. Cicero, *De divinatione* I 3). According to *Discourses* I 11 beginning, not Numa, the founder of the Roman religion, but the senate which elected Numa as Romu-

lus' successor was inspired by heaven.

60. *Florentine Histories* I 9. Cf. Livy IX 46.6-7, a passage which immediately precedes the passage on which the end of the *Discourses* is based.

61. I 19. When re-telling the story of Roman arms and Samnite religion in I 15, Machiavelli does not make any changes except that in summarizing the speech of the consul he changes the order of "gods, citizens, enemies" (Livy X 39.17) in such a way as to bring "gods" into the center, and in enumerating the former allies of the Samnites he changes the order of "Tuscans, Umbrians, French" (Livy X 31.13) in such a way as to bring the French into the center. As for the subject "the French" see note 47 above.

62. Cf. e.g. the treatment accorded to the tyrant Nabis in I 40 with the only earlier reference to him (I 10). None of the six quotations from Livy in I 40 is completely literal. E.g., the first quotation begins in Livy (III 35.6) with *profecto*, for which Machiavelli substitutes *credebant enim*. As regards Appius Claudius as lawgiver, cf. Livy III 56.9, 58.2 and 34.6-7.

63. Cf. page 49 and note 51 above. For the pre-history of this view, cf. Alfarabius, *Compendium Legum Platonis*, IV and V (edited and translated by F. Gabrieli, pp. 17 and 21): *tyrannide . . . opus esse ut legis divinae velut prooemium sit*.

64. In I 7 Machiavelli uses, as he emphasizes, only one Roman example; he uses thereafter two Florentine examples and then, although the previous examples are said to suffice, one ancient Tuscan example; in I 8, the chapter on calumnies, he uses one Roman example and, as he emphasizes, only one Florentine example out of many; in that chapter he refers more clearly to "the histories of Florence" than to Livy, to whom he refers only by speaking of "this text."

"We" in the sense of "we Florentines" occurs for the first time in the *Discourses* in I 8.

65. I 7, III 30 (410); letter to [Ricciardo Bechi], March 8, 1497.

66. I 7-8. Note the reference toward the end of the 7th chapter to the present name of Lombardy: in important respects only the names have changed since antiquity (cf. *Florentine Histories* I 5); for the men who are born in a country preserve through all times more or less the same nature (*Discourses* III 43; cf. II 4 toward the end). Note also the fact that the first quotations from Livy in Latin occur within the context of a Tuscan story (I 12). Cf. page 93 above. In the Livian story about ancient Tuscany to which Machiavelli explicitly refers in I 7, Livy speaks of the violation of the wife of the Tuscan Arruns by another Tuscan (Livy V 33.3) whereas Machiavelli speaks of the violation of the sister of Arruns. Was Machiavelli's Arruns married, or did he live in celibacy, or did he live in incest with his sister like the modern Tuscan Baglioni who is described as a cowardly enemy of a Pope twenty chapters later? At any rate, Arruns called in the French against his fatherland in order to revenge himself, just as the Popes called in the French against the Lombards and other Italian powers (cf. *Florentine Histories* I 9 and 23).

67. I 2 and 9.

68. I 17, 20, 25-26 (cf. III 7), III 30 (409); cf. I 22 and 24 for further criticism of Rome under the kings. As for the praise of Rome in I 28, cf. pages 36-37 above.

69. From this one may understand why Machiavelli's use of Livian passages as pegs in, say, the second half of the First Book does not lead beyond Livy VII.

70. I 31 (Livy V 8) and 32.

71. I 34 (cf. I 33); observe in I 34 (171-172) the four-fold reference to

(dictatorship or) "a similar mode (authority)": dictatorship is not indispensable. Machiavelli draws our attention to the question concerning the maximum time for which the dictator was appointed but does not answer it; he speaks of "a definite time" or "a short time" or "the proper time." Could he have wished to indicate that the temporal limitation of emergency powers is unwise since the length of emergencies cannot be foreseen? At any rate, as is shown by the examples of Sparta and of Venice, one does not run any danger in giving authority to men "for a long time" if one provides for guardians in the Spartan or Venetian manner (I 34-35). Note also the reference in I 34 end to a Roman alternative to dictatorship. Cf. Spinoza, *Tractatus Politicus*, cap. 10.

72. I 37; cf. I 6 (109). As regards Machiavelli's suppressing a part of Livy's account of the misdeeds which the Roman nobility committed in connection with the agrarian law, see pages 103-104 above; cf. also page 37 above.

73. From this we understand why in I 39 the modern example precedes the ancient example.

74. II 13 (265), III 1 (327-328, 331) and I 2 (97). Cf. the deviations from the Roman model in the *Art of War*, II (484-485), III (512, 535) and VI (571), and the remarks on ancient and modern examples *ibid.* III (523 and 530) and VII (606).

75. I 40 (184-185); cf. I 44 beginning. Machiavelli replaces "many errors committed by the senate and the plebs" (I 40 near the beginning) by "the error of the Roman people" (end of the chapter), while using "people" and "plebs" synonymously in the chapter; cf. the allusion to the power of the senate under both dictatorship and decemvirate in I 35 (173). Livy III 32.7, 36.7, IV 3.17.

76. I 49 (199) and 52 beginning.

77. The central example is that of

Saguntum. Saguntum was allied to Rome and was ruined because it adhered to Rome. Machiavelli does not speak of the conduct of the Roman towards the Saguntines; to say the least, that conduct does not prove that the Romans were faithful allies (cf. Livy XXI 16.2 and 19.9-11, also XXXI 7).

78. Cf. page 96 above.

79. Cf. note 19 above.

80. II 1 beginning, 2 (beginning and 238-240). To see the progress of the argument, compare II 2 with the indictment, not of the Roman republic, but of Caesar, the destroyer of the Roman republic in I 10.

81. Cf. I 55 (212).

82. II 14, 19 end, 20; *Prince* chs. 12 (39) and 13 (43-44). Cf. pages 96-97 above.

83. II 20-21, 25. Livy says that the Romans sent prefects to Capua while Machiavelli speaks of a praetor; a few lines later on, Machiavelli speaks of a prefect sent by Rome to Antium whereas Livy speaks of patrons (Livy IX 20.5 and 10); cf. III 12 (371). Machiavelli's silence about the patrons through whom the Romans ruled their subjects is reinforced by the fact that the explicit Latin Livy quotation which follows that silence in II 21 is not quite literal. In I 11, he says of Numa Pompilius that he desired to rule the Romans by "the arts of peace" and therefore turned to religion; cf. I 12 (130). Cf. pages 42-43, 99-102 and 108-110 above.

84. II 18; cf. II 19 (288). "Authority" is mentioned also in the headings of I 34, 44, 54 and III 30. Cf. page 41 above.

85. Cf. ch. 2, note 40 and ch. 3, note 69 above. *Discourses* I 2 (97), 11 (126), 53 (207); *Prince*, ch. 6 (19). Compare the remark about *l'avara natura de'prelati e religiosi* in *Opere* I 680 with the allusion to the avarice of the ancient Roman nobility in *Discourses* I 37.

86. In the spirit of his boundless

praise of the Roman consuls in *Discourses* I 20, Machiavelli suppresses the fact that the imprudent commander was a consul but he points out that the situation was saved by the prudence of a tribune. Cf. the unnecessary reference to the consuls in the third example in which no explicit mention of Roman imprudence occurs.

87. Livy II 45-46.

88. Livy IV 28.4. Cf. pages 52-53 above.

89. Machiavelli sometimes says "he who will read the history," i.e. who will read it after having been tutored by Machiavelli; see I 1 beginning (cf. I pr. [90]), 23 (152), II 13 (264), 18 (283), 20 (290), III 3 (333), 46 towards the end. He conveys the same thought by saying e.g. "he who reads the Bible judiciously, will see"; cf. III 30 (409) with I 28 beginning. The references to "the text" or "this text" or "the text of Livy," especially if they are not preceded by quotations from Livy, indicates the necessity of reading the whole context in Livy; there occur, if I am not mistaken, 18 references to "the text," "this text," or "the text of Livy" in the *Discourses*.

90. Cf. III 6 (351).

91. II 29. The other chapter, the heading of which consists of a Livian statement almost literally translated, is I 57; it follows immediately a chapter which is of utmost importance for what one may call Machiavelli's theology. (The heading of III 36, which reproduces a Livian sentence, differs fundamentally and characteristically from that sentence because it begins with the non-Livian words "The causes why").

92. Cf. e.g. *Discourses* I 7 and 28.

93. Livy IV 23.1-3.

94. I 16 near the beginning; cf. the juxtaposition of "histories" and "memories of ancient things" in I 10 (122); as regards the relation of "histories" and "memories," cf. also

II 4 (242) and 5 (247).

95. See the distinction between "the histories" and what "every one who lives at present knows" in I 29 (160). Consider Machiavelli's use of the expression "everybody knows" which points precisely to the fact that only "the fresh examples" are truly known; cf. I 21 (149), 23 (152)—cf. 24 (154)—56, II 12 (261), 21 (292), III 6 (355) and 43 (436). Cf. also the distinction between what is read and what is seen in III 42 (435); cf. I 58 (217-218). Cf. *Art of War* II (480).

96. I 8 (117), 40 (186), 54, III 26; cf. I 52 beginning and III 38 beginning. In his summary, called by him "this text," of the Livian story of the Decemvirate, Machiavelli says—I 40 (184)—deviating from Livy (III 33.7) that Appius Claudius had taken on "a new nature"; when referring to this remark in I 41, he says that Appius Claudius had "changed nature, as *I* say above" (the emphasis is not in the original). Cf. the reference in the Ep. Ded. to Machiavelli's narratives in the *Discourses* as distinguished from his discourses in that book.

97. I 29 (161), 40 (186); cf. Livy III 44-48. Machiavelli justifies his treatment of the Virginia incident by what he says of the rape of Lucretia in III 5.

98. I 29 (159); the reference to Tacitus contrasts with I 28 beginning, where Machiavelli gathers a certain conclusion from what "he has read of the things done by republics" and then "seeks the cause" of the phenomenon in question. Cf. note 91 above on the heading of III 36.

99. I 37 (175) and 39 beginning. Cf. note 85 above.

100. I 46. Cf. the reference toward the end of the chapter to "the reasons which I stated above," i.e. the reasons not stated by Livy. In this chapter, which opens the section on the plebs or the multitude, Machia-

velli refers twice to what he had said earlier; he thus refers to I 33, the chapter which opens the section on the ruling class or "the princes."

101. I 47. Livy XXIII 2.1-2, 4.

102. I 57. Cf. note 91 above.

103. I 4 (105), 33 (169) and 52 (205).

104. *Prince*, chs. 6 (18) and 11 (36). Cf. *Discourses* I 18 end ("of which we reason in this chapter").

105. No chapter other than *Discourses* I 17 begins with "I judge," whereas there are two chapters beginning with "I believe" (I 18 and II 26). Cf. the "one ought to believe" in the heading of III 48 (see page 36 above). The central scene of *La Mandragola* opens with "I believe that you believe," the second scene with "I believe" (Nicia) and the third scene with "I do not believe" (Ligurio). Two Books of the *Art of War* (II and VI) open with "I believe." Cf. Montesquieu, *Considérations sur les causes de la grandeur des Romains et de leur décadence*, ch. 10.

106. I 58 beginning. Cf. I 10 (124) and *Art of War* IV (550). Cf. pages 41, 107 and 115-116 as well as ch. 2, note 20 above.

107. I 60 and II pr. (230); *Prince* ch. 25 end; *Art of War* I (454, 473) and III (512).

108. I 2 (100-102), 5-6, 16 (139), 37 (178), 44; *Prince* chs. 9 (32) and 8. Note that the *Discourses* end with the praise of an anti-democratic measure.

109. *Prince* ch. 9; *Discourses* I 40 (183, 186-187), 52 end. Observe the contrast in terminology between I 10 and I 16, and the remark about terminology in I 25 end; in II 9 beginning, Machiavelli calls the Roman republic a principality, and in II 12 (263) he calls the Roman republic and the Swiss confederacy kingdoms. *Florentine Histories*, III 13. Livy VI 27.5-6. Cf. page 70 and note 51 above.

110. See pages 112-113 and 124-126

above. Cf. *Florentine Histories* II 34 (104), 36 (109), 37 (112), 41 end, III 17 end, 18 beginning, 20 (157), VI 24 (306). Cf. *Discourses* I 28-29 with *Opere* II (704-707).

111. Consider the meaning of "universal opinion" in II 17 beginning.

112. *Prince* ch. 18 end; *Discourses* I 4 (105), 11 (126), 25 beginning, 47-48, 50 (202), 51 beginning, 53, II 22 beginning, III 14, 34; letter to Guicciardini of March 15, 1525.

113. See the end of I 58 and the heading of I 59; cf. also I 29 to which Machiavelli refers in I 58.

114. I 58 (220); cf. I 9 (120).

115. I 25, 32 heading and beginning, 45 end, 47 (cf. the heading and the beginning with the end of the chapter), II 22 heading and beginning.

116. Voltaire, *Dictionnaire Philosophique*, ed. by Julien Benda, I 165 and 180: "Les empereurs (romains), il est vrai, les grands et les philosophes, n'avaient nulle foi à ces mystères; mais le peuple, qui en fait de religion donne la loi aux grands, leur imposait la nécessité de se conformer en apparence à son culte. Il faut, pour l'enchaîner, paraître porter les mêmes chaînes que lui." ". . . le petit peuple, toujours fanatique et toujours barbare." Cf. *Discourses* I 11 towards the end.

117. *Prince*, Ep. Ded. and ch. 6 (19); *Discourses* I 11 (126), 53 (207), II 13; *Florentine Histories* III 13. Cf. note 49 above.

118. Consider the relation between the analysis of religion in I 11-15 and the condemnation of tyranny in I 9-10, and the relation between the criticism of Christianity in II 2 and the praise of (democratic) republics which surrounds that criticism.

119. Cf. pages 28-29 above.

120. Livy I 7, 10 and 12; *Discourses* I 11 (126) and 2 (98-100).—Compare Aristotle's account of the "natural" genesis and character of the city with what Fustel de Coulanges reports in *La Cité Antique* regarding

the "sacred" city.

121. Livy III 6.5; *Discourses* I 38
(179, 181).

122. Livy III 56.7; *Discourses* I 41
and 45 beginning.

123. Livy V 23.8 and 25.7; *Discourses* I 55 beginning.

124. Livy I 26.12; *Discourses* I 22.

125. Livy V 39.9-12, 40.3-4 and
40.7-10; *Discourses* II 29 (315).

126. Livy V 49.1 (cf. X 16.6); *Discourses* II 30 beginning.

127. Livy VIII 9.10, 13 and 10.7;
Discourses II 16 (270).

128. Livy VIII 13.14; *Discourses* II
23 (296) and II 1 beginning.

129. Cf. *Discourses* I 10 beginning
and end, II 2 (337) and III 18; *Prince*
ch. 13 (43).

130. III 30 (410).

131. Cf. page 122 above.

132. I 46. The only other example
of this kind occurs in II 13 where
Xenophon is said to have "made"
Cyrus do certain things. In the first
two quotations from Dante and Virgil (I 11 and 21), Machiavelli ascribes
to Dante what is said to Dante by
Sordello and he ascribes to Virgil
what is said to Virgil by Anchises.

133. Cf. *Esortazione alla penitenza*
(*Opere* II 801-804).

134. In the First Book, expressions
of this kind occur 6 times, in the
Second Book 7 times, and in the
Third Book 5 times; they all apply
to Livian "texts."

135. There occur 7 such cases. Cf.
also II 2 (239): "Titus Livius confesses it."

136. III 31 beginning; cf. III 12
toward the end.

137. Cf. *Discourses* I 10 (122-123)
and 18 end; *Prince* chs. 6 and 26
(82); see page 42 above.

138. Livy IX 4 and 8-11. The Livian
story is a commentary on the end
of *Discourses* II 13. Cf. *Discourses*
I 15 and III 12 (372-373). See page
117 above.

139. III 12. The expression of Messius-Livy which Machiavelli quotes

is "necessity is the last and greatest
weapon."—Cf. page 120 above.

140. This is not to deny that the
problem of the relation of Christianity to Judaism is somehow present
in the chapter under discussion.
When referring there to the "new
law" of Christianity, Machiavelli
makes us think of "the old law."
Besides, Machiavelli could not help
being aware of the fact that the Roman Church persecuted Judaism as
well as paganism and that it preserved the Latin version of the Old
Testament as much as it preserved
parts of the pagan Latin literature.

141. II 2 (235), 4 (242, 246), 5;
cf. I pr. (90), 10 (122), 12 (129),
III 14 end and 39. See notes 9 and
59 above.

142. Cf. page 141 above with, e.g.,
Psalm 14.1.

143. In *Prince* ch. 26, he calls certain contemporary events which remind us of Biblical miracles, "extraordinary events without example."

144. II 2 (239, 240), 4 (245), 5, 19
(285), III 6 (351-352), 39 (431), 43
(436) and 48 (cf. heading and body).
Cf. pages 40 and 73-74 as well as notes
95-96 above.

145. Livy VIII 11.4 (*Milionium
dixisse ferunt*).

146. In *Discourses* II 18, Machiavelli says that a certain Roman master of the horse fell in the battle
of Sora, which was a Roman victory;
according to Livy, he fell in the battle of Saticula, which was a Roman
victory; but, as Livy mentions immediately afterward, he found in some
sources that he fell in the battle of
Sora and that that battle was a Roman defeat (IX 22 and 23.5). Machiavelli prefers, just as Livy, the version
more favorable to the Romans, but,
differing from Livy, he is silent about
the other version; yet he alludes to
that other version by replacing one
battle by another; he thus shows how
easily undesirable traditions can be
suppressed and how this suppression

can safely be counteracted. See especially Livy IX 22.9-10.

147. I 3 beginning, II 13 (264), 18 (281, 283), III 20 (389), 22 (394) and 30 (410). For the sequel consider II 24 (305).

148. The last word of the chapter is "celebrated"; Machiavelli, in the last sentence, speaks of the fact that poverty has brought honor not only to cities and countries but to religions as well and that "this matter has been celebrated many times by other men."

149. Livy III 12.8, 13.10 (B. O. Foster's translation), 19.2 and 29.1. Cf. *Discourses* I 20 and *Prince* ch. 15.— In *Discourses* III 25 Machiavelli cites Livy's "golden words" in praise of poverty; in III 6 (338) he quotes a "golden sentence" of Tacitus which enjoins obedience to princes; III 26 is the only chapter in which Machiavelli speaks of both Lucretia and Virginia (the great examples of chastity). There occur no other references to golden words or sentences in the *Discourses*.

150. Cf. pages 127-130 above.

151. Cf. *Discourses* III 33 with I 14 and III 32 with I 15; cf. I 12 (128). See also I 47 (197) and III 14; Livy VI 29.1-2.—After having given the two Livy quotations referred to in the text, Machiavelli gives still another Livy quotation; but this time he quotes Livy speaking in his own name; the third quotation has no bearing on "little things." That quotation occurs as a part of a summary of a Livian story (VI 30) in which Machiavelli replaces Livy's "military tribunes with consular power" by "consuls"; as a consequence we here get another Machiavellian example of the early Romans' poor choice of consuls (cf. page 149 above).

152. Livy VIII 30.1-2, 31.1-2 and 8, 32.4-5, 7, 17, 33.3, 11, 13.—Cf. pages 106-107 above.

153. By omitting Livy's *inquit* (VII 32.12) Machiavelli slightly blurs the change from indirect to direct speech, and thus weakens the emphasis on the sentence quoted in the text.

154. III 38. The subject of this chapter as indicated at the end of III 37 is "how the make of a captain ought to be," just as III 36 dealt with "how the make of a good militia ought to be." It appears from the quotations on which the arguments of III 38 and 36 are based, that the good militia must have reverence for the gods, whereas no such demand is made on captains (cf. page 73 above). Both quotations are taken from public speeches.—The description of the subject of III 38 which is given in the heading as well as in the body of that chapter ("how the make of a captain in whom his army can have confidence ought to be") brings out the connection of that chapter with III 33, i.e. the last preceding chapter that was concerned with the difference between Livy and his characters. The description of the subject of III 38 which is given at the end of III 37, conceals that connection. In accordance with this, the words of which Machiavelli says in III 38 that Livy "makes" his character "say" them, are called words of that character at the end of III 37. Machiavelli takes great care here to draw our attention to the connection between two chapters dealing with the difference between Livy and his characters and therewith to that difference itself (cf. the end of the present paragraph of the text on III 39). For the reason stated in the preceding paragraph of the text, he thus also draws our attention to the plan of the *Discourses*.

155. III 37 toward the end and 33 end. Cf. pages 143-144 above.

156. Cf. note 47 above.

157. As appears also from I 23, the captain must be a knower of sites especially in the sense that he must know how to conduct himself in regard to various kinds of sites. For in-

stance, he must know that it is imprudent "to hold difficult places" or
to hold places which are narrow and
in which only a few can stay and
live. Such "malignancy of site" favors
the attacker rather than the defender.
In addition, the attacker will always
find "an unknown road" which is
not guarded by the defender. (This
summary should suffice to dispose
of Guicciardini's objections to the
thesis of the chapter.) Machiavelli
uses the second person singular in I
23 more frequently than in any other
chapter of the First Book; he addresses first the defender with the
counsel to abandon places which are
narrow and in which only a few
can stay, and thereafter he addresses
the attacker with a promise that he
will surely find an unknown road.
Since the example of the country to
be defended or attacked is Italy, he
gives his advice to both the defender
and the would-be foreign conqueror
of Italy.

158. Cf. pages 137-138 above.

159. Livy XXXIX 25: *populum Ro-
manum, qui caritate magis quam metu
adjungere sibi socios mallet....*

160. Cf. pages 103-104 above (on
Discourses I 37).

161. See page 140 above. In III 27,
Machiavelli contrasts a harsh and
effective measure of the Romans with
an ineffective and soft or weak measure of Florence which, being a modern republic, is "a weak republic";
"the weakness of the men of the
present time is caused by their weak
education and little knowledge of
things"; "certain modern opinions of
theirs" which are "altogether remote
from the truth," "arise from the weakness of him who is lord." III 27 deals
with the same "text" as III 26, the
chapter on women. According to
Savonarola (*Prediche sopra Ezechiele*
II), the *savi del mondo* regard the
biblical prophecies as *cose da donne.*
Cf. also III 1 (330), and cf. the discussion of the middle way in I 27

with I 26.

162. Gods are mentioned in the
Second Book only in chapters 1 and
23; the first mention occurs in the
summary of an argument from Plutarch; the last mention occurs in a
quotation from Livy; in the Second
Book Machiavelli himself does not
even speak of gods. In every Book
of the Discourses there occurs a single
quotation from Livy in which gods
are mentioned; see I 13, II 23 and
III 36.—Note the density of "Pope"
and "Church" in II 22, in a chapter
in which no reference to Livy (or
any other writer) occurs.

163. II 23 which contains unusually
extensive quotations from Livy, is the
only chapter in the series II 22-27
which contains references to Livy
(for the meaning of "references to
Livy," see note 21 above). In II 23,
Livy is presented as making Camillus
speak of what the gods have done.
This prepares the remark in III 31
according to which Livy makes Camillus do and say certain things in
order to show what the make of an
excellent man is. The Biblical equivalent of the remark in II 23 would
be that God makes the Biblical writers speak of what God has done or
that the Biblical writers make God
say as to what God has done. Consider III 46 .

164. It appears from Livy (VII
32.13) that the soldiers wrongly accused the commander of the same
error of which Messius rightly accused his soldiers (see pages 140-
141 above).—The quotation from Livy
with which the chapter opens appears, to begin with, as a remedy
for an error which "all men" commit;
the quotation speaks of a captain who
lived long before Livy's time but
Machiavelli speaks of him as though
he were still living in Machiavelli's
time (367; cf. note 44 above). The
quotation speaks less of what the
captain did or said than of what he
thought; that thought is, later in the

chapter, ascribed to Livy; the alleged thought of the captain is known only as Livy's thought.

165. II 18 and III 30. In the heading of III 30 Machiavelli speaks of what a citizen must do if he desires to perform any good deed in his republic on his own authority; the central example given in the chapter is that of Moses who killed "innumerable human beings" in order that his laws and his orders should prosper; according to Machiavelli, Moses did these things on his own authority; according to the Bible it is not clear whether he did them on his own authority or by the authority of God (cf. *Exodus* 32.21-26 with ib. 27-28; cf. *Numbers* 16). Cf. also I 9 (120).—"Author," the grammatical root of "authority," occurs in the sense of "writer," I believe, only in I 25 and in I 58.

166. II 10, 17, 22, III 27.

167. II 17 (274-275): *disputare, rispondendo dico, questo è una massima.*

168. Cf. I 10 end; *Prince* ch. 12 (39); *Art of War* II (485) and IV (539). Cf. pages 41, 119, 157 above.

169. When Machiavelli says in II 27 that he wishes to demonstrate a certain thesis by ancient and modern examples since it cannot be demonstrated with equal distinctness by means of reasons, he does not mean that he does not possess a rational proof of his thesis. He thus certainly draws our attention to his selection of examples. In the preceding chapter he did not use any modern examples but did use an Asiatic example. In II 27 he twice discusses the same three examples; the center is occupied in the first discussion by an Asiatic example and in the second discussion by a modern (Florentine) example. Modernity and Asia are "exchangeable" since the characteristic difference between modernity and classical antiquity is due to the victory of Asiatic thought over classical thought. (See pages 89-90 and notes

16 and 35 above.) The thesis to be proved concerns false hopes for victory (see page 40 above.)

170. III 19. Tacitus is referred to four times in the *Discourses*: I 29 (cf. page 124 above), II 26 (cf. page 50 above), III 6 (cf. note 149 above) and 19. The three last references follow one another at intervals of 13 chapters.

171. Machiavelli introduces the citation with the Latin *ait*: he draws our attention to the fact that he can write Latin; he thus prepares us for his writing some Tacitean Latin. The wording of the citation reminds us of a statement of Tacitus which expresses the opposite opinion to the apocryphal statement that Machiavelli put into Tacitus' mouth. The genuine statement of Tacitus is immediately followed in his work (*Annals* III 55) by a remark which expresses doubt of the moral superiority of the olden times to the present and which reminds one therefore of the argument of *Discourses* II pr.: Machiavelli's treatment of Tacitus as an authority is linked to a reminder of his own criticism of the root of the belief in authority.

172. Machiavelli refers to a statement of his made at another time and adds the remark that that statement is true; the opinion expressed in that statement had been ascribed originally to "the ancient writers" with the understanding that, being the opinion of the ancient writers, it is of course true; he indicates in the repetition that if he refers to authorities, he does not necessarily agree with what the authorities say, even if he does not voice any criticism of what they say; cf. III 21 (390) with I 37 beginning. He notes that "all writers" admire the good order which prevailed in Hannibal's army and implies that those writers were completely ignorant of the cause of that order; cf. III 21 (391) and *Prince* ch. 17 (54). He quotes a prudent man who

said that in order to keep a republic by force, there must be a proportion between him who forces and that which is forced; the prudent man is likely to be Machiavelli himself; cf. III 22 (393) and I 40 (187).

173. Cf. pages 148-149, notes 149 and 165 as well as ch. 1, notes 48 and 68.

174. Livy VII 4.6-7, 5.2, 9.8-10.11. *Exodus* 4.10; I *Samuel* 17. Cf. Machiavelli's reference to the David-Goliath story in *Prince* ch. 13.

175. *Prince* chs. 6 and 13.

176. *Prince* ch. 19 end.

177. Cf. page 41 above.

178. Livy V 23.6 says "to Jupiter and to the Sun." Machiavelli is silent about Camillus' desire to become equal to the highest god. Note that in the heading of III 23 Machiavelli speaks only of one cause of Camillus' exile whereas in the body of the chapter he speaks of three causes. Cf. also *Discourses* III 34 on Manlius Torquatus' concern with being talked about.

179. Livy V 23.1. *Discourses* I 41, III 31 beginning and 46. "Humility" is mentioned in the headings of I 41 and II 14, and in no other headings; the interval between these two chapters is 33. Cf. page 111 above. As regards the connection between the Tacitean subsection and the subsection devoted to the Decemvirate, cf. also the use of "partisans" in III 22 (395) and the reference there to I 43; see I 45 on Savonarola's "ambitious and partisan spirit"; "partisanship" is opposed to "lukewarmness" in *Prince* ch. 6, in the part of the chapter dealing with armed and unarmed prophets; Savonarola's sermons abound with indictments of the lukewarm ones. Cf. *Prince* ch. 20 (67).

180. Cf. pages 105 and 153-153 above. Livy VIII 30.13 and 34.2.

181. Valerius is not, and is, Machiavelli's model (cf. III 37 and 38; see pages 154-155 above). This creates no difficulty; cf. Savonarola, *Prediche*

sopra Ezechiele XXXVII: *Pigliano adunque Nabuchodonosor per la persona di Cristo.—O frate, vo' tu comparare la persona di Cristo a Nabuchodonosor, che fu uno scellerato?—Nota che questo non è inconveniente, perchè nella Scrittura, molte volte, una persona cattiva significa una buona.*

182. Cf. pages 44 and 108 above. Cf. the reference to "every day" need for "new orders" at the end of I 49 with the reference to "every day" need for "new provisions" in the heading of III 49. Cf. also *Florentine Histories* II 28.

183. III 1 (327-330), 8 (362), 11 (368); cf. I 18 (143). Cf. pages 90 and 156-157 above. The central example among the seven Roman examples given in III 1 is that of the execution of Manlius Capitolinus.— Consider the connection between I 26 (the tacit New Testament quotation), II 26 (the only tacit Tacitus quotation) and III 26 (women as the causes of many ruins). Cf. notes 16 and 169 above.—*Principio* or *principii* are mentioned in the headings of I 1, 49, III 1, 28, and 36. In I 49, *principio* and *principii* occur seven times in the body of the chapter; in III 1 they occur ten times in the body of the chapter.

184. I 46 (194). Cf. Savonarola, *Sermone fatto in San Marco a' di 15 Febbraio* 1497/8: *dice il nostro testo: difficile est quod malo inchoatur principio posse ad bonum finem usque perduci. Cioè: che le cose che hanno cattivo principio impossibile è che possino aver mai buon fine.*

185. *Prince* chs. 3 (10), 6 (19), 18 end; *Discourses* I pr. beginning, 11 (126, 128), 12 (129), 18 (145), 25, 58 (217), II pr. (230), 13, III 11 towards the end and 30 (409). Cf. pages 33, 37 and 153-154 above.

186. Machiavelli indicates the subjects of both the chapter on conspiracies (III 6) and of II 32 by saying at the end of the preceding chapters that "it does not seem to (him)

to be outside of his purpose" to discuss "in the following chapter" the subject in question. As he makes clear by a remark near the beginning of III 6 (332), II 32 too deals with a kind of conspiracy. The heading of II 32 draws our attention to the number of modes in which the Romans seized fortified towns; the central mode proves to be "force mixed with fraud" or "furtive violence" or *trattato* or "conspiracy." When discussing this central mode, Machiavelli praises Aratus of Sicyon who, probably owing to "an occult virtue which was in him" was an unrivalled master in "fraudulent and nocturnal" enterprises. We may say that whereas "the occult virtue" through which the people foresees its own good and evil—I 58 (219)—operates in broad daylight so that everyone can judge of the value of that virtue, the "occult virtue" of Aratus operated only in the occult. (Cf. *Florentine Histories* I 3 and VIII 18). Since "furtive violence" or "conspiracy" is a form of faithlessness, we are not surprised to observe that Machiavelli introduces the subject of I 59 at the end of I 58 in the same manner in which he introduces the subjects of II 32 and III 6 at the ends of II 31 and III 5 respectively, for the subject of I 59 may be said to be the problem of Roman faithfulness (see page 117 above). The references at the ends of I 58, II 31 and III 5 are the only ones of their kind in the *Discourses*.

187. II 2 (235), III 1 beginning, 6 (341, 342, 344-346, 354, 355), 8. Cf. *Art of War* VII (609).—Brutus, who simulated folly in order to liberate his fatherland was not a conspirator; hence Machiavelli is silent about his action in the chapter on conspiracies (III, 6) as well as in the sketch of the subject matter of that chapter which he gives at the end of the preceding chapter. As he explains in III 6 (340), one cannot say of a man

who plans to kill or to depose a prince, that he is a conspirator; Brutus kept his plan secret from everyone and patiently waited for his opportunity. At the end of III 5, Machiavelli mentions the arousing of humors against princes as one of the subjects of III 6, while in the repetition at the beginning of III 6 he leaves that subject unmentioned; arousing of humors against a prince was precisely what Brutus did: he turned the desire for revenge upon Sextus Tarquinius, who had violated Lucretia, into desire for revenge upon Sextus' royal father and for the abolition of kingship altogether (Livy I 58.8-10 and 59.1-2). Brutus' long-range plan was the abolition of kingship; the crime of Sextus Tarquinius merely gave him the opportunity. Similarly Machiavelli turns the "given" dissatisfaction with "all prelates" (I 27) into revulsion against the whole traditional order and its ultimate ground.—The difference between conspiratorial and "corrupting" writings is adumbrated by the story of Agis and Cleomenes as told in I 9. Agis, who desired to restore the old Spartan order, was killed by the ephors as one who desired to become a tyrant; through the writings which he left, he aroused the same noble desire in his successor Cleomenes who killed all ephors and thus succeeded in completely restoring the old Spartan order. The action of Cleomenes is described in III 6 (355) as a conspiracy against the fatherland. This conspiracy was originated by writings of Agis. Agis was not hurt by his writings and Cleomenes was greatly helped by them. Cf. II pr. toward the end. Machiavelli indicates the difference between the teacher of conspirators and the conspirator himself by the sole reference to Plato which occurs in either book—*Discourses* III 6 (351)—; two disciples of Plato conspired against two tyrants and killed one of them. He indicates

the same difference by referring in
the same context to Pelopidas' conspiracy against the Theban tyrants
and by his other references to Pelopidas and his friend Epaminondas
(see especially III 18 beginning and
38); the wealthy, married and spirited
Pelopidas delighted in gymnastics and
hunting whereas the poor, unmar-
ried and gentle Epaminondas delighted
in listening and in seeking of wisdom;
Pelopidas had to flee from Thebes
when the tyranny was set up, whereas
Epaminondas could stay because he
was despised as inactive on account
of his concern with wisdom and as
powerless on account of his poverty
(see Plutarch's *Pelopidas*).

188. I pr. (90), 12 (129-130), 13
(133), 17 (141), 19 (147), 20, 55 (211-
212), II 5, 8 (252, 254), III 1 (327,
330) and 17 end. Cf. *Florentine Histories* I 1.—C. Alexandre quotes the
following statement by George of
Trebizond (*Comparatio Platonis et
Aristotelis*) in his introduction to his
edition of Gemistus Plethon's *Traité
des Lois* (Paris 1858, p. xvi): *Audivi
ego ipsum [Plethonem] Florentiae,
venit enim ad concilium cum Graecis,
asserentem unam eandemque religio-
nem uno animo, una mente, una
praedicatione, universum orbem pau-
cis post annis suscepturum. Cumque
rogassem, Christine an Mahumeti? Ne-
utram, inquit, sed non a gentilitate
differentem—. Percepi etiam a non-
nullis Graecis qui ex Peloponneso
huc profugerunt, palam dixisse ipsum, anteaquam mortem obiiset iam
fere triennio, non multis annis post
mortem suam et Machumetum et
Christum lapsum iri. . . .—*Cf. also
Alfarabius, *Compendium legum Platonis*, liber 3, beginning; Roger Bacon, *Moralis Philosophia* (ed. Massa),
193, 215 and 219; and Pico della Mirandola, *Disputationes adversus astrologiam divinatricem* II 5.

189. Cf. Machiavelli's summary of a
sermon of Savonarola in his letter
to [Ricciardo Bechi] of March 8th,

1497. Cf. Savonarola's *Prediche sopra
l'Esodo* XIII on the difference as well
as the similarity between "the war
of Christ" and· "the temporal wars
of the world." Machiavelli would
have agreed with Savonarola's remark
(*Prediche sopra Ezechiele* XXXVI):
*Io ti dico che gli è un piacere a
far guerra.*

190. Cf. *Discourses* III 11 and 12.
Cf. pages 119-120 above.

191. Savonarola *Prediche sopra Ezechiele* XXXIII: *la Chiesa ha el corpo
misto di buoni e di cattivi.*

192. Cf. notes 47 and 66 above as
well as Livy V 46.3. (See *Florentine
Histories* III 7 and V 34.) The dual
meaning of "French" corresponds to
the dual meaning of "Egyptians,"
"Midian," "Jebusites," etc. in the theological tradition. (Cf. Machiavelli's
summary of a sermon of Savonarola
in his letter to [Ricciardo Bechi] of
March 8, 1497). In order to grasp
the moral or mystical meaning of
"Samnites," the third major subject
of *Discourses* III 35-49, one must start
from the fact that the Samnites were
particularly obstinate enemies of the
Romans and resembled the Swiss in
more than one respect (Livy VII
33.16 and IX 13.7; cf. pages 140 and
154 above). The "blind Samnites" are
simply Machiavelli's enemies. At the
command of their captain Pontius,
Samnite soldiers appear "in the guise
of shepherds" and "agree all" on the
same lie which deceives the Roman
consuls and thus brings about a Roman disaster. But Pontius, disobeying
"the counsels of the father" or of
"that old one," chooses "a middle
way," and thus is ruined (III 40 and
II 23 end. Machiavelli does not mention the name of the father and
changes the name of the son which
was Gaius into Claudius; see III 12).
The nameless Samnite father reminds
one of the "old and prudent citizen"
Hanno who did not share Hannibal's
extravagant hopes (II 27). While two
Roman consuls were deceived by a

Samnite, a Roman legate uncovered a similar deception attempted by the Tuscans, at one time allies of the Samnites: the Tuscans sent out some soldiers "in the guise of shepherds" but the legate found out that the speech and the complexion of the alleged shepherds was too refined for shepherds or simple rustics; he discovered the manifest blunder of Rome's enemies which consisted in claiming to be humble and in being at the same time presumptuous (III 48; cf. Livy X 4.9-10).

193. *Discourses* III 45 and 39 end. Livy X 28.13.

Chapter IV

1. Speaking of Walter Scott's *Napoleon*, Goethe says that Scott "speaks as a law-abiding and honest commoner who makes an effort to judge deeds in a pious and conscientious spirit and who strictly guards himself against the whole Machiavellian view without which, however, one would hardly wish to concern oneself with the history of the world." (Letter to Zelter of December 4, 1827). In his *Annalen* (1794) he speaks of Fichte's unguarded utterances "about God and divine things about which subjects one does well to preserve a profound silence." What Goethe understood by Machiavellianism appears from the following sentence (*Maximen und Reflexionen*): "Everything which is Spinozist in the element of poetic production becomes Machiavellian in the element of reflection."

2. Among them is Fichte, who went so far as to call him "a professed pagan." Fichte says that one ought not to defend Machiavelli against the charge of having been an enemy of Christianity but that one ought to try to understand that enmity historically. He concludes this argument with the remark that "in spite of all this, Machiavelli has taken care to depart from life properly supplied with all sacraments of the Church and this no doubt was very good for the children whom he left behind as well as for his writings." (*Machiavelli*, ed. Scholz, 12.)

3. *Florentine Histories*, VII 6; letter to Vettori of April 16, 1527. Cf. *Art of War* I near the beginning.

4. *Discourses* III 30 (410); cf. *Opere* II 802 and pages 17-19 above. See Savonarola, *Prediche sopra Ezechiele* II, V, XXXVI and *Prediche sopra l'Esodo* XX.

5. Cf. page 86 above.

6. Cf. I 10 (124) and 17 (141) with Dante, *Monarchia* I 16 and II 11; *Art of War* I (459).

7. I 1 (96), 11 (125), 12 (129, 130), and 14 (133).

8. II 2 (237-238). Cf. I 12 (130), II 16 (272), and III 1 (330).

9. If we remember correctly, the expression "we believe" never occurs in either of the two books.

10. I 21. Cf. the corresponding use of "first cause" in the two central chapters of the *Prince*, chs. 13 (45) and 14 (46), as well as of "sin" (the sins narrated by Machiavelli as opposed to the sins believed in by Savonarola) in *Prince* ch. 12 (39). See also the remark on "the second cause of our ruin" in *Discourses* I 12 (130); cf. *Discourses* III 33 (417). I 21 may be said to be the central chapter of the central section of I; consider the end of I 22 in the light of ch. 3, note 24 above.—In the only reference to the Bible which occurs in the *Prince* —the reference occurs in the center of the central chapter of the section dealing with arms—Machiavelli avails himself of the authority of the Biblical

story of David in order to prove that only one's own arms are good. The emphasis is on the opposition between one's own arms and the arms of others. Machiavelli completely disregards what the Bible says in the context about Divine assistance to David. Since he had taught at the beginning of the section on arms that good arms are the one thing needful, he can be said to misuse the authority of the Bible in order to establish the anti-Biblical truth par excellence. From his point of view reliance on Divine assistance would be, to say the least, reliance on the arms of others. In his letter to Vettori of June 10, 1514 he speaks of God in the same context in which he speaks of Fortuna in the Epistle Dedicatory to the *Prince*; cf. the thesis of *Prince* ch. 7.

11. III 27 toward the end; I 11 beginning.

12. II 4 (244-245), 19 (285-286), III 9 (362), 16 (381), 21 (390), and 28 end.

13. Cf. ch. 3, note 34 above.

14. Cf. II 2 (239).

15. Cf. pages 68-69, 80 and 110 above.

16. Cf. page 140 above.

17. *Prince* chs. 8 (Cesare was revered by the soldiers) and 19 (Severus was revered by everyone); *Discourses* I 10 (123), II pr. (229) and III 6-7; *Florentine Histories* I 9 beginning. Cf. ch. 1, note 62 and ch. 3, note 86 above.

18. *Discourses* I pr. beginning and II pr. (228-229).

19. *Discourses* II 17-18. The example of Regulus occurs after Machiavelli had indicated that he will use in the sequel only modern examples (283). Cf. *Art of War* II (484-486) and page 159 above.

20. *Prince* ch. 3 (13); *Discourses* I 55 (211-212), II pr. (228), and III 41; *Art of War* I (466); *Florentine Histories* I 17. Cf. ch. 1, note 30 and ch. 2, note 10 above.

21. *Prince* ch. 12 (40); *Discourses* II 2 (238), 3 (241) and 27 (310). Cf. *Prince* ch. 5 and *Discourses* II 32 (323). *Florentine Histories* VI 18.

22. *Prince* ch. 26 (81, 83); *Discourses* I 1 (95), 11 end, 19-20, 26, 45 (192), II 2 (239-240), 8 (252-253), 13, 31; *Florentine Histories* V 34 and III 7; *Art of War* II (506-508) and VI (586-587). Cf. Livy VIII 12.1. Cf. pages 80, 93-94, 112-113, 152-153 and 163 as well as ch. 1, note 68 above.

23. *Prince* chs. 6 (20), 11 beginning and 12 (38-39, 42); *Discourses* II 11, 19 (288), 20 (289) and III 6 (340); *Florentine Histories* I 11, 19, 39 and VIII 5; *Opere* I 648-650 and II 474, 475, 481. Consider the comparison of the state of the Sultan (which is supported by his soldiers so that he can utterly disregard the demands of the people) with the Christian pontificate in *Prince* ch. 19 (65-66).

24. *Timaeus* 24a3-b3; *Politics* 1328-b6-24 and 1329a27-34. Cf. Averroes, *Commentary on Plato's Republic*, ed. E. I. J. Rosenthal, II 17.3-5 and III 5.6.

25. *Prince* ch. 11; *Florentine Histories* I 30, VII 22, VIII 17; *Art of War* II (509). Cf. *Discourses* I 7 (114) and 20 end. Cf. Hume, *History of England* ch. 12 near the beginning: ". . . ecclesiastical power, as it can always cover its operations under a cloak of sanctity, and attacks men on the side where they dare not employ their reason, lies less under control than civil government." Cf. pages 109-110 and 180-181 above.

26. *Discourses* I 12 (130).

27. Cf. ch. 2, note 31 above.

28. *Discourses* I 27. This chapter is the only one which begins with the word "Pope." The preceding chapter is the only one in which the New Testament is quoted.

29. Cf. *Discourses* II 2 (237-238) on the bloody sacrifices of brutes by the ancients and II 16 (270) on Manlius Torquatus by whose command his

son was killed; cf. II 13 end, on the difference between Roman and modern faithlessness.

30. *Prince* chs. 18 end, and 21 beginning. Cf. *Prince* chs. 8 (30) and 19 (62-63); *Discourses* I 10 and 26; *Art of War* II (508-509); letter to Vettori of April 29, 1513. Machiavelli devotes two subsequent chapters of the *Prince* (chs. 17-18) to the subjects of cruelty and faithlessness. In the chapter on cruelty the emphasis is on ancient examples; the only modern example mentioned therein is Cesare Borgia. In the chapter on faithlessness only modern examples occur; the only example mentioned therein by name is that of Pope Alexander VI. In the next chapter Machiavelli discusses the emperor Severus who was outstanding both as a fox and as a lion. In *Discourses* III 21, Hannibal appears as a perfect embodiment of both cruelty and faithlessness or impiety; Hannibal did not combine cruelty and faithlessness with piety. In the parallel in the *Prince* (ch. 17) Machiavelli speaks only of Hannibal's cruelty and his innumerable other virtues, one of the latter probably being his lack of religious hypocrisy. —Pico della Mirandola, *Disputationes adversus astrologiam divinatricem* V 12: *pulsis nuper Judaeis omnibus ex tota Hispania a christianissimo illo rege, numquam certe satis laudato, ubi et numero et divitiis et auctoritate plurimum poterant. Qua eiectione nihil umquam fere vel tristius vel acerbius passos ipsi se non diffitentur, ita multi naufragio, pestilentia quam plurimi, fame maxima pars eorum absumpti, ut nobis, etiam Christianis, in tanta calamitate in qua divinae iustitiae gloria delectabat, homines tamen extrema adeo patientes commiserationem facerent et dolorem.*

31. *Prince* ch. 17 (53). Machiavelli refers there to Dido and immediately before to Cesare Borgia. His reference to Dido in the *Discourses* (II 8) is immediately preceded by a discussion of the conquest of "a part of Syria" by Moses and Joshua.

32. *Discourses* III 21 (cf. *Prince* ch. 17) and 22. Cf. *Discourses* I 10 (124), III 33 beginning and *Opere* II 803. Cf. pages 118 and 162-164 above.

33. Cf. page 49 above.

34. *Prince* ch. 6 (19-20); *Discourses* I 11 (126), II 23 (298), and III 22 (393).

35. Nahum 1.2. Cf. pages 130, 143, 152-153, 156-157 and 166-167 above. In quoting Livy III 53.7 Machiavelli replaces "hatred" by "damning" (*Discourses* I 44).

36. *Discourses* III 1 (330) and 6 (338, 340).

37. *Discourses* I 17 (142), 18 (146), and III 29. Cf.I 24 and the quotation from Dante in I 11.

38. Cf. *Discourses* I 43 and III 22 (395). Cf. ch. 3, note 179 above.

39. *Prince* chs. 6 (18,19) and 26 (82); *Discourses* I 11 (127), 30 beginning, II 24 (303), 33 (325), III 31, and 33 (417). Cf. Savonarola, *Prediche sopra Ezechiele* XXX: *Sathanas ... desiderò (la eccellenzia) per propria virtù e da sè delettazione dello onore proprio. Ib.* XLVII: *il vero cristiano ... è debole quanto alla propria virtù.*

40. Pope Julius II "did everything for the increase of the Church as distinguished from the increase of any private man"; yet everyone aims at his glory and wealth—*Prince* chs. 11 (38) and 25 (79)—; he sought his own glory in making the Church great. Cf. Savonarola, *Prediche sopra l'Esodo* IV: *queste donne disseno la bugia ... e dice qui il testo* [Exodus 1.19-21] *che Dio gli edificò due case.*

41. *Prince* chs. 12, 15, and 25; *Discourses* I 6 (110, 111-112), 29, 37 beginning, 38 (180-181), 40 (184-185, 188), 55 (212-213), II 8 (251-252), 10 (256), 14, 25 (306), III 1 (330), 9, 11 (368), 21, 22, 25 end, and 28. Cf. pages 148-149 and ch. 3, note 85 above.

42. *Prince* ch. 25 (79); *Discourses*

I 11 (125), 29 (161-162), 38 (180-181), 45 (192) and II 25. Cf. Livy XXXIV 15 end and XXXVII 57.15. See pages 42-43, 118-119 and 156-157 above.

43. *Prince* ch. 15 (49); *Discourses* II pr. (227-228), III 25 (400-401) and 31; *Opere* I 643; letter to Vettori of January 31, 1514. Regarding "redemption" cf. *Prince* ch. 26 (84) and page 135 above; see the reference to "the highest Redeemer" in a speech of ambassadors to the Pope in *Florentine Histories* VIII 21.—In the heading of *Discourses* I 41 Machiavelli speaks of "humility"; in the body of the chapter he replaces it by "humanity"; Livy had spoken of *comitas*; see I 40 (184). In the heading and the first line of II 14 Machiavelli speaks of "humility"; in the sequel he substitutes for it "patience" and "modesty" through the mouth of Livy and "cowardice" in his own name. See also III 3 and 9 (363). The emphatically "true example" of humanity given in III 20 is Roman, an action of Camillus. Cf. in III 30 the mention of Camillus' and Piero Soderini's "goodness" with the silence there and elsewhere about the "goodness" of the two other chief characters of III 30, Moses and Savonarola. At the end of *Prince* ch. 11, Machiavelli speaks of the "goodness" of Pope Leo X who had "found" the Christian pontificate most powerful; as for the difference between finding a state already established and founding it, see *Prince* ch. 19 end. See pages 46-47 above, and note 73 below.

44. *Florentine Histories* III 13, VI 20, and VII 23.

45. I 27 (cf. note 28 above). We have tried to preserve the ambiguity of *pietoso rispetto* by speaking of "pious or compassionate respect." Cf. II 28. (In the context to which Machiavelli refers, Livy—V 36.6 and 8, and 37.4—uses *ius gentium* and *ius humanum* synonymously.)

46. I 55 (210-211). In the ancient example Machiavelli mentions Apollo twice (there occurs no reference to Apollo or any other god or to gods in general in the First Book outside the section on the Roman religion, i.e. I 11-15); all the more striking is the silence on God in the modern example.

47. I 30, which is the central chapter of the section on ingratitude. As for the significance of the subject of gratitude, see Machiavelli's *Esortazione alla penitenza*.

48. II 14, 15, and 23 beginning.

49. *Florentine Histories* III 13.

50. III 6 (338, 340, 343, 344, 349-354); cf. III 25 (401). Cf. pages 145-146 above.

51. Cf. III 9 (362) with II 2 (237).

52. The distinction between core and periphery has taken the place of the distinction between the original teaching and later distortions; in the earlier distinction, the original means either the explicit teaching of the Bible or else that part of the Biblical teaching of which a combination of philology and psychology proves that it is the original. Moved by the spirit of this higher criticism, Nietzsche asserts that the notions of guilt and punishment are absent from "the psychology of the 'gospel'." (This assertion occurs in that section of the *Anti-Christ* which by an amazing accident is the 33d section.) The crucial difference between Nietzsche's and Machiavelli's criticism of Christianity is that Machiavelli regards the notions of guilt and punishment as essential to Jesus' teaching.

53. IV 7, VI 20-21, VII 4, 17, 28, VIII 10 and 11.

54. VI 34 and VIII 19-21; cf. I 11. See the following note on VIII 36.—In reading Machiavelli's statements about the prince or a prince, one must always consider what they would mean if they were applied to God.—As regards "good cavalry," cf. page 181 above.

55. As for Machiavelli's opinion of miracles, see pages 73-74 and 145-146 above.—Only if "one" applied "an

extreme force," could a corrupt matter become good; "I do not know whether this has ever happened or whether it is possible for it to happen; for one sees . . . that if it ever happens . . . it happens through the virtue of a human being who is alive at that time": *Discourses* I 17 (142). With a view to the fact that a miracle is an event the cause of which is God, the *causa occulta simpliciter* (cf. Savonarola, *Prediche sopra Ezechiele* XLII), we note that Machiavelli speaks very rarely of occult causes or occult virtues. The occult cause of which he speaks in *Discourses* I 3 is the cause which conceals (*occulta*) a malignity for some time; that cause may be deceit or fear. (See also *Florentine Histories* I 3 end.) In *Discourses* I 58 and II 32 Machiavelli asserts with some qualifications the existence of occult virtues ("it appears" and "one can judge that it was rather by an occult virtue than . . ."); see also *Florentine Histories* VIII 18. In the last section of the *Florentine Histories* (VIII 36), in the eulogy of Lorenzo Magnifico, who was "loved by Fortuna and by God to the highest degree," Machiavelli uses "marvel" or "marvellous" with unusual frequency.—For the meaning of "miracle" see also *Discourses* I 29 (161).

56. *Prince* chs. 11 (36) and 13 (45). Cf. pages 57-58 and 184-185 above.

57. *Prince* chs. 7 (23, 26) and 26 (82).

58. *Discourses* III 6 (341-342, 350).

59. While avoiding in the *Prince* and the *Discourses* the use of *anima*, he uses in the two books *animo* very frequently. (Burckhardt, *Die Kultur der Renaissance in Italien*, 16th ed., 476 refers to a writer who speaks of "his *animo* or *anima*"; Burckhardt adds the remark that at that time philology liked to embarrass theology by that distinction.) The greatest density of *animo* in the *Prince* is to be found in the 7th chapter; in the 7th chapter of the *Discourses*, *animo* is used syn-

onymously with "humors," whereas in I 45 (192) Machiavelli makes a distinction between *animo* and *umori*. Cf. *Art of War* I (470) on Caesar's principle; cf. also the substitution of *animo* for *anima* in *Decameròn* I 7 toward the end with the reference to Epicurus' denial of the eternity of the souls in I 6. *Animo* occurs in *Discourses* III more frequently than in I and II taken together; the greatest densities occur in III 6 (25 times) and 31 (8 times). In III 31 we are struck by the sentence "the vileness of their *animo* made them lose . . . the *animo*"; see also the heading ("the same *animo* and their same dignity") and *Prince* ch. 7 (26). *Spirito* is used in the two books with extreme rarity; *Discourses* III 31 is one of the very few chapters in which *spirito* occurs; for the interpretation of that chapter, consider page 148 above.

60. *Discourses* I 10 end. Cf. with the reference to *sempiterna infamia* the reference to *perpetuo onore* near the beginning of the chapter. In the Christian context of I 27 Machiavelli speaks of "eternal memory"; in the similar context of I 29 he speaks of "eternal infamy."

61. *Prince* ch. 15.

62. *Discourses* III 6 (343).

63. *Discourses* I 2 (98). Cf. Polybius VI 5.4-7.

64. Consider Averroes' *Commentary on Plato's Republic*, ed. cit., I 11.3-6 and II 7.

65. *Discourses* I pr. (90), 11 end, 39 beginning, II 5 beginning and III 43 beginning (cf. ch. 1, note 9 above). Cf. I 10 (124) with Dante, *Paradiso* 7.26. Cf. Thomas Aquinas, *Summa Theologica*, Iq.95a.2. and q.98a.2.

66. *Discourses* II pr. (228).

67. *Discourses* II 5 (246, 248).—Savonarola, *Prediche sopra Ezechiele*, VI says that God created the world as it were a few years ago; the years of the world *sono poco più di sei mila anni o quanti si sieno.*

68. Cf. page 175 above. Regarding

Averroes' assertion that God is the formal and final and not the efficient cause of the world, see Harry A. Wolfson, "Averroes' lost treatise on the prime mover," *The Hebrew Union College Annual*, XXIII 1, pp. 685, 702 and 704-705.—Savonarola, *Prediche sopra l'Esodo*, XX: *Sono diverse scuole, tomisti, scotisti e averroisti intra e'moderni, come erano anche antiche scuole di filosofi Stoici, peripatetici e altri.*

69. *Prince* ch. 18 (56-57); cf. *Discourses* II 13 (265), 22 (294) and III 14 (378).

70. *Discourses* I 49 and III 49. See pages 40, 123, 142-146, 165-167 and note 43 above.

71. *Prince* chs. 6 and 11; cf. the similar remark on Savonarola in *Discourses* I 11 (128). Remarks of this kind occur in the *Prince* rather than in the *Discourses*. Only in the *Prince* does Machiavelli draw our attention so clearly to the presumptuous and temerarious character of his undertaking, as distinguished from its merely dangerous character. This confirms the contention that in some respects the *Prince* is more outspoken than the *Discourses*.

72. Cf. *Prince* ch. 6 with ch. 18 (55). Cf. pages 93-94 and ch. 3, note 165 above. L. A. Burd, *Il Principe*, Oxford, 1891, 55, quotes the following remark by Innocent Gentillet: "Cest atheiste voulant montrer toujours de plus fort qu'il ne croit point aux sainctes Escritures, a bien osé vomir ce blaspheme de dire que Moyse de sa propre vertu et par les armes s'est fait Prince des Hebreux. . . ." Cf. *Discourses* II 5 on the human origin of all religions.

73. *Prince* ch. 7 (21). The titles of *Prince* chs. 6 and 7 suggest in conjunction with the content of these chapters that whereas Moses acquired his principality by virtue, Cesare Borgia acquired his principality by chance. It appears from ch. 7 that Cesare's virtue was decisive for his

success; therefore the example of his actions is the best precept for a new prince which Machiavelli can give. (The reference in *Prince* ch. 13 end to "the four mentioned by me above," i.e. Cesare, Hiero, David and Charles VII to whom Machiavelli now adds Philip of Macedon, makes us also think of "the four mentioned above" in the 6th chapter, i.e. Moses, Cyrus, Romulus and Theseus to whom Machiavelli adds Hiero at the end of that chapter; Cesare occupies the same place in ch. 13 which Moses occupies in ch. 6. When speaking of Hiero in ch. 13, Machiavelli calls him "one of those mentioned by me above.") Cesare, it appears, became great by using among other means dissimulation and fraud. Dissimulation and fraud would thus be required of any new prince or of any founder. They were used by Cyrus (*Discourses* II 13) who is mentioned together with Moses in *Prince* chs. 6 and 26. Machiavelli leaves it to the reader to draw the conclusion regarding Moses. Machiavelli finds similarity between the "actions" of Moses and Cyrus; he does not find similarity between their "lives": in the "life" of Cyrus written by Xenophon Cyrus is presented as a model of "humanity." See *Prince* ch. 14 end as well as *Discourses* III 20 (389) and 22 (394).

74. Cf. *Prince* chs. 6 and 26 with Livy I 4.3-4 and Justinus XXIII 4.

75. *Discourses* I 11, 12 (129) and 13 (133). Cf. I 39 which is linked to I 13 by the example of Terentillus. Cf. pages 74 and 146-147 above.

76. *Discourses* I 8 (116), 49 (199), III 5 (336) and 8 (359). Cf. I 59 (222) with Plutarch, *Demetrius* chs. 10 and 13. Cf. II 31 with Livy VIII 24.1, 6, 14-15. We read in Livy XXXIII 33 that Titus Quinctius was about 33 years old when he was hailed by the Greeks as their liberator; the Greeks expressed the opinion *esse aliquam in terris gentem quae sua impensa, suo labore ac periculo bella*

gerat *pro libertate aliorum . . . maria traiciat ne quod toto orbe terrarum iniustum imperium sit, ubique ius fas lex potentissima sint . . . hoc spe concipere audacis animi fuisse, ad effectum adducere et virtutis et fortunae ingentis.* Cf. ch. 3, note 159 above.

77. See pages 176-177 and 184-185 above. Cf. *Prince* chs. 10 (34), 13 (44) and 19 (60, 61); *Discourses* II 30 end.

78. *Prince* chs. 12 (42) and 22 (74); *Discourses* I 4 (104), 37 end, 45 and 47 (197-198); *Florentine Histories* III 1. Cf. pages 113, 127 and 150-153 above.

79. *Discourses* I 58 (217-218) and 8 (116); cf. II 2 (237). See Livy VI 16.2 and 8, 17.5 and 20.16. Cf. ch. 3, note 178 above.—Machiavelli draws our attention to the *sanguis servatoris* by, shortly after I 58, namely in I 60, making Valerius Corvinus speak of *proemium sanguinis* whereas Livy (VII 32.14) makes him speak of *generis praemium*. Valerius Corvinus whom Machiavelli temporarily calls Publicola is presented in *Discourses* III 22 as the representative of the type of gentle or charitable captain (cf. Livy VII 40.3) in opposition to Manlius Torquatus, the representative of the type of harsh captain. As for the relation in Machiavelli's thought between Manlius Capitolinus and Manlius Torquatus, cf. *Discourses* III 46 as well as pages 163-165 and ch. 3, note 146 above.

80. Cf. I 29 (160-161), 53 (208-209), 58 (221), II 5 beginning, 12 (261) and III 10. See pages 130 and 157 as well as ch. 1, note 48 above.

81. I 58 (219), II 1 beginning, III 1 (330), 2 (332), 23, 29, and 33 (416); *Art of War* VI (591-592). Cf. pages 127-131 and note 46 as well as ch. 3, notes 56 and 162 above.

82. Savonarola, *Prediche sopra l'Esodo X: Tutte le cose che sentono, questi filosofi e astrologi le vogliono risolvere in cause naturali, o attribuirle al cielo più presto che a Dio.*—

Prediche sopra Ezechiele XLVI: *Dice lo astrologo: Ecco il cielo che è mio Dio.* According to Savonarola, even the soul has greater power (*virtù*) than heaven.

83. *Discourses* I pr. (90), 6 (112), 19 (147), II pr. (230), 2 (238), 5, and III 1 beginning.

84. II 29; cf. I 10 end and 11 beginning.

85. Cf. *Discourses* III 1 with Dante, *Inferno* 7.67-96. Cf. note 10 above.

86. I 56 and II 29; each chapter is the fifth before the end of the Book to which it belongs (as for other correspondances between the ends of the First and the Second Book, see ch. 3, note 36 above.) II 29 is the 33d chapter after I 56. The Livian stories on which the arguments of I 56 and II 29 are based belong together; they are all concerned with the war between the Romans and the Gauls led by Brennus. No chapter heading of the *Discourses* mentions God or gods or heaven; *fortuna* is mentioned in six chapter headings (I 23, II 1, 13, 29, III 9, 31) and *accidenti* in seven (I 3, 16, 39, 40, 56, II 5, 23); *caso* occurs only in one chapter heading (I 22) where it means not "chance" but "case."

87. Cf. pages 18-19 and 48 above.

88. Cf. Cicero, *De divinatione* I 64: *tribus modis censet (Posidonius) deorum appulsu homines somniare: uno quod praevideat animus ipse per sese, quippe qui deorum cognatione teneatur, altero quod plenus aër sit immortalium animorum, in quibus tamquam insignitae notae veritatis appareant, tertio quod ipsi di cum dormientibus colloquantur.* Cf. also Pomponazzo, *Tractatus de immortalitate animae,* cap. 14.

89. I 12 (128-129) and II 5.

90. Cf. pages 188-189 above. The intelligences in the air may remind us of "the prince of the power of the air" of *Ephesians* 2.2.—*Discourses* I 58 (219).

91. Regarding the context of I 56,

see also pages 109-110 and 193-194 as well as ch. 1, note 3, ch. 3, note 24 and ch. 4, note 28 above.

92. Savonarola performs the same function regarding the invasion of Italy by the French which the Roman plebeian performs regarding the invasion of Italy by the Gauls. Cf. the correspondence between Savonarola and the plebeian Virginius in *Discourses* I 45.

93. Cf. *Prince* ch. 12 (39).

94. *Discourses* I 34 (171-172).

95. Cf. page 122 above.

96. Cf. *Prince* ch. 26 (82).

97. *Prince*, Ep. ded. and ch. 7 (22); *Discourses* II pr. (229, 230). Cf. *Discourses* II 10 near the beginning (the silence about divine benevolence.) In his letter to Vernacci of June 26, 1513 Machiavelli contrasts "the grace of God" with the deficient kindness of "the heavens" (*e'cieli*).

98. Cf. II 29 with II 28 and III 1 (328). Cf. pages 197-198 and note 76 above.

99. Livy V 37 ff. Cf. page 137 above. Near the beginning of *Discourses* II 30 Machiavelli substitutes *fortuna* for Livy's "gods and men" (V 49.1).

100. *Discourses* II 30 end; *Prince* ch. 25 end. Cf. page 157 above.

101. Machiavelli discusses in III 1 the restoration of mixed bodies in this order: republics, religions, kingdoms.

102. As for the connection between II 29 and III 48, the chapter on the meaning of manifest mistakes, see page 35 above. Cf. also the thesis of I 2 (Rome owed her polity to chance or to "accidents") with the thesis of II 1 (Rome owed her empire to virtue rather than to *fortuna*).

103. Cf. II pr. (230) with II 5 (247-248); cf. II pr. (229) with I 37 beginning. Cf. *Art of War*, near the end.

104. Cf. III 1 beginning and II 5; cf. I 6 (108).

105. II 1. (We may note that II 1, the chapter showing that Rome owed

her greatness to virtue rather than to luck, has the same distance from I 56, the chapter on heavenly signs, which III 1 where *fortuna* is replaced by extrinsic accidents, has from II 29, the chapter on Fortuna as a thinking and willing being through whose election Rome rose to greatness.) Cf. I 2 (97, 101), 4, 11 (127), III 9, and 29; also *Prince* chs. 6 and 7.

106. *Florentine Histories* VIII 36. Machiavelli says that Lorenzo "was loved by fortuna and by God to the highest degree" and he shows by what he says in the sequel regarding the fatal consequences of Lorenzo's death that what he said of Lorenzo cannot be said of Italy or of Florence. Cf. pages 197-198 above.

107. *Discourses* III 9; *Prince* ch. 25.

108. Cf. *Discourses* III 31 with *Prince* ch. 18 end. Cf. the cross reference in *Discourses* III 31 (412) to II 30, the chapter which culminates in the call to "regulate Fortuna." Cf. *ibid.* (413) the reference to "more than 25000." Cf. pages 148-149 and 189-91 above.

109. Cf. *Discourses* III 33 (417) and pages 215-216 above. Cf. also *Prince* chs. 6 (18) and 26 beginning: Machiavelli replaces the distinction between "fortuna-occasion-matter" and "form-virtue" by the distinction between "matter-occasion" and "form-virtue."

110. In *Discourses* III 1 (327-328), Machiavelli distinguishes first between "extrinsic accident" and "intrinsic prudence" and then between "extrinsic accident" and "intrinsic accident"; "intrinsic accidents" are the same as, or at any rate include, "intrinsic prudence."

111. I 11 (126-128), 12 (128-129), 39 beginning, 47, II 22 (293), III 6 (353), 33 (416, 417), and 34 heading. Cf. pages 56-57, 208-209 and 213 above. —When quoting in III 33 (417) two sentences regarding an accident which were put by Livy into the mouth of

a dictator, Machiavelli makes three important changes. Whereas the Livian character speaks of "the fortune of the place," Machiavelli makes him speak of "fortune" and thus indicates the generality of the problem; besides, he omits the intervening sentence in which the dictator ascribes the accident in question to the gods; finally, he omits the prayer of the dictator to the gods, witnesses of the treaty, that they should exact from the enemy the penalties due to them for the violation of the treaty (Livy VI 29.1-2).

112. Cf. *Prince* ch. 20 (68) with ch. 6 (19). As for the context of both statements, cf. pages 58-60 above. See also pages 74 and 187-188 above.

113. Cf. pages 201-203 above.

114. Cf. e.g. Cicero, *De natura deorum* I 33-35 and *Acad. Post.* I 29.

115. *Discourses* I 2 (98, 101), 6 (108), and III 1 (327); Polybius VI 5.1,4, 8; 6.2; 7.1; 9.10, 13-14.

116. Dante, *Inferno* 4.136; cf. Plato, *Laws* 889a4ff.

117. *Discourses* II 5 (248) and III 1 (327). In the *Florentine Histories*, Machiavelli puts the distinction between mixed bodies (i.e. societies) and simple bodies (i.e. living beings) into the mouth of the exiled Rinaldo degli Albizzi who, anxious to return to his fatherland, makes great promises to a foreign prince. Rinaldo says of simple bodies that they frequently require "fire and iron" for their cure and of mixed bodies that they frequently require "iron" for their cure. When he made this distinction, he still had hope of returning to his earthly fatherland. At a later date, after he had lost all hope of returning to his earthly fatherland, he tried to gain the heavenly fatherland. Cf. *Florentine Histories* V 8 and 34 with *Discourses* II 32. Cf. *Discourses* I 47 (197): *le cose e gli accidenti di esse.* Consider also the synonymous use of *animo* and *umori* in *Discourses* I 7 (cf. note 59 above).—Savonarola, *Pre-*

diche sopra Ezechiele XXXVIII: *ogni corpo misto è composto di quattro elementi.*

118. "Superfluous matter": *Discourses* II 5 (248). In the *Prince* and the *Discourses* taken together, "form" occurs 14 times and "matter" 51 times. Cf. *Discourses* III 8 ("he could impress the form of his ambition on the corrupt matter") and 36 ("natural furor and accidental order").

119. 2141. The saying borrowed from the devil in question concerns Lucca, Castruccio's city. Lucca is mentioned in, or in connection with, three sayings of Castruccio: nos. 13, 23, and 33. Machiavelli indicates the plan of the collection of sayings by ascribing the first of the sayings belonging to the Diogenes-section (no. 22), and no other saying, to the young Castruccio.

120. *Prince* chs. 6 (19), 8 (28), 15 (49), and 20 (68); *Discourses* I 11, 12 (128-129), 14 beginning, 19 (147), II 5, 25 (306), and III 1. Cf. pages 139-140, 146-147, 184-185, 189 and 218-220 above.

121. *Prince* chs. 8 (28) and 15 (49); *Discourses* I 10 (121, 124), 11 (126), 12 (129), 14 beginning, 17 (141), and 55 (210-211).

122. *Discourses* I 10 (see the parallel in *Opere* II 538), 11 (126-128), 19, 21, 22, and 23 (151). Cf. page 136 and ch. 1, note 56 above.—The Roman republic was indebted for its empire to a mode and an order discovered by its "first legislator"; that first legislator was either Romulus or Tullus or Appius Claudius but certainly not Numa. Cf. II 1 (231) and 3 (241) with a view to the fact that the event discussed in II 3 took place under the reign of Tullus. Tullus had been called "a most prudent man" in I 21. In II 21 Machiavelli speaks of an event which took place 400 years after the Romans had begun to wage war; the event in question took place 400 years after the beginning of the reign of Numa. This tacit character-

ization of the reign of Numa contradicts the explicit characterization thereof; yet the implicit identification of religion and war can no longer be wholly surprising, especially if one remembers the parallelism between the relation of Livy to the Latin Annius and the relation of the Biblical writers to God (cf. pages 138-147 above). *Discourses* III 21 is the central chapter of the Tacitean subsection. Cf. also II 24 (303) where another "most prudent" man is praised because he put his trust not in fortresses but in his own virtue and prudence.

123. *Discourses* I 10 (123-124), 11 (127), 13 (133), and 55 (211). Cf. the heading of I 12 with the body (130).

124. *Prince* chs. 12 (39), 14 beginning, 15, and 18 (56-57).

125. *Discourses* I 12 (129) and III 29 (407).

126. Cf. the first occurrence of "good" in the *Prince*: ch. 3 (8). Goodness in this sense is relative to the character of the government; see *Discourses* III 1 (329).

127. *Discourses* I 11 (125), 12 (128-129), 13 (132), 14, 15, II 16 (270), III 12, and 32; *Art of War* IV end. Cf. the quotations from Livy which Machiavelli uses for describing the good militia on the one hand and the good captain on the other in *Discourses* III 36 and 38. Cf. pages 38, 119-120, 138-141 and 150 above.

128. *Discourses* I 55 (210-211). There is also this difference between the Roman and the German examples: the Roman plebs did not pay the tithe after all, whereas the German citizens pay the tax. *Discourses* I 11 (125-126), 13 (132-133), 40 (186), and II 25. Cf. also II 28 (312) where it is said that a Roman disaster was due only to the disregard of justice, with III 1 (327-328) where it seems to be said that that disaster was due to the disregard of both religion and justice.

129. *Prince* chs. 9 (31) and 19 (57); *Discourses* I 4 (105), 13 (132), 37 beginning, 53 (206), 54, 60, II 23 (299), 27 (309), and III 40 (433). Consider especially *Florentine Histories* III 13. Cf. page 130 above.

130. *Discourses* I 55 (210-211) and III 1 (327).

131. *Prince* ch. 15 (cf. *Florentine Histories* VII 24); *Discourses* I 18 (143) and 58 (217); letters to Vettori of April 9, and December 10, 1513. See pages 77 and 164 above.

132. *Discourses* III 39 and I 47; cf. the Epp. Dedd. of the *Discourses* and the *Prince*.

133. *Discourses* I 24 (153).—"Ought" ("*debbe*" or "*debet*") occurs in 21 chapter headings of the *Discourses* and in one chapter heading of the *Prince*; three chapters (*Prince* ch. 14, *Discourses* I 21 and III 17) open with ". . . ought."

134. *Prince* chs. 15 (49) and 18 beginning; *Discourses* I 2 (98), 3 beginning, and 10 (122).

135. *Prince* chs. 8 (28, 30), 11 end, 15 (49), 16 (50), 19 (62), and 22 (74); *Discourses* I 2 (98), 9 (119), 11 (127), 18 (144), 27, 29 beginning, 30, III 1 (328, 329), 20, 21 end, and 24. Cf. *Florentine Histories* IV 16.

136. *Prince* chs. 8 (28) and 19 (60-61); *Discourses* I pr. (89), 4 (104), 9-10, 18 (145-146), 27 (158), 29, 58 (218), 59, II 2 (235-236), 21 (292), 24 (301-302), III 16 (380), 20 and 40 beginning. Cf. *Florentine Histories* IV 11 end.

137. *Prince* ch. 9 (31); *Discourses* I 6 (109), 16 (138), 29 (159), 37 (176) and III 25.

138. *Prince* ch. 19 (64); *Discourses* I 6 (112), 33 (168), 58 (218), II 10 (258), 23 (298), 30 (318), III 2 (332), 10 (367), and 31.

139. *Prince* ch. 15 (49). The admittedly incomplete list contains 11 virtues and the corresponding 11 vices. The distinction between the first two virtues (liberality and the virtue of giving) is dropped in the following

chapter; we have then in fact 10 virtues none of which is justice. The number reminds one of the number of virtues in Aristotle's *Nicomachean Ethics* (1106b33-1108b9) where 10 virtues concerned with passions are enumerated; "if one adds justice which is concerned with operations, there will be altogether 11 virtues" (Thomas, *Summa theologica* 1 2, q.60.a.5.c.). By reminding us of Aristotle's ethics, Machiavelli draws our attention to his implicit criticism of that doctrine. His list of 10 virtues seems to lack order completely; for instance, in enumerating the various virtues and the corresponding vices he begins in 5 cases with the virtue and in 5 cases with the vice; this difficulty disappears once one remembers that from his point of view religion cannot be a virtue. At any rate the first half of the list ends with humanity which is Machiavelli's substitute for humility, whereas the second half ends with religion. Machiavelli, one is tempted to say, inverts the order of the two Tables.

140. *Discourses* I 10 (122-123), 47 and II 22; *Prince* ch. 16. Cf. pages 103-104 above.

141. *Discourses* III 40. The last two preceding references to the middle course occur in III 21, the central chapter of the Tacitean subsection, and in III 2. Machiavelli refers in III 40 to the discussion of the middle course in II 23, the central sermon on a Livian text.

142. *Prince* chs. 9 (31), 15 (49), and 17 (52); *Discourses* I 58 (218) and III 31 (411-413). Cf. Livy IX 3.11 and 12.2.

143. *Prince* chs. 15-16.

144. *Discourses* I 6 (110-112); *Prince* ch. 16.

145. As appears from *Discourses* I 2 (98), especially when contrasted with Polybius VI 5.10-6.9, knowledge of justice presupposes positive laws (there is no natural right), whereas knowledge of the honest (the moral)

precedes positive laws. Cf. page 236 above.

146. *Discourses* I 26.

147. *Discourses* III 3 (334), 9 (363-364) and 21; *Prince* ch. 18 (55): *mezzo bestia e mezzo uomo*.

148. Letters to Vettori of August 3, 1514, and of January 31, 1514 (cf. *Prince* ch. 15); *Florentine Histories* VIII 36. Cf. *Discourses* I 6 (111-112).

149. *Prince* chs. 17 (52) and 18 (56); *Discourses* III 21 (390-391). Cf. *Discourses* II 24 (299).

150. *Prince* ch. 8 (30); *Discourses* I 13 (132), 15 (136), and 41. In *Discourses* I 51 Machiavelli speaks of "this prudence well used" but he there means by "prudence" a maxim or rule of prudence; cf. II 26 beginning.

151. *Prince* ch. 8 (28). In *Discourses* I 10 (123), Machiavelli ascribes "virtue" to the "criminal" Severus. In *Discourses* I 17 (141) he distinguishes "goodness" and "virtue" in order to make clear that what is important is virtue. For the distinction between goodness and virtue, see also III 1 (327-328). Cf. also the distinction between the wise and the good in *Florentine Histories* IV 1 and VII 13. In accordance with the change in the meaning of "virtue," "the true life" and "the due means" are also used in an amoral sense; see I 41, 48 and III 9; cf. *Prince* chs. 7 (21) and 12 (40) on Sforza. Cf. page 47 above.

152. In the only reference to the middle course which occurs in a chapter heading, Machiavelli says that the Romans avoided the middle course in passing judgments on their subjects (*Discourses* II 23). In the *Art of War* I (466-467), he recommends the middle course between pure compulsion and pure volunteering in recruiting soldiers (*nè tutta forza nè tutta volontà*; cf. *Discourses* I 23); cf. also *Art of War* III (527). In *Florentine Histories* IV 1 he in fact recommends liberty as the mean between servitude and license. In *Dis-*

courses I 47, he speaks of a middle course taken by the Roman nobles; it consisted in their accepting the substitution of tribunes with consular power for the consuls, a substitution which satisfied them as well as the plebs; this middle course was in fact imposed on the nobility by the plebs; the nobles accepted that middle course because they were certain that they would not incur any serious loss by temporarily accepting it and that it would not work in the long run (cf. *Discourses* I 39 end). In this case the taking of the middle course was judicious. The middle course which the Romans avoided according to *Discourses* II 23 is the mean between forgiving or benefiting the defeated enemy and destroying him; in deciding the fate of the defeated Latins, the Romans decided in the case of each important town whether it ought to be benefited or destroyed; the Romans avoided "the neutral course" which would have consisted in treating each town like every other town; the non-neutral or discerning course which the Romans took is therefore in a sense a middle course between indiscriminate benefiting and indiscriminate destruction; cf. also pages 156-157 above. In *Discourses* III 2, Machiavelli speaks of a middle course which would be "the truest (course) if it could be observed, but . . . I believe that this is impossible"; the course in question consists in staying not so near to princes that one becomes involved in their ruin nor so far from them that one cannot benefit from their ruin; the course recommended by Machiavelli to men who are unable to make open war on a prince is to stay close to the prince and to play the friend of the prince: the course of the concealed enemy is a middle course between the course of the enemy and the course of the friend.

153. Cf. also page 81 and ch. 3, note 179 above.

154. *Opere* II 530-531.

155. *Prince* ch. 21 (73); *Discourses* I 6 (110), 49, III 11 (368), 17 end, and 37 beginning.

156. *Discourses* II 2 (237-238).

157. *Prince* ch. 8 (27-28). Cf. *Discourses* III 31. Compare however *Discourses* II 18 (280) with III 21 .

158. *Discourses* I 58 (220), II 24 (305), III 9, and 13.

159. To the criticism of the middle course in the *Discourses* there corresponds the criticism of neutrality in the *Prince*, ch. 21 (71-73). Machiavelli indicates the connection between "the middle course" and "the neutral course" in *Discourses* II 23 (297), in a chapter preceded by a criticism of a particular form of neutrality (II 22). To understand the passage of the *Prince* on neutrality, one has to consider two things. The criticism of neutrality which occurs in the center of ch. 21 corresponds to the remark on the imitation of Fortuna which occurs in the center of ch. 20; and the criticism of neutrality is based to some extent on faith in the power of justice. In proportion as the faith in the power of justice or in the imitation of Fortuna is weakened, the case for neutrality (or the middle course) is strengthened. Cf. pages 59-60, 82 and 220-221 as well as ch. 2, note 63 above. The difference of treatment of "the neutral course" in the two books illustrates the relation of the two books.

160. *Prince* ch. 25. Cf. pages 215-221 above.—See Thomas Aquinas, *Summa theologica* 1 q.82.a.1.

161. *Discourses* I 2 (100), 6 (111-112), 14 (133-134), 18 (145), 38, and 51.

162. *Prince* chs. 8 (27, 30), 12 (41) and 15 (49); *Discourses* I 9 end, 17 (138), 29 (159), II 10 (256), and III 30 (409).

163. *Discourses* I 10 (122-124), 17 (141), 29 (161), 37 (176), II 6, and III 24-25. Cf. pages 190-191 above.

164. Cf. also the beginning of *Dis-*

courses I 21. *Prince* chs. 7 (24, 26), 13 (45), 18 (55, 57), 21 (71), 22 (74), 23 (76), 24 beginning, and 25; *Discourses* I 14 (133-134), 19 (147), 24 (154), 33 (168), 40 (185), 41-42, III 8 (361), 9, 21 (390, 391), 22 (392-394), and 46 (440). Cf. *Art of War* II (504), VI (586-587), and VII (616-618).

165. *Discourses* III 12. Machiavelli's only reference to moral philosophers concerns their praise of necessity. Cf. I 3 (103), 28, 29 (160-161), 30 (162-163), II 12 (262), and 27 (310-311); *Prince* chs. 12 (42) and 17 (53). Cf. *Florentine Histories* IV 14 and 18.

166. *Discourses* I 2 (98), 3 (103), 37 (175), II 6 (248), 8, III 8 (361), 12 (372), 16 (382), and 30 (409); *Art of War* VI (485) and VII (612). Cf. Livy V 48.6.

167. *Discourses* I 36 (174), 37 (178), II 2 (238), 6, III 6 (339, 341), and 23 (397); *Prince* ch. 17 (53). On the subject of hunger cf. also *Discourses* I 1 (94), 7 (113), 32 (166), and II 5 (247). In re-telling a story in which Livy had spoken only of a plague (V 13-14), Machiavelli adds hunger to the plague: *Discourses* I 13 (131); cf. also Machiavelli's account of the Gallic invasion of Italy in *Discourses* II 8 (251-252) with Livy's account (V 33-34). Cf. Livy III 68.4-6. Cf. page 191 above. In *Discourses* III 26 Machiavelli, modifying Livy's report (IV 9.4-5), makes the woman who gave occasion to civil strife in Ardea a rich heiress: Livy was not sufficiently attentive to the importance of wealth. If there was wealth in Ardea, it can be presumed that there was wealth in Rome at the same period, contrary to what the preceding chapter of the *Discourses* suggests; as regards the ambiguity of the thesis of that chapter, see pages 149-150 above. Consider also the disparagement of liberality in favor of parsimony and even stinginess in *Prince* ch. 17.

168. *Discourses* II 10 (258-259). As Machiavelli asserts, Livy tacitly con-

tends that money is altogether unimportant for winning wars whereas Livy explicitly contends that chance or good luck is important. Elsewhere (II 1) Machiavelli says in explicit criticism of Livy that good soldiers cannot help having good luck; in the present context he says that good soldiers cannot help coming into the possession of money; the status of money is not different from that of chance. As Machiavelli points out on other occasions (I 37, 51, II 6 and III 10), the Roman mode of warfare depended decisively on money, on a full treasury. The need for money is, to say the least, more evident than the need for Fortuna's favor. One is tempted to say that Machiavelli suggests that Fortuna be replaced by money. (As for the connection between Fortuna and money, see *Prince* ch. 7 beginning.) At any rate, from Machiavelli's point of view Livy is not altogether sound regarding causes; cf. the preceding note as well as ch. 3, note 91 and pages 122-125, and 215 above. (Livy, the authority regarding the power and the intention of Fortuna, is introduced in II 10 as the authority vouching for the irrelevance of money and therewith for the relevance of Fortuna, with a view to the particular function of the section—II 11-15—to which II 10 is, as it were, the preface.)

169. *Prince* chs. 17 (53), 22 (74), and 23 near the end; *Discourses* I 1 (94-96), 3 (103), 18 (133, 134), 29 (161), 35 (173), 40 (188), 50 (201), II 5 (248), 25 (306), and III 1 (328-330).

170. *Discourses* I pr. (89), 10 (124), 30 beginning, 31 (164-165), 38, 60 (224), II 8 (251), 17 (277), 24 (301), 33 (325), III 8 (361), 12 (370-371), 16 (381), and 36; *Prince* chs. 6 (18) and 26 (81). Cf. Aristotle *Politics* 1266b38ff. As regards the superiority of choice, see also *Discourses* I 20 which, if read in conjunction with I 11 (127) and 10 (123), says that where-

as nature does not give any guarantee whatever for the succession of excellent rulers, choice or election makes such succession certain provided deception and violence are not allowed to interfere. This extreme praise of "choice" is reasonably followed by an unusually emphatic blame of governments ("they ought to be ashamed of themselves").

171. *Discourses* I 1 (95), 14, 17 (145), 29 (160), 32, 37 (175-176), III 3 (334), 8, 10 (367-368), 11 (370), 12 (371), and 30 (409); *Prince* ch. 3 (12). Cf. *Florentine Histories* II 2 and VII 7. See pages 119-120 above.

172. *Prince* chs. 6 (18) and 26 (81-82); *Discourses* I 1 (95), 17 (142), 18 (145-146), 21 (149), 35 (174), 41, 55 (213), III 8 (361-362), and 16. Cf. Aristotle, *Politics* 1287b37ff.

173. *Discourses* III 35 (422, 423); *Prince* ch. 18 toward the end; *Florentine Histories* VIII 22. Cf. pages 83, 168-172 and 217-218 above.

174. *Prince* ch. 15; *Discourses* I 3 beginning; cf. *Prince* ch. 25 (79) with Aristotle, *Politics* 1311 a30-31; Plato, *Republic* 408 e ff.; Aristotle, *Nicomachean Ethics* 1168b 15-28.

175. *Discourses* I 2 (98), 4 (104), 10 (124), 18 (143), 58 (217), II 5 (248) and III 36 (424); *Prince* ch. 19 end. Cf. Aristotle, *Politics* 1253a 31-37 as well as Plato, *Laws* 680d 1-5 and 782b-c. Cf. pages 46, 70-71 and 133 above.

176. Aristotle, *Nicomachean Ethics* 1102a 5-12 and 1180a 24-28, *Eudemian Ethics* 1248b 38ff.; *Politics* 1264a 1-5, 1293b 1-14, 24-26, 1296a 32-b 2, 1324b 1-28, and 1333b 5-14.—*Discourses* I 9 (119-120), 10 (125), 16 (138), 29 (161), 34 (171-172), II 2 (235-236, 239), III 6 (339) and 8 (359-360). Cf. II 8 (251) with the end of Sallustius' *Bellum Jugurthinum* to which Machiavelli explicitly refers; whereas Sallustius had spoken of the Roman people fighting for glory, Machiavelli speaks of its fighting from ambition.

177. *Discourses* I 16-18, 20, 29 end, 30 (163-164), 34 (171), 35 (174), 58 (219-220), 59 and III 9 (363); *Prince* ch. 5 (17).

178. *Discourses* I 6 (108), 17 (141), 18 (145), 34 (170), 37 (176), 55 (212), II 2 (239-240), 3 (241), 14, 19 (285-286), III 3 (334), 16 (381), 20, 21 (389), 22 (394-396), 23 (397), 25, 28, 30 (408), and 34 (420); *Florentine Histories* I 39, II 42 and III 1; *Opere* II 697-698.

179. Aristotle, *Politics* 1327b 38-1328a 10; Plato, *Republic* 486b 10-13, 537a 4-7 and 619b 7-d 1; *Prince* ch. 17 (52). Cf. pages 191-192 and 239-240 above.

180. *Discourses* I 4, 7, 9, 10 (121), 16 (138), 17 (142), 18 (145-146), 25, 27, 34 (171), 40 (188), 55 (212-213), III 3, 7, 11, 21 (391), 29 (407), 40, 41 (cf. *Florentine Histories* II 5 end) and 44; *Prince* ch. 18 end. Cf. William H. Prescott, *History of the Reign of Ferdinand and Isabella*, ed. J. F. Kirk (Philadelphia 1872), I, 233; Aristotle, *Politics* 1309a 39-b 6.

181. *Discourses* I pr. (89), 1 (95), 4 (105), 5-6, 16 (139), 25, 29 (161), 37 (178), 40 (186-187), 44, 47-48, 49 (200-201), 50 (202), 53, 60, II 2 (235-236, 239), 16 (270), 19 (286), 27 (311), and III 34 (420-421); *Prince* chs. 3 (12), 9 (31-32), and 12 (41); *Florentine Histories* III 1. Cf. ch. 3, note 75 above. Machiavelli succinctly indicates his view of the relation of the great and the people by saying that a civil principality arises when the great make "one of them" or when the people make "one" a prince (*Prince* ch. 9); it is unthinkable to him that the great should make a man of the people (say Mussolini or Hitler) a prince, whereas it makes sense to him that a great man (say Pericles or Caesar) should become prince through the people.

182. *Discourses* I 5, 6 (109-110), 37, 51, 60 (224), II 2 (239-240), 3, 4, 6, 7, 19 (288), III 25 and 49;

Art of War V (563). Cf. page 249 above.

183. *Discourses* I 12 (130), II 4 (243, 246), 13 (265), 21 beginning, III 12 (371) and 24 (399); *Art of War* II (506-509). Cf. page 89 as well as ch. 2, notes 29 and 45 above.

184. *Discourses* I 40 (187) and II 2 (235-236).

185. *Prince* ch. 9 (32); *Discourses* I 32 (166), 37 (176), 38 (179, 181), 51, 53 (206-207), 54, 55 (210-211), 58 (220), 59, II 7, and III 9 (363). Cf. *Prince* ch. 16 with Livy IV 59.10 (and 60.4). Cf. *Discourses* I 44 with Livy III 53. *Florentine Histories* II 34 beginning, 41 end, III 17, 18 beginning, 20 and VI 24. Cf. page 231 and ch. 3, note 41 above.

186. *Discourses* III 13 (375). In order to understand the passage, one must consider the inappropriate character of two of the three examples (Lucullus, Gracchus and Pelopidas), and one must compare I 11 end, and 18 end. Cf. III 16 (380) with I 53 (208). See III 1 (329), 20, 22 (395), and *Prince* ch. 19 (61). Cf. pages 125 and 249 as well as note 126 above.

187. *Discourses* III 20-22 and 7 end.

188. *Discourses* I 40 and III 6 (338, 356, 357). Cf. ch. 3, note 109 above.— "Republic" occurs in 33 chapter headings, "prince" (or "principality") in 20, and "tyranny" in 2 (I 10 and III 28; III 28 is the 121st chapter of the *Discourses*).

189. *Discourses* I 10 (124), 11 (127), 12 (130), 43 (190), and II 2 (239-240); *Florentine Histories* V 1. Cf. Spinoza, *Tractatus politicus* VI 40 and VIII 46 on the different status of religion in monarchies on the one hand and in republics on the other. Cf. page 227 above.

190. *Discourses* I 2 (98-99), 9, 10 (124), 11 (125, 128), 16 (137, 140), 17 (141, 142), 18 (145-146), 23 (151), 55, 58 (220), III 4 (335), 5 (336), and 30. Cf. pages 249 and 252-253 above.

191. *Discourses* I 16 (138-140) and III 30 (409-410); *Prince* ch. 19 (62).

Cf. page 26 above.

192. *Prince* chs. 3 (12), 6 (18-20), 8 (28), 9 (32-33), 15, 18 (56), and 26 beginning; *Discourses* I 9 (120), 10 (123), 17 (141), 20, 27, 58 (220) and III 22 (395-396). Cf. pages 241-242 above.—Machiavelli's view of the status of moral virtue appears most clearly from his utterances and silences regarding chastity. He mentions chastity as the seventh virtue in his enumeration of the moral virtues (*Prince* ch. 15), but whereas he speaks in the four following chapters of all other virtues enumerated in ch. 15, he is silent about chastity, even about the necessity of appearing chaste; for his remark that the prince must abstain from the women and especially from the property of his subjects can hardly be taken as a discussion of chastity; cf. chs. 17 (53), 18 (56) and 19 (57) with the reference to Cyrus' chastity at the end of the preceding section of the *Prince*, i.e. at the end of ch. 14. As for the precept that the prince should abstain from women belonging to his subjects, cf. the silence on this theme in *Discourses* III 6 (341) and 19 (387) with I 37 end. Machiavelli does not mention the rape of Virginia in his enumeration of the mistakes committed by Appius Claudius (*Discourses* I 40). Cf. also the treatment of the Virginia incident in III 5. In III 26 he uses the Lucretia incident and the Virginia incident in order to show that women have done great harm to states (cf. Livy I 57.10). It is in this context and only there that Machiavelli refers explicitly to Aristotle: it seems at first glance that the only teaching of Aristotle with which Machiavelli agrees is the teaching that tyrants ought to avoid hurting their subjects in connection with women; but even regarding this teaching, and precisely regarding this teaching, there is a subtle disagreement. Cf. pages 257-258 above.—The emphasis in the *Prince* (see especially ch. 1) on the kinds of

matter and modes of acquiring principalities as distinguished from the kinds of structures and purpose of principalities is justified by the fundamental character of acquisition.

193. *Discourses* I 3, 37 (176, 178), 40 (187), 46 (193), and III 22 (393-395). Cf. I 50 (201) with III 11.

194. *Prince* chs. 7 (23-24), 8 (27, 29), and 9 (31, 33); *Discourses* I 1 (94), 2 (98), 9 (121), 10 (122-124), 16 (137, 139-140), 25 end, 26, 29 (161), 37 (177, 178), 40 (186, 187), 52 (204, 205), II 2 (235, 236-237), 13, III 4, 6 (354, 355, 356), and 8 (360); *Opere* II 707. Cf. Aristotle, *Politics* 1297b 1-10 and 1308b 33-1309a 9. Cf. Hobbes' assertion that tyranny is merely monarchy "misliked" (*Leviathan* ch. 19). Cf. page 260 above.

195. *Discourses* I 8 (116), 24 (154), and III 8 (360-362). Cf. I pr. beginning, II 2 (237-238), 33 (325) and III 9.

196. *Prince* chs. 19 (61-66) and 20 (67); *Discourses* I 40 (187) and 41.

197. *Discourses* III 2, 3 (334), 6 (338, 340, 346-347, 352, 354, 356), 8 (361-362), 9 (363), 11 end, 22 (392), 23 beginning, 30 (408-409), 34 (419-420), 35, and 42. Cf. Livy I 56.7-12.

198. *Discourses* I 29 (161), 30, 52, and II 28 (313); *Prince* chs. 22 and 23 (76). The chapter containing the discussion of Soderini's possible switch from the cause of freedom to the cause of the Medici (I 52) is located in the middle between the two chapters of the *Discourses* which open with "I believe" (I 18 and II 26). Reflection on the fact that I 52 contains the only density of "Piero" ever occurring in the book will show that it makes sense to describe that chapter as the most important chapter of the *Discourses*. Such reflection presupposes especially a sufficient understanding of I 9. Cf. pages 103-104 and 263 above.

199. *Discourses* I 1 (95), 2 (98), 6 (112), 16 (138), 37 beginning, 46, and III 16 (381).

200. *Prince* chs. 15 (49), 17 (53), and 18 (55-57); *Discourses* I pr. beginning, 3, 9 (120), 26-27, 29 (160-161), 35 (174), 37 beginning, 40 (188), 42, 47-48, 57, 58 (217-219, 221), II pr. (229), III 12 (371), and 29. Cf. Hobbes, *De Cive*, praef. See page 249 above.

201. *Prince* chs. 2 (6), 9 (32), 10 (35), 17 (53), and 20 (69); *Discourses* I 2 (98), 37 (175), 57 end, III 6 (354), 12 (371), 23, 30 (409), 34, and 43 (435). Cf. Polybius VI 6.2-4. In reproducing Livy II 44.7, Machiavelli replaces *res Romana* by *il nome Romano* (*Discourses* II 25 beginning). Cf. page 270 above.

202. *Prince* ch. 17 (53); *Discourses* I 7 (115), 20, 29 (159-160), 30 (163-164), 35-36, 40 (188), 43, 45 end, 48, 60 (224), II 2 (235-236, 239), 24 (301, 303), 33 (325), III 10 beginning, 15 (379), 21 (390), and 28. Cf. III 28 with I 9.

203. *Prince* chs. 6 (19), 7 (26) and 15 (48); *Discourses* I pr. (89), 58 (217), III 2 (333) and 27 (404). Cf. pages 242-244 as well as notes 152 and 159 above.

204. Cf. letter to Vettori of December 10, 1513 with page 241 above.

205. *Discourses* I pr. (89, 90), 2 (100), 10 beginning and end, 38 (179), 58 (219), II 2 (237-238), 13 end, 23 (297-298), 26 (309), 27 (311), 28 (313), 30 (318), 33 (325), III 2 (332, 333), 10 (367-368), 21 (389), 35 (423) and 41; cf. II 10 (258) with *Art of War* IV (546-547), VI (585-586), and VII (612); *Prince* ch. 25 (79); *Opere* II 538-539; letter to Vettori of December 10, 1513. Cf. Thomas Aquinas, *Summa theologica*, 2 2 q. 132. a. 4. ad 2. Cf. pages 281-282 above.

206. *Prince* chs. 3 (12), 18 (57), and 25 (79); *Discourses* I 10 (122-123), 25 beginning, 27 (158), 53, 58 (218), III 2 beginning, 34, 35 (422) and 49 (443); *Florentine Histories* pr.; *Opere* II 538. Cf. page 274 (Severus) as well as pages 44 and 136 above.

207. *Discourses* I 29 (161). Cf. page 253 above.

208. Cf. *Discourses* III 31 beginning with *Prince* ch. 8 (28); *Florentine Histories* V 1 end. Cf. pages 218, 253 and 282-283 above. According to Thomas Aquinas (*Summa theologica* 2 2 q. 80. a. 1. ad 2.), humanity is a virtue regulating our relations with our inferiors. Cf. page 208 above.

209. Cf. pages 279-280 above.

210. Cf. pages 58-59 above.

211. As for Aristippus (cf. page 224 above), see Xenophon, *Memorabilia* II 1.

212. *Nicomachean Ethics* 1181a 12-17.

213. Cf. *Discourses* III 41.

214. *Prince* ch. 3 (12); *Discourses* II 2 (239), III 11 and 30 (409).

215. *Discourses* I 18, 55 and III 26 (cf. note 192 above). Plato, *Laws* 709d 10-710b 2, 711a 6-7 and 735d 2-e 5; cf. 690a 1-c 4.

216. *Discourses* I 58. Cf. also the defense of the people against Livy in *Discourses* III 13 and the corresponding change of a Livian story (IV 31.3-4) in III 15 beginning. Cf. I 49 beginning and end with the plebeian speeches in Livy IV 4.1-4 and 35.5-9. Cf. pages 127-132 above.

217. Cf. also the strange "dependence" of the *Castruccio* on Diogenes Laertius (cf. pages 224-225 above).

218. Cf. pages 241-244, 280 and 282-283 above.

219. The quest for this kind of noble rhetoric, as distinguished from the other kind discussed in the *Phaedrus*, is characteristic of the *Gorgias*. Consider Aristotle, *Metaphysics* 1074b 1-4. Cf. pages 125-126 above.

220. Plato, *Republic* 493a 6-494a 7.

221. Cf. from this point of view Hegel's "Vorrede zu Hinrichs' Religionsphilosophie" (*Berliner Schriften*, ed. Hoffmeister, 78-79) with the parallels in Plato's *Republic*.—Cf. pages 171-173 and 251-253 above.

222. *Discourses* II 5. Cf. Aristotle, *Nicomachean Ethics* 1094a 26-b 7, *Politics* 1268b 22ff. and 1331a 1-18 (cf. [Thomas Aquinas'] *Commentary on the Politics*, VII, lectio IX.); Xenophon, *Hiero* 9.9-10. Cf. ch. 2, note 53 above.

Index

Adams, Henry, 301
Aristippus, 224-225, 345
Aristophanes, 295
Aristotle, 23, 32, 59, 159, 185, 208, 221-222, 224-225, 236, 237-238, 244, 252-253, 254, 255, 258, 270, 273, 290-293, 302, 305, 321, 339, 341-345
Averroes, 202, 330, 333, 334

Bacon, Francis, 176, 301
Bacon, Roger, 328
Bayle, 314
Biondo, 308
Boccaccio, 51, 316, 333
Burckhardt, Jakob, 333
Burd, L. A., 334

Cicero, 95, 107, 125, 290, 291, 317, 335, 337

Dante, 222, 224, 227, 234, 306, 313, 314, 322, 329, 331, 333, 335, 337
Democritus, 222
Diodorus Siculus, 144
Diogenes the Cynic, 224-225
Diogenes Laertius, 224, 345

Epicurus, 203, 222, 292

Fārābī, 318, 328
Fichte, 329
Fustel de Coulanges, 321

Gemistus Plethon, 328
Goethe, 174-175, 329
Guicciardini, 324

Hegel, 345
Herodian, 196
Hobbes, 15, 55, 176, 279, 311, 344
Hume, 330

Jordan, W. K., 311
Justinus, 302, 309, 334

Livy, 24, 29-30, 41, 42, 48, 49, 52, 88-94, 96-115, 121-158, 160, 162-164, 170, 172, 205, 206, 211, 212, 213-214, 215, 228, 259, 263, 275, 291, 303, 305, 307, 308, 310, 311-313, 315-329, 330-332, 334-339, 341, 343-345
Locke, 55

Marlowe, 13
Marsilius of Padua, 317
Marxism, 203
McDonald, A. H., 305
de'Medici, Lorenzo, 305
Montesquieu, 321

Nietzsche, 303, 332

Paine, Thomas, 13, 14
Petrarca, 305
Pico della Mirandola, 328, 331
Plato, 10, 15, 59, 83, 185, 222, 224, 254, 258, 269, 288-294, 304, 327, 337, 342, 345
Plutarch, 137, 311, 324, 328, 334
Polybius, 111, 134, 201, 222, 280, 290-291, 311, 333, 337, 339, 344
Pomponazzo, Pietro, 33, 335

Prescott, William H., 342

Ranke, 308
Rousseau, 26, 294

Sallustius, 124, 137, 167, 342
Savonarola, 18, 58, 72, 92, 112, 175, 183,
    202, 305, 324, 326, 328, 329, 331,
    333, 334, 335, 337
Seneca, 126
Spinoza, 26, 294, 319, 343
Statius, 312
Swift, 309

Tacitus, 50, 124, 160-165, 168, 187, 189,
    195, 199, 320, 323, 325-326, 338, 339
Thomas Aquinas, 333, 339, 340, 344,
    345
Thucydides, 10, 264, 292

Virgil, 313, 322
Voltaire, 321

Wolfson, Harry A., 334

Xenophon, 59, 78, 83, 139, 161, 162,
    163, 291, 293, 307, 322, 345